Colección Támesis

SERIE A: MONOGRAFÍAS, 201

THE ART OF HUMOUR
IN THE *TEATRO BREVE* AND *COMEDIAS* OF
CALDERÓN DE LA BARCA

This book explores the relationship between Calderón's often serious *comedias* and his overwhelmingly funny *teatro breve*, consisting of *mojigangas*, *entremeses*, and *jácaras*. Calderón was able to satisfy his audience's desire for laughter and novelty while injecting blatant parody and satire into the larger and more varied context of the *comedia*. After familiarizing the reader with the *teatro breve* and Calderón's contributions to the genre, this study demonstrates how the playwright incorporated characters, situations and dramatic techniques from these smaller pieces. Thus the burlesque mythology and ridiculous costumes integral to the festive *mojigangas* are re-examined as contributing thematically to Calderón's *comedias*, as well as adding humour. Frantic and popular characters and situations from the *entremés* tradition, thought by many as opposing the *comedias*' main features, are instead shown to join and often dominate these features through the introduction of absurd *figuras*, slapstick, and *burlas*.

Readers will also learn of the *jácara*, its mixture of laughter, violence and criminality, and how this mixture can infuse themes of love, honour and vengeance so prevalent in the *comedia*. By looking at the *teatro breve* as an integral part of Calderón's major works, and not simply a separate 'minor' genre, this book seeks to broaden the reader's knowledge of the playwright's abilities as dramatist and humorist alike.

TED BERGMAN is Professor of Spanish Language and Culture at Soka University of America.

TED L. L. BERGMAN

THE ART OF HUMOUR
IN THE
TEATRO BREVE
AND *COMEDIAS* OF
CALDERÓN DE LA BARCA

TAMESIS

First published 2003
by Tamesis, Woodbridge

ISBN 1 85566 096 2

Tamesis is an imprint of Boydell & Brewer Ltd
PO Box 9, Woodbridge, Suffolk IP12 3DF, UK
and of Boydell & Brewer Inc.
PO Box 41026, Rochester, NY 14604–4126, USA
website: www .boydell.co.uk

A catalogue record for this book is available
from the British Library

Library of Congress Cataloging-in-Publication Data
Bergman, Ted L. L. (Ted Lars Lennart), 1972–
 The art of humour in the teatro breve and comedias of Calderón
de la Barca / Ted L. L. Bergman.
   p. cm. – (Colección Támesis. Serie A, Monografías : 201)
Includes bibliographical references and index.
 ISBN 1–85566–096–2 (hardback : alk. paper)
1. Calderón de la Barca, Pedro, 1600–1681 – Humor. 2. Humor in
literature. I. Title.
 PQ6317.H85 B47 2003
 862'.3 – dc21   2003005013

This publication is printed on acid-free paper

Printed in Great Britain by
Antony Rowe Ltd, Chippenham, Wiltshire

CONTENTS

The author and publishers would like to record their thanks to
the Modern Humanities Research Association
for assistance in the costs of publication of this book.

INTRODUCTION

Studying the Spanish Golden Age *comedia* can be a funny thing. In *comedia* criticism, humour is often mentioned in passing, or in connection with the peculiarities of the genre, but humour as a topic itself rarely takes centrestage. If one mentions the name 'Calderón' to most modern readers and viewers of the *comedia*, they may list several things that made him famous, but while they recite, rarely will you hear these people chuckle, snort or even mention anything related to humour. The number of articles and books written about Calderón de la Barca concerning honour, allegory or court spectacle far exceeds the number written about his sense of humour or capacity to write jokes. Sturgis Leavitt, nearly half a century ago, asked, 'Did Calderón have a sense of humour?' and the answer was a qualified 'No'. Over forty years later, Constance Rose still felt compelled to ask, albeit referring only to a single play, 'Was Calderón serious?'[1]

Beyond answering whether or not Calderón was serious, or if he had a sense of humour, it is more fruitful – and entertaining, which is appropriate for studying the *comedia* – to explain *how* he was funny. Though some may question the value of studying humour up close, its investigation is as legitimate as the careful study of a play's plot, to take a similar example. A single dramatic moment is not independent but connected to themes, genres (along with the expectations they create), staging, the play's overall structure, language and myriad other aspects (some peculiar to theatre, others not) whose relationships to each other, as well as its literary and social contexts, require study for a richer understanding of the work. While the shocking effects of a well-known scene (such as Mencía's *descubrimiento* in *El medico de su honra*) may have vanished with recurrent readings, examining how the surprise operates, exploring its connections with other moments in the play or simultaneous occurrences, adds significance instead of taking it away. The very same can be said of studying humour. Also, as with plot elements, characterisation, setting, etc., this phenomenon and its use in theatre can also

---

[1] Sturgis Leavitt, 'Did Calderón Have a Sense of Humor?', in *Romance Studies Presented to William Morton Dey, Studies in Romance Languages and Literatures XII*, ed. Urban T. Holmes, Jr., Alfred G. Engstrom and Sturgis E. Leavitt (Chapel Hill: University of North Carolina, 1950), pp. 119–21. Constance H. Rose, 'Was Calderón Serious?: Another Look at *Los tres mayores prodigios*', in *Hispanic Essays in Honor of Frank P. Casa*, ed. Robert A. Lauer and Henry W. Sullivan (New York: Peter Lang, 1997), pp. 246–52.

be connected to morals, societal norms, questions of taste, hierarchy, religion, personal attacks, food, drink, clothing and other innumerable ideas, in themselves not immediately associated with laughter.

Because of the well-known fact that humour does not exist in a vacuum, most *comedia* analyses tend to draw our attention farther and farther away from the subject of humour in theatre itself, farther away from the theatrical 'how' of humour and closer to the 'why', or 'to what effect' of broader subjects. As rewarding and invigorating as far-ranging sociological, anthropological, psychological or philosophical studies may be, the objective here is not to explain the wider effects and purposes of humour, nor its deep origins, though these will occasionally be addressed in part. Nor will the following chapters attempt to establish any type of theory regarding humour in Calderón, in the *comedia* or in theatre at large. Nevertheless, such theories will be used, examined and criticised, in order to make us more aware of Calderón's own skill in writing theatre. However, before continuing one must answer the simple question: 'What is meant by humour?' It is, by my own definition, anything with the ultimate goal of making somebody laugh. Naturally, this definition is less than satisfying, but I can offer none better without a precision that has eluded theoreticians for thousands of years. While one must acknowledge that there are different types of humour, a taxonomy of the phenomenon in abstract terms would not be as helpful as a loose categorisation of examples taken from Early Modern Spain. Distinguishing between 'wit', 'the comic', 'joke', 'funny' or the like is not nearly as useful as detailing what aspects specific to Golden Age artistic production may have caused an audience, listener or reader to chuckle, guffaw or smile inwardly. Thus, such terms mentioned above shall correspond to the word 'humour', that is, trying to get a laugh, even if it remains unknown whether or not this goal was ever accomplished. 'Goal' and 'trying' refer to intentionality, another concept fraught with its own particular problems, but again there exists no easy way to escape it, provided that one wishes to remain focused upon methods and conjecturing possible results. A reader who declares it impossible to judge Calderón's intentions may still find amusement in the following chapters, and if not in the 'unintentionally' funny jokes, then surely in the foolhardiness of my declaration of these intentions. Nevertheless, the reader is encouraged to 'humour' these analytical foundations and go along with the stated definition for the time being. While the phenomenon in question, as an abstraction, can oscillate between the particular (obscure) to the universal (obvious), one must have faith that many of Calderón's specific jokes remain sufficiently understandable and persist in being funny, allowing us some chance to grasp their nature.

In the spirit of these previous caveats, the book is structured with sceptics in mind. Chapters 1 and 2 refer nearly exclusively to the *teatro breve*, or short comic works of Calderón de la Barca, specifically his *mojigangas* and *entremeses*. The first purpose then is to introduce the reader to these overwhelmingly humorous sub-genres, and prove that Calderón was trying to get a laugh, and that he relied upon specialised and standardised techniques to do so. The second goal is to familiarise the reader further with the workings of *mojigangas* and *entremeses* by analysing specific examples of demonstrated techniques as they pertain to broader contexts of humour, theatre and occasionally other areas. In one instance, we shall see how costumes can be funny, yet also see how a costume pertains to characterisation, or even geography, and how in turn geography may lend itself to humour. In another case, a joke may be described as a satire or a parody, leading to further discussion of these essential topics. The specific examples in these cases, not all humorous, are taken mostly from theatre, while a few may come from poetry or prose, leading to yet further amplification of the context in which a joke may exist. These first two chapters should make clear that the *teatro breve* is anything but 'teatro menor'. Though it may be overwhelmingly humorous, such a characteristic does not exclude complexity and variety, even among examples taken from solely one author such as Calderón de la Barca.

Chapters 3 and 4 revisit the *teatro breve* as it is found embedded within the *comedia*. A syllogism (in honour of Calderón's Scholastic upbringing) can explain the impetus behind studying this connection between art forms still thought to be quite separate. The genre of the *teatro breve* (represented thus far by the aforementioned sub-genres) is overwhelmingly funny. The *comedia*, while as an entire genre is not overwhelmingly funny, can be funny at times, and always contains parts that are overwhelmingly so. Both the *teatro breve* and the *comedia* are theatrical genres, having much in common structurally. *Ergo*, there must be something in the *comedia* that makes it similar to, and occasionally exactly the same (in part) as the *teatro breve*.

If Calderón's *comedias* and his *teatro breve* are in some respects the same, we must change our opinions of each genre, large and small, especially after questioning the widely held notion that they are entirely distinct. Likewise, what do each genre's differences tell us about Calderón's use of humour, considering that he wrote both genres and that he included the smaller pieces within the larger ones? Chapter 5 introduces a third sub-genre: the *jácara*. Because the *entremés* and the *mojiganga* have much in common, it is natural to fit their respective chapters together. Yet because the *jácara* stands apart from the other two sub-genres (for reasons to be discussed later), and because its theatrical manifestation includes much mixing of sub-genres itself, its analysis seems better placed in chapter 5, thus benefiting from previous discussions in chapters 3 and 4. Chapter 6, as can be guessed, examines the *jácara* as it appears in the *comedia*.

This book is as much about genres as it is about humour, all the while recognising the difficulty in speaking of the phenomenon in essential terms, regardless of how much one may try to avoid relating it to anything else. I must warn the reader that I shall use both 'humour' and 'genre' in occasionally unsubtle, perhaps even naïve, ways. However, concentrating on the *teatro breve* and *comedia* as genres related to humour gives solidity to such a study. I believe that humour can be said to reside in jokes, costumes, motions, etc., and these are subsequently housed in recognisable theatrical genres. These two terms are also helpful in understanding Calderón's artistry and the creative process, ideas that are themselves not entirely easy to grasp. For this reason, the study is titled '*The Art of Humour in the* Teatro Breve *and* Comedias *of Calderón de la Barca*'. For Calderón, as for anybody else, making people laugh was an art form, even if 'art' is reduced to the simple manipulation and alteration of certain recognisable aspects of similarly recognisable genres and sub-genres. Beyond having people agree that Calderón did have a sense of humour, I hope that readers will come to know the artistic possibilities that this trait offers, and subsequently see both the playwright and his world of Golden Age theatre differently. While at the moment it may seem difficult to compare the supposedly austere and humourless Calderón with the witty and often scatological (when he is not being austere) Quevedo, such comparisons should seem quite natural by the time the reader reaches the book's conclusion. The mere fact that Calderón wrote *entremeses* allows us to compare him to Cervantes, the most well-known *entremesista* these days, if not during the seventeenth century. Calderón was no Cervantes, yet by seeing the playwright as a fellow joker (at least on occasion), we become free to analyse his works in ways that were not thought possible before. Once we realise that Calderón himself was freer to create than his reputation would allow us to believe, his creations themselves start to reveal a newfound complexity. I hope that recognition of this complexity, which goes beyond any well-worn stereotype of the Spanish Baroque, will spur further investigations using all the analytical tools and research methods afforded Early Modern Spain's more widely recognised proponents of humour.

1

CALDERÓN AND THE *MOJIGANGA*

THE PLAYFUL SYMBOLISM OF THE *MOJIGANGA*

What is a *mojiganga*? Also called a *fin de fiesta*, which emphasises a constant function of the sub-genre, *mojigangas*[1] would be performed at the end of either a *comedia* or *auto sacramental*. They can be defined as a small dramatic piece meant to complement the larger one, something different to mark the end or to bring closure to an event.[2] The 'fin' aspect of the sub-genre thus remains clear, but 'de fiesta' is somewhat ambiguous, for it can be explained in two ways. 'De fiesta' can signify 'pertaining to the celebration', the celebration being the entire theatrical spectacle; but it can also refer to 'a festive ending', signalling an important aspect of all sub-genres within the *teatro breve*. The festive nature of the *mojiganga* is generally more pronounced than that of the *entremés*, and can be more easily described.[3] The reasons for an increased air of festivity are manifold, and the overall function and history of the festivity are described in both Díez Borque's and Buezo's investigations.[4] Because this chapter is not intended to be an overview of the *mojiganga*, but rather a demonstration of Calderón's use of the form, our focus upon festivity and complementarity will necessarily be narrow and will unavoidably leave out many contexts mentioned by others. In general, however, it is important to keep in mind that happier, louder and more colourful pieces often served to complement the larger theatrical works

---

[1] For a more detailed account of the exact generic characteristics of the *mojiganga* and the history of its development, the reader should consult the following works: Catalina Buezo, *La mojiganga dramática: de la fiesta al teatro* (Kassel: Reichenberger, 1993); Evangelina Rodríguez and Antonio Tordera, 'Intención y morfología de la mojiganga en Calderón de la Barca', in Luciano García Lorenzo (ed.), *Calderón: Actas del Congreso internacional sobre Calderón y el teatro del Siglo de Oro* (Madrid: Consejo Superior de Investigaciones Científicas, 1983), pp. 817–24.

[2] Rodríguez and Tordera, in 'Intención y morfología de la mojiganga en Calderón de la Barca', observe that the *mojiganga* 'es el envés de los dramas de honor o de las obras filosóficas y hasta de sus textos dramáticos teológicos'.

[3] Buezo, p. 21.

[4] Díez Borque in his edition of *Una fiesta sacramental barroca* (Madrid: Taurus, 1984) writes on p. 81 about more than one critic who '. . . hablaba de complementariedad barroca en la representación de conjunto (loa, comedia, entremés, etc.)' before he himself enters the controversy surrounding the possible subversive function of such complementarity.

that, by comparison, were more sombre. The *mojiganga* was often – though not always – a combination of pageantry and comic relief. The four examples chosen here will appear in order of increasing complexity and decreasing complementarity. That is to say, they decreasingly distinguish themselves from the *comedia* if one considers plot, characterisation, setting, dialogue and possibly sobriety to be the hallmarks of the 'greater' genre.[5]

Los sitios de recreación del Rey[6] is undoubtedly the least complicated piece in the Calderonian corpus, excluding his *loas* and *bailes*.[7] The 'plot' consists of the following: various actors, with musical accompaniment, appear onstage, dressed as royal parks or gardens, and each tells how they will bring happiness to the new-born 'Infante' or royal 'niño'. The most obvious aspect of this *mojiganga* is the presence of characters and a setting requiring equal portions of fantasy and suspension of disbelief on the part of the audience. Overall, the *teatro breve* is known for its distortion of reality and the persistent flouting of its laws, for representing something that could never be found in anybody's everyday existence. As an extreme example, *Sitios* pays no regard to mimesis, but in other pieces we will see that the lines between unbelievable fantasy and hard reality become fainter and fainter. In reality, parks cannot speak with a human voice, but making them do so offers great comic possibilities. The association between 'costume' and 'party' is a common one in many cultures, and

---

5 See Buezo, pp. 83–117.

6 All of Calderón's short comic works cited here, unless otherwise expressed, will be taken from Pedro Calderón de la Barca, *Teatro cómico breve*, ed. María Luisa Lobato (Kassel: Reichenberger, 1989). This piece presents an example of the difficulties in establishing authorship, given that Calderón de la Barca himself never attached his name to any separate printed piece of *teatro breve*. Compare María Luisa Lobato's 'Criterios de edición y atribución' (Calderón de la Barca, *Teatro cómico breve*, pp. 22–5) and Buezo's discovery of complicating factors regarding authorship (Buezo, pp. 111–12). I stand by Lobato's arguments for authorship, which on the whole seem more thorough than those of Rodríguez and Tordera, whose justifications are often less detailed and often missing altogether. Only one Calderonian autograph of an independent short comic piece, *El mayorazgo*, is known to exist.

7 Both *loas* and *bailes* can be included under the denomination 'teatro breve', but they have been omitted for the following reasons. During Calderón's time, they were not overwhelmingly funny or heavily laden with jokes. Because most of this study is about humour in Calderón, it appears reasonable that these pieces can be ignored, while recognising that our perspective on the 'teatro breve' as a whole does suffer some reduction. The jokes, almost all wordplay, that can be found in Calderón's *bailes* and *loas*, can also be found in his *entremeses* and *mojigangas*, and thus the humorous conditions of the former sub-genres are contained in the latter. There undoubtedly exist similarities and shared characteristics between many of the sub-genres, between a *loa* and an *entremés* for example, but this leads us back to the blurring of genre distinctions (giving us a *loa entremesada*), which is as obvious a phenomenon as it is an insoluble problem concerning the delimitation of genres. As the differences merely between *mojiganga* and *entremés* themselves are difficult to explain, and because of limitations in the length and scope of this investigation, *bailes* and *loas* as discrete art forms have been omitted.

so is the association between dressing up and acting funny.[8] The incongruity witnessed when seeing a human pretend to be something decidedly inhuman can easily provide humour.[9] In other areas of literature, one need only to think of the clown portraying 'Wall' from the play-within-the-play of *A Midsummer Night's Dream*, or Scout dressed as a ham for a school play in the dramatisation of the novel *To Kill a Mockingbird*.

In *Sitios*, the actor Vallejo enters the stage 'de barba larga vestido', offering a moment of comic suspense before announcing indirectly that he represents the river Tagus (or 'Tajo'). The concept of an 'old man river' was nothing new in literature, but seeing an old man draped in ivy can hardly be called an everyday occurrence, and is inherently incongruous. Incongruities can be exaggerated even further, becoming comical, as shown by the actor Mendoza, 'con una horquilla [a gun mount] y cabeza de jabalí'. Assuming that Mendoza is wearing the boar head, grasping a 'horquilla', the literal instrument of his destruction, allows one incongruity to be layered upon another. His porcine prosthetic and 'horquilla' may carry great symbolic value (as well as fodder for puns), but this value is not undercut by, nor does it attenuate, the laughter caused by such a spectacle. Symbolism is not synonymous with sobriety. Such outlandish costumes may seem extreme, but they lie on a sort of 'continuum' shared by other milder forms of exaggerated dress and behaviour found in other areas of the *teatro breve*. The stage directions 'vestido de ridículo' (which would be redundant in this *mojiganga*) appear in many

---

[8] 'Si le masque suffit à définir une catégorie de fêtes d'une manière pertinente, c'est que son utilisation a un sens por l'ensemble de la fête.' See Marianne Mesnil, 'Mascarades et jeux de signes', in Pier Giovanni d'Ayala and Martine Boiteux (eds), *Carnavals et mascarades* (Paris: Bordas, 1988), p. 22. Mesnil examines the associations from a semiotic perspective, treating the masks (for us, synonymous with costumes) as signs in a larger and more intricate play of signs. Both Buezo (pp. 310–16), and Rodríguez and Tordera in *Entremeses, jácaras y mojigangas* (Madrid: Castalia, 1983), p. 44, explain the semiotics of costumes in the context of the *mojiganga*, but what matters most in this study is the simple association between costumes and the festive and humorous atmosphere that they reinforce. When the time comes to look at *La mojiganga de los guisados*, the notion of Carnival can be included in the discussion.

[9] Henri Bergson in Wylie Sypher (ed.), *Comedy, 'An essay on Comedy' by George Meredith, 'Laughter' by Henri Bergson* (Baltimore: Johns Hopkins University Press, 1980) explains (p. 86) that 'A man in disguise is comical', because it corresponds to Bergson's fundamental and unchanging explanation of 'the comic' as 'something mechanical encrusted on the living'. The word 'mechanical' is linked to Bergson's notion of 'rigidity' in an individual that makes him the target of 'corrective laughter' that ridicules his departure from 'flexible and supple' human behaviour. Bergson contends that this correction is always at work, though it may not be readily apparent to those who laugh. Whether or not the function of laughter is ultimately to invite 'flexible' behaviour is up for debate, but the initial part of his explanation remains one of the most satisfactory explanations to date. Many of Bergson's examples come from the farces of Molière, works of comedy that share many of the same influences (the Italian commedia dell'arte for example) as the *teatro breve*, and that may have even been directly inspired by the Spanish *teatro breve* itself.

pieces that are not properly *mojigangas*, nor exclusively festive. Yet this 'ridículo' is very much part of the 'costume party' atmosphere that runs from smaller pieces like *Sitios* to the larger 'comedia de figurón'.

Regarding the subject of costumes and symbolism, one can easily see how the characters of *Sitios* belong to a long tradition of personification allegory in the Spanish theatre. Though they serve a different purpose, people dressed as places of recreation are not so different from characters like 'Sinagoga', found in Diego Sánchez de Badajoz's *Farsa de la iglesia*. In this piece, a human actor represents Mosaic Law, an abstraction (as is the concept of recreation), but also the Jewish place of worship that is a physical entity (such as a park). A theatrical figure, and a comic one at that, Sánchez de Badajoz's 'Sinagoga' bears close resemblance to the characters found in *Sitios*. Calderón himself would use this personification allegory of a place-name in his *autos sacramentales*, along with those figures representing pure abstraction, such as Love, Knowledge and Faith.[10] While the characters in the *mojiganga* are not strictly personification allegories of abstract concepts, they function similarly. They use the human form to represent something impossible to see in its entirety, not because it is an abstraction, but because of its sheer size and expanse.

Returning to the subject of humour, one might ask: In *Sitios*, who are the butts of jokes? Whom are we laughing at? Humour need not be degrading, and in the case of *Sitios*, it merely stems from playing with the notions of symbolism explained above. A river, impossible to see in its entirety – Menippus and others' fantastic high-altitude journeys in books are quite difficult to duplicate onstage – can make the audience laugh by sporting a long beard, wearing ivy and talking. The audience might have read about an 'old man river' in poetry or mythology, but a river described in a text, and merely in the domain of the reader's imagination, does not suffer the distortion of being represented onstage. The literalisation of the concept produces a river that must walk about (something no 'real' river should do), and perhaps even stoop, wheeze and cough, if we remember that the Tagus in *Sitios* is a 'barba' or old man stock figure. Though not obvious at first glance, the audience is laughing at a visual pun[11]

---

[10] See A. M. Pollin, 'Judaísmo y Sinagoga en Calderón: recreación de un tema alegórico medieval', *Revista de Literatura*, 54 (1992), 149–81.

[11] A visual pun allows one to perceive two things at once through sight, which is not the same thing as seeing two things at once in the same image, though this is one type of visual pun. An example would be two-word meanings stemming from the same image, such as in a rebus. In the case of *Sitios*, the literalisation of an 'old man river' allows the audience to see both 'old man' and 'river' separately *and* at the same time. See pp. 142–8 of Walter Redfern's *Puns* (New York: Basil Blackwell, 1984). Throughout his book, Redfern admirably vindicates a form of joking against which even I harbour deep prejudices. Calderón demonstrates the ingenuity and freshness that can come from skilful punning, a form of joke which Bergson (p. 138) called the 'least reputable' sort of comic inversion. For a good overview of Calderón's verbal joking, see 'La palabra en la estrategia de entretenimiento', in Rodríguez and Tordera's introduction to *Entremeses, jácaras y mojigangas*.

while simultaneously watching a 'river' and a 'barba' onstage. Spectators are made to see the Tagus in a new light, which they find surprising and enjoyable. A more explicit example of this phenomenon is the appearance of Luisa, 'con una olla cubierta', representing the Zarzuela. The double meanings of the word and object 'zarzuela' (park and seafood stew) are exploited by placing the name of the famous recreational area in an ambivalent context. The simplest word-play can produce an ephemeral comic effect, but it can also serve as a 'building block' for even greater jokes. Luisa follows her initial presentation with quips about an 'olla a medio cocer' and an 'olla podrida', and Simón chimes in with further references to Carnival, thus leading to a further double wordplay on swordplay.[12]

Luisa   La Zarzuela, muy casera,
           porque más razón le deis
           les trae a vuestros pucheros
           su olla a medio cocer.
           Aunque pierda mi fiesta
           por esta dicha,
           no me llamen por eso
           olla podrida.

Simón   Por las Carnestolendas
           en mejor parte,
           usté nos dará el lunes
           con la del martes . . .[13]

Words, ideas and costumes are played with as a child plays with toy blocks, mixing them, stacking them, connecting and disconnecting, bringing forth laughter through the marvel of different possibilities and unexpected results. In a fashion, it is a form of *conceptismo*, friendly and easy to understand.[14] However, the *conceptismo* in this case is made richer in a visual context, exploiting the interplay between surprise in the imagination and surprise caused by objects in plain sight. The childlike marvel of costumes and word-play can be considered the humorous equivalent of the religious marvel brought about by the allegorical figures and majestic poetry of the *autos sacramentales*. Nevertheless, it would be incorrect to call *Los sitios de recreación del Rey* a grotesque parody of a 'higher' art form. While laughter

---

[12] See the note on p. 348 of Calderón de la Barca, *Entremeses, jácaras y mojigangas*.

[13] Calderón de la Barca, *Teatro cómico breve*, p. 221, ll. 66–77.

[14] Baltasar Gracián in *Agudeza y arte de ingenio* (Madrid: Cátedra, 1998), writes about elaborate ways in which wit, expressed through *conceptismo*, or the skilful use of poetic conceits, can lead to discovery and greater understanding. The jokes found in the *teatro breve* are rarely of an edifying nature, but they share many of the same 'construction techniques' (allusion, double-meaning, paradox, etc.) named by Gracián.

can be tied to degrading ridicule,[15] a common feature in parody, there is no requirement that laughter itself be degrading, as the jokes in *Sitios* prove. It would be difficult to believe that the audience was meant to look upon the actors, or the places they represented, with derision. This tiny play was performed in celebration of a baby prince's birth. It is a play in honour of an infant and celebrates the future joy he will find in his family's parks and places of leisure. Playfulness without degradation is certainly the most appropriate style for a work of art with such a purpose.

Every character in *Sitios*, except for Simón and the musician, enters the stage and exits before the next character arrives. To a certain degree this mimics a ceremonial procession, a structure upon which many of Spain's more primitive sixteenth-century plays depended. This kind of procession may have links to many social phenomena of the higher classes, such as a parade of heroes, or the incessant visitations of courtiers and visitors as a king or prince holds his audience. Precision, order and even monotony are features associated with a particular type of aristocratic celebration. One could also imagine the orderly serving of courses at a royal banquet, as opposed to the containers of food piled haphazardly together in a common eating situation. The musical introduction that accompanies each figure in *Sitios* – though it comes after the character's speech – is reminiscent of a trumpet blare or public declaration upon the entrance of a worthy person at a high-class social event. People do not stumble onto the scene, but march out in an orderly fashion and leave on a musical cue. All this order, pomp and circumstance does not make the occasion any less of a party, and for this reason we must be careful in defining the term 'festive'. There are different kinds of festivities for different classes of people,[16] yet all intend to be fun; none cease to be full of laughter.

---

[15] More famous than Bergson for commenting on the negative aspect of laughter is Thomas Hobbes, who in *Human Nature* (New York: Oxford University Press, 1994), p. 54, writes: 'I may therefore conclude, that the passion of laughter is nothing else but a sudden glory arising from the sudden conception of some eminency in ourselves, by comparison with the infirmities of others, or with our own.'

[16] This is not the same as saying that there are different types of festive dramatic forms corresponding to different types of audiences. Everything depends upon whether one is speaking of the *mojiganga* as a 'parateatral' phenomenon, as true street theatre, or as a form expressly written and performed for the theatre. Buezo does an excellent job of differentiating between different types of *mojigangas*, their respective participants and audiences, and the transition from street procession to standard dramatic form. See Buezo, pp. 33–95. In the case of Calderón, it would be extremely difficult, for many reasons, to establish a link between the style of festivity in a *mojiganga* and the social class of the audience watching it. Much of Calderón's *teatro breve* was performed in the royal Palacio del Retiro, but this rarely appears to have any direct bearing on the content of the works or the possible crudeness or popular nature of their jokes. At the same time, many of Calderón's *comedias*, featuring the most regal of events and characters, could be performed in a run-of-the-mill *corral*, in front of a 'público popular'. For this investigation, it matters only that *within the works themselves*, one can make a connection between the social class of the people and how they celebrate or have a good time.

The *mojiganga*-as-procession is not only an example of how ceremony and humour mingle; it is also a clear-cut example of comic repetition and climax. While modern stand-up comedians speak of the comic 'rule of threes', another unwritten rule states that any type of repetition can be funny in itself. Without delving too far into the taxonomy of comic terms (something done enough by others), it is evident that repetition is a form of exaggeration or distortion, both terms previously associated with the *teatro breve*. A man dressed as a river is funny, but a man wearing a boar head – further distorting his appearance – is even funnier. A man dressed as a river followed by the fantastic boar-man – displaying one distorted image after another – is even funnier still. No precise comic value can be assigned to each figure, yet they bring more laughter when presented in sequence, rather than in completely separate contexts. While the technique of repetition may appear obvious in *Sitios*, it can be found in forms subtler than those encountered here. A joke may never achieve its goal unless all of its constituent parts work successfully together, especially if each part in itself is not enough to make somebody laugh. Often a joke can consist of a series of completely identical features, with only one small twist at the end. If one were not paying attention to these identical and ostensibly humourless features, one might miss the twist at the end, and the joke would be lost. Such subtler forms of repetition may be at work in the *teatro breve* as it is integrated into the larger *comedia* genre.

> *Sale Juan Rana de moro y otros siguiéndole con instrumentos, todos de moros.*[17]

Here lies a spectacle-within-the-spectacle, a showstopper if you will. Simón stops singing, the musicians silence their instruments, and Juan Rana with his Moorish entourage takes over the scene. Juan Rana the Moor even introduces a new musical refrain to replace the one that all the other characters were singing beforehand. If we consider the costumed characters in *Sitios* to be visual jokes, then Juan Rana's arrival announces the biggest joke of them all. Also known as Cosme Pérez, this comic actor was the toast of Madrid and it was said that he could make the audience burst into laughter by merely walking onto the stage.[18] A great number of interludes and sketches that were written for him carry his name in the title, a name that came from a single *entremés* and later became a permanent fixture.[19] Consequently, any piece

---

[17] Calderón de la Barca, *Teatro cómico breve*, p. 222.

[18] This according to a manuscript quoted in Cotarelo y Mori, *Colección de entremeses, loas, bailes, jácaras y mojigangas desde fines del siglo XVI á mediados del siglo XVIII*, in the series *Nueva biblioteca de autores españoles*, vol. 17 (Madrid: Bailly y Baillere, 1911), p. clxi. This citation is found in a detailed and relatively extensive biographical section on Cosme Pérez.

[19] Hannah Bergman, in *Luis Quiñones de Benavente y sus entremeses* (Madrid: Castalia, 1965), p. 519, writes: 'Creador y creación llegaron a confundirse tan íntimamente que el público, y hasta algunas escrituras legales, llamaban al actor por el nombre del personaje que desempeñaba por excelencia.'

starring Juan Rana cannot help being metatheatrical.[20] Every mention of
his name within the work reminds the audience that he is not only a doctor, a
gentleman or a mayor, but also a famous comedian with adoring fans. Juan
Rana represents perfectly the ambivalence between fantasy and reality so
common in the *teatro breve*. Yet this ambivalence is anything but destabilis-
ing, though it may bring laughter and confusion. Metatheatricality can be a
violent comical rupture of illusion, or a gentle jest that runs parallel to the rest
of the action. In the case of *Sitios* stated above, fiction and truth stand in relationship to each other on stable dramatic ground, just as Juan Rana's (or is it
Cosme Pérez's?) squat figure stands solidly onstage.

Aside from following the tradition of ceremonial processions in *Sitios*,
Calderón de la Barca was copying yet another sub-genre of the *teatro breve*
for his *mojiganga*, namely works invented by Luis Quiñones de Benavente
called *entremeses cantados*.[21] These include *El casamiento de la calle mayor
con el Prado* and *La puente segoviana*, in which actors dressed as famous
Madrid landmarks walk, talk and sing, the same as in *Sitios*. These *entremeses*
differ from *Sitios* in subject matter, as the characters are associated not
with royal pastimes, but instead with working-class situations. Thus, while
the talking streets and bridges are still the product of a festive fantasy, in
Casamiento and *La puente segoviana*, imagination and celebration are tied to
everyday social realities. Humour helps integrate shades of truth (realistic
comments on tariffs, trades, coaches, etc.) with utter fancy, such as a talking
customs gate that jangles pots and pans. These pieces are also structurally
different from *Sitios* in that the characters interact with each other and create
more complex situations, as well as a greater variety of jokes. Both Calderón
and Quiñones de Benavente's pieces are mainly or completely sung
respectively, allowing for a heightened air of festivity but also for musical

---

[20] See Catherine Larson, 'Metatheater and the *Comedia*: Past, Present, and Future', in
The Golden Age Comedia: Text, Theory, and Performance, ed. Charles Ganelin and
Howard Mancing (West Lafayette: Purdue University Press, 1994), pp. 204–21. This is a
helpful survey of the theory of metatheatre in the context of Spanish Golden Age drama,
starting with Abel's original and broad thesis, O'Connor's appropriation and refinement of
the thesis for Spanish drama, and the resultant debate about the use of the term, a debate
that still continues today. I agree with Larson (p. 206) that 'metatheater is not really a
critical methodology per se, or even a theory (except in the most abstract of senses),
although it could certainly be argued that an understanding of the phenomenon is a useful
interpretive tool. Consequently, as a term, "metadrama" is more descriptive than
prescriptive.' See also Margaret Greer, *The Play of Power: Mythological Court Dramas of
Calderón de la Barca* (Princeton: Princeton University Press, 1991), p. 176 for another
example of how Juan Rana's double, or even triple, identity worked onstage.

[21] Luis Quiñones de Benavente, *Joco seria: burlas veras o reprehensión moral festiva
de los desórdenes públicos, recopilados por Manuel Antonio de Vargas* (New York: G. Olms,
1985). The fact that *La mojiganga de los sitios de recreación del Rey* and the *entremeses
cantados* have so much in common provides a clear example of the overlap between *teatro
breve* sub-genres.

parody.[22] The musicians sing the praises of ridiculous costumed figures, all incapable of commanding any real respect from the audience. *Sitios* may at first appear to belong to a simple and limited genre, but when comparing it to the *entremeses cantados*, one begins to see a variety of comic and dramatic possibilities arising from the standard processional structure.

ORDER, CHAOS AND CARNIVAL

La mojiganga de los guisados reveals how the dramatic possibilities of a procession can be further realised, and proves how seemingly limitless jokes and literary devices can be attached to the simple armature of the *mojiganga* form. The basis of many a joke in Golden Age dramatic works is a ridiculous or impossible idea made real onstage. Just as the personified places found in *Los sitios de recreación del Rey* offered comic *asombro* by making a river sing or a park play the guitar, so do the 'guisados' who appear in this *mojiganga*. In this case, differences can be noted from the very beginning because the comic effect is heightened by the frame. Before the personified foodstuffs enter the stage, Don Nuño, listening to Don Gil's 'preview', has declared 'Yo lo oigo y no lo creo.'[23] Don Nuño, possibly sympathising with the audience, offers a moment of resistance against the fantastic creations that threaten to take over the stage.[24] He is a fleeting voice of reason, both a straight man and a straw man, who soberly censures a driving force in the *teatro breve*: silliness and disorder that overrun sobriety and logic.

Los guisados employs the same type of humorous personification as *Sitios*. The device of personification is naturally not exclusive to theatre, and in fact, through it we may see how the *teatro breve* relates to purely read works.[25] Francisco de Quevedo wrote a poem entitled *Boda y acompanamiento del campo*,[26] a simple narration consisting of a list of guests, all fruits and

22 Unfortunately there is not enough space here to explore musical parody, but it is certainly very common in the *teatro breve* and takes different forms.

23 Calderón de la Barca, *Teatro cómico breve*, p. 321, l. 11.

24 Don Nuño's doubt also creates a tiny satire of the stereotypical mad playwright. Much like the English expression 'I can't believe it', his reaction combines disbelief with the disgust he would feel, were the unbelievable to be actually true.

25 André Jolles, in *Einfache Formen* (I use the translation *Las formas simples*, Santiago de Chile: Editorial Universitaria, 1971), explores how larger, more complex literary creations can base themselves on smaller un-literary 'forms' such as myths, fairy tales and even jokes. It is not difficult to see how one could write an *entremés* with no more material than what one received from hearing a joke on the street. At the same time, as Cory Reed has shown (*The Novelist as Playwright: Cervantes and the Entremés Nuevo*, New York: Peter Lang, 1993), larger forms such as the novel can have a profound effect on smaller forms that might have originally come from an oral anecdote. Freely flowing appropriations and associations are at home in the *teatro breve*, but also in the art of the baroque at large.

26 These citations (thanks to a note from Calderón de la Barca, *Teatro cómico breve*, p. 329), come from Francisco de Quevedo y Villegas, *Obras completas*, 2 vols, ed. Felicidad Buendía, vol. 2 (Madrid, Aguilar, 1978), pp. 226–8.

vegetables, invited to the wedding of Don Repollo and Doña Berza. The descriptions of the personified fruits and vegetables can be playful, such as likening Don Rábano to a 'moro de juego de cañas',[27] but the majority of the descriptions take on a strong satiric bent. For example: 'La Granada, deshonesta, / a lo moza cortesana: / desembozo en la hermosura / descarmiento en la gracia,'[28] and 'Don Durazno, a lo invidioso, / mostrando agradable cara, / descubriendo con el trato / malas y duras entrañas.'[29] Quevedo, arch-satirist that he was, made the artistic choice of turning a pleasant country wedding – made even more frivolous by the fact that all the participants are edible plants – into a veiled satirical panorama looking down upon a society where many men are hard-hearted hypocrites and many women are brazen hussies. In fact, the vast majority of the characters described in the poem represent some human failing or negative social type. The use of fruits and vegetables does not soften the satire, though it may add humour.[30] If anything, using a peach to describe hard-heartedness adds pessimism, as there is no hope for the peach-pit ever to soften. Thus, the personified peach becomes a negative type that can experience no change. Satire is full of fixed types,[31] and the use of personification can often intensify the effect by exaggerating the type's chief characteristic. As well as using types to criticise general vices, Quevedo also covers such topical subjects as blood purity (referring to the newlyweds: 'si no caballeros pardos / verdes fidalgos de España') and over-dressed ladies ('Doña Alcachofa, compuesta / a imitación de las flacas: basquiñas y más basquiñas, / carne poca y muchas faldas').[32] The seemingly frivolous and

---

[27] Quevedo, *Obras completas*, vol. 2, p. 227.

[28] Ibid.   [29] Ibid.

[30] Laughter is an integral part of satire: 'Even if the contempt which the satirist feels may grow into furious hatred, he will still express his hatred in terms suitable, not to murderous hostility, but to scorn. Hate alone may be expressed in other kinds of literature; and so may laughter, or the smile of derision. The satirist aims at combining them.' See Gilbert Highet, *The Anatomy of Satire* (Princeton: Princeton University Press, 1962), p. 22. Yet laughter should not always be considered a tempering element that works against destructive urges. 'Murderous scorn' may be conveyed by the laughter itself. See Robert C. Elliot, *The Power of Satire: Magic, Ritual, Art* (Princeton: Princeton University Press, 1960). He writes of cultures where the weight of shame is so great that people have been known to die of ridicule. While it is impossible to believe that Quevedo was trying to kill somebody by comparing him or her to a vegetable, we should never forget the destructive possibilities of ridicule (in its ancient origins and modern manifestations) and the necessary role of laughter.

[31] For a brief yet enlightening discussion of satirical fixed types in the *entremés*, see Eugenio Asensio, *Itinerario del entremés desde Lope de Rueda a Quiñones de Benavente: con cinco entremeses inéditos de D. Francisco de Quevedo* (Madrid: Gredos, 1971), pp. 77–86. Asensio follows Eric Auerbach's designation of the dramatic *figura* as a feature that makes its way into Spanish theatre, including the *teatro breve*. Highet (p. 224) mentions Brant's *Ship of Fools* as an example of this kind of 'descriptive satire'.

[32] Quevedo, *Obras completas*, vol. 2, p. 226. The *Diccionario de autoridades* describes 'caballeros pardos' as those who, without being noble, have gained certain privileges from the king and who aid in the defence of the kingdom. The most reasonable meaning for 'verde hidalgo' would be 'cristiano nuevo', according to my interpretation. The newlyweds are not true nobles, nor possess a family's warrior history to make up for this deficiency.

contrived simplicity of gathering fruits and vegetables for a wedding is an artistic creation that can be articulated in both playful and serious ways. One must remember that Quevedo's poem, though perhaps not a direct influence on Calderón, is of a processional nature (one character presented after another), and has a 'plot' and characterisation that would lend themselves very well to the structure of the *mojiganga*.

Though the simple personifications in *Los guisados* are comparable to those found in Quevedo's poem, there stands one figure who is worthy of separate and particular mention. He is the god Bacchus, or Baco. His presence is representative of two important features of the *teatro breve*, both of which have been briefly mentioned: 'order versus chaos' and parody. Much of the *teatro breve* depends upon a conflict between order and chaos, even if it is on a very small scale. Disorder may take different forms, but it generally stems from the confusion caused by a deception or *burla*, which is integral to the plot. *Mojigangas*, given their processional nature, often lack the dramatic *burla*, but can find other ways to create this type of small-scale comic conflict. Baco, like the dutifully doubting 'straight man' Don Nuño at the beginning, is an order figure, but in a much more significant role. Baco functions as the judge of the tourney and as the master of ceremonies, deciding when the figures are to speak or do battle. At one moment he declares '¿no veis que soy Baco / y a todos presido?'[33] His right of rule comes from the fact that he is the most 'puro', a completely ironic reference to watered-down wine, probably the most repeated topic for jokes used in the *teatro breve*. An order figure like Baco is essential to establishing rules for breaking, structures for tearing down, and order to disrupt, all for hilarious comic effect.

However, Baco is not the typical order figure of the *entremés*, usually an *alguacil* or similar law enforcement official. Yet in a setting where the main characters are a meat stew or a meatball, his presence is appropriate, poetic and humorous, all at the same time. Baco is also a parodic figure. Of all the allegorical and mythological figures, the one that represents getting drunk must be the least edifying.[34] Another way to make fun of appropriated

---

[33] Calderón de la Barca, *Teatro cómico breve*, p. 336.

[34] Calderón is one of innumerable authors who exploit Greek mythology and allegory for humorous purposes. One of the most famous among such authors from the ancient world is Lucian of Somosata, whose second-century satirical *dialogues*, especially *Charon*, were admired and imitated by humanists of the fifteenth and early sixteenth centuries. Erasmus of Rotterdam is famous for his praise of Folly, and David Marsh reminds us of how this allegory herself 'praises the gods under her sway, such as Bacchus or Cupid'. See David Marsh, *Lucian and the Latins: Humor and Humanism in the Early Renaissance* (Ann Arbor: University of Michigan Press, 1998), p. 173. Given the notion (heavily promoted by Bakhtin) that the Renaissance was a time imbued with the 'carnivalesque' spirit of playful, and even raunchy, criticism, Marsh's findings regarding ridiculous gods may surprise us. He writes of the short *Dialogues of the Gods*, stating: 'Since these comic scenes presuppose a thorough knowledge of Homeric mythology, they

mythology in higher art forms (painting, prose, poetry, drama) would be to
have the gods, even of high stature, act ridiculously onstage. A good example
of this can be found in Quiñones de Benavente's *Entremés de los planetas*.[35]
In the piece, Mars 'anda en zelo' after Venus, Venus herself sings *jácaras*, and
the Sun and Moon mock each other with taunting rhymes. Any conventional
significance of these gods is exploited for no other reason than to get a laugh,
reflecting the principal goal of all the *teatro breve* included in this
investigation. Like the words and images that the characters of *Sitios*
represented, in Quiñones de Benavente's piece, themes themselves become
playthings that are tossed about with utter irreverence. War, love, light and
darkness, all ideas that matter deeply in human existence, are drained of any
importance and instead are used as a pretext for jokes and petty squabbling.
The nature of parody is not necessarily to destroy its target, but rather to
transform its appearance, tarring and feathering it in a figurative sense. Such
transformation itself is an act of artistic creation that can involve a great
amount of care, which in turn requires a thorough understanding of the
parodic target's original meaning. In *Los planetas*, the Sun and the Moon do
not just choose any insults for each other, but only ones that correspond
closely to their opposition's nature. In any situation, an insult that hits closest
to its victim's nature is sure to injure the most. This much is obvious. But for
the insult (or parody) to become a successful artistic endeavour, it must be
expressed creatively and ingeniously. Returning to Baco as a parodic figure,
we see that the same types of concerns apply. Choosing the God of Wine as
an arbiter can be seen as a humorous insult and a disregard for the abstraction
of justice potentially represented by Greek gods Zeus or Athena, or a
personified allegorical figure of justice herself. In *Los guisados*, the entire
setting of the tourney is debased (stews instead of knights), and in the
humorous aesthetics of the scene, Baco is the perfect man for the job. As in

---

offered little to charm humanist readers versed primarily in the Latin tradition.' Of the
longer dialogues, which sometimes held interest because of their philosophical themes,
four that take place on Mount Olympus were considered scandalous because: 'A central
comic feature of these works, which paradoxically aroused indignation of Christian
readers, is Lucian's irreverent depiction of the gods, especially Zeus.' Yet it is difficult to
sympathise with such scandal when one considers: 'Mocking traditional authority is part
of the liberating impulse of comedy.' See Marsh, pp. 76–7. Calderón must have been quite
aware of this impulse, and he saw no difficulty in mocking the propriety of an allegory for
authority and justice by electing a drunken god as a judge.

[35] Quiñones de Benavente, *Joco seria*, fols 156a–159a. See also Bergman, *Luis
Quiñones de Benavente y sus entremeses*, p. 331. Bergman explains that this particular
entremés cantado by Quiñones de Benavente is very near to a *mojiganga* in its presentation. She also writes that it bears many resemblances to Quevedo's *La hora de todos* in the
way it presents the gods. For yet another example of the similarity between Quevedo's
prose and the *teatro breve*, compare the gods in the opening chapter of *La hora de todos*
with those in *Los planetas*.

any Greek tragedy, or contemporary mythological play, the gods oversee the affairs of mortals on earth. From the mortals, the gods demand respect, obedience and admiration. So does Baco, but this demand is found in a ridiculous context that turns the relationship between gods and mortals into a silly game. When analysing the relationship between the *teatro breve* and the *comedia*, it will become apparent that joking about mythology can occur just as easily in the larger dramatic genre.

After looking at the literary aspects of *Los guisados*, it is time to make a brief incursion into the anthropological aspects of this *mojiganga*. A fruitful approach used by other critics involves analysing the *teatro breve* from the point of view of Carnival. These observations are borrowed from the great scholar of the 'carnivalesque', Mikhail Bakhtin.[36] Bakhtin relates the pre-Lenten feasts to a time of great permissiveness, 'a temporary suspension of the entire official system with all its prohibitions, and hierarchic barriers'.[37] The temporary nature of this period is important to consider, as Bakhtin does not argue for Carnival as a venue for the permanent overthrow of established social structures. Carnival is a separate and discrete moment that contains its own rules, but does not severely affect the temporally outside world. Rodríguez and Tordera point out how the suspension of time is an important part of the *mojiganga* form.[38] In *Sitios*, time was only measured by the presentation of one figure after another. In *Los guisados*, time obviously passes, but not in any way that corresponds to ordinary human existence.[39] This lack of temporal consciousness is perfectly logical in the realm of personification, as stews and meatballs, just like parks and rivers, have no reason to conceive of time in the same way as humans. Likewise, in Quiñones de Benavente's *Los planetas*, the Sun and the Moon, being markers of time themselves, exist outside of the normal human temporal realm. Personification and the absence of humanly measurable time are closely associated with allegorical dramatic forms such as Calderón's *autos*. Theatrical personification is synonymous with dressing up in a costume, and absence of time, by definition, means acting outside of conventional constraints. These two ambivalent features can easily be exploited in a carnivalesque atmosphere. Both Carnival and dramatic allegory can use the same artistic devices to achieve different ends, and Calderón de la Barca is the perfect example of someone who knew how to achieve both. One form (the *mojiganga*) is overwhelmingly funny, and the other (the *auto sacramental*) is not; and this type of contrast reaches

36 Mikhail M. Bakhtin, *Rabelais and His World*, ed. Hélène Iswolsky (Bloomington: Indiana University Press, 1984).   37 Bakhtin, *Rabelais*, p. 89.
38 Rodríguez and Tordera, 'Intención y morfología', p. 823.
39 Unlike *mojigangas*, most *entremeses* remain closely connected with 'real-time' as the *entremesil* characters and their activities are firmly rooted in day-to-day activities, such as buying, selling, stealing, eating, gossiping, etc., in recognisable mundane environs.

the heart of the matter when approaching humour from an aesthetic point of view.[40]

Another important aspect of Carnival found in many a *mojiganga* is a spirit of mockery closely related to parody. Examples that Bakhtin lists include: the jester-as-king, 'the Will of the Ass' and 'the drunkards' mass',[41] all of which poke fun at venerated institutions. In the case of *Los guisados* it is clear that the tourney between the stews is a degraded ritual ordinarily associated with the nobility. However, one must also recognise that an onstage competition of any sort offers a pretext for conflict, and captures the attention of the audience in a theatrical piece without any plot. It would be excessive to claim that a major purpose of *Los guisados* is to make a mockery of noble forms of competition, though this is partly the intention and contributes to the general humour of the piece. It is more fruitful to look at this mock tourney as the transformation of a violent conflict into something light-hearted and festive. In a literary sense, this *mojiganga* bears close resemblance to the mock epic, but in an anthropological sense, it is a close relative of carnivalesque battles. Bakhtin often names Carnival as an occasion that celebrates life and regeneration. Death is of little concern, and when mentioned, it is laughed at and seen as only another part of the cycle of life, death and rebirth.[42] Everything continues, consuming, expelling,

[40] From the perspective of dressing up, the lines between genres are easily blurred, even in comparing a *mojiganga* with an *auto sacramental*. We are lucky to have stage directions that offer at least some idea of the visual effects that came from costumes. Here are three examples. *Los guisados* states (between lines 34 and 35): '*Sale por . . . otro lado don Estofado y doña Olla, que estas figuras se pueden hacer o vestirlas ridículamente como suenan o con verdaderas ollas y pucheros.*' Later Don Mondongo (between lines 197 and 198): '*Descúbrese y estará vestido con morcillas y manos.*' In Calderón's *auto*, *La cena del rey Baltasar*, in Pedro Calderón de la Barca, *Obras completas*, vol. 3, ed. Ángel Valbuena Briones (Madrid: Aguilar, 1960–7), p. 155, the comic figure Pensamiento is described as '*vestido de loco, de muchos colores*'. In yet another *auto*, *A tu prójimo como a ti*, Culpa is '*vestida a lo bandolero, con capa gascona, montera, chupa, y pistolas*' (*Obras completas*, vol. 3, p. 1889). At what point does one costume become a cause for laughter, or at least an aid in getting people to giggle? Naturally, the costumes need not work autonomously, and their function as sign (as the semioticians would say) can vary as it is integrated with the words and actions of the characters onstage. The Bandit-Culpa, the Patchwork-Pensamiento, also carry a 'semiotic tradition' with them that may come from the theatre itself, and not solely from masquerades or Carnival. As one may guess, integrating a study of the *auto sacramental* at this point would create too wide an area of debate, but the genre is useful as a point of reference regarding costume and celebration. 'Dressing up' in *comedia* criticism is inevitably placed in the context of disguise, deception and social role-playing, while costumes in the *teatro breve* (considered by critics to be more representative of popular sentiment) are associated with joking and Carnival. These types of paradigms (which may or may not have guided Calderón's thinking) can easily lead one to missing humorous moments.

[41] Bakhtin, *Rabelais*, pp. 81, 85 and 295, respectively.

[42] See Bakhtin, *Rabelais*, pp. 197–211, for Bakhtin's vision of carnivalesque violence. He concludes (p. 211) that Rabelais wrote from a tradition where 'Bloodshed, dismemberment, burning, death, beatings, blows, curses, and abuses – all these elements are steeped in "merry time", time which kills and gives birth, which allows nothing old to be perpetuated and never ceases to regenerate the new and the youthful.' Calderón's 'guisados', while violent, are not exactly agents of regeneration, and do not appear to fit into this vision.

living, dying and springing anew into the world in order to do it all again. The fact that humans never die in the *teatro breve* supports the notion that it is an art form that follows the carnivalesque tradition. In *Los guisados*, foods repeatedly fall dead under the blade of Don Estofado, but who can be sad about this when everybody was planning to eat the hapless victims all along? In the *comedia*, the 'galanes' are the victims of dangerous, and often mortal, swordplay. In the *teatro breve*, people are the victims of a 'palo' or a well-placed slap to the face. In the spirit of real-life (not fictional or Rabelaisian) Carnival, people are bopped, bumped and bounced around, but nobody gets hurt in the end.

The third and most obvious link between *Los guisados* and Carnival is the overwhelming presence of food and wine. Bakhtin used the image of a pre-Lenten feast as the connecting point between literature and anthropology. The banquet sequences in *Gargantua and Pantagruel* were a key to understanding Rabelais' writing in terms of a social phenomenon. It is thus tempting to look for glimmers of Carnival wherever a substantial quantity of food can be found. In *Los guisados*, one certainly finds a great many things to eat: beef stew, meatballs, minced beef, tripe, salad, roast lamb, minced lamb, parsleyed lamb, etc. To a certain degree, the festivities of Carnival have been brought on to the stage. We should be careful, however, in calling the *mojiganga* a mere appropriation of a pre-existing social event, even if *Los guisados* contains elements that can be used to support a Bakhtinian point of view.

Calderón's *mojiganga* has more in common with Quevedo's poem than merely the use of personified things to eat. I have been careful so far to avoid claiming that *Los guisados* presents an abolition or reversal of social order. The noble hierarchy established among the 'guisados' is laughable – we would never imagine following orders or doffing our hat to a meatball – but the hierarchy does not lose significance despite its humorous context. One may recall that in Quevedo's *Boda y acompañamiento del campo*, Don Repollo and Doña Berza were described in terms of their matching 'casta'. It is funny to think of cabbages belonging to a certain bloodline, just as it is funny to give any vegetable an honorific title; but this type of humour lies some distance away from Carnival. In Quevedo, social conventions are not overthrown or turned upside-down for a good laugh. Instead, conventions are emphasised for a good laugh as they are incongruously applied to leafy greens. This incongruity gains coherence as it is applied across the board and a comically logical (as opposed to riotously disorderly) universe is created. A similar universe is created in *Los guisados*. A coherent incongruity, while remaining funny, allows for strong contact with the real world, no matter how absurdly it is portrayed. That is, order in itself can still be funny, unlike Carnival, where disorder and abandon are causes for laughter. This order is not constant throughout our entire *mojiganga*, but it exists to the extent that the piece cannot be called wholly carnivalesque. This might seem like quibbling over details, but these details reveal a satire, based on a standard hierarchy, which runs completely against the spirit of Carnival, both in Quevedo and in Calderón's piece.

In Quevedo, as should be expected, the satire is endemic and runs throughout the work, saturating every description with some form of negative comment about the various vegetable representatives of human nature. Every fruit, every green, every bulb, every tuber bears some vice or defect that merits mention. In *Los guisados*, the dishes are held in high esteem, even as they fall dead trying to prove their worth, until an unwanted stranger steps on to the scene.

Gallega y Asturiana	Otro Príncipe, señor, encubierto y disfrazado va entrando por el palenque.
Gallega	El olor no es nada sano.
Baco	Ea, descubra quién es.

Descúbrese y estará vestido con morcillas y manos

Menudo	Soy don Mondongo.
Baco	Ahí callo. ¿Y quién es vuestra Princesa?
Menudo	Doña Chanfaina Livianos, legítima esposa mía.
Estofado	Pues ¿cómo es esto, villano? ¿Cómo a aparecer te atreves entre tan nobles guisados? ¡Hola! ¡Matadle, prendedle, deudos, amigos, vasallos![43]

The scene is obviously ridiculous, and it seems unlikely that anybody in the audience would worry much about Don Mondongo's death. After all, he is nothing but blood sausage and hacked-up tripe to begin with. However, the audience must be laughing at more than just food-as-nobility. They laugh at a criticism, they participate in a satire, of Don Mondongo, the hopelessly ignoble noble. Don Mondongo enters the scene, according to Gallega and Asturiana, 'encubierto y disfrazado'. When he is unmasked, and when he reveals the name of his spouse, he is decried as 'villano', not worthy of being among 'tan nobles guisados'. What was once a simple form of incongruity in the relation between stews and noblemen has suddenly become something more elaborate. Don Mondongo represents the 'villano' trying to pass for a 'noble' and failing miserably. At this moment, the audience is probably laughing as much at failed social climbing as they are at a man adorned with hoofs and blood sausages. When the target of laughter is social behaviour, we have social ridicule, that is, social criticism employing laughter, which fits a good definition of

---

43 Calderón de la Barca, *Teatro cómico breve*, p. 321, ll. 193–206.

satire.[44] This satire finds its root in a comic conflict based on exclusion, an element that is completely contrary to the spirit of Carnival.[45]

Calderón's comic talent is evident in his ability to strike a balance between carnivalesque festivity and ultimately destructive violence, emphasising one or another aspect at different times and finally allowing one side to triumph over the other. Calling this or any *mojiganga* a purely festive form would require us to overlook many important details.[46] *Los guisados* is overwhelmingly funny, as jokes abound everywhere in the work's movement and conversation. Yet even in this small piece, one may speak of comic eruptions, of moments where humour and disorder overrun the contrasting forces of sober logic and scepticism. It occurred at the beginning as Don Nuño's 'Yo lo oigo y no lo creo' was buried beneath an avalanche of absurd scenes that followed. In the *comedia*, we will see that the case is the opposite and that sobriety and reason are overwhelming, and the comic eruptions are smaller and dispersed throughout the larger work. One should not expect that these small comic scenes in the *comedia* are any less complex than those in the *mojigangas* we have seen so far. Festivity is not a straightforward notion; neither is Carnival, nor comic violence, nor metatheatricality, nor parody, nor satire, nor order figures. Each notion has its own separate aspects that can be used for different comic effects, and their uses become increasingly complex as they are integrated into a larger piece, where the vague notion of 'comic relief' becomes an increasingly loaded term.

THE INCREASING COMPLEXITY OF THE *MOJIGANGA*

La mojiganga de la muerte, like the previous pieces, makes humorous use of metatheatricality. In this case, the phenomenon is much more extensive, starting from the very beginning of the piece and continuing throughout. At the same time, the framing is more subtle and more elaborate. In *La muerte*, the

---

44 Despite Highet's title, *Anatomy of satire*, he admits (p. 233) that, 'The function of satire has been variously, and never quite satisfactorily defined.' Also see Alvin Kernan, *The Cankered Muse: Satire of the English Renaissance* (New Haven: Yale University Press, 1959), p. 7. He writes of the ancient origin of satire (a word which comes from *satura*, meaning mixture or medley) and its long pedigree: 'The protean nature of satire has interfered with any precise definition of its conventions.' However, he also states: '. . . satire must be a definite kind of attack'. Few seem to disagree with the notion of satire as an attack, least of all Elliot, but Highet is wise to point out the element of 'laughter' or at least a 'smile of derision', which keeps satire from being something else, such as a simple letter of complaint or a fire-and-brimstone sermon.

45 To see clearly how Bakhtin is not always applicable, compare his positive portrayal of tripe (*Rabelais*, pp. 224–5) to the derision heaped upon Don Mondongo in *Los guisados*.

46 To see that contemporary writers and critics were aware of the various functions of humour in the *teatro breve*, it only suffices to contemplate the title of Luis Quiñones de Benavente's strangely titled collection: *Joco seria: burlas veras o reprehensión moral festiva de los desórdenes públicos*.

musicians sing: 'Vaya de fiesta, vaya de gira, / vaya de baile, vaya de chanza, / vaya y venga la mojiganga.'[47] This shout would seem like a more elementary frame than the one erected by the pre-tourney conversation found in *Los guisados* if it were not for the words of the Carretero that follow: 'El Señor sea loado, / que ya la mojiganga se ha acabado.'[48] It is a case of theatre-within-theatre, but the piece in question has supposedly come to an end, instead of beginning, as indicated by the first three lines. What has occurred is a startlingly funny, paradoxical and self-conscious expression of the piece's presence through the ironic denial of its own existence. Starting with the ending (quite different from *in medias res*) does not have to be inherently comic, as Calderón proves in his *auto sacramental* titled *Lo que va del hombre a Dios*.[49] However, when a particular type of attention is paid to this feature, belief can be momentarily suspended in a feat of anti-verisimilitude used for comic effect. Calderón's serious *auto* begins with Christ ascending triumphantly into heaven, a scene normally reserved for the end. As it happens, the comical allegorical figure of Placer points out the peculiarity of this beginning and contributes a humorous perspective to a sober and climactic event. It is Placer's consciousness of his presence in a dramatic work that breaks the illusion, breaks the rules of the game unexpectedly, and gives the audience a reason to laugh. In *La mojiganga de la muerte*, the dramatic illusion is not ruptured by any direct reference but rather through a massive contradiction that the audience could not possibly have missed. No piece of *teatro breve*, no matter how brief, lasts ten seconds, and the statement that the 'la mojiganga se ha acabado' makes no sense unless there is a separate theatre-within-the-theatre. Instead of having a character remind us outright that we are watching a work of dramatic fiction, Calderón tells the joke through the juxtaposition of a character's statement against the audience's expectations for further action, which require them to look outside the dramatic illusion. The frame is rather complex, but its function is simple. Notions of beginnings and endings are toyed with and tossed about, but the singing announcement still rings clear and has the tradition of a recognisable generic form behind it. The audience is about to watch a costume party onstage.

Margaret Greer has written a lucid and thorough article that explores the nature of parody in *La mojiganga de la muerte*,[50] and for that reason I shall

[47] Calderón de la Barca, *Teatro cómico breve*, p. 353, ll. 1–3.
[48] Ibid., p. 353, ll. 6–7.
[49] 'Pues ¿qué me ha de entristecer, / sino ver un argumento vuelto lo de abajo arriba?' See Calderón de la Barca, *Obras completas*, vol. 3, p. 277. For this observation and analysis of the *auto*, I am indebted to Barbara E. Kurtz, 'Guilty Pleasure: The Comic, the Sacred, and Placer(es) in the Autos Sacramentales of Calderón de la Barca', in *Play, Literature, Religion: Essays in Cultural Intertextuality*, eds Virgi Nemoianu and Robert Royal (Albany: State University of New York Press, 1992), pp. 61–75.
[50] Margaret R. Greer, ' "¿La vida es sueño? ¿o risa?" Calderón Parodies the *Auto*', *Bulletin of Hispanic Studies*, 73 (1995), 313–25.

not examine parody in any detail here. However, it remains important to keep in mind that this piece's main parody employs a metatheatrical joke of a very common sort: the citation of a play within a play. The moment in question, which is examined in Greer's article, occurs when the drunken Caminante, upon seeing Death and other figures pass before him, declares, 'pues estoy / viendo que la vida es sueño'.[51] This misplaced phrase is sure to cause a laugh because, when the play's title (in this case referring to the *auto sacramental*, not the *comedia*) and theme are quoted, the audience is shaken slightly from its absorption in the dramatic illusion. Previously, when Carretero explains to Caminante that Demonio has broken his leg in an accident, Caminante responds 'Pues será el diablo cojuelo,'[52] alluding to the novel by Luis Vélez de Guevara. The *teatro breve* is replete with such name-dropping, and citing the titles of *comedias* is a gag that is repeated time and again. An extreme example of this species of punning can be found in a series of *entremeses*, whose entire premise is to name as many *comedia* titles as possible.[53] In a more blatant case of metatheatricality that operates on a more general plane, Caminante asks in an aside, '¿Si soy hombre de Auto Viejo, / pues que me hallo contrastado / del Ángel mal y del bueno?'[54] For the moment, the audience is not laughing at human failings, ugliness or silly costumes when such references are made. It would also be difficult to say that the audience is meant to laugh at an exaggeration or distortion. The audience is most likely laughing at an art form that makes fun of itself; they laugh at a surprising act of artistic self-consciousness. This *mojiganga*, like many other art forms, is able to derive humour from mere appearances, yet *La muerte* is also able to combine simple jokes in rather sophisticated ways.

While *Los sitios de recreación del Rey* and *Los guisados* contained some similarities to allegorical drama, the text of *La muerte* refers explicitly to this poetic device, although the device *per se* is not used. It is not true allegory as found in an *auto sacramental* because the actors are mostly out of character

---

[51] Calderón de la Barca, *Teatro cómico breve*, p. 359, ll. 183–4. Along with Greer, Lobato, as well as Rodríguez and Tordera, have noted the significance of these lines.

[52] Ibid., p. 359; p. 357, l. 106.

[53] *Entremés de los títulos de las comedias*, in *Rasgos de Ocio, en diferentes bayles, entremeses, y loas de diversos avtores, Segunda parte* (Madrid: García Morras, a costa de Domingo de Palacio y Villegas, 1644), pp. 189–99. *Loa sacramental de los títulos de las Comedias* in *Autos sacramentales, con qvatro Comedias nvevas ys sus loas, y entremeses* (Madrid: María de Quiñones, a costa de Juan de Valdés, 1655), fols 151r–152r. *Loa de los títulos de las comedias sacramental de Lope de Vega* [this is different than the last *loa*], in *Flor de entremeses, Bayles y Loas, Escogidas de los mejores Ingenios de España* (Zaragoza: Diego Dormer, 1676), pp. 27–35. There are dozens upon dozens of these thematic 'sub-sub-genres' within the sub-genres of the *teatro breve*, and an entire separate study would be required to detail the features of each theme, from 'poetas locos' to 'versos esdrújulos'. Suffice it say that the audience of the time would be familiar with many sub-sub-genres and would recognise them instantly.

[54] Calderón de la Barca, *Teatro cómico breve*, p. 358, ll. 150–2.

and the setting is one of definite temporality. Let us return to the beginning of
the piece. The *mojiganga*-within-the-*mojiganga* has finished. Carretero is
waiting to transport the actors. They must get to the next performance by
noon, as the Autor does not wish his actors to waste all afternoon changing
costumes. Caminante enters the scene, talks about the high sun, and decides
to sleep for a moment. We are obviously no longer speaking of a suspended
or eternal allegorical time. But while still in 'real time', the actors remain in
costume, allowing them to play with their appearance just as other personifications did in the previous *mojigangas*. In the universe of this piece, the
mojiganga is officially over, but the costume party spirit remains. While in
Sitios and *Los guisados*, the costumes served to clarify the identities of those
present onstage, in *La muerte*, the costumes are better described as disguises,
as the actors onstage take on a double identity. The audience knows that underneath each costume hides an actor, but the drunken Caminante is not aware of
this. Thus a split develops between the audience's perception and Caminante's,
leading the audience to laugh at the short-sightedness of Caminante and thus
feel superior in its clearer view of the situation.[55] In this case, however, the
costumes become a form of trickery or 'burla', essential to many scenes within
the *teatro breve*, especially the more complex *entremés*. A greater number of
points of view can lead to greater confusion. As long as the audience can keep
things clear in its imagination, it can derive pleasure in appreciation of the
increased comic complexity.

Calderón is also able to stretch a joke further by simultaneously working
with and against audience expectations. When the characters mount the cart
offstage, their seating order provides constant fodder for puns. 'El alma es lo
primero' and 'echadla con el Diablo'[56] are normal figurative expressions that
now take on literal significance as the allegorical characters find their places
in the cart. This silly game reappears in another form when Cuerpo and Alma
step onto the scene. Unfortunately for the shaken Alma, Cuerpo must leave in
search of a safe place, 'si hay por aquí en qué albergarte'.[57] While the notion
that the body carries the soul is acceptable, it is made funny by its literal
representation onstage. One might imagine the glowing light of a soul housed
in the body, but a body staggering around with a fairly substantial soul in its
arms makes an awkward scene and gives occasion to laugh. The true surprise
occurs when the body decides to give up the soul, not because of the presence
of death (who in this *mojiganga* has yet to enter the stage), but because it
would be too tiresome to carry the soul while searching for help. The joke
stretches even further as Cuerpo tells Caminante: 'Hombre, en tus manos te
dejo / el Alma, cuídame de ella / mientras yo por ella vuelvo.'[58] It makes sense
that the body should give up the soul, but taking it back shortly afterwards

[55] See Greer, ' "¿La vida es sueño?" ', p. 314.
[56] Calderón de la Barca, *Teatro cómico breve*, p. 354, l. 47.
[57] Ibid., p. 359, l. 159.   [58] Ibid., p. 359, ll. 160–2.

does not, thus defying our expectations of how an allegorical figure ought to behave. But supposing in real life, for whatever reason, the body did have to give up its soul for a moment, what should it do? Should it not give up its soul to another body for temporary safe keeping? This is exactly what Cuerpo does, entrusting his 'Alma' to 'Hombre', that is, Caminante. Funny, unexpected and yet somehow full of sense, the jokes (simple puns turned into elaborate twists of logic) demonstrate Calderón's already proven mastery of allegory, his ability to play with concepts for a laugh as well as for the public's edification.

La muerte is undoubtedly more complex in its plotting than the previously examined pieces, despite maintaining the structure of a procession. From the very beginning, the sequence of events anticipates Caminante's arrival, playing with the audience's expectations and perceptions that are soon to be confused and contradicted by those of the central character. In *Sitios* and *Los guisados*, or in the *entremeses cantados* by Quiñones de Benavente, the spectator is immediately confronted with a visual representation of some unreal incongruous entity during an extraordinary event. A stew fights to the death, a bridge sings that it will not let wine pass. When visual puns are introduced, such as Zarzuela carrying an 'olla', laughter stems from an immediate confluence of what is imagined ('Zarzuela' has a double meaning) and what is seen onstage (a woman portraying a park also holds a pot). As seen in previous splits in perception or alternate points of view in *La muerte*, there exists a split between the imagination and vision. Long before the costumed actors enter the stage, they carry on a conversation with Autor and Carretero who remain onstage. The cart in which they travel is offstage. This leads to two important considerations. First of all, a purely imaginative scene, using space offstage[59] allows for the portrayal of events that would be difficult to dramatise without a major theatrical apparatus or 'special effects'. While it may be possible for the carriage to be flipped over onstage, it is much easier to act out the sounds, shouts and groans from offstage and allow the audience's imagination to fill in the rest. Also, when the piece relies on the visual imagination, there occurs a sort of temporary generic metamorphosis, where elements essential to the dramatic art are eliminated and the form in which the 'story' of this *mojiganga* is told reverts to the oral tradition. The story is told by multiple people, but at the moment it is told mostly through words and not actions. Autor and Carretero are, in a fashion, story-tellers, accompanied by the occasional offstage shouts of the *comediantes* and the 'special effects' of '*ruido de carretería y campanillas*'. The story they tell,

[59] I refer the reader to chapter 5 of Michael Issacharoff, *Discourse as Performance* (Stanford: Stanford University Press, 1989). He explains (p. 58) that, 'There are two major forms of dramatic space: onstage and offstage (mimetic and diegetic), the theatrical equivalent of the narratologists' showing-versus-telling dichotomy.' This is part of Issacharoff's greater theoretical framework, which can be guessed from the title.

a sort of 'back story', is the first part of *La muerte*'s plot. After Caminante
appears, drinks and falls asleep, Carretero and Autor, now offstage, carry out
a more complex dialogue with the 'comediantes', and the story-telling
becomes more of a drama. This is the second part of the plot. The use of an
imagined offstage space is nothing new in the dramatic art form, but in *La
muerte* it is deliberately linked to jokes that bring the imagined to life, and
also refers to the relationship between non-dramatic and dramatic art forms,
all the while telling a story.

The use of offstage space to portray the allegorical figures in our imagination before their appearance also creates suspense, something difficult to
achieve were this *mojiganga* merely a parade of characters. While it was likely
that this piece was performed during Corpus Christi festivities,[60] and even
though the audience would have seen plenty of people in costume, the element
of suspense still remains. The entrance of the figures is delayed, but their presence is constantly the subject of conversation, making the audience wait until
these figures finally appear. In *Sitios*, the personified figures are announced and
march onto the stage without a moment's delay. In *Los guisados*, the
introductory frame presented by Don Gil and Don Nuño's conversation about
'comedias caseras' establishes an air of anticipation, which quickly evaporates
as the dishes make their appearance a few moments later. In *La muerte*, no
costumed figure makes an entrance until line 115 of the piece's 280, though
the 'comediantes' speak their first words in line 30. The audience must have
been eager to see the figures that shout, joke and jostle each other, and fall
victim to accidents, but when they finally show themselves, a complicating
factor has been added: Caminante. Now it is not only a question of how the
audience will react, but also how Caminante himself will react to the entrance
of the figures. A new element of suspense is added, as one point of view and
one set of expectations are multiplied. In *La muerte*, humour takes on greater
complexity as the relative intricacy of the piece's plotting becomes greater than
that found in *Sitios* or *Los guisados*.

As the wineskin dries up and the intoxicating liquor disappears, so does the
relatively festive fantasyland created by the costumed allegorical figures.
Carretero enters the stage and announces that the cart has been righted and it
is time to go, signalling an apparent end to this *mojiganga*-within-the-
mojiganga. Yet Demonio, Cuerpo and Alma, joking still, refuse to enter the
cart for fear that they will be injured again. Cuerpo accuses Carretero of being
drunk, and the shouting match between them soon turns into a full-fledged
flailing fight. Demonio and Muerte attempt to break up the fight, but the
whole scene threatens to devolve into violent chaos, much like the narrowly
avoided massacre at the end of *Los guisados*. As in our previous *mojiganga*,
something occurs to stop the bloodshed. But instead of the introduction of an
order figure, another comic event occurs to prevent self-annihilation.

---

[60] See Calderón de la Barca, *Teatro cómico breve*, p. 352.

Suddenly, a group of 'gallegos' shouts offstage using a comic dialect, letting everybody know that they are followed by a group of 'gitanos'. Likewise the 'gitanos' shout (though not in a 'habla deformado') about their intentions to follow the 'gallegos'. The surprising entrance of these two groups serves several functions.[61] First of all, it serves to put an end to the bickering among the 'comediantes'. Fighting between characters onstage has limited comic possibilities. There are ways of stretching out the action of a comic battle, generally through the use of verbal attacks or manoeuvring onstage, both of which depend on steadily increasing ingenuity. But when the fighting consists mostly of simple shouts and 'embestir', there is little material to go on. Thankfully, the 'gallegos' and 'gitanos' arrive before the shouting and grappling become monotonous. Their arrival can be considered a 'plot point', an event that changes the action onstage. Their arrival also provides an instant joke that requires no elaboration or preparation and these stereotyped figures could easily be called a 'cheap laugh'. While the 'gallegos' offer merely a 'cheap laugh', the 'gitanos' offer something else, an instantaneous element of suspense. In the *teatro breve*, gypsies are synonymous with trickery, deception and pranks. As the comedy of Caminante's illusion grows anaemic, the presence of the 'gitanos' injects more lifeblood into the body of this *mojiganga*. They gleefully announce: 'Aunque se junten con otros / no importa, llegar podemos, / que a más moros, más ganancia.'[62] They are referring to the fact that no matter what came before them, they will take advantage of the situation with their wiles. In terms of the plot, they are also announcing that no matter what monotonous conflict transpired before their arrival, they are sure to bring fun and trickery back into the picture.

In a strange twist of expectations, the figures who first appear threatening to reap the benefits of disorder decide to establish an order of their own through happy dancing and singing. Running parallel to the expectation that 'gitanos' are purveyors of trickery and deception is the expectation that a *mojiganga* should end in song and dance. The 'gitanos' fulfil the latter expectation rather than the former. They shout 'troquemos / en regocijo el espanto',[63] and remind both the audience and the characters onstage: '. . . pues todas las mojigangas / tienen un fin, advirtiendo / que es disparatar adrede, / tal vez gala del ingenio'.[64] The 'gitanos', threatening to cause further disruption, albeit fresh and comic, instead bring closure to the work, recalling the reference to 'mojiganga' at the very beginning. They call on everybody to sing and dance, and make this *mojiganga* true to its name, fulfilling the implied promise of festivity at the start of the work. The end is finally made definite as everybody sings in unison '¡Ay por aquí, por aquí acabemos!'[65] announcing the finish to this varied and complex 'fin de fiesta'.

61 See Greer, ' "¿La vida es sueño?" ', pp. 318–19, for even more functions. Some that I list here are included in her analysis.

62 Calderón de la Barca, *Teatro cómico breve*, p. 361, ll. 235–7.

63 Ibid., p. 361, ll. 250–1.   64 Ibid., p. 361, ll. 254–8.

65 Ibid., p. 363, l. 280.

BETWEEN *MOJIGANGA* AND *ENTREMÉS*

El pésame de la viuda is a *mojiganga* that approaches the other end of the spectrum first represented by *Los sitios de recreación del Rey*. The two pieces have much in common, but in the areas of plot, characterisation, setting and dialogue, *Pésame* lies much closer to the *comedia*. In *Sitios* and *Los guisados*, no setting is mentioned in the stage directions. The situation is the same in *La muerte*, until the arrival of Caminante, where the directions state 'campo y camino'. One does not always find the setting explicitly described in *acotaciones* of the *teatro breve* (or in the *comedia* for that matter), because it is often indicated by the characters' appearance and conversation. However, in the case of *Sitios* and *Los guisados* one can see that the characters do not offer any elaboration on the setting, leaving it as an ill-defined imaginary space for the presentation of personified figures.[66] The audience knows that the parks will sing, and that the dishes will stage a tourney, but few more expectations remain. The setting in the beginning of *La muerte*, though not explicitly defined, was roughly described through the conversation between Autor, Carretero and the 'comediantes'. They are in a town, ready to leave for another. Later, the presence of Caminante, his monologue, and the stage directions, set the scene of the baking hot countryside where the fantastic visions will appear before him. The stage directions for *Pésame* are not explicit, but Rodríguez and Tordera venture a guess regarding where the action should take place.[67] Despite the absence of any explicit stage directions indicating a setting, the location and the implied surroundings become abundantly recognisable in the first few moments, through the appearance and conversation of the characters, along with the props that are employed onstage.

Sale María de Prado de viuda, un escudero y Jerónima.[68]

Audience expectations are immediately heightened as an obviously upper-class widow named Doña Clara enters the scene. According to social conventions, a widow was required to behave in a certain way, and it is with these conventions that the *mojiganga* will play. The costume of the widow may not be 'ridículo', nor may it involve dangling sausages or a brightly painted sun, but it still creates expectations that the following action may fulfil or defy for comic effect, as seen in the personification costumes of previous *mojigangas*.

The plot of *Pésame* is quite simple and mainly consists of various visitors calling upon the widow. This follows a general pattern found in *mojigangas*, in which a series of characters appear onstage with a single minimal pretext

---

[66] *Los guisados* does explicitly take place in a 'estacada', but this is the location of any 'torneo', by default, and has no connection to any recognisable geographical confines.

[67] Calderón de la Barca, *Entremeses, jácaras y mojigangas*, p. 354.

[68] Calderón, *Teatro cómico breve*, p. 289.

for their arrival. The monotony of the event contains the echoes of a parade or a celebration, something I have called processional and festive aspects. While these aspects may retreat to the background for part of the piece, they never disappear entirely and inevitably come to the forefront at the end when everybody joins in a song-and-dance routine. This pattern can also be found in works titled *entremés*, and in *Pésame* we begin to see the blurring of the distinction between these two sub-genres of *teatro breve*. In *Pésame*, unlike *Sitios*, the visitors do more than just sing a little song and exit the stage. They do more than state their name, nature, function and then do battle, as in *Los guisados*. The characters do much more than the simple punning and shouting carried out by the 'comediantes' in *La muerte*. While the pretext for the guests' arrival is simple and unchanging, its ramifications are complicated as the actions and settings are joined to a more complex reflection of reality.

Among the conversations between characters, we find the repeated refrain (stated by various characters): 'El diablo pensara / de un pésame hacer una mojiganga.' This statement breaks through the plotting and the conversation that, by their more 'realistic' play-like style, suppress the festive and processional nature of the theatre piece. Rodríguez and Tordera note that: 'La idea del paso de una situación de pesadumbre a otra mucho más festiva es característica de la mojiganga.'[69] In the same note they also mention that in one edition of *Pésame*, the refrain was eliminated and the piece was called an *entremés*, demonstrating conclusively that the two types of *teatro breve* could indeed be interchangeable. The refrain also reminds us of the extremely self-conscious nature of the *mojiganga*, and that it can even 'play around' with its own definition. With an extreme feeling of metatheatricality, the piece itself dares to become serious, thus causing a generic catastrophe and cancelling itself out as a *mojiganga*. In a related example, Quiñones de Benavente writes a *jácara* that actually is no *jácara* at all, but merely a playful and teasing promise that one will be performed, though it never comes into being.[70] While *Pésame* plays with the nature of its own existence as an art form, as did *La muerte*, it also makes a self-conscious reference to the nature of humorous dramatic forms in general. That is to say, it plays with the oscillation between tragedy and comedy. While I have called the *teatro breve* an 'overwhelmingly humorous' dramatic form, there always remains room for serious contrast, and not only in the presence of a 'straight man'. Sometimes a negative or oppressive atmosphere can persist until, through a joke, a burst of laughter dissolves all sad or sombre feelings on the stage. Often, however, a comic contrast is made without banishing the anti-comic forces. The serious character or

---

[69] Calderón de la Barca, *Entremeses, jácaras y mojigangas*, p. 355.

[70] Hannah E. Bergman, *Luis Quiñones de Benavente* (New York: Twayne, 1972), p. 75. This book is similarly titled to the Castalia book, the latter including 'y sus entremeses', which I shall include in order to distinguish between the two.

setting remains as jokes are bounced against it, mocking its sobriety but thriving on the tension that exists between the serious and comic sides of the same situation. This is the how the comic plot works in *Pésame*, and the line, 'El diablo pensara / de un pésame hacer una mojiganga', refers to this tension, this constant battle in which laughter thrives upon the serious, yet does not immediately seek to vanquish it. This tension, or oscillation, has its counterpart in the *comedia*, but rarely in such a compact form that leads to a rapid succession of jokes.

While the 'plots' of *Sitios*, *Los guisados* and even *La muerte* may be threadbare, they give a pretext for various comic occurrences with respectively increasing complexity. *Sitios* did have a pretext for dressing up its characters in silly costumes and singing, something intended to bring laughter and amusement no doubt. In *Los guisados*, one found a similar pretext, but shouting matches and battling with wooden spoons added to the laughter and enjoyment. *La muerte* featured silly costumes, occasional singing, punning and fighting, but also the introduction of multiple points of view and *burlas* by pitting the outsider Caminante against the rest of the 'comediantes'. These interactions brought us closer to situational comedy, a hallmark of the *comedia*, which gets more laughs through the actions and movement of the characters than through their words or static visual displays such as costumes. Every piece of theatre has some aspect of situational comedy, but it is often scarcely noticeable or important. I started this chapter with *Sitios* because it offered few complicating factors in this respect. The characters made their entrance, said their piece and marched off. In *Pésame*, where no humour is derived from costumes alone, the characters can draw laughter from the audience as much through what they do as through what they say. Situational humour does not necessarily depend upon an interaction between characters but it does depend on a character's physical reaction to their surroundings, whether it includes other characters or not. The main influence upon the plot of *Pésame*, that is, the way the characters behave, is the widow's insistence on keeping up appearances while she yearns to do what is forbidden to her by custom.

Doña Clara finally convinces herself – with the help of her servants – that she should be allowed to eat 'huevos y torreznos' and 'chocolate de Guajaca', as these can be considered 'duelos y quebrantos' and will not break an ecclesiastical fast. But Doña Clara realises that eating these morsels still violates the spirit of her mourning, and she runs the risk of public shame if her neighbours spot her eating with gusto in a well-lighted house, violating what she calls here 'viudedad'. Therefore, panic erupts when Doña Aldonza comes to visit while Doña Clara is enjoying her meal. In a moment of desperation, after asking for the lights to be snuffed out, Doña Clara hides all her food in the closest available container, which happens to be her skirt. The extinguished light is perhaps one of the most common devices in Spanish Golden Age theatre used to create surprising situations, both in the *comedia* and the *teatro breve*. However, one should not always associate darkness with instant

comedy, as obscured appearances can also lead to the most tragic of mis-
understandings, as is the case in Calderón's larger works of theatre. In this
mojiganga, hilarity ensues after all is dark, and the darkness is used more than
once, repeatedly causing people to behave in a ridiculous fashion. Doña
Aldonza inadvertently sits down on the water jug and glasses, overturning them
and leaving a giant wet spot on the chair where she once sat, and quite possibly on her dress. Though leaving a big wet spot is a joke that works by itself,
it is tied to a series of previous events and qualifies as situational comedy.
Aside from the hilarious stain that the dampened 'dama' must have created, the
event leads to further jokes between the characters watching the scene. The
physical humour, or slapstick, that stemmed from the situation produces jokes
about water together with other wordplay. In the *teatro breve*, when wine is
mentioned, when water is the topic, a seemingly obligatory joke about 'vino
aguado' is made. The stage directions give us some idea about the characters'
movements onstage, but there is much that must be inferred from the conversation and references made by the characters themselves. Rodríguez and
Tordera have sought to find ways of envisioning possible actions by looking at
stage directions and embedded descriptions in Calderón's texts and outside
sources.[71] Though it may be difficult to appreciate the performance in the
mind's eye, since many details of the piece's staging are missing, there are
other reasons to admire the use of slapstick. Calderón is widely recognised for
his elaborate stage decorations in his longer works, and though his *teatro breve*
is humble and on a small scale, it is evident in *Pésame* that the simple setting
(a sitting room) and meagre props (water, food, furniture, candles) are
employed ingeniously for surprising comic effect. Calderón also admirably
integrates jokes of various types, switching seamlessly from the situational and
physical to topical comedy in a natural fashion. Pratfalls are not gratuitous in
this case, and neither is the satire of diluted wine, though either could stand as
an independent joke. All are integrated into a comic framework that shows no
holes or gaps. If a piece of *teatro breve* has a plot of some substance, combining joke-types under a narrative structure becomes possible, a feat that is
actually more difficult in the simpler *mojiganga*. The *entremés*, which often
contains a narrative based on a *burla* or deception, can use various types
of jokes and often present a moment of comic climax based entirely on physical humour. Humour in the *comedia*, as stated before, is mainly driven by
situations, all of which require some form of plot to connect them. In this
sense, *comedias* are closer to *entremeses* than to most *mojigangas*. Consequently aspects more commonly associated with the *entremés* may function
differently or create a different effect when used in a *comedia*, compared to
aspects reminiscent of a *mojiganga*. After carefully determining that a simple

---

[71] Evangelina Rodríguez and Antonio Tordera, *Calderón de la Barca y la dramaturgia
corta del siglo XVII* (London: Tamesis, 1985).

pratfall[72] in *El pésame* is not structurally isolated or gratuitous, similar precautions should be taken while analysing the supposed 'cheap laughs' and *disparates* found in the larger *comedia*.

While physical humour is commonly associated with the *teatro breve*, comic contradiction is another type of humour that is equally noticeable. A specific example of this comic contradiction is found in the tension that stems from a psychological contradiction, as when Doña Clara's inward desires conflict with the pressures of society, making her act in a comic fashion. Maxime Chevalier puts it best when referring to the stock figure of the widow:

> El contraste entre la alegría desordenada que infunde en el alma de la viuda y la ansiada libertad y el anhelo que demuestra por contraer nueva unión no deja de sorprender y parece implicar cierta contradicción, pero acaso no convenga exigir coherencia rigurosa en una representación tan claramente festiva.[73]

Doña Clara has the light on when she knows she should not, and she eats when she should be fasting. After Doña Aldonza's visit and her subsequent wetting with water, Doña Quiteria calls on the widow and adds even more tension by provoking further contradictions in the widow's behaviour. Doña Quiteria, without mincing words, exclaims to the recently widowed Doña Clara, '¡Qué novio te traigo, amiga!'[74] Doña Clara's immediate response is, '¿Ahora en eso me hablas? / ¡No lo quiera Dios! Mas dime, / ¿quién es y cómo se llama?'[75] The living contradiction of the widow's behaviour is expressed compactly in those three lines. The same joke is soon repeated, as she hears about the suitors' houses and cries again, 'No me hables de eso, ¡ay de mí! / ¿Pero, a qué barrio son?'[76] Soon the joke collapses into the single expression from Doña Clara, '¡Ay mísera!' and the response of all the ladies present, who chime in, '¡Ay desdicha!' The exterior 'mísera' would represent the pain of the widow's loss, but we all know that in the interior her sighs represent a longing, not for the past husband, but rather for the future suitor. The fact that all the women sigh in chorus betrays the notion that they are perfectly aware of the hypocrisy as well. Any doubts about their awareness are eliminated when they collectively recite the emblematic phrase of this

---

[72] Let us not forget that acts of tripping, stumbling and falling are ambivalent events that need not be funny. We need only think of Enrique's fall from his horse in *El médico de su honra*, and likewise Rosaura's fall in *La vida es sueño*. In Calderón's *El príncipe constante*, this ambiguous nature is even addressed by one of the characters, in Fernando's positive outlook on Enrique's misfortune as he falls from his boat at the beginning of the play.

[73] Maxime Chevalier, *Tipos cómicos y folklore (siglos XVI–XVII)* (Madrid: EDI-6, 1982), p. 86.

[74] Calderón de la Barca, *Teatro cómico breve*, p. 295, l. 161.

[75] Ibid., p. 295, ll. 162–4.   [76] Ibid., p. 297, ll. 176–7.

piece, which before was uttered only individually: 'El diablo pensara / de un pésame hacer una mojiganga.' After the men have entered the scene and after they have had their misadventures finding a place to sit in the dark, they eventually insist in unison 'Sí que una señora rica / y moza y de buena cara / no está bien sola,'[77] making it clear that they too are in on the joke. After all, Doña Clara's attempt to keep up appearances is one massive, multi-faceted joke (based on a contradiction) that makes up the substance of the entire *mojiganga*. Though the *mojiganga* takes place during a period of mourning, every sad moment is quickly contradicted and made funny. A sort of party runs parallel to this ostensibly sombre occasion, as if the celebration were just waiting to break through and overrun the tenuously dominant sobriety. Everybody seems to be aware of this, and though the festive forces of disorder are slow to take over, they win in the end.

Doña Clara announces that she would indeed move in with Don Lesmes if it were not for her tender little son, who should not have a stepfather at such an early age. This final excuse momentarily threatens to postpone the party for at least a few years, much longer than this tiny theatre piece will last onstage. The tension builds as the baby, who only seconds before lived in the audience's imagination, is called forth. The directions read: 'Sale Morales vestido de Niño de la Rollona,[78] con un pan de Vallecas en la mano.'[79] In order to help you, gentle reader, imagine the scene, it only warrants mentioning that Morales is a grown man, who now enters gurgling: 'Mama, coco, coco.' Instantly the tension is shattered, and the *mojiganga* wins over mourning, as a one-man costume party makes his way onto the scene. The final comic blow is struck when the man-baby, hearing that his 'mother' will remarry, declares:

> ¿Qué es casarse? ¡Voto a Cristo
> que la reviente a patadas
> a ella, a la casamentera,
> al novio, a cuantos y cuantas
> intentaren en casa
> de un pésame hacer una mojiganga![80]

Two men applaud, one saying '¡Qué gracia!' the other '¡Qué donosura!', piling one unexpected response upon another, making the situation even more absurd and throwing off the equilibrium felt through the previous dramatic

---

[77] Calderón de la Barca, *Teatro cómico breve*, p. 297, ll. 261–2.

[78] See Calderón de la Barca, *Entremeses, jácaras y mojigangas*, p. 366, for a thorough discussion of the *niño de la rollona* or *hijo de la rollona*. One characteristic of such a 'mimado' is that he 'tiene siete años y mama aún ahora'. They were spoiled rotten and had a temper to match.

[79] Calderón de la Barca, *Teatro cómico breve*, p. 300.

[80] Ibid., p. 300, ll. 288–93.

tension surrounding the widow's behaviour. At that moment, the women call for a dance and the newly engaged couple sing nonsense rhymes. The festive spirit shows itself victorious, something that could have been anticipated from the very beginning of the *mojiganga*.

The widow from *Pésame* is our first express example of a comic type, a phenomenon that we shall encounter frequently while looking at Calderón's *entremeses*. Maxime Chevalier, in his book titled *Tipos cómicos y folklore (siglos XVI–XVII)*, cites the hypocritical widow as a standard figure from folklore. His thesis proposes that many character types in fiction – many who appear in the *teatro breve* – originally come from an oral tradition and somehow find their way into written literature. About the 'viuda' he writes: 'Hay que aceptar la evidencia: la viuda literaria es personaje calcado sobre la viuda alegre de los refranes y de los cuentos tradicionales.'[81] Those who wish to contest this thesis can battle against Chevalier on his own terms (and while reading his books), but I believe most would admit that rarely is anything purely the creation of a single author's imagination. What matters most is that the 'viudita alegre' is yet another example of a figure from popular culture and the oral tradition (many of whom, perhaps like the 'bobo aldeano lopesco', 'nace en el campo'[82]) that finds itself a repeated topic of written literature as well.

Rodríguez and Tordera have noted similarities between *El pésame de la viuda* and two works by Francisco de Quevedo (one in prose and the other an *entremés*), adding more items to the list of connections between Calderón and the famous satirical poet:

> Si comparamos esta obra con el pasaje – casi idéntico – de Quevedo en *El mundo por de dentro* (*Sueños y discursos*, ed. Felipe C. R. Maldonado, Madrid, Castalia, 1972), se observa que Calderón ha intuido la poderosa fuerza corrosiva que la crítica puede alcanzar vertida dramáticamente, con la posibilidad de dos niveles escénicos simultáneos, poniendo así de manifiesto la sentencia quevediana: 'Oye, verás esta viuda, que por de fuera tiene un cuerpo de responsos, cómo por de dentro tiene una ánima de aleluyas, las tocas y hechizo, tendiendo los ojos hechos una yesca . . .' No en vano el mismo Quevedo aprovechó hábilmente este pasaje en su *Entremés de Diego Moreno*.[83]

Indeed, after reading the portion of the Quevedo quote omitted by Rodríguez and Tordera, one learns that Quevedo included a brief imaginary conversation between the widow and the nosy 'amigas que harán su oficio'. They encourage her, one after the other, not to waste her youth and to instead seek a new man. The satirist also describes how the widow, first taking half a bite

---

81 Chevalier, *Tipos cómicos y folklore*, p. 87.
82 Ibid., p. 126.
83 See the 'nota previa' to this piece in *Entremeses, jácaras y mojigangas*.

to eat (think of Doña Clara compromising on her chocolate), later eats everything, claiming it turns to poison inside her. Already in this piece of prose, Quevedo has staged a dialogue similar to that which we find in the *teatro breve*. This is perhaps one of narrowest gaps to be found between prose and theatre and proves that a leap between genres need not be very great.

After this comparison with Quevedo, it should be obvious that the image of the widow in the Calderonian *mojiganga* is undoubtedly a satire, though satire itself does not come to dominate the entire piece. Satire is not required to permeate an entire work of literature, even though this is often the case in Quevedo. By keeping in mind Maxime Chevalier's observations, one is also reminded how this piece has its origins in folklore types. From this perspective, Calderón was also a competent dramatist when it came to drawing inspiration from the oral tradition. Such can be said (and so Chevalier himself wrote) about Quevedo, but neither is made any less of a satirist by including folklore sources in his artistic palette. Satire passes negative judgment on some human failing, singular or collective. Sometimes this critical voice is not harsh, or even judgmental, depending upon one's interpretation. Rodríguez and Tordera seized on Quevedo's reputation as a harsh satirist, saying Calderón employed the same 'poderosa fuerza corrosiva'. James Crosby, in his notes to *El mundo por de dentro*, problematises the widow's supposed hypocrisy by writing:

> Sin embargo, un criterio psicológico podría llevarnos a atribuir las contradicciones en el comportamiento de la viudas no tanto a la hipocresía sino a un estado emocional ambivalente o francamente conflictivo, bien conocido en las personas recién enviudadas.[84]

While the corrosiveness of the satire of the widow may be in dispute, there is agreement that it involves ambivalence and conflict, two features that lend themselves very well to comic situations. When the possibility of psychological interpretations applied to satire arises, it becomes apparent that we have come a long way from simple parades of dancing parks and singing Moors. The greater panorama of a social reality comes into view, and the conflicts and ambivalence born of the human condition become more apparent, though the silly costumes, onslaught of puns and occasionally impossible situations are still likely to appear. To explore further these intersections between the real and the absurd, between the mimetically flimsy and the dramatically robust, our investigation enters the realm of Calderón's *entremeses*.

---

[84] Francisco de Quevedo y Villegas, *Sueños y discursos*, ed. James O. Crosby, vol. 2 (Madrid: Editorial Castalia, 1993), p. 1348.

2

CALDERÓN AND THE *ENTREMÉS*

El reloj y los genios de la venta is an *entremés* that maintains a somewhat processional atmosphere, making it similar to many *mojigangas*, while its setting and characters also resemble those used by Spain's famous satirist Francisco de Quevedo. Rodríguez and Tordera, along with Lobato, have observed how *Genios* resembles Quevedo's interlude *La venta*,[1] and thus provides the opportunity to demonstrate the flexibility of the *teatro breve* in treating the same theme. Calderón's *El reloj y los genios de la venta* opens with the stage directions: 'Sale Pedro, mozo de mulas, muy guapo.'[2] Pedro has come to meet his lover Juana, and he hears her singing from within. The young couple exchanges fanciful songs mocking inns, and they trade some witticisms about caring for the mules. Most commonly, *entremés* couples (married or not) are antagonistic pairings whose sniping and manipulation are a cause for laughter.[3] The teasing between these two, apparently both friends and lovers, is of a strictly playful nature:

> Juana   ¿Acomodaste las bestias?
> Pedro   Cierto que eres mentecata,
>   ¿pues tú dónde no has visto bestias
>   que no estén acomodadas?[4]

The epithet 'mentecata' carries very little derision, as he scolds Juana for no other reason than to 'set up' a pun that satirises the well-known sluggishness of Spain's rented mules. If anything were the target in this exchange, it would

---

[1] Calderón de la Barca, *Teatro cómico breve*, p. 137 and *Entremeses, jácaras, mojigangas*, p. 173.   [2] Ibid., *Teatro cómico breve*, p. 129.

[3] Couples are almost never together for reasons related to love. In fact, Hannah Bergman writes (Bergman, *Quiñones de Benavente*, p. 28): ' "Love" serves merely as a pretext for the complicated stratagems devised to circumvent the watchfulness of the girl's father, brother, or husband. Lack of true love or affection within the family is equally marked; wives cannot abide their husbands, fathers find daughters merely a burden, girls connive to escape paternal or brotherly supervision.'

[4] Calderón de la Barca, *Teatro cómico breve*, p. 130, ll. 27–30.

have to be the 'bestias'.[5] The joking serves to demonstrate the togetherness of the lovers instead of signalling irreconcilable differences that are found in many other male–female relationships in the *entremés*. At the end of Francisco de Quevedo's *Entremés de la venta*, there is a similar brief scene featuring a 'moza de la venta', Grajal, and a 'mozo de mulas'. Grajal and the 'mozo' exchange witticisms. The basis of the exchange is Grajal's cynical response to the 'mozo's advances, which begin with '¡Qué lindo torbellino de mozona!' and are followed by trite comparisons that today could only be called 'pick-up lines'. Grajal dismisses the earthy 'mozo' and offers a veiled threat that the innkeeper may cut him up and offer him to guests for dinner. Yet this is only a small scene at the end of the piece. The main male–female interaction in Quevedo's *La venta* is between Grajal and the innkeeper Corneja, and their employer–employee relationship is not any more uplifting than the interaction between Grajal and the 'mozo de mulas'. In the very beginning, as Corneja finishes his rosary, the first words to come out of Grajal's mouth are sung:

> ¿Es ventero Corneja?
> Todos se guarden,
> que hasta el nombre le tiene
> de malas aves.
> ¿Qué harán las ollas
> adonde las lechuzas
> pasan por pollas?[6]

From the first few lines of the *entremés*, an antagonistic relationship is exposed, one that will offer plenty of opportunities for Grajal to poke fun at Corneja's pitiful and disgusting inn. It should be noted that both Calderón's and Quevedo's interludes begin with singing, and in both cases, it is of a taunting nature. This is a perfect example of how music can play a role in intensifying the humour of a situation. Anybody who, as a child, frolicked on a school playground, will remember how the taunts of the greatest power (and childlike elegance) were those that were sung and rhymed.[7] In Calderón's *Genios*, the singing is confined to tiny fanciful melodies that make oblique references to the unsatisfying conditions of the inn. That is, in *Genios* the singing is a burlesque yet endearing communication between lovers, while in

---

5 Highet, *The Anatomy of Satire*, p. 226, points out that women, in general, have been the favourite target of satire for many writers. However, because nearly everybody is the subject of ridicule in *entremeses*, it is often difficult to determine whether women, at any particular moment, are being singled out and separated as the specific target of a satire, though this certainly can occur.

6 Quevedo, *Obras completas*, vol. 2, p. 538.

7 In archaic traditions, Elliot writes (*The Power of Satire*, pp. 15, 38) that rhyming could have magical and even deadly effects when used in a verbal attack.

La venta Grajal's singing is meant to irritate an employer. Thus we find a significant difference between the two *entremeses* that quickly contradicts
Lobato's notion that 'Todo el entremés citado de Quevedo, tiene una línea
argumental semejante al calderoniano.'[8] *Genios* has no 'ventero'. Consequently, the satire of the inn in Calderón's *entremés* is unanswered, unlike in
Quevedo, where the object of mockery and barbed remarks appears onstage
and interacts with the attacker. Because this interaction makes up half of the
La venta's plot,[9] it is incorrect to claim that the 'líneas argumentales' are the
same. Grajal's satire of the inn is twice as long as Juana's (54 versus 27 lines)
and does more than merely list grotesque food substitutions. In fact, the
impudent 'moza de venta's monologue is all the more vivid and critical as it
contains tiny scenes within it. Another difference is that Calderón drops the
inn-satire quickly and moves on to something else, never to bring up the subject again. This tendency to quickly switch from one joke to the next can be
seen as a frequent feature of Calderón's *entremeses*.

The comparison between *Genios* and *La venta* recalls our previous one
made between *La mojiganga de los guisados* and Quevedo's poem *Acompañamiento y boda del campo*. The possibility of using food for satire was
readily apparent to Calderón, but he chose not to elaborate the concept to the
same degree as Quevedo. As a rule, Spain's arch-satirist seems more concerned
with setting the scene in his works, more concerned with creating the sprawl-
ing and jumbling mess fundamental to his blend of harsh criticism, humour and
artistic expression.[10] It is worth noting that Quevedo's *entremeses* resemble
much more his prose than other *entremeses* by Quiñones de Benavente or
Calderón de la Barca. At the same time, critics seem to unequivocally consider
entremeses as the Golden Age's most satirical dramatic form before the advent
of full-length satirical plays.[11] Therefore, studying Quevedo's short comic

8 *Teatro cómico breve*, p. 137.
9 Alvin Kernan (*The Cankered Muse* (p. 31)), writes that the 'plot' of satire consists of
a type of stasis that defies any type of change or forward movement. He also writes on
p. 205 how playwrights in the past have attempted to integrate satire into a work that
depends heavily upon changing circumstances. It would be fair to say that Quevedo has
done more to integrate the satire into the action of the work, compared to Calderón who
presents Juana's comments almost as though they were a short satirical poem inserted into
the *entremés*.
10 Kernan writes (p. 7): 'The scene of satire is always disorderly and crowded, packed
to the very point of bursting.' This effect is certainly easy to accomplish while writing
poetry or prose, but as can be expected, the *teatro breve*, which rarely has more than five
or six actors, does not lend itself well to creating a crowd scene. If Kernan is correct, he
offers a compelling reason for why dramatic satire cannot achieve the same effect as purely
written satire.
11 See Albrecht von Kalnein in 'Teatro y política: Calderón como arma polémica en las
sátiras de los años 1670', *Teatro del Siglo de Oro: homenaje a Alberto Navarro* (Kassel,
Reichenberger, 1990). He explains that these crude yet scathing plays were put on in
response to the political and financial scandals of the time. Not only did these satirists steal

works should demonstrate the ultimate capabilities of dramatic satire and, through comparison, to what measure these capabilities were exploited by Calderón and others.

After line 72 of *Genios*, the inn-satire comes to an end and Juana asks the 'mozo' Pedro whom he has brought with him by mule. He answers, 'Traigo figuras extrañas / y mientras que se adereza, / por reírte, has de escucharlas,'[12] instantly erecting a 'frame', as did Don Gil when he announced the antici-pated 'torneo' in *La mojiganga de los guisados*. Pedro also enthusiastically lists all the 'figuras' and their distinguishing quirks. The satire on inns sud-denly has changed into a satire of a different nature: a parade of caricaturesque figures. Eugenio Asensio called Quevedo 'Teofrasto del hampa cortesana',[13] noting the affinity between the early modern Spaniard and the ancient Greek in painting a series of 'caracteres' or 'figuras'. Pedro's mention of 'figuras' in Calderón's *Genios* instantly draws the audience's imagination back to the realm of Quevedo's creations and those of the ancient satirists that preceded him. Yet Calderón follows neither Quevedo nor the ancients in the presenta-tion of his figures onstage. Both Spanish artists' works feature fixed types, but by comparing them, one can see the variable nature of satire, particularly as it takes dramatic form.

The characters of Quevedo's *La venta* follow the spirit of most *entremeses* in that they correspond to recognised social stereotypes mostly related to professions, while Calderón's *El reloj y los genios de la venta* makes a somewhat unusual departure. The social or 'costumbrista' aspect is not very strong.[14] In place of Quevedo's stock figures,

> Uno hay con hipocondría,
> y otro hay que siempre habla
> de su lugar, y en su tierra
> cuanto hay en el mundo, pasa.
> Y otro preciado de hacer
> vestidos, y que los traza
> y que los guisa de buen gusto,

the names from Calderón's *comedias* for use in a humorous context, but von Kalnein contends that they also found inspiration in Calderón's occasional criticisms or comments on life outside of the theatre (p. 309), though Calderón himself was not a satirist *per se*.

12 *Teatro cómico breve*, p. 131, l. 74.   13 *Itinerario*, p. 184.

14 Eugenio Asensio, in his *Itinerario* (p. 140), is careful to point out the particular brand of Spanish 'costumbrismo' of the time that was later poorly interpreted by the Romantics: 'No podría compilarse, con pretensiones objetivas, una obra como *Los españoles pintados por sí mismos*. En el Siglo de Oro, prevalecen, a lo que creo, otros enfoques descriptivos: la observación maravillada a lo Ulises, la evocación de fiestas y la crítica moral.' This supports further Auerbach's view that the mimesis, or realism, of this literature (and we include the *teatro breve*, with its many street scenes and common folk) was a means to something else and not a descriptive end in itself. See Erich Auerbach, *Mimesis*, trans. Willard Trask (New York: Anchor, 1953), p. 292.

> y de aquesto sólo trata.
> Otro hay que trae un reloj
> y cada instante le saca,
> y que venga o que no venga
> la hora que es nos encaja.[15]

Looking over these types, and later seeing how they correspondingly and predictably behave within the piece, one may have difficulty in calling them satirical figures. However, Rodríguez and Tordera have no difficulty in doing so. Here is what they write in the 'nota preliminar' of their edition:

> Toda la obra gira en torno a un doble registro satírico: el de las condiciones precarias y el recorrido por diversas 'figuras extrañas' cuyo genio ('genio' tiene en la época la acepción de la natural inclinación por alguna cosa) transmuta la venta, en ciertos pasajes, en un hospital de locos. En este asunto recuerda el entremés *El Portugués* de Cáncer y Velasco, con la ventaja, en el caso de Calderón, de captar los síntomas de diversos temas de lo que podríamos denominar semántica del Barroco, tales como la obsesión por el tiempo, la incipiente caracterización del hipocondríaco o melancólico y otros más convencionalizados como el lindo [referring to the tailor].[16]

Rodríguez and Tordera's analogy of a 'hospital de locos' is appropriate, but this could be said about many *entremeses* if a laughable obsession is the criterion for madness. Also, to be precise, it must be mentioned that the characters never actually enter the inn because all the beds are taken. Thus, while the image of the inn-as-madhouse has a certain charm, it does not technically apply to this piece. I have no argument with the first 'registro satírico' named by Rodríguez and Tordera, but in the second 'registro' they seem to be forcibly applying a decorum that does not necessarily stick. The man who always speaks of his town is not 'convencionalizado' in the *teatro breve*, according to what I have read. Likewise, the 'lindo' is certainly a stock character, but while most 'lindos' are obsessed with their appearance (including their clothes, to be sure), none that I have ever met in Golden Age fiction were so concerned with garments that it became *all* they thought about. While the character in *Genios* may have a bit of 'lindo' in him, he is not merely narcissistic. He also concerns himself with the appearance of others and feels the need to tailor their clothing against their will. The man with the watch may represent a 'baroque' obsession with the passage of time, but he may also merely be a 'personaje orgulloso de su reloj',[17] much as people today are fond of putting their newly purchased electronic gadgetry (I am thinking of mobile telephones and Personal Digital Assistants) to very conspicuous use. The melancholy

---

[15] Calderón de la Barca, *Teatro cómico breve*, p. 131, ll. 77–89.
[16] Ibid., *Entremeses, jácaras y mojigangas*, p. 172.
[17] Ibid., *Teatro cómico breve*, p. 129.

hypochondriac seems to be the most evident satirical figure in that he clearly represents a human failing that is relatively common compared to the bizarre habits of the others. All in all, Calderón offers a 'mixed bag' of characters, few of them fitting into the standard moulds employed by Quevedo and many *entremesistas*, including Calderón himself in other works. This motley crew carries with it some of the spirit of the *mojiganga*, where little explanation is needed for the characters, not because they rest on the foundation of every-day reality, but because the festive point-of-view looks unfavourably upon any justification other than to have a good time. Pedro, the 'mozo de mulas', is practically metatheatrically aware of this fact. His announcement to Juana that the 'figuras' are here 'por reirte' is also an announcement directed obliquely to the audience, similar to the framing of the action in *Los guisados*.

The processional aspect of the piece is condensed, as all the characters appear *en masse*, and in this respect it bears no obvious resemblance to most *mojigangas*. Still, some similarities remain, stemming mainly from the mechan-ical and repetitious behaviour of the 'genios'. In this case, comic repetition works on the crudest level, rehashing the same joke over and over again. Luckily, Pedro Calderón de la Barca, a connoisseur of comic effects and their limitations, saw the advantage of having the characters interact. This interaction is more elaborate than simply having them continuously spout statements corresponding to their one-dimensional personalities.

Hipocóndrico	¿Saben ustedes, que he notado hoy día que no se estima ya la hipocondría?
Juana	O es dada y solamente al entendido.
El de los vestidos	De hipocondría tengo yo un vestido.
Hipocóndrico	Este es un triste mal y es barbarismo decir aqueso.
El de los vestidos	Pues por eso mismo, que es una tela de un color muy triste, que vella sólo da melancolía, y por eso se llama hipocondría.[18]

The obsessive clotheshorse chimes in, relating the other's complaints to his singular point of view. But instead of mechanically uttering a complaint simi-lar to his previous one, the hypochondriac responds to his companion's state-ment, simultaneously complaining and setting up the final punch line of the joke. Comic value is achieved from more than a mere exhibition of the char-acters' foibles. Their collaborative dialogue, though slightly argumentative, works to create a bigger joke. This type of interaction also tends to soften the mechanical quality of their behaviour that would be the central focus of a critic like Bergson. Seemingly contrary to Bergson's notion, the characters'

---

[18] Calderón de la Barca, *Teatro cómico breve*, p. 133, ll. 113–21.

flexibility or willingness to integrate each other's existences (obsessive as
they may be) is the cause for laughter here. 'El de los Vestidos's final quip
incites laughter through a strange sense of momentary absorption into (or reconciliation with) the other's melancholic point of view.

All the same, 'flexibility', humanness or normality are relative terms, and
compared to the young lovers of this sketch, the 'genios' are extremely odd;
they are rather 'rigid' and 'mechanical' in the Bergsonian sense. What makes
Genios an unusual *entremés* is the unusually sincere relationship between
Juana and Pedro that seems out of place in such a farcical and mocking genre.
Many rustic characters in the *comedia* are seen as comic relief, but also as a
representation of the earthier and less complicated side of human relations,
especially between men and women. Pedro and Juana seem related to this
tradition, and while their tryst may be nothing more than a brief encounter,
the focus is not upon their unbridled lust, nor any cynical point of view, as in
Quevedo, but instead upon their being together. All the beds at the inn are
taken, and all present must make 'rancho' outdoors. Pedro looks up at the sky,
counting the 'cabrillas' (Pleiades), and one can imagine Juana looking up at
the stars with him, as she says she can only see six, while he sees seven. This
is an extremely intimate, human and mimetic moment, rarely found in the
entremeses, where, in general, characters' actions are aimed relentlessly
towards satisfying the needs of their obsessive stock personalities. Pedro is
not trying to seduce Juana – they already know each other intimately – he is
just making pleasant conversation. Upon hearing that 'Siete son', the man
with the watch breaks in:

El del reloj   Esa porfía presto se remedia,
               sí serán en verdad, y aún siete y media.

Pedro   ¿Siete y media? ¡Jesús! ¿Qué está diciendo?
               ¿Quién oyó desatino tan horrendo?
               ¿En el reloj cabrillas? ¿Es esfera?[19]

This type of comic misunderstanding is one of dozens of common
devices[20] used in the *teatro breve*. However, much would be lost if our
investigation stopped at naming the device and offering a brief explanation of

[19] Calderón de la Barca, *Teatro cómico breve*, pp. 133–4, ll. 130–2.

[20] I have avoided providing a list of comic devices, but if the reader is interested, a good
overview of them can be found in Calderón de la Barca, *Entremeses, jácaras y mojigangas*,
pp. 26–49, or much more extensively in Bergman, *Quiñones de Benavente y sus entremeses*, pp. 91–157. Other critics have listed the comic devices to be found in the *comedia*. See
Jakob Kellenberger, *Calderón de la Barca und das Komische: unter besonderer Berücksichtigung der ernsten Schauspiele* (Frankfurt: Peter Lang, 1975), and Alberto Navarro
González, 'Comicidad del lenguaje en el teatro de Calderón', in *Iberoromania*, 14 (1981),
116–32, and Ignacio Arellano, 'La comicidad escénica en Calderón', *Bulletin Hispanique*,
88 (1986), 47–92.

its function. It is more valuable to address a larger context in order to appreciate Calderón's full exploitation of the joke. Pedro and Juana's world of normal human interaction has been suddenly invaded by the chatter of one of the obsessive *entremés* characters. The misunderstanding is not only inherently funny, but also funny as the point of contact between two worlds, one outrageous and nonsensical, and the other relatively serious. Again, comic forces – while not the embodiment of disorder, certainly lacking everyday sobriety – begin to invade a normal reality. As soon as the man with the watch tries to explain himself, 'El de su lugar' adds automatically 'Para eso de relojes, Villalpando', seeking whatever pretext he can to mention his home town, thus pushing further the incursion of the 'genios' with his mindless comment.

At that moment, however, Pedro's feeling of surprise becomes pure pleasure as he says he cannot help but laugh at such a wild 'disparate'. This directs the audience's thoughts back to Pedro's original statement about bringing the 'figuras' forward to get a laugh. But Pedro's comment is not an aside to the audience or a sideways remark to Juana as before. The hypochondriac hears the comment and, as he seized upon 'El de los vestidos's statements before, remarks bitterly that he himself has no reason to laugh. He even complains about his son, who, despite his father's desires to the contrary, 'es un picarillo que se alegra'.[21] What was once obsessive chattering filled with knee-jerk responses becomes an involved yet light-hearted discussion about melancholy, thanks to Pedro's intervention. Despite the absurdity of his complaints, the mere fact that the hypochondriac has a son makes him a slightly more human figure. Of course, no element, farcical, fantastic, human, realistic or otherwise dominates in this *entremés*. Instead it is the 'mixed bag', the mess, the *satura* that makes the piece so entertaining. From melancholy to family problems, to the need for happiness, Pedro steers the conversation towards a solution and orders 'Vea uced bailes, vea mojigangas, / perderá este color verde y cetrino'.[22] This reference, similar to the one proclaiming the arrival of the 'figuras', is metatheatrical, though more subtle, as Pedro's advice is effectively being followed by the audience that is witnessing that advice being given. The self-conscious nature of the *teatro breve* reveals itself momentarily while remaining solidly rooted in the substance of the conversation.

[21] Calderón de la Barca, *Teatro cómico breve*, p. 134, l. 149.
[22] Ibid., p. 134, ll. 153–4. The *Diccionario de Autoridades* defines 'cetrino' as a colour associated with melancholy. 'Verde' is generally associated with youth and vigour, but can also connote bitterness, as in unripe grapes. Evangelina Rodríguez cites Doctor Estevan Pujasol's *El sol solo, y para todos sol, de la Filosofía sagaz y Anatomía de ingenios* (1637), who states: ' "el color del rostro verdugado, y cetrino [. . .] significa colérico y arrojado [. . .] a causa del melancólico humor" '. See Evangelina Rodríguez, 'Gesto, movimiento, palabra: el actor en el entremés del Siglo de Oro', *Los géneros menores en el teatro español del Siglo de Oro (Jornadas de Almagro 1987)*, ed. Luciano García Lorenzo (Madrid: Ministerio de Cultura, 1988), p. 60.

The *entremés* enters a brief period of normalcy as Pedro asks Juana and the others to pray with him so that the mule-cart can make it safely down the hill, a journey which almost cost him his life before:

Juana	El Ángel de la Guarda anda en aqueso y a todas horas nos está velando.
El de su lugar	Para Ángeles de la Guarda, Villalpando.
Juana	(*Ap.* No he tenido jamás noche tan buena)[23]

A moment of sobriety is once again broken up, and Juana and Pedro are very amused, and not the least bit irritated. They enjoy the show, and it is now evident that they are 'egging on' their strange guests to say and do strange things for their nightly entertainment. The man obsessed with clothing is encouraged to offer a tailoring demonstration when he hears the word 'guisar' in reference to the upcoming dinner. He stabs some fabric here and slices some material there, but unfortunately he also, 'Hace la demostración en la cara de Perico.'[24] Pedro ('Perico') takes offence that this 'genio/figura' has decided to physically incorporate the product of his madness into Pedro's personal space in a dangerous fashion, and the young muleteer responds by hitting back. Naturally, an obsessive personality will not quit his behaviour so easily, and Pedro sees himself forced to pummel the mad tailor into submission. Finally, the lover of clothes submits and cries out 'se me han quebrado los brahones', perhaps a fate worse than broken bones, from his point of view. Following the great *entremés* tradition, the scene has devolved into one of shouting and violence. But before the stage is consumed in a flurry of screaming and pummelling, Juana launches into a song that recalls the peaceful beginnings of the sketch. Women, in the background, answer in chorus. Pedro sings 'Mozos que bailar sabéis . . .',[25] and all the men answer in the same fashion as the women. Upon the mention of 'bailar' one can imagine the men and women pairing off and getting into a dance-formation, ending the *entremés* on a happy and orderly note.

After looking carefully at *Genios* it is difficult to claim that Calderón's piece about an inn 'sigue la línea argumental' of Quevedo's *entremeses*, but comparisons do reveal important similarities, particularly those concerning the ending. Quevedo's *La venta* also ends with fighting, more verbal than physical, as the student and Corneja square off in a war of words:

| Estudiante | En esta pobre choza todos somos Hurtados sin Mendoza. |

---

23 Calderón de la Barca, *Teatro cómico breve*, p. 135, l. 170.
24 Ibid., p. 135, l. 176.   25 Ibid., p. 136, l. 190.

Corneja	Miente el picaño.
Estudiante	Ladrón, protoladrón, archiladrillo y tátara Pilatos, casamentero infame de estómagos y gatos.
Corneja	Infame, espera, calla, calla, que quien no mata con morcilla rabo, menos me matará con una bala.[26]

In order to prevent an escalation, Guevara, the director of a visiting theatre troupe, invites the two squabblers to become friends and asks that his musicians strike up a happy tune. While music served a negative, irritating and conflictive purpose at the beginning of *La venta*, here it serves to soothe tensions by integrating everybody into a contrived song-and-dance routine. It is a practical requirement of the structure in most *teatro breve* pieces; the shouting and slapping and pummelling and cursing can only go on for so long. There must be music to give a sense of closure,[27] to construct a final frame around the piece which, while more plot-driven than the *mojiganga*, is still a festive onstage spectacle in its own right. At the end of Calderón's *Genios*, Pedro sings an answer to the chorus' question, '¿Qué queréis?':

> Que cantando, tañendo y bailando,
> figuras tan grandes aquí celebréis.[28]

It is a final reminder that throughout the conversation, serious and ludicrous, throughout all the interaction, realistic and contrived, peaceful and violent, *El reloj y los genios de la venta* has been a self-conscious parade of 'figuras' in an ingeniously altered form.

CALDERÓN AND THE TRADITIONAL *ENTREMÉS*

El dragoncillo could be considered the consummate example of Calderón's complete understanding and mastery of the *entremés* form. In a way, *El dragoncillo* is the consummate *entremés* because it includes four prominent distinguishing characteristics that bind this sub-genre together: heavy borrowing

[26] Quevedo, *Obras completas*, vol. 2, p. 541.
[27] There is a long tradition of ending an *entremés* with *palos*, or beatings, which seems to have died out at the beginning of the seventeenth century. One finds many violent and dramatically unresolved endings in the sixteenth-century examples of Cotarelo's *colección*, but by the time that Quiñones de Benavente reached prominence, the ending with *palos* was practically unheard of, if surviving pieces give us any indication.
[28] Calderón de la Barca, *Teatro cómico breve*, p. 136, ll. 192–3.

from folkloric themes, a rogue's gallery of stock figures, suspenseful yet fast-paced action and the all-important *burla* or deception that is the centrepiece of the work. In this *entremés*, a wife convinces her husband to leave the house by warning him of the arrival of 'la justicia' (in reality just the mayor) who surely wants to arrest him for a bad debt. After the husband hides, the wife learns that the mayor has only come to secure lodging for a visiting soldier of a company that is staying in town. The wife explains that the house has no food, but this does not disappoint the newly arrived soldier, who immediately makes advances towards her. She rebuffs him as her husband returns, shuts him up in the hay loft with her husband's encouragement, and when the husband departs a second time, she greets her lover, a 'sacristan' (sexton) who comes loaded with food. When the husband returns unexpectedly, the sexton hides under the table with his food, and the clever soldier explains to the husband that he can conjure forth dinner. He does so by blackmailing the 'spirit' hidden under the table in order that he may obtain the goods that the sexton-lover has brought. While the food appears magically from underneath the table, both the sexton and the soldier snatch it away from the husband before he can eat it. The sketch ends with the sexton setting off an explosive and knocking out the lights, an act followed by wild pummelling in the dark, before everybody marches off stage in separate directions.

This story certainly stretches far back into the history of both literature and folklore. In her notes on the piece in question, Lobato lists various observations made by other critics about antecedents to *El dragoncillo*.[29] An obvious comparison can be made with Cervantes' *entremés* titled *La Cueva de Salamanca*. Jean Canavaggio, an expert on Cervantine interludes and also an astute examiner of Calderón, has written a brief but authoritative article comparing the two works that looks again at Rodríguez and Tordera's notion that *El dragoncillo* is a 'reescritura' of the Cervantine interlude. Canavaggio's main criticism is that Rodríguez and Tordera neglected to take into account other literary antecedents, aside from Cervantes, and that the Valencian critics failed to acknowledge the vast reservoir of folklore from which both artists may have drawn:

> Dos tratamientos distintos de un mismo motivo tradicional: así nos aparecen *La cueva de Salamanca* y *El dragoncillo*; así se explican las semejanzas observadas por la crítica y que, a la verdad, se derivan de la identidad del tema; así se aclaran las diferencias que revela el mero cotejo de los dos textos, siendo éstos, a fin de cuentas, dos «literarizaciones» de un mismo fondo mostrenco . . .[30]

---

[29] Calderón de la Barca, *Teatro cómico breve*, p. 214.

[30] Jean Canavaggio, 'En torno al "Dragoncillo": nuevo examen de una reescritura', in *Estudios sobre Calderón, Actas del Coloquio Calderoniano. Salamanca 1985*, ed. Alberto Navarro González (Salamanca: Universidad de Salamanca, 1985), p. 14.

Though Maxime Chevalier's name is barely mentioned in this article, Canavaggio's statement resembles Chevalier's warnings about neglecting the importance of folklore in the origin of the widow or the country bumpkin in Spanish theatre. While Chevalier's main concern about these characters was the lack of data required to give a social and economic foundation to their literary existence[31] – for the widow and bumpkin respectively – Canavaggio feels that critics have placed too much emphasis on the similarities between Cervantes and Calderón while glossing over the differences. Franco Meregalli, in 'Cervantes in Calderón', ten years after Canavaggio made his subtle yet important distinctions, writes: 'Il caso più chiaro della presenza di Cervantes in Calderón è quello di *El dragoncillo*, derivante inequivocabilmente da *La cueva de Salamanca*.'[32] Ignoring differences also means ignoring information that connects the two works to others (as shown by Lobato and Canavaggio), proving once again that Calderón did not simply 'rewrite' *La cueva de Salamanca*. At the same time, critics are correct in pointing out that Calderón must have read Cervantes' works and was indebted to them,[33] but this is not to say that Calderón was slavishly copying Cervantes, just as Asensio reminds us that 'Quevedo no siguió esclavizado al módulo de Teofrasto' in the realm of satire.[34]

While debating Cervantes' influence and Calderón's originality may seem like a minor point of contention, this type of argument has relevance on a greater scale. Such a debate points to the special nature of the *entremés* that is often ignored, perhaps paradoxically because of its overwhelming presence. The *entremés* exhibits amazing flexibility in its ability to appropriate various forms from oral and written literature, from all social and cultural registers. The *entremés* truly corresponds to the original Latin definition of *satura*, and is the dramatic 'clearing house' of everything from epic poems to fart jokes. In a way, the *entremés* is the dramatic equivalent of a joke, a powerful creative tool that can absorb and transform nearly any concept or artistic creation.[35]

[31] Chevalier, *Tipos cómicos y folklore*, p. 126.

[32] Franco Meregalli, 'Cervantes in Calderón', *Atti delle giornate cervantine* (Padova: Unipress, 1995), p. 131.

[33] Meregalli, p. 131; Canvaggio, p. 15; Edward M. Wilson, 'Calderón y Cervantes', *Archivum Calderonianum, Hacia Calderón: Quinto Coloquio Anglogermano, Oxford 1978* (Wiesbaden: Franz Steiner, 1982), p. 10.

[34] Asensio, *Itinerario*, p. 189.

[35] In their conclusion to *Dramaturgia*, Rodríguez and Tordera write (p. 213): '. . . el entremés de Calderón no es un mundo bizarro y aparte, sino un *mundo abreviado* en el que todos o la mayor parte de los motivos y obsesiones de su obra seria se perfilan, por su reducción no sólo de los temas, sino de los propios procedimientos de su dramaturgia.' This same property can be observed about the joke in a much more general sense as well. For Jolles, the joke occupies a special place in his series of *einfache Formen* (Jolles, p. 227): 'Si vamos más lejos, notaremos que no sólo pueden desatarse en el chiste, lengua, lógica, ética y similares; también puede desligarse todo aquello que a lo largo de este trabajo hemos denominado simple.'

Travelling along a 'mini-itinerario' of short comic theatre, one will notice
many appearances of the 'malmaridada' in the *teatro breve*. Thus, while it is
reasonable to argue that *El dragoncillo* and *La cueva de Salamanca* have a
special affinity and belong to a sub-sub-genre because they share the use of
magical conjuring, one must not neglect distinguishing characteristics
between the two pieces that make each resemble other works. *La cueva* is very
similar to Lope de Rueda's *Paso 3°* (first published in 1567), called by later
critics *Cornudo y contento*. The husband Pancracio in the Cervantine
entremés is like the husband in *Cornudo y contento* because he is completely
oblivious to his wife's infidelity, even though he knows a student is staying
with her. In contrast, the husband's suspicions in Calderón's *El dragoncillo*
are constantly gnawing away at his conscience. In what seems like an admis-
sion of his wife's infidelity, he grumbles '¿Tanto en esconderse tardan?'[36]
upon entering the stage after what was doubtlessly a noisy scramble for the
sexton-lover to hide himself. This cynical and pained outlook of the 'marido
sufrido' (as opposed to the oblivious cuckold) bears resemblance to Diego
Moreno's attitude in the *Primera parte* of Quevedo's *entremés* that bears this
character's name. *El dragoncillo*'s husband suspects his wife, bickers with
her, but always makes sufficient noise to give warning before he enters the
house, lest he discover her *in flagrante*, in bed with another man. How does
Luis Quiñones de Benavente, the most famed contemporary *entremesista*, fit
into this itinerary of dramatic cuckoldry? Hannah Bergman writes two sentences about his adultery sketches: 'Las intrigas adúlteras (menos frecuentes
en Benavente que en otros entremesistas) muestran notas comunes.' However, she continues to explain that: 'Forman el motivo principal de sólo tres
piezas [out of a minimum of one hundred fifty], ninguna de atribución muy
segura.'[37] This observation reveals an unexpected feature of Calderón's
entremeses, that from at least one point of view, statistically speaking, they
are more *risqué* than those by Benavente. *El dragoncillo* is a classic *entremés*
founded on an old theme. This tradition is also a backdrop against which one
may notice particular details and distinctions crafted by Calderón.

The characters are as old as the plot in which they all play a part. Searching
for the origins of the stock figures would lead to debates equivalent to those
carried out in the Cervantes–Calderón controversy noted above. What matters
is that the *entremés*, more than any other dramatic form, offers a literal
rogues' gallery of characters of a very standard sort. There always exists a
tension between the exaggerated nature of *entremés* characters and the
constraints of the fictional world in which they live. Satire, a major function
of *entremeses*, is greatly aided by demonstrating vices in a real-world setting.
Parody can also depend upon realism as it seeks to lay low transcendental
notions that strive beyond the mundane. The everyday world is also the plane

[36] Calderón de la Barca, *Teatro cómico breve*, p. 206, l. 184.
[37] Bergman, *Quiñones de Benavente y sus entremeses*, p. 79.

of crudeness and bodily necessity, and the street is an appropriate setting to let fly scatological and sexual jokes. One begins to see that the setting itself is conducive to laughter, provided that the characters' appearance and behaviour exploit the comic possibilities through exaggeration. The tension between the outlandish and the everyday is not necessarily one of opposition. This is the value of stereotypes and caricature, inherently exaggerating and distorting features of reality, never beyond recognition, occasionally making these features clearer and more distinct than is ordinarily witnessed.

The dependence upon stereotypes raises another curious question about the nature of decorum. In the world of the *teatro breve*, abundant *disparates* rule. Crazy schemes that would never work in real life (such as magically turning a man into a dog[38]) are easily brought to fruition. Language loses its shape as wordplay, rather than the need to convey meaning, becomes the foundation of discourse. Occasionally, words lose their meaning entirely, as speech devolves into verbal gobbledygook.[39] People bop each other over the head and shout insults, only to make amends and dance together at the end. The heavy emphasis on nonsense would seem to demand the primacy of the unpredictable, but the characters from the *entremés* rogues' gallery subscribe to a fairly rigid order.[40] The ultimate decorum, in a sense a 'theorem' of decorum in the *entremés*, could be stated as 'make 'em laugh' or 'knock 'em dead', an exhortation to burst the collective belly of the audience. The 'preceptistas' of the time made no mention of standards for writing *teatro breve*, and the unwritten rules used by *entremesistas* (subsets or 'lemmas' of the 'theorem' stated above) seem to have developed by themselves. That is not to say that no 'preceptista' ever commented on this form. Indeed, Anthony Close has pointed out how one of the characters in López Pinciano's treatise *Philosophia antigua poetica* uses Lope de Rueda, the sixteenth century's most renowned *entremesista*, as a 'favoured source' while discussing the notion of comedy with his friends. Close explains how Rueda's *entremeses* are related to the 'native [Spanish] traditions of humour', and are greatly valued by 'El Pinciano' as examples of mastering the comic in theatre. The modern critic writes:

> The most vivid testimony of this traditionalism is the extraordinary encomium of the stereotyped figure of the rustic simpleton as an invention by which Spanish dramatists have supposedly outstripped all the comic playwrights of antiquity. By portraying this clown as a fusion of

[38] *El sueño del perro*, by Quiñones de Benavente, in Cotarelo, *Colección de entremeses*, vol. 18, pp. 780–3.

[39] See the end of the previously cited *Entremés de los planetas*, p. 16.

[40] Aside from Chevalier's work on folkloric types, see also Lope de Rueda, *Pasos*, ed. José Luis Canet Vallés (Madrid: Castalia, 1992). Canet Vallés lists the main characteristics of stock figures found in *entremeses* one hundred years previous to those of Calderón. Though new characters appear, and slight variations occur, there is little difference in the 'gallery' over this time period.

ignorance, foolishness, malice, and uncouth sensuousness, they have
managed to cram all the essential features of 'ugliness' [conforming to
the Aristotelian terms of *deformitas et turpitudo*] into one package, thus
achieving a maximum of risibility.[41]

While *entremeses* serve as useful examples for reflecting on certain types of
humour, no questions arise in *Philosophia antigua* as to *how* these pieces
themselves are written, nor does the work mention any specific rules for doing
so. We find the works examined in the wider context of discussions concerning 'ugliness', decorum, etc. Nevertheless, El Pinciano was correct in recognising a conscious process in the production of *teatro breve*. In reading his
appreciation of the genre, and Close's analysis, we see that Spanish comic
traditions, including 'old chestnuts', could be distilled in the *teatro breve* by
simply combining and exaggerating well-known laughable qualities, without
following an express set of precepts. I believe that for Lope de Rueda, both
the popular tradition and his audience's reaction were the main sources
informing his artistic production, rather than an adherence to neo-Aristotelian
dicta, even though the results of the first approach could often coincide with
the latter and still provide good examples for theoretical treatises.

Close has mentioned the invention of the simpleton, or 'bobo', a figure who
represents the epitome of *entremés* characterisation, meaning that his every
characteristic is intended to get a laugh. This character is one among many who
populate the universe of the *teatro breve*, and many of whom have solidified into
fixed types as their comic success has been demonstrated time and again.
Beyond possessing the common knowledge that these characters must be 'ugly'
in some way – in this genre meaning exaggerated, vicious, stupid, clumsy, etc. –
the playwrights of the time developed their own unwritten rules concerning
the inherent qualities of their creations and how each would interact with the
other onstage. It was always best to include well-known characters, ones that

---

[41] Anthony Close, *Cervantes and the Comic Mind of his Age* (Oxford: Oxford
University Press, 2000), p. 253. Close goes on to discuss 'El Pinciano's concern with the
separation between *burlas* and *veras*, the comicity of *entremeses* belonging to the first
category but not to the latter. Were he alive when the edited works of Luis Quiñones de
Benavente were published, it would have be interesting to know what 'El Pinciano' might
have thought of a book titled *Joco seria* and subtitled *Burlas veras*. The fascination at the
time (1645) with combining these previously irreconcilable elements is evident in the
work's introduction. The praise and commentary that precede the *entremeses* in *Joco seria*
demonstrate a contemporary artistic appreciation of an art form, still as 'ugly' as in the
previous century, yet which now supposedly has a value beyond making people laugh. As
with 'El Pinciano's distinct praise in 1596, such appreciation still lacks any instruction or
manifesto on *how* to write the *teatro breve*, a corresponding equivalent (ironic or not) to
Lope's *Arte nuevo de hacer comedias*. In fact, it would probably be fruitless to search for
such a source. Asensio writes (Asensio, *Itinerario*, p. 125) that Quiñones de Benavente, the
master of the genre, was, 'guiado no por teorías, sino por el espíritu e instinto de su época
que engendró la ópera italiana y la zarzuela española'. The same can be said for Calderón,
who followed in Quiñones de Benavente's footsteps.

are inherently funny, and force them (quite easily, given their nature) into absurd situations. A knowledge of these types (explicitly called 'figuras' in a manuscript copy of one of Quevedo's *entremeses*,[42] as well as in many pieces found in Cotarelo's collection) relaxes the audience because they find themselves in familiar circumstances. Such preparatory knowledge promotes a sort of comic verisimilitude, into which the consciousness of the audience is partially subsumed, always leaving room for the ever-present metatheatrical layering or self-conscious outburst. These are aspects of decorum and verisimilitude of which the 'preceptistas' were not aware, but which *entremesistas* dutifully acknowledged and used to great advantage.

Stereotypes are indispensable in the structure of the *entremés*. Familiarity with stock characteristics provides a type of dramatic shorthand where no character development is necessary beyond, for example, a student saying: 'Pobre estudiante soy.' It would be even more economical for a student to say nothing at all and simply step on to the stage in a ragged cap and tattered robes. Stereotypes also function as discrete components that can be mixed and matched to create different scenes. The playwright can put a sexton together with a soldier, or a miser together with a muleteer, or throw an astrologer, a widow and a Frenchman all into a room and see what happens. This artistic strategy was most evident in *El reloj y los genios de la venta*. *El dragoncillo* features a 'gracioso' (more a descendant of sixteenth-century 'bobos' than Lope de Vega's creation), a 'malmaridada', a sexton and a soldier, all characters that could happily exist in other *entremeses*. Looking ahead to the *comedia*, we see that it too features stock figures of a sort, and many fewer from which to choose, compared to the *entremés*. Does this mean that there are fewer situational possibilities for the *comedia* than for the *entremés*? Everything depends upon the number of possible actions that the individual characters types are capable of, and not only the sheer number and variety of the characters themselves; but these comparisons between the two types of characters from each genre will be saved for later analysis.

Examining social stereotypes in a genre that mercilessly mocks dramatic convention obliges us to think of metatheatre in its social dimensions. Jonathan Thacker has written an excellent study on the subject of metatheatre, in which he adopts the notion promoted by the social anthropologist Erving Goffman (and other 'role-play' theoreticians) that sees life as 'a dramatically enacted thing'. He argues that because Early Modern Spanish audiences were aware of this idea in their own time, self-reflection on roles (social, sexual or otherwise) in the *comedia* gave the audience and playwright a venue in which to reflect upon (or debate to a certain degree) the established roles in society at large.[43] Can the same be said of the *teatro breve*? After all, it is an

---

[42] Asensio, *Itinerario*, p. 259.

[43] Jonathan Thacker, *Role-Play and the World as Stage in the Comedia* (Liverpool: Liverpool University Press, 2002), p. 10.

immensely self-reflexive genre and it is packed full with well-established roles. Curiously enough, for all the mockery and free-wheeling treatment of convention that exists in the *teatro breve*, little of it serves to criticise the constraining aspect of social roles themselves. Much of this is owing to the status and permissible actions of the characters. I offer one example. A 'estudiante capigorrón' is a theatrical role that reflects a social one, and the character himself may be aware of the role he plays in the theatre piece, but he is unable to do much in order to question this role or shake himself free of it. This is because his (comic) entertainment value depends upon an adherence to a dramatic convention initially sprung from a social environment. By tricking, begging, seducing, stealing, in however mad and topsy-turvy a fashion, he is actually following, in a vague way, what society expects of him. In the comedies mentioned by Thacker, powerful manipulation by women and the world-turned-upside-down offer entertainment as they simultaneously give the audience pause to consider the societal values in an obvious representational mode and in reality. In the case of the *teatro breve*, there is little that the 'capigorrón' can do to give his audience an occasion to examine more closely the environment that has produced him. Nevertheless, as the characters and situations in the *teatro breve* approach the social standing and relative realism of their counterparts in the *comedia*, we would do well to contemplate the significance of their role-play within the theatre and without. We have seen already in *La mojiganga del pésame de la viuda* how a simple farce can actually provide commentary on the agony created by excessively harsh social expectations.[44]

Comedias, particularly those called 'de capa y espada', are known for their fast-paced action, but nothing can compare to the velocity at which most *entremeses* run. Reviewing the first sixty lines of *El dragoncillo* offers a prime example. The interlude begins with Teresa, the Gracioso's wife, saying, 'Huid, marido, que viene la Justicia,'[45] immediately creating suspense and action. To further this, the husband (both a dolt and a sceptic) instead of auto-matically hiding, reasons for a moment with his wife to verify that she knows of what she speaks. Additionally, the husband moves slowly, heightening the tension before the arrival of the 'justicia'. He hides just in time as the mayor comes forth, ostensibly to search for the delinquent Gracioso. This notion is dispelled as the mayor declares: '. . . pues yo a eso no venía . . .'[46] and the action takes an extremely short 'breather'. Then, in the next line, the mayor announces the arrival of the rag-tag soldier, setting the action in motion once again. Now begins the banter between 'Juan-soldado' and the 'malcasada', which starts on the subject of food but moves towards something else as the

---

[44] See Thacker, pp. 109–31, to observe the complexity and true questioning of norms that can be achieved when the theme of the free-spirited widow is used in the *comedia*.

[45] Calderón de la Barca, *Teatro cómico breve*, p. 198, l. 1.

[46] Ibid., p. 200, l. 31.

leering soldier sings: '¿Qué importa que no tengas, / patrona mía / más regalo, si tienes / esa carilla?'[47] At this moment of tension, we hear the singing of the husband who is arriving home to surprise Teresa, whom he thought he had left alone. The level of suspense is brought up one notch further. All these examples of the motion between suspense and calm, these quick jumps and oscillations, have been taken from only the first sixty lines of the sketch.

The term *teatro breve* is useful not only for avoiding the connotation of inferior quality that comes from the expression *teatro menor*, but also for focusing on the idea of acceleration, brevity and rapid-fire motion. The *entremés*, true to the function implied in its name, had to be quick, under the definition of 'intermission', an activity that is short by nature even today. I believe there exists some confusion in assuming that, in the context of the *teatro breve*, less means worse or inferior. No place seems more appropriate for the use of the cliché 'less is more' than that of the *entremés*. There is more plot, at least on a per-line or per-minute basis. There is also more variety in conversation as many topics are crammed into the dialogue in the form of witticisms and jokes. If one is merely looking for jokes themselves, there are certainly more in the *teatro breve*, per-line, per-minute, as the language itself can often be a language of jokes, much like the modern Marx Brothers spoke to each other continuously in puns and 'equívocos'. Of course, less can also mean less, and there is certainly less character development, less involved personal relationships, less emotional involvement between characters and less (or close to no) treatment of ethical or philosophical themes in either a thoughtful or edifying fashion.[48] Unfortunately, 'less is less' is the most intuitive response to the *teatro breve*, and most critics have failed to see the other side of the coin. Increased action and suspense are the most obvious examples of a 'less is more' strategy in writing theatre, and they are easy to witness in *El dragoncillo*.

The key element of most *entremés* plots is the *burla*, or deception. The Caminante of *La muerte* was easily deceived because of his drunken grogginess and the unexpected arrival of costumed characters. The *burla* of *El dragoncillo* relies upon the agency of the tricksters, the stupidity of the victim being merely a convenience. *Burla* has multiple meanings in Spanish, just as 'joke' or 'trick' do in English. In this case, I refer to a meaning that corresponds to the notion of a 'practical joke', not a play on words or a simple ironic or false statement. We are speaking of a joke that is the trick which drives the plot, the trick that is central to the action, not merely a brief occasion

---

47 Calderón de la Barca, *Teatro cómico breve*, p. 201, ll. 54–7.

48 I cite the comment from *Itinerario* (p. 234) that is the origin of a common expression among scholars of the *teatro breve*: 'Respondiendo a los mismos instintos antisociales [mentioned by a *gracioso* in *El castigo sin venganza* by Lope], el entremés, amparado por sus festivos privilegios, nos brinda este cuadro: justicia apaleada, engañados, maridos burlados, ingenuos chasqueados, en una palabra: vacaciones morales.'

for a laugh among many similar such occasions in the piece. The soldier's trick
is the centrepiece of *El dragoncillo*, and is therefore worth examining in detail.
The wife, wary of the soldier's advances, and expecting the arrival of her lover
the sexton, 'lodges' the *dragoncillo* (locks him up) in the hay loft, thanks to the
key ('la llave de mi honor'[49]) given to her by her jealous husband. This time,
Teresa has momentarily tricked the soldier, manipulated him to her advantage.
As often occurs in the *entremés*, the trickster is himself tricked.[50] Thus, the
soldier, upon being released by the returned husband, devises an ingenious
plan. Like the student of Cervantes' *La cueva de Salamanca*, he claims to be a
master of the black arts and will conjure food from out of thin air. He asks that
all be made dark, allowing him to secretly draw food from under the table,
where the terrified sexton is hiding himself and his victuals. 'Conjuring' the
food from the sexton is a hilarious form of blackmail, as nothing damaging
about the situation is revealed, though the permeating precariousness is
perfectly understood by everyone. Everyone that is, except the husband, who,
as the object of the *burla*, is made an outsider. In some *entremeses*, deceptions
are carried out for the sake of fun, but most *burlas* are motivated by material
desires, generally involving money, food, alcohol, sex, or any combination
thereof. The wife Teresa tricks both her husband and the soldier to satisfy her
sexual appetite, while the soldier himself tricks everybody so that he may fill
his empty stomach. For both wife and soldier, there also exists an element of
gamesmanship involving the thrill of manipulating others, an activity
corresponding to the purely playful qualities of a *burla*.

I have implied that the *entremés* is dramatic art's answer to the joke in all
senses of the word, from wordplay to deception. A skilfully written synopsis
of *El dragoncillo*, with all of its important comic moments intact, would prove
this by reversing the paradigm. Most *entremeses* can be retold as funny stories.
Fooling somebody is a common basis for jokes, particularly those centred on
a stereotyped character considered to be particularly witless. These types of
joke also generally involve a canny individual, perhaps representing another
stereotype, who is responsible for the manipulation.[51] These 'individuals' that

---

[49] Calderón de la Barca, *Teatro cómico breve*, p. 203, l. 121.

[50] Bergson, in Sypher, p. 122, writes that the surprising twist on a familiar situation
reminds us of its original repetitive quality. 'It casts over a host of other scenes a reflection
of the comic element it contains.' The Italian Renaissance theoretician of humour,
Castelvetro, assigned this 'rivolgimento' to one of his four categories for trickery in jokes.
See Enrico Mussachio and Sandro Cordeschi, eds, *Il riso nelle poetiche rinascimentali*,
(Bologna: Lapelli, 1985), p. 82.

[51] I derive this notion from Christie Davies, *Ethnic Humor Around the World: A
Comparative Analysis* (Bloomington: Indiana University Press, 1990). She writes on p. 10:
'Although the ethnic jokes told in many societies throughout the world pin a wide range of
comic attributes onto a great variety of peoples and ethnic groups, one pair of ethnic jokes
seems to be far more widespread, more numerous, and more durable than any other. This
pair comprises on the one hand jokes about groups depicted as stupid, inept and ignorant,
and on the other, as if in opposition, jokes about groups portrayed as canny, calculating,

appear in jokes are actually the same stereotypes found in the world of the *entremés*, two characters based mostly on the elemental features of trickster and dupe. How necessary are these stereotypes in the function of the theatrical *burla*? What occurs when characters are not inherently tricky, when, for example, their material desires do not motivate them to fool and manipulate others? What do we have when a dramatic piece features trickery without any students conspiring to get a free meal, without soldiers stealing change purses, without wives reaching for physical satisfaction outside of their marriage? What happens when people still attempt to trick one another for other reasons and through other means? I would argue that contemplating this type of less materialistic piece brings our gaze closer to the *comedia*, where the *burla* also reigns supreme but in a distinct manner. Doors, disguises and blackouts abound and offer plenty of opportunities for confusion and power plays, just as can be found in the *entremés*. Upon brief examination, one can even find base desire driving the intrigue and trickery of many 'capa y espada' plays as well. The driving force is love, or lust, depending on one's moral angle and which prominent seventeenth-century moralist one sides with. The trickery and schemes of the *comedias* are called 'burlas' in Spanish,[52] but also 'engaños', bringing to the forefront a great baroque theme. In chapter 4, when looking at Calderón's *El astrólogo fingido*, the connections between the *entremés* and the *comedia* by way of the *burla* will become readily apparent.

The *El dragoncillo* is a classic *entremés* in most aspects, but the ending is a bit odd. While many *entremeses* during and before Cervantes' time ended with 'palos' or blows, by the time Quiñones de Benavente's model reached prominence, the overwhelming majority of *entremeses* and *mojigangas* ended with a song and a dance. The pieces that have been examined so far offer a good representative sample, corroborating the existence of this norm. In *El dragoncillo*, when the sexton sets off an explosive, the lights go out, and he says, 'De este soldadillo tengo / de vengarme,'[53] after which all three men rain blows upon each other in the dark. If *El dragoncillo* were to follow the scheme of most pieces, somebody would have brought out a candle and started singing. Everybody would have joined in, and a final dance would have

and craftily stingy. Such jokes far outnumber jokes based on any other comic trait ascribed to any group of people, whether nation, ethnic group, or regional minority.' I see no difficulty in transferring these observations about ethnic and regional groups to the professional, marital and economic groups that make up much of the *dramatis personae* in the *teatro breve*.

[52] See Max Oppenheimer Jr, 'The *Burla* in Calderón's *El astrólogo fingido*', *Philological Quarterly*, 27 (1948), 241–63. For Oppenheimer, all the deceptive schemes of a *comedia* can be called *burlas*. While he relates the subtlety of a *burla* to casuistic reasoning, nowhere in his article does he mention the *burla* as something funny. Obviously *comedias* can contain funny *burlas*, even funny casuistry, and one aspect of the *burla* need not exclude others.

[53] Calderón de la Barca, *Teatro cómico breve*, p. 212, ll. 343–4.

signalled the end of the interlude. Instead, the following sequence ensues after the last blow:

Criada   Yo me voy a mi cocina.

Teresa   Yo debajo mi cama.

Sacristan   Yo me voy a mi *profundis*.

Soldado   Y yo a mi Cuerpo de Guardia.

Gracioso   Y yo a mi guarda de cuerpo.
            Y pues nadie a escuras baila,
            a buscar un baile voy
            que sirva de mojiganga.[54]

It seems extremely unlikely that a *mojiganga* would follow an *entremés* and therefore this is definitely the end. With the ultimate self-conscious flourish, the Gracioso, thought to be the biggest idiot of the bunch, expresses his disgust for being trapped in an all-too-traditional *entremés*. He goes off seeking an alternative ending better fitting the contemporary style, one where beatings are always countered with happy singing and dancing. It can only be that Calderón was aware of the traditional nature of this *entremés*, and in order to demonstrate this awareness, he gave his audience a metatheatrical wink by denying the traditional ending.

THE *ENTREMÉS* AS A VEHICLE FOR PARODY AND SATIRE

The next *entremés* is *El toreador*, a tiny masterpiece of comic theatre, which by itself provides enough material for an entire separate investigation. Rodríguez and Tordera wrote a short (65 pages of analysis) book on the staging and semiotics of this one piece alone.[55] Their attention is mainly directed towards the work's representation onstage and its relation to greater themes, and the critics use ingenious painting analogies that fit well with Calderón's way of thinking. Among the many areas of interest in their study, Rodríguez and Tordera's observations about mimesis and its rupture are extremely valuable,[56] but the present analysis will look at other aspects of the piece. Every *entremés* features parody, but few can match *El toreador* in the sheer concentrated amount of this feature. The following examples are not all new, and Rodríguez and Tordera, as well as Lobato and other critics, have ably noted many of them. I do not pretend to make any great revelations,

[54] Calderón de la Barca, *Teatro cómico breve*, p. 213, ll. 349–55, these being the last lines of the piece.

[55] Rodríguez Evangelina and Antonio Tordera, *Escritura y palacio: El toreador de Calderón* (Kassel: Reichenberger, 1985).

[56] See Rodríguez and Tordera, *Escritura y palacio*, chapter 6, 'Espejo o retrato o ventana: la epifanía barroca de la imagen'.

rather simply to enumerate the series of mini-parodies and their targets in order to demonstrate the astounding capacity of the *entremés*-structure in housing and presenting jokes. Also, parody is often tied into satire, and *El toreador* offers several examples of this synthetic operation.

Parody (we are naturally speaking of the humorous sort) is a special type of mockery that alters a recognised form or places it into an unusual context so that, while the form remains recognisable, the changes effected make it the object of laughter. Because forms do not really travel (even in the figurative sense) from one place to another, parodying involves a duplicating process or 'mimicry'. Mikhail Bakhtin writes:

> For any and every straightforward genre, any and every direct discourse – epic, tragic, lyric, philosophical – may and indeed must itself become the object of representation, the object of a parodic travestying 'mimicry'. . . . Parodic-travestying literature introduces the permanent corrective of laughter, of a critique on the one-sided seriousness of the lofty direct word, the corrective of reality that is always richer, more fundamental and most importantly *too contradictory and heteroglot* to be fit into a high and straightforward genre.[57]

This notion of 'fit' corresponds to the absorbing capacity of a joke, a capacity that is shared with the *entremés* sub-genre. The *entremés* seizes upon most any idea and makes fun of it. In this particular case the object of ridicule, picked up and played with, is the 'one-sided seriousness' of both literary and social conventions. A classic conundrum in the study of Golden Age theatre concerns the separation between literary creation and social reality, between what people actually did under the reign of Philip IV, and what people (then and today) merely read in books and plays written at the time.[58] Though these problems are often impossible to resolve, one can often distinguish the blurry line between fiction and reality when comparing literary parody to satire. In fact, part of defining these techniques depends upon recognising whether the targets are real (social) or imagined (literary).

As mentioned before, Calderón delights in exploiting the rapid movements of the *entremés* by making jokes of a passing referential nature. While parody can be a drawn-out process, Calderón chooses to touch on one parody for only moments before leaping to the next. Let us review the plot of *El toreador*, examining the parodies in 'slow motion'. The stage directions indicate: 'Sale Juan Rana vestido de caballero ridículo muy triste, dos criados, dándole de vestir, y Músicos cantando.' 'Caballero ridículo' is itself a parodic expression, as 'caballero' in the context of Spanish theatre would ordinarily connote

---

[57] Mikhail M. Bakhtin, *The Dialogic Imagination*, translated and edited by Caryl Emerson and Michael Holmquist (Austin: University of Texas Press, 1989), p. 55.

[58] See the conclusion of José María Díez Borque, *Sociología de la comedia española del siglo XVII* (Madrid: Cátedra, 1976).

dignity, sobriety and obvious nobility, all features that run contrary to the accompanying adjective in this case. Juan Rana's outfit reveals the laugh-filled decorum of *El toreador*, as much of what follows is the result of mock-gentlemanly behaviour. While the musicians sing a song of pained love, Juan Rana cries out:

> ¡Ay, que rabio de amor otra vez digo:
> llamadme un confesor, Dios sea conmigo![59]

Dying of love has always been a powerful theme in literature, from the ancients, to Petrarch, to Diego de San Pedro's *Cárcel de amor*; but it is clear from this couplet that the 'lofty word' has been brought down to earth by rather earthy details. 'Rabiar' can mean rage, but it can also refer to 'hidrofobia', literally rabies, a deadly condition. The immediacy of true corporeal death is highlighted by the call for a confessor. Juan Rana is taking his love much too seriously, at which point the exaggeration of the theme makes it laughable.

A moment later, the capricious 'caballero' decides he cannot stand the accompanying sad music any longer and thus asks the singers and musicians to shut up, lest he toss them out of the window,

> . . . que cuando un gran señor está llorando
> no han de estar cuatro pícaros cantando.[60]

The romantic notion of the lovelorn gentleman whose heart is soothed by gentle music is quickly dispelled as the sad songs piped into his ear do nothing but irritate the distraught Juan Rana.

After the musicians leave, he launches into a tiny monologue, declaring his love for Doña Bernarda. Juan Rana has never seen her face to face, but he once glimpsed her portrait, after which he became hopelessly enamoured of her. The notion of being in love with a portrait is a common one during the age, two famous examples being found in Lope's *Peribáñez* and Calderón's own *Pintor de su deshonra*. Since Calderón himself used the concept, one could consider this to be a self-parody, but it is not exclusively such.[61] Upon finishing his tiny yet anguished speech with '¡. . . que me muero totalmente de amor!'[62] Juan Rana bursts into tears (intensifying the parody of the

---

[59] Calderón de la Barca, *Teatro cómico breve*, p. 181, ll. 12–13.

[60] Ibid., p. 182, ll. 19–20.

[61] Calderón seems to poke fun at his own artistic creations more than any other dramatist I know. See Claire Pailler, 'El gracioso y los "guiños" de Calderón: Apuntes sobre la "autoburla" e ironía crítica', *Risa y sociedad en el teatro español del Siglo de Oro/ Rire et société dans le théâtre espagnol du Siècle d'Or* (Paris: Centre Nat. de la Recherche Scientifique, 1980), pp. 33–48.

[62] Calderón de la Barca, *Teatro cómico breve*, p. 156, l. 27.

lovesick courtesan), but before he can entirely abandon himself to emotion, one of his servants quickly steps forward to announce an unexpected visitor, shaking Juan Rana from his self-absorption. The guest who has invited himself in, simply known as 'Caballero', introduces two related parodies of common literary occurrences. One is the phenomenon of anagnorisis, which manifests itself as the unwanted guest addresses the dumbfounded Juan Rana as 'Primo de mi Alma'. This type of surprising recognition is a staple of the Byzantine romance, where long-lost lovers and relatives are reunited in tears and jubilation. In Calderón's *entremés*, Juan Rana is less than thrilled, and even made uncomfortable by the constant hugging.

> Hombre, si eres mi primo como dices
> los primos no remachan las narices.[63]

This statement points out the contradiction between the heightened emotional state of the visitor and his inferior status in the hierarchy of participants in literary anagnorisis. He is not a lover, nor a parent, nor a sibling, just a cousin (or so he claims) who has happened to pass by. The grand notion of a fantastic family reunion has been brought low by making it nothing more than a visit by an unknown and annoying relative.

However, the cousin has come to do more than just hug Juan Rana to the point of discomfort. He also claims to be his long-lost heir. The question of inheritance can be the subject of great drama and tragedy as in *King Lear*, but here the question instantly becomes ridiculous in the same manner that the anagnorisis was made base: the heir is unknown to the benefactor. What is more, the heir is a cousin, rarely a figure involved in traditional stories that make the distribution of material goods the centre of the plot. The notion appears even more ridiculous if we keep in mind that, moments before, the Caballero reminisced about Juan Rana as 'tamañito, / vestido a lo alemán de frailecito'.[64] Has anybody heard of an *older* cousin being an heir to the younger, particularly the 'sucesor más inmediato', 'por línea recta'?

Juan Rana goes on to explain his infatuation with Doña Bernarda to his newly discovered cousin and the conversation proceeds to cram in one parodic reference after another, mostly rehashing the jokes told at the beginning:

Caballero   ¿Sin verlas, hay quien quiera a las mujeres?
Rana   Señor mío, este amor fue por poderes.[65]

'Por poderes' refers to a marriage arranged by a higher authority, which makes little sense in this case, until one realises that Calderón, through the

---

[63] Calderón de la Barca, *Teatro cómico breve*, p. 157, ll. 43–4.
[64] Ibid., p. 156, ll. 37–8.   [65] Ibid., p. 157, ll. 62–3.

mouth of Juan Rana, plays with the notion of 'poderes' of a magical or even transcendental nature, referring to the original theme (the power of love) that is the object of mockery. In this exchange between the two men, we were able to admire the rapid-fire execution of jokes, foreshadowing the dialogue of joking that became so popular in American vaudeville and was brought to the silver screen by the Marx brothers.[66] Sometimes a comic shorthand is developed in the process of trading quips:

> Caballero   ¿Y ella es hermosa?
>
> Rana   ¡Ay, primo, es muy perfecta!
>
> Caballero   ¿Y habéisla escrito?
>
> Rana   Sí, por la estafeta.[67]

'Estafeta' refers to mail carried on horseback by the standardised Royal Postal Service across Spain. In the worlds of the *novela sentimental* and the *comedia*, letters are lovingly and urgently carried by trusty pages and lackeys, not in huge sacks shipped across the dusty plains of Castile. When the Caballero asks '¿Y habéisla escrito?' he is asking 'Do you follow the vast literary tradition of writing love letters?' and Juan Rana is answering 'Yes and no.' The Caballero's seemingly simple question is extremely loaded and pitches Juan Rana's character against the massive weight of classic love stories. In a nimble feat of literary 'judo', Juan Rana uses tradition's weight against itself and figuratively throws it to the floor with this ambivalent and yet deflating response. The motions from both parties are extremely deft, and much of the joke lies beneath the superficial meaning of the words, not in plain view. However, before subtle witticisms come to dominate the discourse, Juan Rana is soon bursting into tears, reminding everybody, for the third time, that he is consumed by ('me abraso') and dying of love.

> Caballero   Que son congojas, Dios os las reciba.
>
> Rana   Son flatos que el amor me sube arriba.[68]

Pedro Calderón de la Barca, a skilful a playwright as Velásquez was a painter, takes full advantage of his dramatist's palette and throws in a joke about bad gas, cutting away any dignity that might have remained in Juan Rana's

---

[66] See Joe Laurie Jr, *Vaudeville: From the Honky-Tonks to the Palace* (New York: Henry Holt and Co., 1953), p. 82. We learn that, 'Most of the old-time two-man acts had belly-laugh material. Their comedy was broad, physical, and rowdy. They could use gags that the mixed [man-and-woman] couldn't use. They could get bigger laughs than the average single act, because they could feed each other and so build up the gags.' The exact same can be said of two-man acts in *entremeses*.

[67] Calderón de la Barca, *Teatro cómico breve*, p. 158, ll. 64–5.

[68] Ibid., ll. 71–2.

lovelorn moaning. This 'carnivalesque' style of parody is much more direct than the previous example, which could have been described as 'agudeza y ingenio';[69] however, in the end both parodies achieve the same effect. Curiously enough, through all of Rodríguez and Tordera's analysis of the text, I find no reference to the 'flatos' joke. While its obvious nature may have precluded the need for comment, it would have been a good time to examine the limits of taste that were established in dramatic representations staged in front of the court of Felipe IV. Calderón, the court's playwright, known by most today as dogmatic and strait-laced, did not seem to think it inappropriate to write belch jokes for a work celebrating the birth of a prince.[70]

Juan Rana decides to court the subject of his favourite portrait, and for this he enlists the help of his 'cousin'. This is an occasion for a tiny parody on both the social phenomenon of courting and its representation in the *comedia*. Courtship in an urban environment meant roaming the streets, which meant two things for the *madrileño* of the seventeenth century: being well-armed and looking one's best.

Sale un criado con un estoque largo y un broquel, el mayor que se pueda.[71]

It helps to remember that Cosme Pérez ('a.k.a.' Juan Rana) was short and squat, and the bigger the *accoutrements*, the funnier they would look on him, adding further to the courtier's previously indicated 'ridículo' appearance. To squeeze an extra bit of comic juice out of this tiny scene, Calderón adds confusion when the servant who brings the gear is unable to remember where to put the buckler shield. Juan Rana offers directions, prefaced by 'Siempre os lo acuerdo . . .', which leads one to believe that the servant will not get it right this time either. This adds yet a third (or fourth, considering Pérez's famous stoutness and sluggishness) layer of visual mockery that completely undercuts the notion of the dapper *galán de comedia* strutting about the streets of Madrid, breaking hearts wherever he goes.

---

[69] Shakespeare's Polonius is famous for saying, 'Brevity is the soul of wit.' Sophocles is thought to have said, 'A short saying oft contains much wisdom.' Not to be outdone, Baltasar Gracián in *Agudeza y arte de ingenio*, lists among his many poetic devices, 'las respuestas prontas ingeniosas', which nowadays would be translated as 'snappy comebacks'. While I contend (as Asensio writes of Benavente) that Calderón wrote 'sin teorías', Gracián's observations on separate poetic devices are applicable, and indeed I follow his method in my own investigation. In making a comparison, it is easy to see that my concern with Calderón's 'mixing and matching' and combining jokes bears great similarity to Gracián's idea of the 'agudeza compuesta'. His words on p. 377 state: 'Auméntase en la composición la Agudeza [compuesta], porque la virtud unida crece, y la que a solas apenas fuera mediocridad, por la correspondencia con la otra llega a ser delicadeza. No sólo no carece de variedad, sino que antes la multiplica, ya por las muchas convinaciones de las Agudezas parciales, ya por la multitud de modos y de géneros de uniones.'

[70] See the 'cronología' on p. 154 of Calderón de la Barca, *Teatro cómico breve*.

[71] Calderón de la Barca, *Teatro cómico breve*, p. 159.

When Juan Rana and his cousin finally arrive at Doña Bernarda's house, there ensues a further parody of the courtship ritual. Sex-roles are temporarily reversed as Juan Rana fears being spotted speaking on the street, lest his honour be injured. When he explains to Doña Bernarda that he has rented a balcony for the next day's bullfight, she asks for one small favour: that her newly declared lover risk his life in the bullring in her honour. While Lope de Vega's Don Alonso gains prestige and the admiration of the ladies through bullfighting in *El caballero de Olmedo*, Doña Bernarda's choice of Juan Rana as a 'champion' ('Lo que habéis de hacer por mí, / si es que os obliga mi amor / es torear en mi nombre'[72]) clearly undercuts the gallant neo-chivalric tradition.

Given his mission, Juan Rana is on the verge of panic, but his (now very helpful) 'cousin' offers some soothing advice by explaining how he should behave, from his entrance into the *plaza* to the reverences he should make before the king and his court. These instructions offer an opportune occasion for yet another parody, one that combines the target of bullfighting with that of fencing manuals. These objects of ridicule have precedents, like all our other examples, and I will indulge in two instances of cross-referencing in order to demonstrate again how the *entremés* freely absorbs any joke that it can. Eugenio Asensio writes about Quevedo's non-dramatic caricatures and explains that: 'Los novelistas y los cómicos de la época entraron a saco en estas producciones, bienes mostrencos, pues circulaban en manuscritos convidando al plagio.'[73] An example of a caricature mentioned by Asensio can be found in 'Para ser toreador sin desgracia ni gasto . . .' that appears at the end of Quevedo's *Libro de todas las cosas y otras muchas más*. Here is the complete citation:

> Para ser toreador sin desgracia ni gasto, lo primero caballo prestado, porque el gusto toque al dueño y no al toreador; entrar con un lacayo solo, que, por lo menos dirán que es único de lacayo; andarse por la plaza hecho caballero antípoda del toro; si le dijeren que cómo no hace suertes, diga que esto de suertes está vedado. Mire las ventanas, que en eso no hay riesgo. Si hubiere socorro de caballero, no se dé por entendido. En viéndole desjarretado entre pícaros y mulas, haga puntería y salga diciendo siempre: «No me quieren». Y en secreto diga: «Pagados estamos». Y con esto toreará sin toros y sin caballos.[74]

The mere notion of simple, easy-to-follow instructions for this feat parodies the belief that bullfighting is a matter of bravado and lightning reflexes,

---

[72] Calderón de la Barca, *Teatro cómico breve*, p. 160, ll. 113–15.

[73] *Itinerario*, p. 191.

[74] Quevedo, *Obras completas*, vol. 1, p. 116. For the *entremesil* manifestation of this prose see *Toreador de Babiles* and *Mentiras de cazadores y toreadores* in Francisco Bernardo de Quirós' *Obras*, ed. Celsa Carmen García Valdés (Madrid: Instituto de Estudios Madrileños, 1984).

something impossible to learn in a minute or two. While most of the comic weight of Quevedo's passage comes from the satire against hypocritical bull-fighting *poseurs*, the aspect that Calderón exploits in *El toreador* is that of the juxtaposition between matter-of-fact instructions and the complex and deadly ballet that is the reality of a bullfight. The Caballero explains to Juan Rana:

> Terciar la capa con gentil decoro,
> empuñar el rejón, salir al toro,
> aguardarle cubierto,
> darle en la nuca y ¡zas! dejarle muerto . . .[75]

Killing a bull is made to sound as easy as slicing a piece of bread. Let us compare this last passage to one from Calderón's *El desafío de Juan Rana*, where Bernarda demonstrates to her husband how he is to defeat his challenger in a duel:

Bernarda	Mirad marido, cuanto a lo primero,
	os habéis de calar bien el sombrero,
	sacar la espada con gentil despecho,
	entrar el pie derecho,
	poneros recto, firme, y perfilado . . .
Cosme [Rana]	¿Qué importe si él me pone de cuadrado?
Bernarda	Y luego, echalle un tajo con gran tiento,
	recoger el aliento,
	y con brío, que en vos no es maravilla,
	¡zas!, tiradle a matar por la tetilla.[76]

This passage bears a striking resemblance to the previous one, right down to the emphatic '¡zas!' when going in for the kill. Seventeenth-century books on how to fight bulls actually existed, but their audience would be small and the parody seems much more a socio-cultural than literary one.[77] On the other hand, there were a great number of fencing instruction manuals. One of the most famous was the *Libro de las Grandezas de la espada* by Luis Pacheco Narvaez. This work, which attempted to teach fencing with scientific and geometrical rigour, was grotesquely parodied by Quevedo in the first chapter of the second book of *El buscón*, along with other aspects relevant to Spain's 'espadachín' sub-culture. Sword-fighting and bull-fighting, and the violent 'machismo' for which they stand, are deflated as the phlegmatic and cowardly Juan Rana is forced into adopting the role of a lance-wielding 'matador'. The climactic final scene of *El toreador* is pure slapstick (and still parody, of

[75] Calderón de la Barca, *Teatro cómico breve*, p. 161, ll. 137–40.
[76] Ibid., pp. 183–4, ll. 57–66.
[77] Daniel Tapia Bolívar, in his *Breve historia del toreo* (México: Editorial México, 1947), p. 16, writes of one such manual by Don Juan de Gaspar.

course) as Juan Rana, decked out in feathers and ridiculous clothing, sits astride his hobbyhorse and nervously attempts to negotiate with the oncoming bull. Unable to show any bravado, he hopes to stall his adversary's advance by asking if they can be friends. The reluctant 'toreador' is thrown from his steed and he shouts from the ground that he is at death's door. In the final parody of the piece, Bernarda promises to save his life if he will only marry her. Thus the love of a woman saves the life of a man in burlesque fashion, and everybody lines up to sing and dance in honour of the prince and the royal family.

When comparing Calderón's joke about bullfighting with the one written by Quevedo in the *Libro de todas las cosas*, it was evident that Calderón was undercutting the brave tradition of 'tauromaquia', while the main butt of Quevedo's joke was the hypocrisy on the part of 'toreros falsos'. Following our loose definitions, one would say that Calderón was more concerned with parody in this case, and Quevedo was more concerned with satire. Yet while *El toreador* is crammed full with parodical references, it also contains moments of a greater satirical nature, which poke fun at human failings rather than literary or social conventions. As with the bullfighting jokes, the two realms of comic effect can overlap. The habit of 'rondar' is a staple activity of *comedia* plots, but also a social custom. Featuring a 'caballero a lo ridículo' transforms the custom into a parody, but it also mocks the vanity of real practitioners of the custom, and is therefore somewhat satirical as well. Let us look at three examples of primarily satirical elements in *El toreador*.

Our first joke might go by undeciphered by modern readers. The 'Caballero' assumes that he and Juan Rana will be heading out into the streets by coach:

Caballero	Digo que iré con vos. Pongan el coche.
Rana	¿El coche?
Caballero	Sí, ¿en aqueso qué se pierde?
Rana	No es posible.
Caballero	¿Por qué?
Rana	Le tengo en Verde.[78]

This snappy dialogue leads to a punch line, which Lobato explains thus: '. . . se refiere a la fiesta de Santiago el Verde . . . la nota característica de ese día era ir en coche, bien fuera propio o prestado, dejando Madrid vacío de ellos . . .'[79] Juan Rana's response must be ironic, as are his later descriptions of the fine horses that he supposedly owns. Juan Rana the 'caballero ridículo' has no coach, and his lie makes a satirical reference to the many 'hidalgos' of

---

[78] Calderón de la Barca, *Teatro cómico breve*, pp. 158–9, ll. 82–4.
[79] Ibid., p. 164.

the time who had to keep up appearances through all forms of deception. The satire in the punch line also refers to the obsession with coaches in Madrid at the time, how men and women would do all they could to show up in a coach at the social watering holes of the *corte*.[80] Much of Golden Age satire rings true today as anybody who has read Quevedo's poetry can attest. By the same token, some of Quevedo's works, such as the poem that starts 'Érase una nariz . . .' are extremely topical and lose much of their power through the absence of what was once an obvious point of reference. The mockery of the nose is easy to grasp, but without knowing the intended victim, the context of the 'attack' is lost. With social satire, knowledge of the target is indispensable, especially when the satire is contained within brief, yet deftly told, referential jokes of a rapid-fire fashion, as found in the *entremés*.

Another satire, lengthier than the last, is a simple criticism of crowded theatre seating. Doña Bernarda and her female friends make the wearying journey up several flights of stairs in order to reach the balcony that Juan Rana has rented for them:

Bernarda	Amigas, no lo creo, aunque llegamos,
	¡gracias a Dios que en el balcón estamos!
Mujer 1ª	Día de juicio es toros en la villa.
Bernarda	¡Jesús, y qué penosa escalerilla!
Mujer 2ª	Yo vengo muerta a puros empellones.
Bernarda	Amigas, aún me dura el sobresalto
	¡Jesús, no más balcón en cuarto alto![81]

In this case, the slight mention of a bustling city that was given in Juan Rana's references to coaches is now fully brought to life as the three women complain about the inconsiderate and jostling viewing public. There is little room in this study for examining the staging of this *entremés* (or others, since our focus is mainly structural), but fortunately Rodríguez and Tordera cover this aspect admirably in their small book dedicated specifically to *El toreador*. All the same, it is still worth mentioning that this piece was performed in the Coliseo del Buen Retiro, and the women were undoubtedly speaking from the theatre seats at this moment, giving extra emphasis to the satire by having

[80] In her notes to *El entremés de los coches* Hannah Bergman writes: 'El entremés se ríe del afán de las mujeres por andar en coche; es probable que se escribiera en alguno de los años en que hubo premática contra los coches, aunque el texto no alude explícitamente a tal prohibición. La sátira contra los coches es constante en la primera mitad del siglo.' See Bergman, *Quiñones de Benavente y sus entremeses*, pp. 397–8, The idea that 'el afán por andar en coche' was a female concern could add another dimension to Juan Rana and his 'cousin', both of whom could have represented their roles in an effeminate fashion, possibly for greater comic effect.

[81] Calderón de la Barca, *Teatro cómico breve*, p. 152, ll. 153–60.

their actions and location correspond to their complaints. Turning the actors
into spectators is also a blatant example of metatheatre. This scene within the
entremés demonstrates once again how Calderón exploited comic possibilities
by combining elements, instead of remaining satisfied with exhibiting only
one at a time.

The third and last example of satire is contained within the character of
Doña Bernarda herself. A favourite target of satire is woman, her supposed
capriciousness, controlling nature or great desire to manipulate men to
her advantage. The sub-genre of the *entremés* is full of these women who
lead men into awkward, dangerous and inevitably laughable situations. The
manipulative woman bears close resemblance to the 'malcasada' who also
uses her feminine wiles to dupe men. Though Doña Bernarda is not a
grotesquely deformed caricature, she belongs to a class of stereotypical
women called 'mujeres pedigüeñas', or more commonly, 'busconas'.[82] These
women would try to get what they could from a man, out of necessity, but also
seemingly out of sport, an idea that lends itself well to the battle of the sexes
that is often the centre of the action in an *entremés*. In *El toreador*, Doña
Bernarda asks Juan Rana to be her champion, explaining that this feat will
serve as a token of his love for her. But as she looks on, and chats with her
lady companions, it becomes clear to the audience that she also expects her
courtier to put on a good show and to entertain her friends.

> Bernarda   El sale, verle es vicio.
>   Amigas, hoy será día de juicio.[83]

It is a test of Juan Rana's entertainment value as much as it is of his bravery
or love. Doña Bernarda also points out to her friends the high cost of the seats,
highlighting a major tendency of the 'mujer pedigüeña' to conflate affection
with money, as well as with sport. Doña Bernarda enjoys the monetary
benefits of Juan Rana's infatuation, getting a free balcony for the 'corrida',
and she does not hesitate to brag about it to her friends. The *entremés*, with
an emphasis on material concerns and the relations between the sexes,
combined with little concern for true love, has always been said to contrast
sharply with the idealistic world of the *comedia* where love conquers all.
However, it appears that some examples of Calderón's *teatro breve* offer

---

[82] Justo Oblanca Fernández writes in *Literatura y sociedad en los entremeses del siglo
XVII* (Universidad de Oviedo: Servicio de Publicaciones, 1992), p. 265: 'Dada la tendencia al estereotipo que presenta el género entremesil hay una serie de motivos que, según
vamos a tener ocasión de comprobar, se reiteran constantemente a la hora de presentar y
caracterizar estas figuras femeninas: tienen la "enfermedad" de pedir, se proponen (y casi
siempre lo consiguen) engañar y burlarse de los hombres, y también muestran muy a
menudo una apetencia desmesurada por galas, comidas, celebraciones o por seguir una
moda ridícula en vestidos o cosmética, por ejemplo.'

[83] Calderón de la Barca, *Teatro cómico breve*, p. 163, ll. 172–3.

small yet noticeable exceptions to this rule. Despite Doña Bernarda's capricious manipulation of the love-struck Juan Rana, she promises to marry him at the end.

Naturally, strong threads of mockery, irony and self-consciousness run throughout *El toreador* and, as the ending has already been explained in terms of parody, it may be difficult to take their love seriously. But light-hearted mockery is not the same as pessimistic cynicism, and in a sub-genre that tries to get a laugh at every moment, seriousness can only be measured in very relative terms. Both bitter and warm laughter can function as a form of dismissal, but the former is more likely to have a negating effect than the latter. Laughter can carry with it the notion of affirmation. While the *entremés* may (much like the *mojiganga*) present itself as one big party, where anything goes and nothing matters, the tentative grip that it has on human reality always offers the possibility for a positive lesson, just as satire teaches through negative example. Calderón wrote short pieces containing different types of moments, some comically critical, and others completely carefree and inconsequential. Many moments lie between the extreme cases of sardonic criticism and frivolous celebration, and the next *entremés* is the embodiment of such a moment.

THE *ENTREMÉS* AS AN ABBREVIATED *COMEDIA*

Agustín de la Granja wrote that, for Calderón, the *entremés* was equal to a 'comedia breve',[84] containing an intriguing plot but with situations (and one would also guess characters) that constantly bring the audience to laugh. Here, the plot will be of main concern, but the characters and the setting, and how they are attached to the plot, will also be studied. Let us begin with the briefest possible plot synopsis for *El mayorazgo*. Don Cosme, a 'caballero ridículo', wishes to marry the young Marisabidilla, with whom he is in love. Marisabidilla's father, Don Pánfilo, is a wretched miser who has lent Don Cosme money. Don Cosme, who could not repay the debt, was forced to sell off his future inheritance ('el mayorazgo'), and without any money of his own is now unable to marry the miser's daughter. Don Pánfilo cares obsessively about Don Cosme's well-being, but only because the young man is a source of money. He gives the would-be suitor all forms of prosthetic devices and medications, and goes so far as to hire a doctor to check constantly on Don Cosme's health. During a consultation, two of Don Cosme's friends (who had planned with him earlier) suddenly jump forth and pretend to stab him to death with their swords. Don Pánfilo cries over the death of his money, and Marisabidilla over her lover, but both parties' sadness turn to shock as Don Cosme (after being dragged offstage) appears back from the dead, dressed in

---

[84] Pedro Calderón de la Barca, *Entremeses y mojigangas de Calderón para sus autos sacramentales*, ed. Agustín de la Granja (Granada: Universidad de Granada, Curso de Estudios Hispánicos, 1981), p. 33.

all his medical devices. He demands the hand of Marisabidilla and the return of his inheritance, if he is to return to life. Don Pánfilo will give the first, but not the latter, and consequently Don Cosme pretends to bring the willing Marisabidilla along with him into the realm of the dead. At last, Don Pánfilo grudgingly gives in and plays along with the *burla*, and his remaining anger is quickly drowned out by the singing and dancing at the end of the piece.

There are many different ways to look at this plot, but one of the most fruitful would be to compare it to classical antecedents. Northrop Frye's famous essay on comedy makes the principal claim that comedy concerns the restoration of social order, often in the form of a marriage contract.[85] Frye also states that the structure of such a comedy, aside from containing the requisite young lovers destined to marry, also features the older blocking character (a monomaniac 'humour'), who is responsible for the dramatic tension of the work. In this respect, the plot of *El mayorazgo* follows the tradition of classical comedy rather closely. At the same time, it is easy to see that this piece is not a shameless imitation of Plautus or Terence. Calderón has written a work in which the characters are different from their classical predecessors, not only because of a change in setting, but also because of a change in plot structure that makes the characters act differently.

Don Cosme is not completely analogous to a Roman slave or a young Greek lover. He is a 'caballero ridículo', a special brand of Spanish character who lies somewhere between the *galán*, the *gracioso* and the *figurón*.[86] He cannot be a complete laughingstock, or there could be no real concern in the audience for the outcome of this *entremés*. Idiocy and extremism, though causes for great laughter, are usually punished in this art form. Cunning and daring, also causes for great laughter, are rewarded. Don Cosme is not punished for his attempts and cannot be considered a complete laughingstock. *El alcalde de Zalamea* features a 'caballero ridículo' (one could also call him a 'figurón', as will be observed in chapter 6) who is obviously much more the object of ridicule. To further illustrate the point that not all 'caballeros ridículos' are created equal, one should compare Don Cosme to Juan Rana in his role as the love-struck and foolish gentleman in *El toreador*. Both characters cry and lament in the beginning, but Juan Rana carries on to the extreme, and his soul-searing lovesickness reaches grotesque proportions. Don Cosme does

[85] Northrop Frye, *Anatomy of Criticism: Four Essays* (Princeton: Princeton University Press, 1957), p. 163.

[86] The *galán* and the *gracioso* make up the famous pair in most *comedias* that follow Lope's example. In vaudevillian terms, the *gracioso* is obviously the 'joker', and the *galán* is the 'straight man'. The 'figurón', as a character-type, has not received much attention in *comedia* studies, even though he has an entire sub-genre of *comedias* dedicated to him. One such play is *El lindo don Diego*, by Agustín Moreto. The *figurón* is an upper-class (at least in appearance) gentleman who makes a fool of himself through excessive vanity, bravado, sentimentality or noble pretence. He is not necessarily a 'lindo', though he may be. The *figurón* will be discussed in detail in chapter 4.

sigh 'tengo y no tengo' in the beginning, yet while this lament parodies the angst-ridden love lyrics common to the *comedia*, it also intends to set up the description of the plot complication that is to follow: he has love but he has no money. In fact, in the 'over-the-top' farcical world of the *teatro breve*, Don Cosme's affliction appears downright reasonable and may even offer a glimmer of sincere love. Money is also an object in classical comedy, but Don Cosme's financial situation features a particularly early modern Spanish slant. His problem stems from his inability to access his inheritance, the sole source of his wealth. While the sub-genre of the *entremés* demands that he be 'ridículo', his simultaneous 'caballero' nature does not merely function as a comic contrast. His noble status, which prevents him from earning money except by sitting around and collecting rent, works perfectly to get him into the bind that drives the intrigue of this miniature comedy. Don Cosme belongs to an urban setting that is prevalent in many *entremeses*, the domain of pimps, prostitutes, soldiers, fishmongers, doctors and constables; but also that of another sector of society. He belongs among the idle and barely landed gentry who came swarming to the 'corte' in hopes of maintaining their status, or at least making enough money to survive. The 'caballero' is thought to belong solely to the *comedia* in the form of the *galán*, but his presence in the *teatro menor* raises interesting questions about the connection between both larger and smaller forms.[87]

The central character of this *entremés* is Don Pánfilo Ronoso the miser:

> . . . un viejo tan avaro, tan celoso,
> que casi, casi, exagerarlo quiero,
> guarda a su hija como a su dinero . . .[88]

He is not the first miser to appear in a comedy, nor is he the last, and for this reason it would be appropriate to compare him to Euclio in Plautus' *Aulularia* and also to Harpagon in Molière's *L'Avare*. There also exist Golden Age literary misers who serve as useful points of comparison. Don Pánfilo corresponds to Northrop Frye's archetypal 'blocking' character. Even if not a father, this character is inevitably '. . . a rival with less youth and more money'.[89] According to Segal, who cites Meredith (who borrows from Rabelais), the miser character is a spoilsport belonging to the 'agelasts', averse to any fun or happiness. Therefore, in the context of *El mayorazgo* and comedies of some resemblance,

---

[87] As it happens, the *mayorazgo* is a common plot device in comedias. Calderón's *El pintor de su deshonra, Dar tiempo al tiempo, Mañana será otro día, Guárdate del agua mansa* and *Las tres justicias en una*, to name a few, make varying use of this socio-economic phenomenon. Sometimes an inheritance may be the central theme, such as in Lope's *El mayorazgo dudoso* or Alonso Castillo Solórzano's *El mayorazgo figura*.

[88] Calderón de la Barca, *Teatro cómico breve*, p. 64, ll. 24–6.

[89] Frye, p. 165.

the miser is driven by nature to discourage the plans of the young lovers.[90] Don Pánfilo resembles Plautus' Euclio beyond the fact that both are obsessively concerned with money. They are both fathers whose daughter's marriage is entirely contingent upon a financial outcome, directly linking their monomania[91] to the workings of the plot. The situation in *Aulularia* is different than *El mayorazgo* because the Roman miser Euclio refuses to marry his daughter off to *anybody*, not even the wealthy Megadorus, for fear that such a union would leave his treasured pot of gold ('aulularia') open to attack from a possibly greedy son-in-law. Don Pánfilo of *El mayorazgo* is slightly less delirious with greed and more practical. He has actually lent money to Don Cosme and this, in effect, is the cause of the dramatic conflict. The complexity of the plot in *El mayorazgo*, in the relationship between the father and the possible son-in-law, is greater than that involving the suitors and the father in *Aulularia*. This increased complexity corresponds to Calderón's more intricate and yet more 'flexible' version of the miser stock figure that is a product of the Spanish society at the time.

Luis Quiñones de Benavente also wrote an *entremés* about a miser called, appropriately, *El miserable*,[92] featuring the tight-fisted Don Peralvillo as the central character. 'El miserable' of the title is little more than a drawn-out caricature of a stock figure, a anthropomorphic list that details the absurd lengths to which somebody will go to save money. Don Peralvillo saves the oil from his salads so that it can be used for lamp fuel. He carefully measures out a dozen lentils, allocating half to be served for dinner, seasoned with a single grain of salt. He is so miserly that he even holds fast to his dreams at night so that they will not escape him. Though no clear dichotomy exists, one can see a rough division between the style of *El mayorazgo* and *El miserable*, the latter exploiting the stock character in a more 'quevedesque' fashion. Don Peravillo, in his presentation onstage, appears similar to the notorious *licenciado* Cabra in *El Buscón*, when one regards his grotesquely exaggerated

---

[90] Erich Segal, *Roman Laughter: The Comedy of Plautus* (Cambridge, Mass., Harvard University Press, 1968), pp. 70, 76.

[91] Monomania, or the *idée fixe*, is of major importance to Bergson and fits squarely into his theory of the mechanical encrusted upon the living. He also describes how an obsession is not inherently comical: '[This is] the essential difference between comedy and drama. A drama, even when portraying passions or vices that bear that name, so completely incorporates them in the person that their names are forgotten, their general characteristics effaced, and we no longer think of them at all, but rather of the person in whom they are assimilated; hence, the title of a drama can seldom be anything else than a proper noun. On the other hand, many comedies have a common noun as their title . . .' See Bergson in Sypher, p. 70. Reading the table of contents of any collection of *entremeses* will corroborate this assertion. Of course, even the most frivolous of *comedias*, such as *El lindo don Diego*, may have a proper name, a fact which may make us question Bergson's assertion. But *comedias* are not necessarily overwhelmingly laughable, like Molière's farces, which Bergson had in mind. When comparing the *entremés* to the *comedia*, it will become apparent that Bergson's notions may not always apply.

[92] Cotarelo, *Colección de entremeses*, vol. 18, pp. 773–5.

behaviour. This comic effect is derived from repetition, from heaping one vicious characteristic upon another, in the form of a list, similar in a way to Quevedo's satirical poems. Calderón's version of this satire uses the exaggeration only as a point of departure for the intrigue of the play, and instead he chooses to include fresh and surprising comic devices that spring from the well-worn topic of stinginess.

It is difficult to see Don Pánfilo as merely a self-contained stock figure, a type of strange creature with a dramatic animal instinct forcing his behaviour. Regarding a similar subject, Erich Segal points out a fact that is ignored by even some experts on Plautus' work.[93] The Roman playwright saw the ridiculous portrayal of the 'agelast', including the miser, as a way of poking fun at the historically famous *gravitas* of his fellow citizens, an institution that included a no-nonsense approach to money. Calderón's Don Pánfilo, though his exact profession is unknown, is certainly representative of an urban class concerned with the efficient use of capital and its investment. He stands for a group of people who gain their money through cunning, as opposed to the dispossessed *caballero* Don Cosme who came across his money by dumb luck. But the cunning of Don Pánfilo is not the kind that is rewarded in the *teatro breve*. This is because it is cold and calculating, devoid of improvisation and happy ingenuity, and certainly not the kind of inventiveness that would bring applause from the audience. Money-lending, no matter how skilful, is not very exciting, nor does it garner much sympathy from a seventeenth-century audience. Despite Don Pánfilo's connection to the 'real world', his behaviour is not without its grotesque manifestations, especially in his personal treatment of Don Cosme. On different occasions, Don Pánfilo confuses either Don Cosme's health or his person with 'dinero' or a 'talego vivo' respectively. These moments, with the miser's requisite 'mugging' (making faces) and exclamations, were sure to draw laughs, owing to the 'cosificación' of poor Don Cosme, what Bergson would call encrusting the mechanical (the action of counting cold cash) upon the living. Molière's Harpagon much more resembles Euclio than Don Pánfilo, though he comes only decades after Calderón's piece.[94] His wild paranoia and his love affair with a cash box make him a dead ringer for a Roman comedic stock figure. However, there is a major difference between Rome and the setting of seventeenth-century Paris, and how this concerns the plot cannot be ignored. The love intrigues that play such a great role in Molière's bourgeois comedies

---

93 I am comparing p. xiv of Plautus, *The Pot of Gold* [*Aulularia*], trans. and ed. Peter D. Arnott (Arlington Heights: AHM, 1967), which speaks of 'the sturdy common sense and instinct for order which was one of the finest characteristics of the Roman Republic', with Segal, *Roman Laughter*, p. 11, who demonstrates Plautus' point of view that the Romans clung maniacally to their *gravitas*, partially because of a sense of inadequacy in the face of the ostensible perfection of their ancestors.

94 *El mayorazgo* was most likely performed soon after it was written in May of 1642. See Calderón de la Barca, *Teatro cómico breve*, p. 64. *L'avare* by Molière was first performed on 9 September 1668. See Molière, *Five Plays* (London: Methuen, 1981), p. 28.

bring *L'Avare* somewhat closer to *El mayorazgo*, though most similarities are shared with the Plautine model.

A common plot device in *entremeses* is nothing more than the simple interaction between two stock figures. Regarding the conflict and subsequent actions between characters, an *entremés* can be the dramatic equivalent of putting two insects in a jar and watching them fight mindlessly as spectators jubilantly look on. Often, however, stock figures can cooperate instead of doing battle, and this can lead to equally rewarding comic possibilities. In *El mayorazgo,* the inclusion of the 'Doctor' adds mirth to the production, and presents another example of an interlude-within-the-interlude, demonstrating the often multi-layered nature of the supposedly rudimentary 'teatro menor'. Though a satire of the physician could stand alone as a comic scene, the character is woven into the plot. Molière's *Le malade imaginaire* incorporates the role of a quack, though more thoroughly than in *El mayorazgo* because the French full-length play makes medicine the main subject. On the other hand, Calderón in *El mayorazgo*, always finding ways to abbreviate jokes, keeps his satire elementary. In both plays, short and long, Spanish and French, the sickness is imagined or, at the most, heavily exaggerated. Don Cosme complains to his friends that Don Pánfilo worries so much about his debtor's health, that:

> para cobrar la renta
> mi salud ha tomado por su cuenta
> guardándome de suerte
> que teme más mi muerte que su muerte.
> En mis más leves males
> los catarros se le hacen sincopales.[95]

In *Le malade imaginaire*, Argan is an extreme hypochondriac (a distant cousin of the melancholy traveller in *El reloj y los genios de la venta*), and his own ailments are mainly the products of his deranged imagination, one that receives unhealthy stimulus from the quack doctor Diaforius Senior. In both cases, the jokes centre on the great contradiction between the true state of health of each character and what they imagine their bodily status to be. The harmlessness of the affair allows for laughter. An actor sincerely suffering the effects of illness onstage would unlikely be much of a pleasure to watch.[96] In both pieces, marriage concerns the role of the doctor, as in both cases he is being married into the family so that the patriarch can exploit him for free medical services. In both the French and Spanish farces, the marriage of the daughter to the doctor prevents the young lover from having her hand in

---

95 Calderón de la Barca, *Teatro cómico breve*, p. 64, ll. 43–8.

96 It is well known that when a deathly ill Molière himself collapsed onstage, in the role of Argan, people thought that it was all part of the act and, one can imagine, funny. They might have thought differently had they known the truth.

marriage. Molière used this plot twist to forward the intrigue of the play, but in *El mayorazgo*, because the doctor is somewhat of a peripheral figure, the problem of Marisabidilla being married off to a quack quickly fades into the background.

Like the miser, the doctor of *El mayorazgo* is not the first nor the last of his kind. The quack is a stock figure that has existed since antiquity and lives on to this day, as evidenced by the (now-forgotten) pop song parody 'Like a Surgeon' by 'Weird Al' Yankovic. The figure is so common that he inevitably arrives with his own easily anticipated stereotyped behaviour and series of jokes. Though Quevedo did not invent the 'galeno' character-type, nor perhaps give him any improvements or innovations, it is still informative to read his 'how-to' manual explaining the path to becoming a quack doctor:

> La ciencia es esta: dos refranes para entrar en casa: el *¿Qué tenemos?* ordinario; *Venga el pulso;* inclinar el oído; *¿Ha tenido frío?* Y si él dice que sí primero, decir luego «Se echa de ver. ¿Duró mucho?» Y aguardar que diga cuánto, y luego decir: «Bien se conoce. Cene poquito, escarolitas; una ayuda». Y si dice que no la puede recibir, decir: «Pues haga por recibilla». Recetar lamedores, jarabes y purgas, para que tenga que vender el boticario y que padecer el enfermo.[97]

As stated before, little of *El mayorazgo* reaches 'quevedesque' levels of satire, and Calderón's doctor does not carry out all the instructions listed above. However, he still manages to perform two classic quack duties: analysing the patient's pulse and asking what he had for dinner.

Throughout this scene, one is reminded that while the doctor's role predominates, the satirical figure of the miser is never excluded. He is constantly worried about the prospects of his money, embodied by Don Cosme, whose death would make it impossible for Don Pánfilo to exploit the inheritance. The relation between the two stock figures is relatively complex, given the complications of the plot, but the jokes remain obvious as Don Pánfilo frets onstage about the possible loss of his 'talego vivo'.

As observed in previous examples of his *teatro breve*, Calderón did not frown upon slapstick. While he may not have been as crass as Quevedo, or Molière with Monsieur Purgon's enema, he could exploit imagined sickness for purely visual comic effects. In an exercise of multiplying comic possibilities, Calderón includes a scene of medical mischief even before the doctor arrives onstage. Any description, even a verbatim quote of the stage directions, cannot possibly do justice to the sight of Don Pánfilo slapping one prosthetic after another onto the hapless Don Cosme. A bonnet, spectacles, crutches, stomach plaster are all stuck onto the 'caballero', making even further laughable his 'ridículo' appearance. It

---

[97] These instructions can be found a few paragraphs before those outlining how to be a bullfighter, in Quevedo, *Obras completas*, vol. 1, p. 115.

is another case of 'cosificación', where the somewhat human *entremés* gentleman is degraded and dehumanised through the miracles of Early Modern science. Bergson's arguments about the comic certainly gain weight when one
considers the laughter Don Cosme must have provoked while tottering about on
crutches, vision blurred, stomach plastered, with his head safely and warmly
bundled up on a sultry summer afternoon. A friend's comment, 'Por Dios que os
ha dejado / muy bien el tal Don Pánfilo alhajado,'[98] only adds to the humiliation
and resultant laughter.

Few good *entremeses* would be without a *burla*, and *El mayorazgo* is no
exception, even though the deception itself does not take place until halfway
through the piece. Even when the *burla* does occur, it is clear that most of the
action does not rely on the deception itself. While the *burla* in Calderón's
entremés does spawn jokes and affects the characters' behaviour, it is, as the
title implies, the status of the *mayorazgo*, rather than the trick played by Don
Cosme and his friends, that has a greater effect on the plot. The trick in
question involves having Don Cosme avoid paying his debt by faking his own
death. While the premise is simple, Calderón adds a dash of suspense to what
could have been a straightforward procedure. He does this by dividing the
action into two parts. First Don Cosme complains, and his friends console
him with some useful advice. 'Hombre 1°' is about to explain how to pull off
the helpful stunt when he is interrupted by the sudden appearance of Don
Pánfilo and the doctor. The audience is left on the edge of its seat, with only
partial information about planned future events. Everybody knows that Don
Pánfilo will be tricked, that Don Cosme's death will be faked, and that the two
plotting 'hombres' will be involved, but nobody knows how, not even Don
Cosme. This combination of anticipation and surprise is similar to that found
in *La muerte* in which the characters identify themselves offstage, and both
protagonist and audience must wait before the tension concerning the figures'
appearance is finally resolved. The Caminante in *La muerte* was in the same
situation as the audience until the characters entered the scene. At that
moment, when he thinks he is seeing devils and angels, the audience is able
to laugh at the Caminante's folly because they all possess information that he
does not. In *El mayorazgo*, the audience shares, for a split-second, a moment
of surprise with Don Cosme when the two 'hombres traidores' burst onto the
scene and pretend to slay the 'caballero ridículo'. After that split-second, both
the audience and Don Cosme realise what has happened. Now, who is the
object of folly? The answer is simple: Don Pánfilo, who must be present to
witness the faked death. He plays the same role as the Caminante who
believes he is seeing visions of death before him. Don Pánfilo sees one
situation (a dead *caballero*, and the loss of his money) and the audience sees
something else: a live gentleman who has just outwitted a shrewd old man,
now seen panicking and crying. While the *burla* first appeared to be divided

---

[98] Quevedo, *Obras completas*, p. 67, ll. 127–8.

into only two parts, it now becomes clear that there is more to come. Don Cosme cannot remain 'dead', or he will never find his way back into the arms of Marisabidilla. The *burla* is not quite complete, and suspense is reintroduced. This brings us to the subject of death in the *entremés*.

Seventeenth-century Spain, like many cultures, was not a time or place where death was celebrated joyously. This very fact was fodder for many jokes in *La mojiganga del pésame de la viuda*. The party atmosphere often found in *entremeses* and *mojigangas* would seem to stand quite contrary to a sombre vision of death. Thus, it can be said without reservation that in the *entremés*, unlike the *comedia*, death is ridiculed and vanquished on a regular basis.[99] In the *comedia*, the intrigue of the plot is often accompanied by a lingering threat of death that hangs in the air. One false move, one miscommunication, could lead to a deadly duel with a vengeful brother or to a dutiful slashing at the hands of the night watch, always ready to keep the streets rid of trouble-makers. One finds plenty of intrigue and risk-taking in the *entremés*, but death is never a consequence of this behaviour. The fake stabbing that Don Cosme endures is a joke unto itself, and the contrived shouts of '¡Muera!' in such an obviously non-threatening context were sure to have elicited plenty of guffaws. The worst that any victim in the *teatro breve* can expect is to be the recipient of 'palos' or to be laughed off the stage. *Entremeses* in which characters die are inexistent to my knowledge. In the most severe example that I can find, the fourth part of *Los alcaldes encontrados*,[100] the supposed death is not even violent. Attenuating the sobriety of such circumstances even further, the deceased *alcalde* Domingo is later 'resuscitated' and the audience finally learns that he was never dead at all.

El mayorazgo ends with a happy marriage. Following Frye's archetypal 'mythos of spring', the true love between Don Cosme and Marisabidilla is rewarded, the absurdly immoral 'ritual bondage' of Don Pánfilo is thwarted, and 'a kind of moral norm, a pragmatically free society' is created in place of the miser's financial and marital manipulations.[101] It is a free and happy time, guided by a youthful 'stable and harmonious order'. In this sense,

---

[99] This has been said about comedy as a whole as well, something which we shall consider later while looking at Calderón's full-length plays: '. . . it is in this deep and nearly universal aversion to death that comedy finds its opportunity. Comedy thus is anti-tragedy in the sense that its prime instinct is to put dying out of mind. It is an absurd but endearing attempt to exorcise the inevitable.' See Robert ter Horst, 'The Origin and Meaning of Comedy in Calderón', in *Studies in Honor of Everett W. Hesse*, eds William C. McCrary and Jose A. Madrigal (Lincoln, Nebraska: Society of Spanish and Spanish-American Studies, 1981), p. 147.

[100] Although Hannah Bergman states that the piece is not Quiñones de Benavente's (Bergman, *Quiñones de Benavente y sus entremeses*, p. 375), I cite from a work from Luis Quiñones de Benavente, *Colección de piezas dramáticas (entremeses, loas, y jácaras) escritas por el licenciado Luis Quiñones de Benavente*, vol. 2 (Madrid: Librería de Biliófilos, 1874). [101] Frye, *Anatomy*, p. 169.

El mayorazgo's marriage-ending follows classical endings, as well as the pattern of the *comedia*, not to mention Molière's farces. Yet Maurice Slawinski has another point of view about the social order established by a marriage at the end of the show.[102] In his example, marriage is seen as a commercial contract more than anything else, where desire is opposed to a social order that depends primarily on reliable social transactions. While this may be the case in Italian Renaissance comedy, *El mayorazgo* appears to lend itself more easily to Frye's archetype than to Slawinski's. Still, one is left wondering, at a time when marriage in the 'real world' was so dependent upon monetary concerns, why are finances mocked in *El mayorazgo*? One could argue that it is not the financial aspect of the marriage contract that is mocked, but instead Don Pánfilo's twisted exploitation of it for his own gain. However, nowhere do the lovers mention to each other their class status or any question of money, proving unequivocally that what brings them together is love and nothing else. The furthest one could argue is that money is ambivalent, and in any case not as important as love. It can be expected that an *entremés* is out of step with the 'real world' (after all the *teatro breve* gets its laughs by distorting reality), but it may surprise us that, as an *entremés*, this piece is also unusual in its treatment of love. Hannah Bergman, one of the foremost authorities on the *entremés*, wrote that love is very rarely taken seriously in this sub-genre. She also explains how Calderón pokes fun in all possible ways at the tradition of marriage, making jokes in his own *comedias*.[103] Juan Rana's marriage to Doña Bernarda in *El toreador* was contrived, and, though not filled with cynicism, was not based on an obvious mutual love between the two characters. The weeping and pining of the young lovers in *El mayorazgo* may be laughable, but in the relative terms of the *entremés*, they may form one of the most serious couples to date.

Don Cosme cannot come close to equalling Juan Rana in the absurd expression of his love. He is not the bearer of one parodic gesture after another, nor are his emotions reduced to grotesque bawling. Don Cosme is funny, but he is no clown. Neither does he correspond to other versions of lovers found in *entremeses*, ones motivated purely by lust or by the root of all evil: the love of money. Marisabidilla shows no indication of being a scheming manipulator of the 'mujer pedigüeña' type like Doña Bernarda. She is not after money, nor food, nor sport, nor even a good time. She just wants to be with her beloved, though her melodramatic lamentations may bring laughter. She is a lover from the comedy tradition of all ages, prevented by her father from getting the one thing in life that she truly wants. Marisabidilla even bears close

---

[102] Maurice Slawinski, 'Comedy of Words and Comedy of Things: A Renaissance Commedia and its Plautine Models', *New Comparison*, 3 (1987), 5–18.

[103] Hannah E. Bergman, 'Ironic Views of Marriage in Calderón', in *Approaches to the Theatre of Calderón*, ed. Michael D. McGaha (Lanham: University Press of America, 1982), pp. 65–74.

resemblance to the *dama de comedia* in two important ways. First, she has a faithful maid who acts as a go-between and who arranges the lovers' secret trysts. Second, though her lamentations may border on parody, they are lamentations all the same. They are still manifestations of an inner strife that mirror the long monologues found in the *comedia*. Because we are in the realm of the *entremés*, the lament will therefore be short and made to get laughs. But among all the possible caricaturesque attitudes that Calderón could have chosen for Marisabidilla, he chose an exaggerated yet unwavering love instead of cold cynicism or capricious 'mudanza'. Calderón intentionally avoided the easy satire of women in order to create an atmosphere capable of approaching that of the *comedia*. Even in the *comedia*, considered the era's most serious secular dramatic genre, marriages at the end seemed contrived, and the lovers' laments could often reach exaggerated, if not absurd, levels of emotional distress.

El mayorazgo is as close as one can come to a *comedia* in less than 350 lines of verse. It is overwhelmingly funny, but within the fabric of its many jokes there are different registers of humour that run from the absurdly and unbelievably grotesque to the healthy and hearty laughter that smiles in the face of death. One even finds moments of sorrow and tenderness that are not completely swamped in a torrent of guffaws. Humour is relative in dozens of ways, many of which lie within the text itself. Putting the audience aside (and putting aside whether they were drunk, sober, friendly, few, tired, bored, visiting from out of town, etc.) jokes can be measured against their context within the work itself. Both *El mayorazgo* and *El toreador* are love stories to a certain degree, and both certainly feature parody, satire, silly costumes and mock violence; but they are obviously not the same piece. Something about *El mayorazgo* makes it truly worthy of the epithet 'comedia breve'. In it, Calderón takes full advantage of the relative shades of humour, how laughter can be mixed with love, tragedy and fear. The *entremés*-within-the-*entremés* involving Don Pánfilo's application of medical prosthetics and the arrival of the satirical doctor make this clear. The joking of this tiny scene appears almost gratuitous compared to the rest of the dramatic action, yet how can one speak of 'comic relief' in a work where everything is meant to be funny? Many of Calderón's *comedias* in urban settings are full of wacky escapades, but critics have no difficulty in separating out moments of 'comic relief' from the portions of the main action. The various types of humour that Calderón employs in his *entremés* cannot be generalised as a constant stream of comic relief. Jokes for Calderón were yet another form of art (along with allegory, stage design, etc.) for him to master and exploit, as he constantly sought new ways to use them.

3

CALDERÓN AND THE *MOJIGANGA* WITHIN THE *COMEDIA*

THE *FIESTA BURLESCA*, *MOJIGANGA* AND OPERA

The best place to start examining the *teatro breve*'s presence in the *comedia* is the *comedia burlesca*, its often-ignored counterpart.[1] While the *comedia burlesca* shares characteristics with the *entremés*, it is the *mojiganga* that offers the best point of comparison because of its dramatic structure and overwhelmingly festive elements[2] (all of which take precedence over plot and *burla*, in the sense of an extended practical joke), which correspond to the *comedia burlesca*'s negation of structuring narrative elements and utter lack of serious moments onstage. Both the *mojiganga* and the *comedia burlesca* are much more of a party than a story told in dramatic fashion.[3] Calderón's *comedia burlesca*, *Céfalo y Pocris*,[4] is a masterpiece of non-stop joking that

---

[1] The *comedia burlesca* is a genre commonly found in the context of an entire *fiesta burlesca*. See *Una fiesta burlesca del siglo de oro*: Las bodas de Orlando *(comedia, loa, y entremeses)*, ed. Javier Huerta Calvo (Lucca: Mauro Baroni, 1997). The relationship between the *comedia burlesca* and *entremés* has been studied by other critics. See Loly Holgueras Pecharromán, 'La comedia burlesca: estado actual de la investigación', in *Diálogos Hispánicos de Amsterdam 8*, vol. 2, ed. Javier Huerta Calvo, Harm den Boer and Fermín Sierra Martínez (Atlanta: Rodopi, 1989), particularly p. 472. Buezo, pp. 163–8, sees many similarities between the *comedia burlesca* and what she calls the 'mojiganga burlesca de asunto histórico-literario', although she states that the latter places greater emphasis on 'paraverbal' elements such as music, singing and dancing. This last hypothesis is somewhat questionable, as Buezo uses the two burlesque generic manifestations of *Los amantes de Teruel* as examples to show how a travesty of a similar theme is produced differently, supposedly according to different generic norms. These norms are put in question as soon as we read a burlesque comedy such as *Céfalo y Pocris*, which uses music in a way that is not necessarily 'antidramático'. Eugenio Asensio, in his *Itinerario del entremés*, pp. 39–40, compares the standard *comedia* with the *entremés*, which happens to be the subject of chapter 4 in our study.

[2] That is not to say that the *entremés* is not festive in its own right, though the elements that make it so are structured differently. See Asensio, *Itinerario*, pp. 18–24.

[3] Despite the formal aspect of the dramatic *mojiganga*, I do not believe that, in relative terms, it has suffered the 'creciente literatización del género' that Asensio ascribes to the *entremés*. It is precisely the survival of aspects eliminated from the *entremés* over time that maintains the distinction of the *mojiganga*.

[4] Pedro Calderón de la Barca, *Céfalo y Pocris*, ed. Alberto Navarro González (Salamanca: Almar, 1979). Not too long ago, the authorship of this play was rather disputed, but every year more people attribute it to Calderón. Vera Tassis included it in his list, and while never named

exceeds in mirth any *mojiganga* by fourfold, and can match any piece of *teatro breve* in its sheer concentration of jokes.

Céfalo y Pocris contains far too many jokes to mention, the majority of them parodies. Attempting to categorise these parodies alone, while mentioning select examples, occupies half of Alberto Navarro González's introduction to his edition. Therefore, I shall avoid specifically commenting on the parodies found within the play, for they are explained well enough by the editor. The continuous stream of parodic references can be compared to those listed in our analysis of *El toreador*, but they are far greater in number and variety, given the length of this *comedia burlesca*. Yet *Céfalo y Pocris* has barely a narrative thread, and in this sense cannot be compared to any relatively well-plotted *entremés*. Leaving aside the extremely tenuous marriage plot, the only relevant narrative element of the play is the moment (anticipated by the audience) in which Céfalo shoots Pocris accidentally. However, when this event occurs, it is little more than another excuse to make jokes, one more

by Calderón as a spurious play, neither was it mentioned in the playwright's own list. The Reichenberger bibliography says that 'criticism' has put the authenticity in doubt. The citation of this 'criticism' refers to Ángel Valbuena Briones' *Perspectiva crítica del los dramas de Calderón* (Madrid: Rialp, 1965), but when we find this citation, it is nothing but a small footnote stating the 'autenticidad ha sido puesta seriamente en duda' (p. 325), without any justification whatsoever. Regalado, in his massive two-tome study on every aspect of Calderonian theatre, writes: 'Este crítico, encariñado con un Calderón dueño de un estilo elegante y una visión aristocrática del mundo, no se ha hecho a una obra tan atrevida y desenfadada como *Céfalo y Procris*, única razón posible para la excepción que hace de esta comedia.' He also points out (p. 722) how Edward M. Wilson and Jack Sage, in *Poesías líricas en las obras dramáticas de Calderón* (London: Tamesis, 1964), though they did not attribute the work to Calderón, still used thirty-four examples (many which quote the playwright's own work) taken from *Céfalo y Procris* in their book on the lyric in Calderón. See Antonio Regalado García, *Calderón: los orígenes de la modernidad en la España del Siglo de Oro*, vol. 2 (Barcelona: Ediciones Destino, 1995), p. 72. Also see Eloy R. González, in 'Carnival on the Stage: *Céfalo y Pocris*, a *Comedia Burlesca*', *Bulletin of the Comediantes*, 30 (1978), 4. He refuses to commit either way, but finds the arguments against its authenticity not very strong. Greer, in *The Play of Power*, p. 199, writes that, 'A definitive answer to whether Calderón is really the author of this parodic mythological play has yet to be given.' Alberto Navarro González (the editor of our modern edition), in *Calderón de la Barca de lo trágico a lo grotesco* (Kassel: Reichenberger, 1984), pp. 147–52, has no doubts about attributing the work to Calderón, and neither does Jose Manuel Pedrosa in his recent article 'La oración del peregrino y la comedia de *Céfalo y Procris* de Calderón', *Neophilologus*, 82 (1998), 403–10. Ignacio Arellano has published a collection of *Comedias burlescas del Siglo de Oro* (Madrid: Espasa-Calpe, 1999), in which Calderón is named as the author. In October of 2000, I had the honour of visiting the 'Calderón 2000' conference in Pamplona, where talks about *Céfalo y Pocris* were given; indicating that Calderón's authorship of the piece is accepted among the majority nowadays. If there remains any risk in attributing the play to Calderón, I feel the risk is well worth it, for as Greer writes in *The Play of Power*, p. 199, 'an affirmative answer would add another layer of complexity to Calderón's manipulation of the conventions of court drama'. Studying the presence of the *teatro breve* in the *comedia* is precisely concerned with this type of layering, witnessed in many plays outside of *Céfalo y Pocris*, and is a phenomenon that can only be studied with greater precision with the inclusion of this piece.

ridiculous scene among dozens, quickly assembled onstage and replaced just as quickly by the next in line. The same is true of the tenuous love intrigues that whimsically appear out of nowhere. The main purpose of these intrigues is to parody the melodramatic exploits of the *comedia de capa y espada*. Aside from featuring degraded protagonists who gain no sympathy from the audience, the situations themselves are dramatically degraded in their sheer lack of relevance to any plot. Instead of a motor for the dramatic movement of the piece, love intrigues (if they can be called such) are fleeting and soon replaced by some other type of joke as the *comedia burlesca* grinds on, getting a laugh however it can. Thus, the processional and festive atmosphere of the *mojiganga* is maintained, yet with even less attention paid to contriving a frame. Gone are the introductory frames as found in the celebration of the Prince's birthday in *Sitios*, the tourney of the foods in *Los guisados*, a drunken traveller's confusion in *La muerte*, or the collective mourning in *El pésame de la viuda*. No frame, except the mere designation of *fiesta*, can contain all the delightful nonsense that is struggling to burst free. *Céfalo y Pocris* best fits Bakhtin's definition of the carnivalesque[5] and it should come as no surprise that the play itself 'se representó a Sus Majestades día de carnestolendas'.[6]

Aided by Rodríguez and Tordera's 'morfología de la mojiganga', one can detect how the complete disregard for plot corresponds to the carnivalesque suspension of time.[7] Also present are costumes, a feature seen in three out of four of the *mojiganga* examples in chapter 1. Aside from the undoubtedly 'ridículo' appearance of all of the characters, there exist *figuras* whose extraordinary appearance heightens the carnivalesque atmosphere of the piece even further. First, there is the vulgar king, described by the editor as 'rotivestido',[8] practically a walking affront to Lope's famous phrase: 'entremés de rey jamás se ha visto';[9] and second, one encounters a guardian giant who is alternately

---

[5] The relatively complete freedom, the near over-saturation of innocuous mockery, the propensity for scatology and body-related humour, all with little concern for any structuring elements, correspond to Bakhtin's notion of Carnival as a time of liberation. Although this play remains a court spectacle, and is inarguably surrounded by controlling hierarchical elements (the courtly audience, the literal structure of the noble palace walls), the play remains as faithful to Bakhtinian Carnival as one can achieve in such a setting.

[6] Calderón de la Barca, *Céfalo y Pocris*, p. 3. Also hence the title of the article by Eloy R. González, who uses Caro Baroja's observations on Spanish Carnival, instead of Bakhtin's universalising anthropological perspective.

[7] Rodríguez and Tordera, 'Intención y morfología', p. 823.

[8] *Céfalo y Pocris*, p. xxv.

[9] Fernando de Toro-Garland, 'El "entremés" como origen de la "comedia nueva" según Lope', *Lope de Vega y los orígenes del teatro español: actas del I congreso internacional sobre Lope de Vega* (Madrid: EDI-6, 1981), p. 104. This line from the *Arte nuevo de hacer comedias* is quoted by critics almost as often as the famous 'gusto/justo' rhyme used by Lope to justify his style to the *academia*. Much of the *Arte Nuevo* itself is tongue in cheek (Did Lope really 'lock away' Terence and Plautus when writing his comedies?) and it should not surprise us to find more than one piece of *teatro breve* with a completely ridiculous king. See Henri Recoules, 'Les intermèdes des collections imprimées: vision

described as 'monstruo de tan mal cuerpo',[10] 'ruin Gigantillo, hijo de enano y giganta'[11] and 'chico gigante',[12] probably referring to the fact that the costume that indicated his role was far from terrifying. The choice of a giant and a king – both figures of great stature and power in respectively literal and figurative meanings – as ridiculous figures not only corresponds to the abstract theory of Carnival,[13] but also to a particular tradition of costumed characters that lives on in Spain to this day. The giant-sized figure itself was a common sight in Corpus Christi festival processions,[14] used to represent different 'nations' of the world by featuring such figures as gypsies, 'Ethiopians' and 'Romans'. The dramatic use of giant and king costumes[15] must have borne a natural association with these festive street processions, also called *mojigangas*.[16] This connection between theatre and street spectacle could not have been lost on the audience, even though there are no (until the end, as we shall see) traditional cries of '¡vaya de fiesta! ¡vaya de mojiganga!'

In both *entremeses* and *comedias*, costumes, beyond their basic use as clothing, are often used as a disguise. The *mojiganga*, on the other hand, mainly uses costumes to produce an isolated comical effect independent of furthering the plot. This is true in *Céfalo y Pocris* as well. In one scene in the first act, the Capitán of the guard takes some of the principal characters captive and orders that 'carantamaulas' (grotesque masks) be slapped on the prisoners' faces in order that 'nadie los conozca'.[17] The Capitán gives a practical reason for putting on the masks, but it seems little more than a pretext for making the characters look even sillier. Even the arrest, the original pretext, is but another way to make light of a character's appearance. The Capitán says he is arresting Aura because she is ugly, and he offers absurd yet compelling reasons relying on wordplay.[18]

caricaturale de la société espagnole au XVIIᵉ siecle', vol. 1 (Lille: Service de reproduction des thèses, Université de Lille III, 1973), pp. 61–2.

    [10] Calderón de la Barca, *Céfalo y Pocris*, p. 14.
    [11] Ibid., p. 17.   [12] Ibid., p. 45.
    [13] The notion of 'el mundo al revés' has also been called a universal phenomenon. See Helen F. Grant, 'El mundo al revés', *Hispanic Studies in Honour of Joseph Manson*, eds Dorothy M. Atkinson and Anthony H. Clarke (Oxford: Dolphin, 1972), pp. 119–38.
    [14] Buezo, pp. 47, 48, 72, does not cite any examples from Calderón's time, but plenty can be found instead in Javier Portús Pérez, *La antigua procesión del Corpus Christi en Madrid* (Madrid: Consejería de Educación y Cultura, 1993), pp. 155–84.
    [15] For another example of the costumed king, one may think of the 'King of Epiphany', a tradition still popular in Spain and France. See Julio Caro Baroja in *El carnaval*: *análisis histórico-cultural* (Madrid: Taurus, 1965), pp. 307–10. He names examples of the 'Rey de la fava', one being from 1383 and another from the 1930s.
    [16] Portús Pérez, p. 158.
    [17] Calderón de la Barca, *Céfalo y Pocris*, p. 21.
    [18] He says (Calderón de la Barca, *Céfalo y Pocris*, p. 21): 'Por fea: / que es precisa circunstancia, / pues es fea, ser prendida.' The *Diccionario de Autoridades* (Madrid: 1734) lists several definitions for 'prender'. One definition is: 'Vale también adornar, ataviar y engalanar las mugeres.' Another definition is 'Se toma tambien por exercer los brutos el acto de generación', which allows for the possibility of additional misogyny to be included in the joke.

When the prisoners are brought before the king, their masks are promptly removed,[19] without any use of the masks for games of trickery or deception as might happen in an *entremés*, such as Lope de Rueda's *Carátula*. In another scene, also particularly degrading to the female characters,[20] the king asks Céfalo to choose between his two daughters Pocris and Filis for marriage:

> Cómo en peras, escoged
> entre esas dos hijas bellas;
> y dando al amor tributo,
> vaya el diablo para puto,
> y casaos con una dellas.[21]

Céfalo is sceptical about their appearance, seeing that beauty can be superficial, and he demands a closer inspection, finally asking 'Hola, aquí / ropa fuera'. At this moment, clothing and its threatened removal are used to make jokes about misleading appearances, but not in any sense that drives the plot; it is merely a means to humiliation. In the previous act, Céfalo himself was dragged onto the stage half naked. As Pocris and Filis desperately fight each other over who gets to *avoid* being married to Céfalo, the argument becomes violent and they are left clawing away at each other's head coverings.

Beyond the masquerade aspect of this onstage *fiesta*, one must also pay attention to the great number of moments when a character sings[22] or even dances. Singing and dancing in public belong to the tradition of the celebratory street procession. By way of the *mojiganga*, such a tradition takes on a discrete theatrical form as it appears on a closed stage. The insertion of song or dance into a larger work occurs in all the theatrical genres mentioned thus far,[23] and need

[19] Calderón de la Barca, *Céfalo y Pocris*, p. 36. Aura says she is afraid to reveal her face, saying she suffers 'vergüenza'. Antistes then responds, naming her and saying, 'Y aún desvergüenza', indicating the mask has been removed.

[20] There is often an overlap between the commonplace misogyny of satire and the literary parody of the pristine and esteemed 'dama de comedia' who, in the universe of the play, is dazzlingly beautiful and beyond reproach.

[21] Calderón de la Barca, *Céfalo y Pocris*, p. 65.

[22] See Wilson and Sage.

[23] With regard to song, entire *comedias* can be based on the *romancero* tradition. Consequently, Lope's *El caballero de Olmedo* used a few lines from a song for stunning dramatic effect. It is worth noting that the lines in question actually first appeared as they do in the *comedia*, in a 'baile que bailaron unos representantes'. See Lope de Vega, *El caballero de Olmedo*, ed. Francisco Rico (Madrid: Cátedra, 1981), p. 46. The *comedia* can borrow from the *teatro breve* tradition as much as it can from the *romances*. Further regarding dance, Calderón's *El maestro de danzar* capitalises on the popularity of dance lessons by having its characters perform the latest moves. A beautiful example of the full integration of an entire 'minor' genre into the *comedia* is the opening of the third act of Calderón's *comedia novelesca*, *El castillo de Lindabridis*. It has a *sarao*, full of dancing and singing about love, in which the main characters sing back and forth with a chorus. The scene is not meant to be funny, however, and therefore I offer it only as a very general example.

not be inherently funny. However *Céfalo y Pocris* is such an enormous 'grab-bag' of jokes, ranging from the basest toilet humour[24] to the wittiest parody of literary forms, that inevitably popular songs and verses appear among the many targets for laughter. At the same time, not everybody in the play bursts into song for the same reason, though the desired effect of laughter is always the same. Singing can be used for parody when the words of well-known poems[25] are twisted, or when somebody sings 'straight', while the surrounding action of the play remains contrary to the mood of the song, or when the mood of the song clashes with the inherent subject matter.[26] Expressing oneself in a musical fashion can also comically highlight a character's response in conversation by offering an unnaturally melodious answer, unexpected *stile recitativo*,[27] or a sweetly melodious song juxtaposed to melodramatic weeping for the sake of comic contrast.[28] Also, a song can be used as a whimsical rhetorical device in order to reinforce an argument, where the well-known lyrics function as a type of authority.[29] In the most noticeable and significant sense, a song can break out of its role as simple embellishment and take on the identity of a sub-genre, as is the case of the *jácara* in *Céfalo y Pocris*.

The *jácara* already enjoyed a history of participating in mixed genres such as the *jácaras entremesadas*.[30] The narrative form and guaranteed drama of the original ballad genre's storylines lent themselves well to theatrical performance. At the same time, as evidenced by many examples found in printed editions, the audience would have been satisfied if only to hear an actress[31] come out onstage and sing a *jácara* without any internal justification surrounding the event. In *Céfalo y Pocris*, Calderón plays with the notion of inserted genres by having the noblewoman Aura sing a *jácara* about her misfortunes. The scene, itself a broad joke with multiple layers, serves as a good example of the purely associative joking style of the *comedia burlesca* genre. The first step is the 'set-up'. After arriving at a mysterious castle and being frightened off by the guardian 'ruin gigantillo', Céfalo and his crew of *graciosos* try a second door. Behind the door one hears shouts of 'échala fuera', to which Céfalo responds: 'Jácara piden adentro / pues "échala fuera" claman.'[32] Céfalo confuses the

---

[24] Céfalo's *calzas* become 'dos veces necesarias' (p. 15 in the Navarro González edition) when he sees the giant. The King's practice of sorcery includes 'una clara en su orinal'. See Eloy R. González, p. 9.

[25] Calderón de la Barca, *Céfalo y Pocris*, p. 27.

[26] Ibid., p. 12. [27] Ibid., p. 8.

[28] Ibid., p. 13 [29] Ibid., p. 14.

[30] See Evangelina Rodríguez, 'Del teatro tosco al melodrama: la jácara', in *Actas de las jornadas sobre teatro popular en España*, ed. Joaquin Alvarez Barrientos and Antonio Cea Gutiérrez (Madrid: CSIC, 1987), p. 227. She describes the sub-genre as 'un teatro burdo, de mezcla de estilos, antipretencioso, heredero de una naciente vocación musical'. A more thorough description of the *jácara* as ballad and as theatre will take place in chapter 5.

[31] Of the examples I have collected from *jácaras* sung in the theatre, the performers are overwhelmingly women.

[32] Calderón de la Barca, *Céfalo y Pocris*, p. 18. Note that the 'hero' is joking here, and not one of the *graciosos*.

shouts from within the castle with the extra-theatrical shouts that traditionally come from the audience members who demand that an actress perform an impromptu *jácara*.[33] Suddenly, out steps Aura, singing a *jácara* about her very own misfortunes. The joke that Céfalo made, one that could have been lost among the many dozens of jokes in the play, has suddenly taken on unexpected life and affected the action. After being interrupted momentarily by some encouraging words from the absurd hero Céfalo ('. . . que quien canta mal sus males, / muy mal sus males espanta . . .'),[34] Aura continues. However, before she can mention her identity, she describes the awful scene of the castle's social life, consisting of the king's caprices and the princesses' constant feuding. By impulsively describing her surroundings, Aura violates an unwritten rule of the *jácara*: the song must start with the introduction of its protagonist. Upon finally reaching the subject of herself in the song, Aura makes a small slip-up:

> . . . y vamos a mí, que entre ellas
> estoy vendida y comprada.
> Yo soy hija de Luis López . . .
>> [*Representa*]
>
> Mas, ¡ay de mí! ¡Qué ignorancia!
> ¡Como si fuera en mi casa!
>> [*Canta*]
>
> Hija soy de Antistes, que hoy
> tiene del rey la privanza;
> y pues él es el privado,
> su hija será la privada.
>> [*Representa*]
>
> Mi nombre es María . . . ,¿qué digo?
> Es Aura; que estoy turbada
>> [*Canta*][35]

---

[33] While it is naturally difficult to find evidence of an impromptu *jácara* in printed form, both *Jácara que se cantó en la compañía de Olmedo* (Cotarelo, *Colección de entremeses*, vol. 18, p. 514) and *Jácara que se cantó en la compañía de Bartólome Romero* (Quiñones de Benavente, *Jocoseria*, fols 109–11) explicitly mention the audience's demand for the performance in question.

[34] Calderón de la Barca, *Céfalo y Pocris*, p. 18.

[35] Ibid., p. 19. The search for the 'historical reality' behind many jokes can become surprisingly convoluted. According to Hugo Albert Rennert, in *The Spanish Stage in the Time of Lope de Vega* (New York: Hispanic Society, 1909), pp. 510, 512, there was an actor named Luis López who had an actress daughter named María, and she even had the *entremés La sacristán mujer* written for her by Calderón. See Calderón de la Barca, *Teatro cómico breve*, p. 110. Rennert also writes that María died in 1651. However, Ángel Valbuena Briones (Calderón de la Barca, *Obras*, vol. 1, p. 1785) writes that *Celos, aun del aire matan* premiered on 5 December 1660, and nowhere is a 'María López' listed (though she may have been married by then) on the exceptional extant cast list. Thus, either *Céfalo y Pocris* was written long before it supposedly premiered (even the editor is not sure of the date, although he supposes it was Carnival of 1661; see p. xvi), or news of María's death

Watching the flustered actress drop out of character must have been funny in itself, but this obviously intentional act is also meant to poke fun at the technique of mixing genres. Calderón has intentionally forced, in a sloppy yet comical fashion, an entire discrete *jácara*, full of self-conscious references to the *comedia*'s adoption of the form,[36] into the loosely structured action of the main play. Poor Aura cannot be sure to which genre she belongs. Is she a character with a singing part in a mythological *comedia*? Or is she the figuratively unmasked actress who makes a special singing performance after an act has come to a close? The choice of singing a *jácara* is not purely capricious, nor merely supported by Céfalo's ironic 'set-up'. Aura is, after all, 'enjaulada'[37] in a castle, and correspondingly *jácaras* often took the form of prisoner's laments. Singing a song associated with urban crime in a mysterious and secluded castle may seem a bit incongruous, but the playwright tries to 'aid' (ironically, leading to further incongruity) the audience in reconciling the disparate elements by introducing the Capitán, part and parcel of the greater *justicia*. The arrival of law-enforcement officials is a theatrical commonplace in both *comedias* and *entremeses* alike. In the *comedia*, the *justicia* often arrive at night to break up the nocturnal skirmishes of prowling *galanes*. As can be anticipated from the topsy-turvy nature of *Céfalo y Pocris*, this scene is meant to take place in broad daylight. Let us look at the ensuing dialogue, as silly, mocking and self-conscious as any other found in *Céfalo y Pocris*:

Tabaco	¿Linternas con luz tan clara?
Capitán	Pues ¿qué se os da a vos? ¿No es mi cera la que se gasta? ¿Es bueno escandalizando estar aquí con jácaras la vecindad?
Pastel	Pues, ¿quién es vecino desta montaña?
Capitán	Aquel risco. [. . .][38]

was greatly exaggerated, or this is a different comic actress named María with a father coincidentally named Luis López, or Calderón is writing an inside joke to which none of us may ever be privy.

[36] *Celos, aun el aire matan* contains a straightforward *jácara* sung by the *gracioso* Clarín. The jaunty tone may have contrasted with the rest of the opera's *stile recitativo*, but this contrast in tone would have been welcome and easily reconciled as Clarín is a ruffian of sorts and his attitude is harmoniously reflected in the melody of the *jácara* he sings.

[37] Calderón de la Barca, *Céfalo y Pocris*, p. 20.

[38] Ibid., p. 21. It is possible that, for *la justicia*, carrying lanterns was such a commonplace that the devices became an integral part of their costume. For this reason, Calderón may be playing with this notion by putting them in a context that renders part of their costume superfluous and ridiculous. Another possibility, pointed out by Eloy R. González, is that the reference to the daylight is a metatheatrical reference to the common flimsy artifice of establishing that it is night-time (though the play is performed in daylight) through the use of costumes, characters' references to their surroundings or, as we see here, the carrying of lanterns or candles.

The Capitán asserts his authority, and insists on switching the setting to an urban one. The impertinent *gracioso* Pastel naturally questions the notion of a 'vecindad', observing that there are no houses to be seen. Aside from the playful battle of wits, there is also a parallel battle between genres. Pastel represents the 'reality' of the scene's obvious *caballeresco* setting, with castles and giants, and the Capitán in turn represents the danger associated with night-time adventures commonly found in the *comedia*. Considering this conflict, it seems odd that the Capitán would want to end the *jácara* since, in a sense, it was this song that brought him into existence on the dramatic plane. This contradiction constitutes yet another part of the joke that begins with Céfalo's seemingly offhand *jácara* reference and ends with the Capitán taking the protagonists prisoner and slapping masks upon their faces, bringing us to the masquerade scene described above.[39] The devil-may-care spirit of a *comedia burlesca* allows for the introduction of jokes with a minimum amount of justification. One needs nothing more than a single word in a conversation, which another character seizes in order to make a quick pun. Some jokes may flash briefly and then fade away, some may slide into other jokes through word association or concretisation; and some jokes (again, starting with a single word) may grow to become mini-interludes in themselves. Cases like this latest one can take advantage of theatrical conventions, especially those of the *teatro breve*, piecing together entire genres or sub-genres with apparently reckless abandon while holding everything together with the versatile adhesives of good humour and free association. Adding to this, one must also consider the self-conscious nature of the process, making fun of itself as it progresses, thus demonstrating to us modern readers that explaining a joke (at least in oblique terms) can add humour instead of taking it away.

Though *Céfalo y Pocris* is not precisely a *mojiganga* stretched out to two thousand lines, it does bear many resemblances to the smaller genre, as shown. If this is so, then what do we make of the explicitly named *mojiganga* that comes at the end of the piece? What role does an overwhelmingly funny *small* piece play in finishing off an overwhelmingly (one could even say exclusively) funny *large* piece? It cannot be that the notion of 'comic relief' is relevant in this case, and therefore we shall have to look for other explanations. In the last scene, instead of Céfalo shooting Pocris because of a tragic mistake, he fires at her for peeping at him from behind some bushes. The event is naturally all in good fun, as she asks him to be careful and not miss. When he fires, she fakes being injured and falls to the floor. After a comical exchange between the lovers, she expires and Céfalo lets loose a

---

[39] Lest we merely associate masks with Carnival, let us also remember that there exists a long tradition of costumes and silly (for spectators, not wearers) hats associated with the penal system and the Inquisition. It is possible that this humiliating aspect of dressing up is also being evoked in this scene.

burlesque grieving rant, calling on the forces of nature, as well as 'pavos, perdices, gallinas, / morcillas, manos, cuajar . . .'[40] to come and mourn her untimely death. His lament ends with him calling upon everyone to intone these sorrowful words: "Su moño descanse en paz."[41] The king immediately enters the scene, but considers the killing well done since his highness harbours an aversion to Peeping Toms. He orders that his daughter be carried away:

> Ese cadáver llevada,
> y a su merecida muerte
> sea pompa funeral
> una grande mojiganga;
> que no se ha de celebrar
> esta infelice tragedia
> como todas las demás.[42]

Everybody asks '¿Mojiganga?' in mock surprise, and the king answers 'Mojiganga . . .', making it abundantly clear what is about to proceed. The jolly king fetches himself a guitar hanging from a tree, '. . . que cada día las cuelgan / los pastores',[43] and he leads the rest of the company in a song-and-dance routine ('Vaya, vaya de mojiganga')[44] so fresh and lively that his *canas* literally disappear by means of an airborne wire, yanking away his costume's beard and wig. After the giant and the ladies dance a *guineo*,[45] everybody joins together (perhaps even including the dead Pocris) in a massive 'baile de matachines'.[46] In this way, the spectacular *fin de fiesta* concludes. In one sense, this *mojiganga* fulfils the role of any other; it marks the definitive end of the spectacle, the *fin* for the *fiesta*, a dancing and singing curtain call. This *mojiganga* is also a final slap in the face of convention in what must be the most unconventional (one may even say anti-conventional) of *comedias*. The king himself says he refuses to allow an ending 'como todas las demás'. In a play that seeks to thwart every expectation through twisting every well-known dramatic situation into new grotesque shapes, singing and dancing in celebration of somebody's death is absurd yet appropriate. But is it a surprise? Are any expectations thwarted in the final moment? Only a few, considering

---

[40] Calderón de la Barca, *Céfalo y Pocris*, p. 89.
[41] Ibid., p. 89.   [42] Ibid., p. 90.
[43] Ibid., p. 90.   [44] Ibid., p. 91.
[45] *Autoridades* states that to perform this dance, 'se ejecuta con movimientos prestos y accelerados, y gestos ridículos y poco decentes'.
[46] According to *Autoridades*, a 'matachín' is a 'Hombre disfrazado ridículamente con carátula, y vestido ajustado al cuerpo desde la cabeza a los pies, hecho de varios colores, y alternadas las piezas de que se compone: como un cuarto amarillo y otro colorado. Fórmase destas figura una danza entre cuatro, seis u ocho, que llaman los Matachines, y al son de un tañido alegre hacen diferentes muecas y se dan golpes con espadas de palo y vejigas de vaca llenas de aire.'

that all except Rosicler (who states: 'Muera quien muerte la da')[47] had
appeared either neutral or jovial in the face of Pocris's death, preparing the
audience for a less-than-tragic finish to the play. Also by the end, the insistent
theme of 'el mundo al revés' would have been so drilled into the minds of the
audience that a happy ending to this 'tragedy' could hardly have come as a
great surprise. The surprises lie in the details,[48] for it is the king, instead of
the *graciosos*, who leads the song and dance; and he sets up the small jokes
that pepper the final scene, such as the conveniently hung guitar and his
prosthetic hair that flies away into the air.

Though the scene is full of grotesque images, nothing is so shocking or disruptive that it alters the sense of closure instilled by the theatrical *mojiganga*,
even when Rosicler has asked that Céfalo be killed. The last moment of dramatic tension in the entire piece, the last obstacle that stands in anybody's way
before the final festivities can begin, is a death threat. Yet both death and the
sadness associated with it are overpowered by the sheer happiness of the
mojiganga, in the form of the king's mandate, itself a parody of the royally
sanctioned *deus ex machina* endings of the *comedia*. At the same time, there
can be no victory over sadness by joy without a real threat and, as in *El
pésame de la viuda*, one is not far from the other, though the latter must
always triumph. The king declares before strumming his guitar:

> Vaya, vaya de mojiganga,
> de alegría y de pesar;
> que quien llora con placer,
> siente bien cualquiera mal.[49]

[47] Calderón de la Barca, *Céfalo y Pocris*, p. 89.

[48] This is also the case in Lope's *tragi-comedia El caballero de Olmedo*. Everyone is
expected to know the song that inspired the play, and also know that Don Alonso must die
at the end. Of course, the information that is missing is why, where, when, and how he
must die; hence the suspense. But even all this suspense can be eliminated and still defeat
expectations, as seen in the burlesque version by Francisco Antonio de Monteser,
El caballero de Olmedo, ed. Celsa Carmen García Valdés (Pamplona: Universidad de
Navarra, 1991), p. 253, ll. 1547–52). The *comedia burlesca* as a genre always leaves room
for surprise.

D. Rodrigo	¿Así os estáis, don Alonso,
	cuando yo y diez compañeros
	a mataros esperamos
	en el camino de Olmedo?
D. Alonso	Perdonad; no lo sabía.
D. Rodrigo	¿Venís?
D. Alonso	Sí.
D. Rodrigo	Pues allá espero.

[49] Calderón de la Barca, *Céfalo y Pocris*, p. 91.

The culmination of this joyous *fiesta* is also a reflective moment that invokes sadness, an evil necessary for joy's victory. It is also a moment to reflect light-heartedly upon the entire play itself, a non-stop parade of laughs that never allowed sadness a single advantage. As the play draws to an end and the laughter dies down, the *mojiganga* reminds us to keep on singing and laughing in the real world. Just as the *mojiganga* is a laughable point in time, so is the greater performance of the *comedia burlesca*, a fleeting moment in the everyday lives of the audience.[50] Likewise, the days of Carnival are fleeting. What is not fleeting is the ability to laugh and be happy. As this ability concerns brief moments, such as the *mojiganga*, so can the ability be stretched further and applied for hours on end as in the *comedia burlesca*. Likewise, gaiety and laughter can fill the time over days during Carnival. The message of any *mojiganga* is to have a good time in the 'here and now'. The message of a *mojiganga* in a *comedia burlesca* may be to laugh whenever you can, even if it means laughing and crying at the same time.

Let us now review the opera *Celos, aun del aire matan* and compare its less abundant comic scenes with the non-stop flow of theatrical jollity that was found in *Céfalo y Pocris*. Rather than examine the express objects of parody,[51] it would be of greater interest to look at the comic scenes and how they function as a type of *teatro breve* within the greater structure of the play. The scenes in question invariably involve the three *gracioso* characters in the play: Rústico, Floreta and Clarín. Though entirely sung, this opera is otherwise similar to a *comedia* and follows the genre's conventions with regard to the decorum of its characters. The rustics crack the jokes, while the nobles (in this case, mythological characters and heroes) do not make light of any situation.[52] In *Celos, aun al aire matan*, while the *graciosos* interact with the

---

[50] I realise that the audience consisted of nobles whose 'everyday lives' may have consisted of sumptuous luxury and the complete absence of care. Still, I find it likely to believe that even nobles have bad days and that no amount of luxury can take away the fear of death and disease. An idea I would wish to develop later in another study is that of the greater relationship between humour and *desengaño*. The common association is that the comic use of disguises teaches us that appearances are deceiving. A broader outlook would examine laughter as a reaction to the realisation that everything soon dies, decays and withers, though at the time it may appear thriving and beautiful. This would not necessarily follow the Bakhtinian carnivalesque theme of life cycles and regeneration, though it may involve the temporary banishment of fear in the face of death.

[51] See González and the introduction of *Céfalo y Pocris*.

[52] Alberto Navarro González, 'Comicidad del lenguaje en el teatro de Calderón', p. 131. He concludes: 'La comicidad del lenguaje corre casi exclusivamente a cargo de los graciosos de sus Comedias y Autos.' One would have to ask what is meant by 'casi exclusivamente'. As we will see in the following *comedia-entremés* section, there are plenty of exceptions and 'grey areas' that do not support decorum. There are plays where the *gracioso* has less of a comic role than the nobles themselves. Ignacio Arellano writes in 'La comicidad escénica en Calderón', *Bulletin Hispanique*, 88 (1986), 89, a more subtle account of *comedia* decorum, concluding: '. . . para los nobles se desarrollan otras zonas de lo cómico, que se pueden denominar genéricamente "medios cómicos ingeniosos",

serious characters of the play, their sober superiors are not 'dragged down' (provoked to throw tantrums, incited to rant and slap or left trembling with comic rage) to a baser level, despite the antics of their inferiors. There seems to exist a clear separation between the world of the comic and that of the serious. This is the argument that Alfredo Hermenegildo makes in his article 'La marginación del Carnaval: *Celos, aun del aire matan* de Pedro Calderón de la Barca',[53] which states:

> Nuestra hipótesis – en el caso de *Celos, aun del aire matan*. – es que, respondiendo en su estructura a las mismas fuerzas de organización interna, el gracioso, sin embargo, asume una función marginada, subalterna y semi-desligada de la articulación fundamental de la comedia.[54]

> [el *gracioso*] es la encarnación dramática de un complejo mecanismo, de carnavalización/descarnavalización, y de neutralización o, mejor, de marginación de su carácter festivo y popular.[55]

Hermenegildo appears to make a distinction between the word 'fiesta', relating it to the 'tono etéreo'[56] of the 'fiesta cortesana', and the crude 'carácter festivo' mentioned above. All encounters between these two 'caracteres' or 'tonos' are described in terms of 'choques', or clashes. These clashes are subsequently described in terms of language and the ability to influence action. Clarín's offhand and bawdy language clashes with the 'discurso noble, subyacente en las palabras y los gestos de Céfalo'.[57] Secondly, in a dramatic scene where Diana is about to kill Aura with a javelin, Céfalo's attempt at rescue is momentarily diverted by Clarín's cynical request that Diana be allowed to hit her target:

> ¿[. . .] hubiera fiesta
> como ver asaetar todas las hembras
> cuanto más una?[58]

Naturally, Céfalo does not follow the advice of the uncouth clown, calling him 'vil'. According to Hermenegildo, this rejection of Clarín's attempt to influence the plot further demonstrates the complete inefficacy of all the *gracioso* characters in contributing to the narrative, and thus leaving no dramatic imprint on the play as a whole. If we apply Hermenegildo's interpretation to

en los cuales lo risible escénico tiene muy poco papel'. He also mentions the *figurón*, a character that we shall look at later in chapter 4.

[53] Alfredo Hermenegildo, 'La marginación del carnaval: *Celos, aun del aire matan* de Pedro Calderón de la Barca', *Bulletin of the Comediantes*, 40 (1988), 103–20.

[54] Hermenegildo, p. 103.   [55] Ibid., p. 105.

[56] Ibid., p. 106.   [57] Ibid., p. 109.

[58] Calderón de la Barca, *Celos, aun del aire matan*, *Obras*, vol. 1, p. 1787.

our global view of the *comedia* and the *teatro breve*, we would have to assume that there exists practically no interpenetration of the genres in *Celos*. Supposedly, when any of the *graciosos* attempt to enter the other generic realm, they are promptly rejected, producing a clash, a shock to the audience, an announcement that the world of the *comedia* and the world of the *entremés* or *mojiganga* are irreconcilable. To push the point further (though Hermenegildo does not go this far), it is as though any comic moment, through its 'marginación', is reduced to the status of all delimited *teatro breve*, that of standing outside as a contrast, as a relief, rarely having any relevance to the action of the main play. It is crucial to consider the merits of this line of thinking when examining the ubiquitous comic episodes and stock figures of any *comedia* – found within the genre's inevitably episodic structure and equally inevitable gallery of stock characters – and their relation to discrete pieces called *teatro breve* and their cast of characters.

Hermenegildo's argument appears sound, well argued, and indeed some of its points are irrefutable. However, it is worthwhile to look closer at the argument as well as some items that may have been overlooked. Such an exercise can be helpful later when contemplating the 'bigger picture' of *comedia* and *teatro breve* relationships. In fairness to Hermenegildo, one cannot forget that he is only concerned with the 'marginación de carnaval' in *Celos* and no other play. But his contention that this play represents the continuation of the 'triunfo del discurso dominante'[59] over rebellious fools, from Juan del Encina on down to Calderón, seems to hint at a more global point of view.[60] With regard to *Celos*, Hermenegildo contends that Rústico, played by the famous *gracioso* Antonio de Escamilla, would have caused a shock in an opera where all the other characters, male and female alike, are played by women who establish a 'tono etéreo'.[61] However, Clarín, another character chosen by Hermenegildo as an example of attempted comic insurrection, has the voice of a woman. Indeed, this

[59] Hermenegildo, p. 103.

[60] See also David Gómez-Torres, 'La función de la risa en el discurso de la comedia: absorción y manipulación de los rasgos grotescos y carnavalescos' (PhD Dissertation, University of Tennessee, 1994). Gómez-Torres goes slightly against Hermenegildo's ideas by suggesting that the 'dominant discourse' was not always so dominant, using the *Égloga del Carnaval* (a 'Renaissance piece') by the very same Encina as an example. After looking at another such piece, and three 'baroque plays', he sums up in his abstract: '. . . as Bakhtin has shown for other European literatures, in post-Renaissance Spanish literature, laughter undergoes a process of devaluation. It no longer shows positive aspects of the world, but negative aspects of certain individuals.' It is unfortunate that Gómez-Torres would include an early *égloga*, which is not, properly speaking, a *comedia*, without choosing any *teatro breve* for his later examples. There, the carnivalesque spirit is alive and well, as we have seen. We may even see it contaminate the *comedia*, without being excluded, as I am trying to prove. Bakhtin's theory of Carnival is remarkably useful, but one should never forget his fascination with hybridisation, which may allow us to imagine a coexistence of 'dominant' and 'carnivalesque' 'discourses' instead of some sort of battle between them.   [61] Hermenegildo, p. 106.

gracioso is played by Mariana de Borja,[62] a singer, harpist and actor in many of the *autor* Escamilla's theatrical productions.[63] Given the company she kept onstage in *entremeses, jácaras* and *mojigangas*,[64] Mariana de Borja surely would have fit the bill in playing a 'cynical, crude . . . dishonest . . . street-smart ruffian who abuses women and delights in macabre jokes and violent language'.[65] One should not automatically assume that the presence of a woman, singing or not, contributes to a 'tono etéreo'. This contradiction between the actor's gender and the *persona* of a *jaque* onstage could be explained by a separate and topsy-turvy nature of the carnivalesque, but only with difficulty. First of all, the world of the *hampa* is hardly carnivalesque, as we shall see in chapter 5, and Clarín the *jaque* would be an unlikely representative. Secondly, if one were to include Clarín under the rubric of the carnivalesque, would his 'spirit' really remain separate from all the other women dressed as men? Is the 'tono etéreo, sin aristas, de gran fiesta cortesana' so great that the cross-dressing of the serious characters is made to seem natural? When *Celos, aun del aire matan* was played the night before *Céfalo y Pocris* during Carnival, was it possible for the audience to disassociate completely the nearly all-female cast from the costume-happy spirit of the previous day's celebration? Though other elements, such as an overabundance of food and drink, along with scatology, may be absent, cannot the costumes bear some sort of correspondence to Carnival? When Clarín speaks of the *fiesta* above, is he referring to the 'fiesta cortesana', the spectacle as a whole, or to his own crude 'festivo' version, with which he tries to interfere? Or is he confusing both versions of *fiesta*?

Hermenegildo writes that Clarín's demand that Céfalo step out of the path of Diana's javelin is ineffectual. This is true. On the whole, the notion that the *graciosos* of *Celos* do not affect the actions of the major characters is unassailable. Yet, this inefficacy, at this moment of the play, is not solely a characteristic of the comic characters. The critic carefully lines up Céfalo and Clarín's verses (respectively noble for the rescuer and cynical for the jeering onlooker), but he strategically neglects to mention Diana's lines. I shall reproduce more of the dialogue in order to demonstrate the true effect of Clarín's taunts:

Diana   . . . Aparta
Céfalo   Advierte, considera
         que no es querer que viva
         pedirte que yo muera.

---

62 Calderón de la Barca, *Obras*, vol. 1, p. 1785.

63 Rennert, p. 436.

64 Hill, p. 186. According to Rennert (p. 436), she played 'fourth parts', which usually refer to those of the *graciosas*, and actresses in the *teatro breve*. She appears in Calderón's *Sitios*, and possibly also his *Mojiganga de la muerte*. See Calderón de la Barca, *Teatro cómico breve*, pp. 218, 352.

65 Louise K. Stein, *Songs of Mortals, Dialogues of the Gods: Music and Theatre in Seventeenth-Century Spain* (Oxford: Clarendon, 1993), p. 232.

Clarín   Apártate, señor,
         y que la tiren deja:
         tendrás un lindo rato.

Céfalo   ¿Eso, vil, aconsejas?

Clarín   ¿Pues dime, hubiera fiesta
         como ver asaetear todas las hembras,
         cuanto más una?

Diana   Aparta
         digo otra vez.[66]

Clarín and the goddess Diana are ganging up together against Céfalo; they are of the same mind. As much as Clarín fails, Diana fails. Since even a goddess could not influence Céfalo at the end of this scene, it seems a bit unfair to explain Clarín's inefficacy merely in terms of 'la marginación de carnaval'. Clarín's jeering may have no effect, but this may not have even been a real concern of his. More than asserting his own will, he is mockingly supporting the goddess. His *jacarandino* nature (inherited from old ballads and the *teatro breve*), despite its joking tones, is not at odds with the severe Diana's actions. He wants to see blood. His misogynist impulses (which again may have seemed strange coming from Mariana de Borja) coincide nicely with Diana's unbridled vengeance against those who violate her vow of chastity and treacherously give themselves over to Venus. From Clarín's point of view, it is as though he has stumbled across a street fight, a 'showdown', transported from its Spanish urban setting to a Greek mythological landscape. Not a carnivalesque scene, to be sure, but neither one that excludes Clarín and the *teatro breve* tradition that he represents. I would even venture to say that Clarín's sarcastic jeers heighten the dramatic tension, though they might be somewhat jesting. Hermenegildo is correct in stating that the *gracioso* does not affect the narrative thread, but seeing the above dialogue in its entirety does put into question his 'conclusión #5': 'El gracioso ha sido reducido a la condición de simple vehículo de una comicidad no integrada de modo orgánico en el conjunto de la obra dramática.'[67] This does not appear to be the case.

The scenes that are of most interest to Hermenegildo, and to our study, are those involving the love triangle between Clarín, Rústico and Floreta. 'En ellas se muestran muchos de los rasgos salidos de la fiesta popular y que conforman un microcosmos paralelo al de los señores.'[68] I would like to replace the term 'fiesta popular' with *mojiganga* and 'microcosmos paralelo al de los señores' with *entremés*. Indeed, that is very much what these generic terms had come to represent in Calderón's time. The *entremés* aspect of the love triangle is most obviously represented by Clarín's persistent advances

---

[66] Calderón de la Barca, *Obras*, vol. 1, p. 1788.
[67] Hermenegildo, p. 119.   [68] Ibid., p. 112.

towards Floreta (who is married to Rústico) and the *criada*'s coquettish reciprocation. Such adulterous situations are the basis for hundreds of *entremés* plots, including that of *El dragoncillo*, studied earlier. They are 'un microcosmos paralelo' that mocks the strict fidelity ostensibly demanded by the 'honour code' controlling the *comedia*'s husbands and wives. Of the two relatively major scenes involving Clarín and Floreta's flirtations, the second is rather tame. Floreta hides behind some branches and Clarín, not knowing to whom the voice belongs, beckons her to come forward: 'Que nos queramos / por pasatiempo.'[69] After Clarín reassures the unrecognised voice that Floreta is 'yesterday's news', 'ninfa de baratillo, / la amé una tarde', Floreta reveals herself in order to scold him, only to have her husband also step out of the forest to recriminate both wife and lover. This scene of confused identities, listening while hiding and mildly scandalous behaviour is more akin to the plays of Calderón's urban *comedias*[70] than the bawdier *entremeses*, but can still be said to function as a 'microcosmos paralelo'. The truly scandalous scene is the previous one in which Clarín embraces Floreta directly in front of his master Rústico's face. Their flirtations solidify in a physical interaction that pushes the limits of any theatrical genre's decorum, though, 'even when it appears that an adultery may be consummated, the tone . . . remains light, in *entremés* style'.[71]

According to Hermenegildo, each *entremesil* scene is alike in that it is an extension of the *gracioso* type, manifested in three characters. This type in *Celos* '. . . no sirve para reafirmar la verdad oficial. Queda excluido de la problemática que llega a plantear tal reafirmación. Su finalidad dramática es la de provocar la risa de diversión, de gratuito entretenimiento.'[72] Yet, one must also read what Hannah Bergman wrote six years earlier:

> What I propose to examine here, however, is not so much how a comic turn successful in interludes was transferred to three-act plays to add humour but rather how the dramatist integrated the motif into the thematic structure of more ambitious works, and to what extent it may provide further evidence concerning his attitude towards marriage.[73]
>
> . . . the fact that [Rústico] is presented as a husband and not as a simple suitor to Floreta emphasises the contrast between a plebeian (but in this

69 Calderón de la Barca, *Obras*, vol. 1, p. 1809.
70 The upper class in literature, even in seventeenth-century Spanish drama, was no stranger to scandalous behaviour. Calderón's *Mañanas de abril y mayo* is a consummate example of both *damas* and *caballeros*, married and single, entertaining two or three lovers. As can be expected, social order is restored at the end through marriage.
71 Hannah E. Bergman, 'Ironic views of marriage in Calderón', p. 71.
72 Hermenegildo, p. 119.
73 Bergman, 'Ironic views of marriage', p. 65.

case, not mismatched) couple, where not even the strongest provocation inspires real jealousy, and the noble pair which in spite of the tenderest declarations of love cannot resist the threat of imaginary jealousy, jealousy of the air itself.[74]

In an opera such as *Celos, aun del aire matan*, the importance of individual plot points is subservient to the overall theme, and one should not ignore the thematic connections that bring both *comedia* and *entremés* together, creating a 'comicidad integrada' whose existence Hermenegildo denies.

In the other significant adulterous scene, Clarín and Floreta have an affair directly in front of the enraged Rústico. Why does the husband have difficulty intervening in such a scandalous situation? The answer is simple. Rústico has been turned into a dog. This brings us to the *mojiganga* side of things. The goddess Diana, enraged by Rústico's assistance to Eróstrato, subjects the hapless *gracioso* to a 'serie de seis zoomorfosis'[75] as an act of revenge:

> Hoy he de vengarme
> de un villano con su muerte.
> Mas darle muerte es desaire;
> que no merece castigo tan noble
> el rústico objeto de un pecho cobarde.
> A Acteón mudé la forma
> en venganza de otro ultraje,
> y a aqueste he de hacer que nadie le vea
> que en forma distinta de bruto no le halle.[76]

That the function of this punishment is 'puramente instrumental y no significativa desde el punto de vista de la dramaticidad',[77] is arguable if one considers such scenes of transformation solely in the context of the dramatic *mojiganga* tradition. Before he is transformed into a dog, Rústico's first metamorphosis[78] is represented by a costume of animal skins and 'una cabeza de cuatro caras de animales diferentes'.[79] At first, Floreta sees her husband Rústico as a lion and is frightened by his menacing teeth and claws. Secondly, Rústico changes into a bear, wreaking further havoc as Pocris enters the stage and, with Floreta, shouts for help. Third and fourth, Rústico passes from bear to wolf and then tiger, as Céfalo threatens to kill this challenging game,

---

[74] Bergman, 'Ironic views of marriage', p. 72.

[75] Hermenegildo, p. 116.

[76] Calderón de la Barca, *Obras*, vol. 1, p. 1792.

[77] Hermenegildo, p. 117.

[78] According to Valbuena Briones, 'El argumento está tomado de la fábula de Cephalus y Procris que Ovidius Naso cuenta en el libro siete de las *Metamorphoses* (vv. 690–865).' See Calderón de la Barca, *Obras*, vol. 1, p. 1785.

[79] Calderón de la Barca, *Obras*, vol. 1, p. 1792.

consequently scaring the poly-zoomorphic Rústico offstage. After an extended period of being in dog form ('con máscara de lebrel y collar y pieles'[80]), Rústico makes his final appearance as a wild boar, 'con cabeza de jabalí',[81] recalling a vision already witnessed by us readers, and perhaps even by some in the royal audience, in the *mojiganga Sitios*. The extreme grotesqueness of these costume changes[82] far exceeds the simple costumes and disguises used to deceive others in any *entremés*. Rústico has become a one-man costume party, a one-man *mojiganga*. The mythological tradition of a metamorphosis is exaggerated so that six animals can successively parade onstage as the onlookers in the dramatic action express their fear, surprise or appreciation. That these transformations do little to affect the 'dramaticidad' should come as no surprise because the *mojiganga* is a very anti-dramatic sub-genre. It revels in silly costumes and making noise, not in weaving plots and creating great tension. The *mojiganga* as a discrete genre invariably comes at the end of a play, and it has no purpose in feeding the audience further intrigue. Dislocated from the end of a *comedia* or *auto sacramental* and placed inside the larger form, in this case an opera, the genre can be expected to retain this festive atmosphere whose last concern is 'dramaticidad'.

Concerning the presence of the *entremés* in *Celos*, the happy ending between Rústico and Floreta does not affect the greater 'dramaticidad' of the work in terms of the main narrative thread. Yet in all the thousands of *comedias* written during the Golden Age, when did the sub-sub-plot of a *criado* love affair ever affect the outcome of the principal characters' storyline?[83] Calderón knew the *comedia* conventions inside and out, as well as those of the *teatro breve*. While he did not violate the plotline decorum in this case, he did play with convention in order to create tension *thematically*, affecting the 'dramaticidad' in a way that would go unnoticed by any critic if narrative were

---

80 Calderón de la Barca, *Obras*, vol. 1, p. 1796.

81 Ibid., p. 1801.

82 While one may imagine that a transformed-human masquerade is a restrictively specific sub-sub-genre of theatre, Arellano ('Comicidad escénica', p. 78) points out that even so there exists room for variety. He describes the masquerade found in *El mayor encanto amor* by writing: 'Este ballet animal es una danza ornamental, más que cómica.' Instead of the creatures in *El mayor encanto amor*, Rústico's transformations and multiple visages in *Celos* have more in common with the transformed victims of *El golfo de las sirenas* (a harpy, serpent and other fierce creatures), a *zarzuela* that we shall examine later in our study.

83 Lope's *El perro del hortelano* is a famous example in which a *gracioso*'s schemes change the social status of the hero and thus the outcome of the play. Calderón's *Mañanas de abril y mayo* has a hero that courts a *criada* (among three women), but this does not strongly affect the outcome of the play. Often in the *comedia*, *criados* commit errors that lead to confusion and further plot complication, but generally the final dramatic outcome is in the hands of the heroines and heroes of the play.

the only concern. Calderón's trick was not ignored by Hannah Bergman, who dedicated much of her life to studying the *teatro breve*:

> The rather close integration of the comic subplot with the serious main action . . . is carried even further in *Celos, aun del aire matan*, where there are married couples on both levels. The triangle formed by the principals has a tragic outcome, while that of the servants is grotesque. I do not mean to suggest a mechanical parallelism between the two actions . . . Although obviously the grotesque transformation of Rústico echoes that of Aura at the beginning and foreshadows that of Céfalo at the end, and gives rise to some very funny scenes . . .[84]

Though the married *graciosos'* reunion does not end in a song-and-dance routine like most *entremeses*,[85] the spirit of reconciliation is definitely similar. While the *entremés*, in general, is thought to mock the serious *comedia* by means of comic variations of similar themes, the comic alternative in *Celos* appears to have a somewhat serious message, namely that jealousy can be overcome and need not lead to disaster if husband and wife are truly compatible and understand each other. Placed in a greater context, the *entremés*-type characters and situations become the other side of a tragi-comic coin, and they take on thematic significance. And as Bergman writes, none of this implicit moralising is at the expense of the 'very funny scenes'. Looking at the *graciosos* in this light, it would be difficult to see them as marginalised characters: severed, neutralised and figuratively swept into a corner of the play's structure. It seems as though the audience could not ignore the tension and connections between the two plotlines (and also the contrasting genres), even if one plot did not influence the other directly.

THE MIXING OF HUMOROUS AND SERIOUS GENRES

Calderón de la Barca is generally credited with inventing the genre of the *zarzuela*, a musical theatre piece with both sung and spoken parts.[86] While Calderón did not contribute any major innovations to the realm of the *teatro breve*, he is recognised by all for his contributions to musical theatre. His willingness to experiment with different generic forms, and to join and blend those forms in various combinations, gave rise to entirely new genres such as the *zarzuela*. *El golfo de las sirenas* is such a piece in which

---

[84] Bergman, 'Ironic views of marriage', pp. 71–2.
[85] We witnessed this in *El mayorazgo*, *El pésame de la viuda* (which could have qualified as an *entremés*), and it was alluded to in *El dragoncillo*.
[86] Calderón de la Barca, Pedro, *El golfo de las sirenas*, ed. Sandra L. Nielsen (Kassel: Reichenberger, 1989), p. 26.

theatrical experimentation, the *comedia, teatro breve*, singing and humour all combine.

The entire theatrical *fiesta*[87] of *El golfo de las sirenas* consists of a *loa*, a one-act *comedia*, and a *mojiganga*, all explicitly named as such.[88] The repetition of characters and setting indicate beyond any doubt that the three pieces were meant to be performed together, despite Valbuena Briones' contention that the smaller 'festive' ones need not be included 'por no guardar relación directa con el mito de la pieza'.[89] Sandra L. Nielsen's later edition contains all the pieces, for she was aware of their importance in the production as a whole. Nielsen details the blatant metatheatrical aspects that show themselves in the *mojiganga* of *Golfo*, and she concludes: 'The *loa*, the play, and the *mojiganga* together constitute a formal parody of a standard three-act *comedia*.'[90] A self-awareness pertaining to the parody is not exclusively the domain of the comic characters, though it is mostly they who point out the spectacle's contrived nature.[91] Nielsen lists several examples in which the *gracioso* Alfeo, who appears in both the *comedia* and the *mojiganga*, makes references to his role as expositor upon landing ashore. Alfeo mockingly quotes a Calderón *comedia* title (one of Calderón's *graciosos*' favourite types of joke[92]), and refers obliquely to his actor's pseudonym, as he also comments on the theatre's location and changes in stage scenery. He ruptures the dramatic illusion even further by referring to the duration of the work in which he performs, telling the audience that it will last 'hora y media'.[93] Alfeo's wife and comic *teatro breve* partner, Celfa, is equally circumspect of her role and theatrically self-conscious, as she uses wordplay to call attention to the *zarzuela*'s emphasis on music, does a burlesque of the famous prisoner Segismundo, and makes a descent to the stage in a 'nube de mojiganga', mocking the fanciful flights of deities in Calderón's mythological *comedias*.[94] It is important to note that

---

[87] Even though the title does not contain the word 'fiesta', the event is called such by one of the fishermen in the *loa*. See Calderón de la Barca, *Golfo*, p. 74. See also p. 9 of this edition for notes on the *fiesta* as a whole.

[88] On p. 78, Alfeo states 'aquí acabará la Loa, / y empeçara [sic] la Comedia'. On p. 119, Sileno says: 'empieça la mojiganga'.

[89] Calderón de la Barca, *Obras*, vol. 1, p. 1724.

[90] Ibid., *Golfo*, p. 30.

[91] Nielsen writes, pp. 34–5: 'Even minor characters participate in this metatheater. In the *loa* a fisherman speaks to the shepherdesses, alluding to the Zarzuela [the location from which the genre derived its name] . . . Astrea has already made allusions to the members of the royal family and brought them down to her rustic level . . . The four elements are also self-referring characters in this *zarzuela*. In the *loa* the four choruses sing, complaining about the terrible weather in January. However, they change their tone and become happy as soon as they are conscious of the royal presence.'

[92] Claire Pailler, 'El gracioso y los "guiños" de Calderón', pp. 33–48.

[93] Calderón de la Barca, *Golfo*, pp. 32–3.   [94] Ibid., pp. 33–4.

metatheatrical references are made by the *graciosos* not only in the *mojiganga*, but also in the main play itself.[95]

This mockery of convention, which could be gentle or sarcastic, was obvious in all four of Calderón's *mojigangas* examined in chapter 1. As in *Sitios*, in *Golfo* one finds an express recognition of the royal family's presence and the reiteration that this is a festive occasion in their honour. Likewise, as in *Sitios*, here Juan Rana is the comic centrepiece, his persona as an actor shining through to such an extent that his character Alfeo cannot help but declare: 'Aunque soy un Juan Rana / miren que no sé nadar.'[96] His presence throughout *El golfo de las sirenas* would have been a constant reminder that the retelling of the Ulysses myth was only a fanciful show. The *loa* for any Golden Age theatre piece works as a sort of frame but as with *Los guisados* (a *mojiganga* that contained its own frame), the *comedia* portion of the *Golfo* spectacle contains its own framing devices, independent of the adjacent pieces. *Los guisados* promoted most unabashedly the carnivalesque spirit, but the spectacle of *Golfo* does not share the same love of food and drink and absurd costumes as *Los guisados*. Yet, at the same time, the play must be somewhat related in spirit, for it was staged a second time during Carnival the same year it premiered.[97] The figurative unmasking that occurs during the transition between *comedia* and *mojiganga*, where the legendary island of Trinacria (Sicily) gives way to the hills and brambles of the Zarzuela, is reminiscent of the mockery of theatre-within-theatre (and also the *auto sacramental La vida es sueño*) as seen in the *La mojiganga de la muerte*. Alfeo's cry, '¿Qué mojiganga? esperad, / oid; ¡el Cielo me valga! / agora que caygo en ello, / ¿dónde estoy?'[98] reminds us of the confused Caminante of *La muerte* who finally understands that he has been the subject of a theatrical illusion. The mythological 'égloga piscatoria' that is *Golfo* may seem to have little to do with a piece such as *La mojiganga del pésame de la viuda*, the least festive and parade-like of our examples. However, the main play and *mojiganga* contain matrimonial bickering and the mention of urban settings,[99] which is more like

---

[95] We may again think back to Thacker's thesis regarding metatheatre and its social dimensions. In a case such as *Golfo*, given the high level of artifice and fantasy in the staging, plot, characterisation and setting, it may be difficult to see Celfa and Alfeo's extreme self-awareness as bearing social significance. However, we would do well to keep Thacker in mind when studying the *teatro breve*, as it thrives on self-relection, especially when the pieces are set in recognisable contemporary contexts, as are the majority of *entremeses*. At the moment, the metatheatricality of *Golfo* seems more concerned with literary and artistic conventions, rather than the social roles of its characters, who are either fishermen or figures from Greek mythology. See page 51.

[96] Calderón de la Barca, *Golfo*, p. 112.

[97] The piece premiered on 17 January 1657. See Ángel Valbuena Briones, 'Calderón y las fiestas de carnaval', *Bulletin of the Comediantes*, 39 (1987), 167.

[98] Calderón de la Barca, *Golfo*, p. 119.   [99] Ibid., p. 32.

Pésame, though there is no mistaking the *mojiganga* of *Golfo* for an *entremés*, unlike *Pésame*, which qualifies as both. Nielsen noted the strange hybrid nature of *Golfo* and wrote: 'This unusual *zarzuela* has all the farcical elements of the *entremés* and "carnivalisation" of the *mojiganga*,'[100] confirming what we have just observed in these juxtapositions. This notion of hybridisation is much more appealing, and I would say more correct, than Valbuena Briones' conception of a separate nature that makes the *teatro breve* portions unnecessary to publish nowadays. Hybridisation also relates to the humour inherent in the entire theatrical spectacle. Humour is far from relegated to the discrete pieces of *teatro breve*. It may even come to dominate over the play's more serious side. As Nielsen observes: 'Even the climax of the serious plot, Ulysses' escape, is overshadowed by the comic antics of Alfeo, who has been commandeered to row the escape ship.'[101]

We shall now look at the relationship between the *teatro breve* and the main play itself, though at times it is impossible to extricate one from the other, leaving aside the notions of parody and metatheatricality already covered thoroughly by Nielsen in her introduction. In the opening *loa* of *Golfo*, the *villana* Astrea (who plays only a minor role in the main play and the *mojiganga*) provides a long monologue, extending an invitation for the royal family to enjoy the performance:

> A nuestro mísero albergue
> descienden, que la grandeza
> tal vez se divierte afable
> entre la humilde simpleza
> de lo rústico, porque
> cotejando diferencias,
> ver lo que son, y no son,
> les suele servir de fiesta.[102]

This speech is many things. It is most obviously a *captatio benevolentiae* for the audience, where the entire production personified (with Astrea and metonymically the *loa* as mouthpiece) humbles itself before the royal family, asking them to 'descend' to the modest level of the spectacle. As with most similar introductions, the claims to modesty are accompanied by the promise of enjoyment, assuring the reader, listener or viewer that the attention paid will be worthwhile.[103] But the choice of words such as *humilde* and *rústico* are not chosen merely as rhetorical devices; they refer to a specific reality that is the Zarzuela as fiesta. The location, in the brambly woods and hills of the

---

100 Calderón de la Barca, *Golfo*, p. 30.
101 Ibid., p. 32   102 Ibid., p. 72.
103 See Jean-Louis Flecniakoska, *La loa* (Madrid: Sociedad General Español de Librería, S. A., 1975), pp. 64–6, for details on the *captatio benevolentiae*.

Pardo, would have been constantly on the minds of the spectators; thus, instead of begging them to forget their surroundings, Astrea asks them to find solace and enjoyment in the rugged environment. This portion of the *loa* also calls upon the audience's imagination to compare and reconcile the *diferencias* they encounter, not only in the setting and the royal presence, but in the play which the *loa* itself frames. This very reconciliation can provide the key to appreciating the *fiesta*. Just as *Apolo* (Felipe IV) can descend and rest comfortably in the rugged setting, so can the humble *rústico* fishermen and women conversely make themselves at home in the legendary tale of the shipwrecked Ulises, a story that in turn takes the wilds of the Zarzuela and changes them into the fabulous island of Trinacria. The *rústicos* are different from the noble Ulises, and different from the supernatural and powerful Caribdis and Escila, but their presence is not an anomaly. Nor is the *teatro breve* genre jarring or out of place, as it is represented by the chief *rústicos*, the *graciosos* Celfa and Alfeo. Audience, venue, setting, staging, cast, generic forms: all are harmonised, despite conceivable incongruities, in the synthetic whole that is the *fiesta*.

We must look closely at Alfeo's essential role in *El golfo de las sirenas* if we are to understand the extent to which the *teatro breve* and *comedia* are integrated in *Golfo*. This fisherman played by Juan Rana appears in the *loa*, *comedia* and *mojiganga* that combine to make up the spectacle. Nielsen writes that consequently:

> He appears earlier than Ulysses, speaks more lines, and remains in the drama until the end . . . Alfeo becomes the most important character in the *zarzuela* as a whole, and the comic sub-plot takes on more importance than the serious main plot. Ulysses' story becomes a play-within-a-play, one that takes place in Sicily (called Trinacria here) within a comic play that is being performed in the Zarzuela Palace itself.[104]

These observations are concerned with how this relationship produces elements of metatheatre, but they also beg the question if there is any difference between Alfeo's role in either the *loa, comedia* or *mojiganga* portions of the spectacle. Do the discrete genres constrain the behaviour of the famously transgressive figure of the *gracioso*, particularly when he is played by the era's most famous comic actor? The answer would appear to be 'No'. The popular and comic constancy granted to both Alfeo and Celfa is unwavering. The *loa* itself, which is meant to frame the following play and capture the audience's attention and benevolence, does not begin with anybody calling for quiet or announcing the royal presence. Instead, the *loa* begins with Celfa and Alfeo bickering onstage. He complains about his bad luck fishing and the chore of coming home to her. She berates him in return,

---

[104] Calderón de la Barca, *Golfo*, p. 30.

having already called him 'bestia'.[105] If we or the audience did not know any better, we might think that the *zarzuela* was starting with an *entremés*. The *loa* eventually conforms to a more traditional format,[106] but not before Alfeo and Celfa establish the roles that they will play consistently throughout the entire spectacle. When the *comedia* portion approaches its climax, Ulises and his companions demand that Alfeo row them away from their attackers to safety. Alfeo does not want to anger Caribdis or Escila, with whom he shares the island, and he begs to be left alone. In a desperate plea, he asks Celfa to support him, but nothing has changed since their very introduction onstage:

Alfeo	Celfa, pues eres mujer,
	ruégales tú que me dexen.
Celfa	Señores, no le llevéis,
	que es tonto, y no sabe más
	que remar, y conocer
	los bajos de aqueste puerto,
	sin dar en ningún través,
	por más bravo que ande el mar.
Alfeo	Muy buenas señas pardiez
	para dejarme; ¿qué dices?
Celfa	Digo lo que verdad es;
	¿sabéis otra cosa vos,
	que en dos paladas, o tres
	atravesar todo el golfo?
Alfeo	Que me destruyes, mujer.
Celfa	Por eso lo digo yo.[107]

This scene-within-the-scene is not clearly separated from the rest of the play by virtue of being comic. In fact, quite the opposite is true. Here, the humorous fighting that could have been found in hundreds of *entremeses* is perfectly integrated into the action of the play. Ulises and his men impatiently wait until Alfeo, their only means of escape from the island, is browbeaten into submission. Without the stock character of the shrewish wife, and the extraneous help she offers, these ancient Greek heroes would have been left stranded. The *graciosos'* bickering relationship and the comic consequences thereof continue in *Golfo*'s *mojiganga* and persist to the very end of the spectacle until the chorus shouts: 'Quedo, quedo, sed amigos, / cantando y

105 Calderón de la Barca, *Golfo*, p. 67.

106 Flecniakoska, pp. 15–50, provides a thorough study of the origins of the *loa* genre, from the Roman *prologus*, to the Italian *prologo*, to the *introitos*, *prólogos* and *argumentos* of sixteenth-century Spanish theatre. These 'proto-*loas*' (my word) were commonly represented by *rústicos* and *pastores bobos*.

107 Calderón de la Barca, *Golfo*, pp. 104–5.

bailando.'[108] In this way, the traditional reconciliation of the *teatro breve* is finally achieved. In each portion of the *zarzuela* as a whole, Alfeo and Celfa offer much more than mere comic relief. They are a source of continuity, but this does not mean that they always do the same thing, nor that they are trapped in performing only one function within the work. Their first words in the *loa*, while following a particular comic tradition, make explicit reference to fishing, thus establishing the setting for the entire 'égloga piscatoria'. This establishment coincides nicely with the framing function of the *loa* genre, and is only one example among many where Alfeo and Celfa are free to play within the confines of particular generic conventions, asserting their function as they joke about their assigned roles. In the *comedia* portion, the *graciosos* are not merely parodic clowns added for comic relief, but rather figures whose crude behaviour still manages to mix well with the surrounding action. In fact, Alfeo and (to some extent) Celfa are the very centre of attention, and on the whole it is much more Alfeo's *fiesta* than anybody else's.

Even if one of the island's fishermen were not to conclude the *comedia* with the words 'empieza la mojiganga',[109] there would still be little confusion about the generic classification of the long comic scene that finishes the whole spectacle. The only dramatic element in the ending scene is Celfa 'encantada', trapped high in a tower and whom Alfeo must rescue. The only significant action is Celfa lowering herself down in a basket, Alfeo riding up afterwards, and consequently falling to the floor when the aforementioned basket is suddenly released, much to his shock. The rest of the *mojiganga* concerns witty banter between *gracioso* husband and wife, both joined in conversation by an eloquent *salvaje* who guards the tower. The rescue of a damsel in distress evokes the world of chivalry, but there is little corresponding action to mimic this world effectively. Instead, the masquerade element of the *mojiganga* is emphasised through the nearly obligatory parade of costumed characters – hardly dramatic action in itself – under the pretext of showing humans transformed into animals, held captive on the island like Celfa in her tower. The people were the victims of Escila the enchantress. It is not entirely clear why they have suffered such a fate until after they parade onto the scene, and after Alfeo defeats the *salvaje* in a burlesque battle of wits. Each creature – harpy, wolf, serpent, lion, tiger, catamount, magpie, wild boar – was previously a character whose vices matched the behaviour of the animal into which he or she was transformed. Anyone familiar with Greek mythology will recognise that this punishment can be found in the legend of Circe and Ulysses. In fact, as Ignacio Arellano points out, Calderón used a similar procession of animal-humans in *El mayor encanto, amor*, which is loosely based on the Circe stories found in the *Iliad* and Ovid's *Metamorphoses*.[110] Arellano states that in *El mayor encanto, amor*, 'Este

---

[108] Calderón de la Barca, *Golfo*, p. 126.   [109] Ibid., p. 119.
[110] Ibid., *Obras*, vol. 1, p. 1508.

ballet animal es una danza ornamental, más que cómica', while the dance in *Golfo* is comical and grotesque.[111] One might add to this observation that the scene of the transformed animals in *Golfo* is also satirical to some degree, for it criticises, though perhaps superficially, vices in a humorous tone. Satire as we know it in Western literature began with the classical Greek and Roman writers, and their use of gods, heroes and supernatural beings (including Circe[112]) was continued through Calderón's time by playwrights fascinated with classical antecedents. Likewise, gods could appear in another genre that had its origins in Spain's street processions, demonstrated by Bacchus' role in *La mojiganga de los guisados*, a work that combined a mythological figure with a 'motivo caballeresco' and social satire.

Finally, it is worth mentioning that the relationship between allegory and the *mojiganga*, one that may have seemed tenuous in *Los sitios de la recreación del Rey*, now becomes more apparent when the element of broad satire is present.[113] While the masquerade in *Golfo* corresponds to specific circumstances of a specific myth, the transformed characters still represent vices of a transcendent nature. At times the vices are only implied through the animal, but sometimes they are explicitly stated, such as the man who, because of self-interest, was changed into a mountain lion. Either way, the characters are not complex individuals (they have no names beyond 'hombre primero' or 'mujer tercera', etc.), but rather the essential embodiment of a vice, much like the common personification allegory found in the *autos sacramentales*. The relation between costumes, jokes, and allegory that could be found in Calderón's separate *mojigangas* appears once again in both the

111 Arellano, 'Comicidad escénica', p. 78.

112 Gelli's *Circe* was a popular treatise on the nature of man that used animals for comparison, and took the form of dialogues between Ulysses and the beasts. Gelli himself was no doubt inspired by Aristotle, Pliny, Plutarch, Lucretius, Lucian and Seneca, among others. See Armand L. de Gaetano, 'Gelli's *Circe* and Boaistuau's *Theatrum mundi*', *Forum Italicum*, 7 (1973), 441–54. In this treatise (which was translated into Spanish in a Valladolid edition in 1551) '. . . the comparison between the conduct of man and that of the beasts differs from most bestiaries in that it is used essentially as a means to make man conscious that his behavior is not consonant with his divine attributes'. See Gaetano, p. 443. Calderón's use of the Circe myth for Escila's enchantments can hardly be said to aspire to the same level of sophistication, precisely because it is more festive, and less philosophical than Gelli's.

113 As an allegorical drama, Thomas O'Connor has called *Golfo* a 'failed dramatic experiment'. See Thomas Austin O'Connor, 'Formula Thinking/Formula Writing in Calderón de la Barca's *El golfo de las sirenas*', *Bulletin of the Comediantes*, 38 (1986), 35. His ideas are further explained in his section on *Golfo* in Thomas Austin O'Connor, *Myth and Mythology In the Theater of Pedro Calderón de la Barca* (San Antonio: Trinity University Press, 1988), pp. 184–7. Nielsen's judgment is less harsh, as she writes (Calderón de la Barca, *Golfo*, p. 48) that Ulises not only appears in *Golfo* and *El mayor encanto*, but also in the *auto sacramental Los encantos de la culpa*, and that, 'The allegorical interpretation implicit in the first two becomes explicit in the *auto*.'

comedia portion of *El golfo de las sirenas* and the integrated *mojiganga* that brings the spectacle to a close.

El laurel de Apolo is a two-act *zarzuela* that can fruitfully be compared with *El golfo de las sirenas*. While it does not approach allegory in its use of mythological figures, it does have a similar thread of humour that runs through it. Thomas Austin O'Connor relates this humour to a self-conscious irony about the genre's novelty and perhaps its debased nature:

> What suffuses *Laurel* is its ironic tone, a tongue-in-cheek attitude that masks the text's exposure as a novelty. The ironic stance is in fact a defense mechanism by which the text asserts its difference at the same time as it acknowledges its hesitancy to full commitment.[114]

I believe that to claim that irony (often inextricably linked to the humorous situations) is used for 'self-defense' may be an overstatement of the *zarzuela*'s inferiority complex. O'Connor refers to the personified Zarzuela's speech in the *loa* that states:

> No es comedia, sino sólo
> una fábula pequeña
> en que a imitación de Italia
> se canta y se representa;
> que allí había de servir
> como acaso, sin que tenga
> más nombre que fiesta acaso.[115]

Yet if we think back to all the examples of the *mojiganga* examined beforehand, we remember them as rife with ironic references. A very self-conscious (synonymous with ironic in this particular case) act may actually be a call for celebration, lest one forget the shout of '¡vaya, vaya la mojiganga!' *Laurel* does not go this far, but it is safe to assume that its irony is just as much an inherent part of the celebratory *fiesta* as it is a 'defense mechanism'. *Laurel* also features comic *rústicos* similar to those found in our previous *zarzuela*, though O'Connor writes, 'What in *Golfo* is an obvious contrast between the comic emphasis of the minor forms and the serious nature of the main play, becomes in *Laurel* a more integrated effort,' arguing that this 'more integrated effort' would 'stress the more light-hearted nature of the genre'.[116] This is not necessarily the case, after considering the plenitude of integrated comedy in the form of the constant presence of Alfeo and Celfa throughout the *loa*, *comedia* and *mojiganga* of *Golfo*. Consider also Nielsen's well-founded statement[117] that Ulises' serious story is actually a play-within-a-comic-play, overwhelmed by Alfeo's antics.

---

[114] O'Connor, *Myth and Mythology*, p. 121.
[115] Ibid., p. 120.   [116] Ibid., p. 184.
[117] Calderón de la Barca, *Golfo*, p. 30.

Regardless of which *zarzuela* has more integrated humour, in *El laurel de Apolo* the *gracioso* Rústico's big scene, that is 'the core of *Laurel's* comedic stance',[118] has much to do with the genre of the *mojiganga*. The scene recalls that of another Rústico, from *Celos, aun del aire matan*, in that he is transformed by an angry god, albeit this time into a tree and not many different animals. An obvious parody of the classical Daphne and Apollo myth (the subject of this *zarzuela*) is played for maximum laughs, as Rústico must suffer all sorts of indignities owing to his newly acquired arboreal status. Changed into a tree, he echoes the performances of all the other costumed comic characters seen in previous *mojigangas*. Like any character from the *teatro breve*, and like Alfeo swallowed and regurgitated by a giant fish in *Golfo*, Rústico comically defies death in his new form. For example, lovers inscribe *motes* into his back, yet he is unharmed. The humour is heightened further as he turns his back so that the next lover will not see what a previous rival had left behind. His country cousins make the poor Rústico a target for practising with their slings, and while they hit him directly in the eye, he suffers no permanent damage. When this 'tree' lets out a shout and starts to hop away, the would-be shooters are frightened off. The fact that Rústico the tree can hop about undercuts the classical Daphne myth. What is the point of becoming a tree, punished with ostensible fixedness, if one can still move from one place to another? The other Rústico's punishment in *Celos, aun del aire matan* was without a direct correlation to a specific victim taken from mythology. He was likened to one victim out of many among the mass human-to-animal transformations of the Circe myth. In *Laurel*, the transformation is a direct imitation of Dafne's, which belongs to a unique story of metamorphosis. Does this comic reproduction of Dafne's demise mean that Apolo would turn whomever he wanted into a tree? In a fashion, Rústico's similar fate makes Dafne no longer unique and therefore cheapens the dramatic nature of the metamorphosis. It is also significant that this is a parody *avant la lettre*, foreshadowing Dafne's fate, and therefore may be even more effective in undercutting the sombre nature of the punishment by preceding it. In this case, the *mojiganga* takes on even greater importance as it is no longer merely a *fin de fiesta*, an afterthought, but instead a force working internally.

THE *FIESTA* AND THE FESTIVE HERCULES

When one thinks of cracking jokes, throwing parties and generally having a good time, the Jesuits and their *colegios* do not immediately come to mind. Yet all these things, to one degree or another, did occur, thanks to the celebration of *fiestas literarias*[119] within the confines of the educational institutions that

118 O'Connor, *Myth and Mythology*, p. 129.
119 Nigel Griffin, 'Some Aspects of Jesuit School Drama: 1550–1600' (PhD Dissertation, Oxford: 1975), pp. 13–26. In his study, Griffin gives a great account of the phenomenon, from the sumptuousness of the costumes and set decoration, to the notion of *ludus* or play, considered a vital ingredient for the proceedings.

were the legacy of Saint Ignatius of Loyola. It was at these institutions where many of Spain's most famous authors, poets and playwrights studied while young,[120] and they must have learned much about the dramatic craft while probably participating in, and certainly attending, such *fiestas*.[121] While very little has been written about the connection between Jesuit theatre and the other 'branches',[122] particularly that of professional performances held in *corrales*,

---

[120] See Ignacio Elizalde, 'El teatro escolar jesuítico en el siglo XVII', in *Teatro del siglo de oro: homenaje a Alberto Navarro González*, ed. Víctor G. de la Concha, Jean Canavaggio, Theodor Berchem and María-Luisa Lobato (Kassel: Reichenberger, 1990), p. 119. 'Estas comedias humanísticas, colegiales, ejercieron extraordinaria influencia en los orígenes y formación de nuestro teatro nacional. En adelante, no podremos llenar el vacío que hay entre los dos Lope con media docena de nombres, o salir al paso diciendo que el genio portentoso del Fénix de los Ingenios sacó de la nada el teatro español.' Another critic is more cautious. See Cayo González Gutiérrez, *El teatro escolar de los jesuitas: 1555–1640 y edición de la Tragedia de San Hermenegildo* (Universidad de Oviedo: Servicio de Publicaciones, 1997), p. 288. 'Sería presuntuoso, y además falso, decir que Cervantes, Lope, Calderón y Quevedo deben su técnica y su método a los Padres de la Compañía de Jesús. Pero sí es lógico suponer y admitir que aprendieron bastante del sistema teológico de la Orden y que su entusiasmo por las letras se vio estimulado por las prácticas del Colegio y la influencia de los educadores.' I believe that somebody like Calderón, who so blatantly exploited theatre for didactic purposes, did learn some of his techniques from the Jesuits. See also Barbara Ellen Kurtz, *The Play of Allegory in the Autos Sacramentales of Pedro Calderón de la Barca* (Washington, D. C.: Catholic University of America Press, 1991). The major argument of Kurtz's book proposes that Calderón takes Saint Ignatius' idea of *composito loci* from the *Spiritual Exercises* and uses it in his *autos*. Yet, even she admits (Kurtz, p. 12), along with all other critics who have commented upon this issue, '. . . there is little or no evidence that Calderón directly imitated any of these dramas; as of now, any mutual influence between *auto* and Jesuit theatre remains a hypothesis, although a highly probable one, especially given Calderón's close association with the Society.'

[121] According to Cotarelo, Calderón spent five years at the Jesuit Colegio Imperial in Madrid, finishing in 1614 and continuing on to the Universidad de Alcalá de Henares. He would later go on to study at the Universidad de Salamanca. See Emilio Cotarelo y Mori, *Ensayo sobre la vida y obras de D. Pedro Calderón de la Barca, Parte primera (Biografía)* (Madrid: Tip. de la 'Rev. de Arch., Bibl. y Museos', 1924), pp. 62, 71. The play, whose *entretenimiento* we shall study in detail, was possibly performed in Madrid in 1617. See *La Tragedia de San Hermengildo*, ed. Julio Alonso Asenjo, vol. 2 (Madrid: UNED, 1995), p. 474. Coincidentally, it was likely that Calderón stayed a year in the city of Madrid until October 1617 (Cotarelo, *Ensayo*, p. 81). Thus it is possible that Calderón had contact with the play in question, though such an occurrence is still very much in the realm of speculation.

[122] Justo García Soriano, 'El teatro de colegio en España', *Boletín de la Real Academia Española*, found in several sections spread out over vols 14, 15, 16 and 19. I now refer to p. 397 of vol. 15. García Soriano speaks of different authors and currents '. . . que habrán de convergir más tarde a la integración de nuestro glorioso Teatro: la popular y religiosa, la profana semiculta y la humanística del Renacimiento. Fueron luego perfeccionando las dos primeras tendencias otros felices continuadores, que sacaron ya sus obras del ámbito escolar al aire libre de las plazas y de los primeros corrales de comedias. Sólo la tendencia humanística, la más sabia y artificiosa, permaneció dentro de los *generales* y paraninfos universitarios, únicos lugares propicios para su cultivo y desarrollo.' García Soriano's study lists numerous examples from Jesuit theatre, most of which remain unedited and unpublished, and a few of which contain humorous situations and characters equal to those found in any piece of *teatro breve*.

it seems that from the very outset one should imagine these branches as not being separate but rather as intertwined. There are certainly a great many connections between the Jesuit drama and humanistic university theatre of the time, though a slight distinction between the two can be made by demonstrating that the former had a tendency to moralise as well as educate, while the latter was didactic on a strictly intellectual level.[123] This distinction does nothing to diminish a great number of shared characteristics, including the use of humour, allegory and a variegated mix of genres. If one eliminates the respectively didactic and moralising nature of university and Jesuit theatre, one is left with costumes, staging, characterisation, verse, singing and 'special effects', that is, features shared with the non-didactic and secular theatre. By the same token, secular theatre need not ignore moral, theological or (though less likely) book learning.[124] Each venue (*colegio*, university, *corral*, royal palace) can put on a show that shares characteristics (in text and in presentation) taken from a common pool of dramaturgical knowledge. Thanks to these 'family resemblances', one may speak of Calderón's mythological plays as 'secularized *autos*',[125] or acknowledge that his 'comedias de santos' could play successfully to an audience outside the patio of a Jesuit *colegio*. An example of this secular–moralistic–theological overlap that relates directly to Calderón's use of humour and allegory is the figure of Hercules. Before looking at Calderón's own works, it would be worthwhile to look at one example taken from the Jesuit tradition in which the playwright was steeped.

The work in question is not actually the full-length play of *La tragedia de San Hermenegildo*, but rather the three-part *entretenimiento* that broke up the five acts of that very work. The *tragedia* and the *entretenimiento*[126] were written by the Jesuit Father Hernando de Ávila, and premiered in the *colegio* of San Hermenegildo, in Seville, on 25 January 1591.[127] The *tragedia* is 7,877 lines long, including the *entretenimiento*, which consists of 1,902 lines, or 24 percent of the entire dramatic spectacle. Needless to say, such a ponderous drama would have lasted several hours, and the *entretenimiento* must have been very welcome to all involved. The play, together with its interludes, contains parts for forty-six actors,[128] not all of them speaking, of course.

---

[123] Jesús Menéndez Peláez, *Los jesuitas y el teatro en el Siglo de Oro* (Oviedo: Servicio de Publicaciones de la Universidad de Oviedo, 1995), p. 29.

[124] Thus the propensity in the Golden Age to cite Horace's 'omne tulit punctum qui miscuit utile dulci' (such as in the foreword to Quiñones de Benavente's *Jocoseria*) or simply to refer to 'deleitar aprovechando'.

[125] O'Connor, *Myth and Mythology*, p. 191.

[126] The *entretenimiento* filled the role of the traditional *entremeses*. See Asenjo, p. 465.

[127] Asenjo, p. 462.

[128] One must keep in mind that these events held at the *colegios* were partially intended to show parents what their children had learned and to show patrons that the money they gave to the school was well spent. This type of 'showcase' often tried to display the talents of as many students as possible, and this explains why some Jesuit plays' *dramatis*

The main play contains portions of Latin spoken mainly by Hortensio the Byzantine ambassador (called 'Roman' in the historical sources, and consequently in the play[129]) and other 'Roman' soldiers. Fortunately for much of the audience, when Hortensio speaks to Hermenegildo and others citizens of Hispania, he is accompanied by an interpreter who translates his Latin into clear sixteenth-century Castilian. In Act II, scene 4, one encounters a *disputa* concerning the Incarnation held entirely in Latin, what Asenjo calls a 'concesión a las necesidades pedagógicas de los estudiantes'.[130] The *entretenimiento*, like the greater part of the *tragedia*, is entirely in Castilian verse, and while mostly humorous and bearing no relation in subject matter, is not entirely divorced from the moralising nature and political message of the main play.[131] The hero of these small pieces is Hércules, in an allegorical mode, subjugating passions and fighting against ignorance. Taken from Greco-Roman myth, he is *virtus* personified, using his strength to battle vices, equally personified, who appear onstage. In many ways, these interludes are similar to the *autos sacramentales* in their mode of communication, their setting, characters and important message for the audience. Yet, despite its great symbolism, the *entretenimiento* remains above all else a piece closely related to the *entremés* genre, as we shall see.

Hércules faces two kinds of rivals in these Jesuit interludes. He must defeat the Bárbaros, brutes who represent ignorance, and who have locked up Sciencia in a tower. Hércules must also contend with Amor Sensual and Amor Interessal, distracting passions, which seek to thwart his every move. The allegory of savages locking up Science is straightforward enough, but the personifications of the evil types of love – as opposed to Hércules' unembellished allegorical helpers Amor de Sciencia (the child of the captured Sciencia) and Amor de Honor – feature a curiously effective twist: they are both gypsies. On a primary level of meaning, within the order of the *teatro breve*, gypsies represent both fun and troublemaking.[132] They are guaranteed to please the audience with dancing, singing or some form of tomfoolery commonly associated with this stock figure. The *entremés* gypsy was also popularly associated with deception and thieving, the most common plot devices producing hilarity in short comic theatre pieces. However, the notion of deception *per se*

---

personae contain fifty or more parts and why the greater *fiestas*, 'with a whole multitude of smaller verse compositions, short dramatic offerings, and disputations', could last hours upon hours, if not over the span of two days or more (Griffin, pp. 80–2).

129 Asenjo, p. 442.   130 Ibid., p. 443.

131 Ibid., p. 437. *San Hermenegildo* is a prime example of the mixed purposes of Jesuit theatre. At the moment of the play's premiere, the Colegio de San Hermenegildo en Sevilla was performing an act of defensive propaganda. Father Hernando de Ávila wanted to produce an elaborate display of the Company's educational merit, while thanking the city for its generous contributions and simultaneously quieting those critics who saw such contributions as excessive.

132 Recall the gypsies that appear at the end of *El reloj y los genios de la venta*.

is extremely abstract, as is the concept of the *burla* itself,[133] and the play's author takes advantage of this fact by constructing connections between 'concrete' racial stereotypes and more general moral failings through the use of a personification allegory that is both humorous and serious.

The '"evil" Amores' first meet with the characters they have come to replace, the good 'Amores'. The first comic effect stems from the evil ones' appearance, namely their gaily coloured exotic clothes,[134] contrasting with the good ones' attire.[135] The second effect is manifest as soon as they open their mouths, for they speak with a constant 'ceceo' that is typical of the 'voz deformada' characteristic of the ethnic and national stereotypes that populate the *teatro breve*. The joking starts early as Amor Sensual exclaims mockingly, '¡Oh qué buen año de amores!',[136] commenting on the seemingly auspicious meeting of four 'Amores'. After trading *sententiae* regarding their identities, the evil ones bring the level of discourse (and the altruism of the exchange) down to a baser level by asking the good 'Amores' to spare them a *quarto*. Playing his stereotype to the hilt, Amor Sensual next insists on reading Amor de Sciencia's palm. Upon grabbing the unwilling Amor de Sciencia's hand, Amor Sensual spits into it, causing the enraged allegory to shout back indelicately: '¡Oh, hi de puxa, gitano!'[137] The burlesque palm reading continues and Amor Sensual manages to convince Amor de Sciencia to drop his hand, whereby he promptly hits his stooping victim. Menacing fist-waving ensues, followed by beard-pulling ending in an all-out melee, with the good 'Amores' arising victorious. So far, the *entretemiento* has been half allegory and half comical street fight. Later, a ridiculously armed, *sayagués*-speaking, tough-talking Bárbaro adds to the mirth by warning of the oncoming rescuer 'Miércoles' (i.e., Hércules, one of the Bárbaro's many malapropisms), and he also menaces Sciencia, or as he calls her, 'doña Sabïonda'.

Much mirth and merriment mixed with allegory is found in these pieces, and the 'concentration' of humour throughout remains consistent with the examples mentioned above. In the interest of saving space and sharpening our argument, we will leave aside the example of a broken cat-filled crock[138] and look at the comical scenes involving the allegorical Hércules himself. In the beginning of the second interlude, he proudly recites his legendary role in the foundation of Seville (a city he now represents), and his present role in liberating Sciencia, which in turn represents the 'diez y siete mil ducados'[139] given

---

133 A *burla* can involve means of trickery ranging from the simplest to the most complex, from hiding under a table to using the most sophisticated casuistic theology. The simple we have seen already; for the more complex, see Oppenheimer.

134 Asenjo, p. 540.   135 Ibid., p. 619.

136 Ibid., p. 540.   137 Ibid., p. 543.

138 Ibid., p. 728. The *entretenimiento* is not without its scenes of completely gratuitous absurdity, but most of the comic devices are relatively well structured, with cause-and-effect occurrences.   139 Ibid., p. 610.

by the municipality to the Colegio de San Hermenegildo. However, serious discourse is soon superseded by the return of Amor Sensual and Amor Interessal, who mischievously follow the good 'Amores', who themselves have been ordered by Hércules to fetch him a glass of water. This leaves our hero to face the Bárbaro of the last act, who this time has disguised himself as a gypsy. If the Bárbaro were still wearing his protective gear, his triple-layered costume (savage, man-at-arms, gypsy) would rival any past or future *teatro breve* character's appearance, even that of the prosthetic-laden *caballero ridículo* of Calderón's *El mayorazgo*. Hércules' circumspect 'straight man' reaction to such a sight is equally funny. Never have Barbarism and Virtue faced off in such a ridiculous fashion. Hércules finds the Bárbaro's language 'gracioso' (it is a grotesquely parodic *sayagués–gitano* hybrid), calls him ironically 'donoso',[140] but obviously sees through the laughable disguise. The hero remains in control of the situation.

Yet, soon Amor Sensual and Amor Interessal appear on the scene, dressed as their virtuous counterparts (Amor de Sciencia and Amor de Honor respectively), a disguise that does not immediately betray its nature to Hércules. They begin to sermonise in verse on the virtues of the love that they supposedly represent. They argue that Hércules should give up his quest and return to the riches of Seville: '. . . está en tu poder / gozar de tanto regalo, / esta sciencia te señalo, / que el gozar de esto es saber.'[141] They also advise: 'Pues, si a caso buscas honra, / señor, pesuadirte quiero, / que no ai honra sin dinero, / ni con dinero deshonra.'[142] The message to the audience is clear: there is evil in succumbing to vicious love disguised as good. After a comical and fruitless effort to sort out who is who, the evil 'Amores' end up collaborating with Bárbaro, and the serious examination that sought to differentiate between vice and virtue devolves into a mess of children's games, false noses, soaked costumes and, as a *finale*, 'magic flutes' that explode with clouds of charcoal in the faces of the hapless good 'Amores'. Though the twin allegories of virtue are the constant victims, Hércules looks quite stupid and helpless through association. Only at the end of the second part does the fog of confusion begin to clear as Hércules menaces the evil 'Amores' with his club, chasing them offstage. In the third part, the villains get their just desserts. As they start mocking the hero once again, he quickly grabs each in a headlock and strangles them to death. An attack featuring an onslaught of Bárbaros follows, but Hércules dispatches them effortlessly as well, despite their release of successive 'secret weapons', a lion and a bear.

What can be learned by reading the *entretenimiento* of Hércules? Ambivalence and humour can be a major part of allegory and moralising, categories that are generally associated with one-sidedness and seriousness. Consequently, Hércules himself can be seen as an ambivalent figure. He represents

---

140 Asenjo, p. 615.

141 Ibid., p. 622.

142 Ibid., p. 623.

Virtue's subjugation of the passions and the power to liberate Science from the threat of Barbarism. Yet he also represents indecision (though momentary) as well as pride. He also represents money, itself an ambivalent object that can be used for good or evil. His serious demeanour reflected in his opening speech carries weight as he stands accompanied only by the good 'Amores', but his image as a problem-solver and man-of-action is seriously tainted for the greater part of the *entretenimiento*, as he falls prey to trickery and is fig-uratively yanked this way and that by the whimsical manipulations of his clownish adversaries. He is a 'straight man' who wins in the end, but not before being laughably and unwittingly humiliated in a way that fits his char-acter best. He is forced to succumb to inaction. This portrait of Hercules, part of a great spectacle that was a predecessor of the 'huge allegorical entertain-ments'[143] to come, was much more flattering than his future portrayals. To see how he reappears in a surprisingly negative fashion, let us return to the works of Calderón de la Barca, where one can detect various features of the Jesuit *entretenimiento* repeated.

In drama, there have always existed mythological figures of an ambivalent nature. Corresponding to his thesis that any serious genre is quickly accompanied by a parodic or travestying counterpart, Mikhail Bakhtin writes of the ancient Greek satyr play and of

> Hercules, the powerful and simple servant to the cowardly, weak and false king Euristheus; Hercules, who had conquered death in battle and had descended into the netherworld; Hercules the monstrous glutton, the play-boy, the drunk and scrapper, but especially Hercules the madman – such were the motifs that lent a comic aspect to his image. In this comic aspect, heroism and strength are retained, but they are combined with laughter and with images from the material life of the body . . . The comic Hercules is one of the most profound folk images for a cheerful and simple heroism, and had an enormous influence on all of world literature.[144]

Lawrence Nees, tracing the use of the Hercules figure in the Middle Ages, writes:

> Even within the classical tradition itself Hercules could be a difficult and ambivalent figure. Sometimes he stood for virtue, but he also represented the vulgar muscle man, the fool seduced by his own lust, the drunkard, and in general the gross embodiment of coarse and merely physical elements of humanity, as for example in Attic drama and in the Roman poetry of Ovid and Propertius.[145]

143 Griffin, p. 63.

144 Bakhtin, *The Dialogic Imagination*, pp. 54–5.

145 Lawrence Nees, *A Tainted Mantle: Hercules and the Classical Tradition at Carolingian Court* (Philadelphia: University of Pennsylvania Press, 1991), p. 160.

Some scholars have pointed out that, during the Middle Ages, even Hercules as *virtus* was ambivalent and not necessarily seen in a positive light, as he was considered too pagan a figure to be reconciled with Christian conceptions of good and evil.[146] However, by Calderón's time, the stigma of Hercules had long since worn off and the hero was readily adopted as an allegorical figure.

At the same time, what was once simple ambivalence was now becoming practically polysemous. Much can change in a century or two. One can merely compare Enrique de Villena's treatise *Los doce trabajos de Hércules*,[147] written in 1417 (though printed in 1483) with Juan Pérez de Moya's *Philosophía secreta de la gentilidad*,[148] printed in 1635. The esteemed Hispanist Emilio Cotarelo y Mori, who edited Enrique de Villena's work, criticises him for making what we nowadays call 'too tight a fit'. Using the Hercules myth to make moral observations was certainly an innovation, but using an extremely narrow interpretation of each of the hero's labours and subsequently equating them with particular sectors of Castilian society was a rather forced didactic method of little value.[149] In the much later *Philosofía secreta de la gentilidad*, however, Pérez de Moya's varied and disparate points of view of each Herculean feat left room for various interpretations. Using an analytical method more scholarly than Villena's, Pérez de Moya manages to, in the editor's words, 'interpretar discretamente todas las tradiciones mitológicas rehaciendo en una nueva enciclopedia las corrientes dispersas . . .'[150] While the later work is more sophisticated, in every case listed in both *Los doce trabajos* and *Philosofía secreta*, Hercules' allegorical role changes in relation to the varied natures of his allegorical opponent, thus making him a multifaceted symbolic figure. He is always exemplary, but in two particular stories found in the later *Philosofía secreta*, he functions as a negative example; Hercules becomes the conquered instead of the conqueror. These two examples correspond to the only two extant uses of the Hercules figure in the *comedias* of Calderón.[151] It is useful to keep in mind the theatrical Hercules' comical and ambivalent nature, his utility in the *fiesta* setting and the early *teatro breve*, along with the

---

[146] Theodor E. Mommsen, 'Pertrarch and the Story of the Choice of Hercules', in *Medieval and Renaissance Studies*, ed. Eugene F. Rice, Jr (Ithaca: Cornell University Press, 1959), p. 173.

[147] Enrique de Found in Villena, *Obras completas*, ed. Pedro M. Cátedra, vol. 1 (Madrid: Turner, 1991).

[148] Juan Pérez de Moya, *Philosofía secreta de la gentilidad*, ed. Carlos Clavería (Madrid: Cátedra, 1995).

[149] Emilio Cotarelo y Mori, *Don Enrique de Villena: su vida y obras* (Madrid: Sucesores de Rivadeneyra, 1896), p. 55. See also Villena, *Obras completas*, vol. 1, p. xx.

[150] Pérez de Moya, p. 29.

[151] This is according to Richard W. Tyler and Sergio D. Elizondo, *The Characters, Plots, and Settings of Calderón's Comedias* (Lincoln, Nebraska: Society of Spanish and Spanish-American Studies, 1981). Hercules appears in Calderón's *auto sacramental El divino Jasón*, not as the main character, but rather as an explicit proxy for Saint Peter the Apostle.

encyclopaedic accumulation of allegorical meanings attached to him. These meanings include that of negative exemplar, and it should not surprise us that Calderón, the consummate baroque playwright, seized upon the richness of such a character that could be articulated in both tragic and humorously grotesque ways.

Fieras afemina Amor is subtitled *Fiesta que se representó a los siempre felizes años de la Serenísima Cathólica Magestad doña Maria-Anna en El Real Coliseo de Buen Retiro*.[152] It is a *fiesta* in multiple senses. Like most *comedia* performances, *Fieras* harkens back to the Jesuit tradition of the *fiesta literaria* in that it is a comprehensive spectacle consisting not only of the *comedia*, but also of an introductory *loa*, intermediate *entremés* and *sainete*, and a *fin de fiesta* that follows the final act. The *fiesta* is synonymously cele-bratory and its purpose is similar to that which was seen in *Los sitios de recreación del Rey*, the very first example in this entire investigation. Like-wise, the *fiesta* now in question is overall a cheerful event, and that cheerful-ness is not merely indicated by words such as 'felizes años' and the presence of the comic sketches and singing and dancing, but also by the testament of successive performances of *Fieras afemina Amor* that associate this spectacle with a general air of festivity.[153] Yet the centrepiece of the spectacle, the *comedia* itself, is far removed from the burlesque *Céfalo y Pocris*, and though Juan Rana does star in the first *entremés*, he is separate from the main play and cannot be said, at first glance, to have a direct influence on its tone. We are thus left to examine Hércules, the *fiera* of the *comedia*'s title and how he fits into this celebratory and happy atmosphere surrounding the *comedia*.

Borrowing freely from various sources,[154] Calderón retells the story of how Hércules, decrying love, has angered both Cupid and Venus, who seek revenge by making him fall helplessly in love with Yole. Owing to a compli-cated love triangle that leads to the death of her true love – a situation based on well-known legendary characters and stories associated with Hércules – Yole finds herself unhappily promised by her father to the brutish yet some-what domesticated hero. The revenge of both the mortal woman and the gods takes its final form as Yole, with the help of the Hesperides, braids the sleeping Hércules' hair with ribbons, giving the muscleman a ridiculously feminised appearance. The play ends with the hero disgraced, pained and contrite, conceding complete subservience to Love's power. While from this description it may appear that Hércules is only made ridiculous at the end, rarely is he portrayed in a flattering or positively exemplary fashion.

[152] Calderón de la Barca, *Fieras afemina amor*, ed. Edward M. Wilson (Kassel: Reichenberger, 1984).
[153] Ibid., *Fieras*, p. 19.   [154] Ibid., pp. 23–5.

Thomas O'Connor even singles out *Fieras afemina Amor* as a sort of exception that should not obscure an overall vision of the mythological plays:

> Calderón demythologizes Hércules, 'the hero above all other heroes', as Richmond Y. Hathorn characterizes him, in *Fieras afemina Amor*. To stop at this phase, or to concentrate exclusively upon this negative aspect of demythologizing in Calderonian theatre, is to fail to see the forest for the trees.[155]

Yet it is this 'demythologizing' (these distracting 'trees in the forest') that is such an integral part of much of the *teatro breve* and that allows us to make connections between the longer and shorter genres. O'Connor writes that plays such as *Fieras* and *Los tres mayores prodigios* (which we shall look at next) 'problematize our expectations' by 'respecting, though transcending' the genres of *comedia palaciega* and *drama de honor*,[156] the generic categories into which each play respectively falls. Cannot this transcendence be more complex than the mere defeat of expectations? Cannot transcending genres also refer to a play that simultaneously crosses over into different theatrical genres, particularly into those that pride themselves (if one will permit the Bakhtinian personification) on laying low the high-and-mighty? In listing the instances of comic cross-dressing males in Calderonian *comedias*, Ignacio Arellano points out that they are all *graciosos*, with the exception of Hércules in *Fieras afemina Amor*.[157] Does this make the Hércules of *Fieras* ultimately akin to a *gracioso*? Not quite, although the comparison is worthy, and not only in the context of the feminised Hércules at the end of the piece. The Calderonian critic E. M. Wilson wrote about the figure that ought to be, according to the audience's generic expectations, the principal comic figure of the play:

> Licas is the *gracioso*, the anti-hero, the man who shows how fantastically absurd his master's conduct is. He is like most of Calderón's *graciosos*, gluttonous and cowardly, but this is only a very minor feature in his part. His real function in the play is to put forward normal human attitudes as a contrast to his master's inhuman heroics.[158]

On one level this relationship does fulfil the requirements of the standard *criado–amo* pairing that is the stock in trade of the *comedia palaciega*. Yet, while the *gracioso* may be the foil for his master's lovelorn musings or courtship rituals, the typical *amo*'s behaviour is never described by critics as 'fantastically absurd', nor his heroics as 'inhuman'. Wilson is effectively, and practically by definition, calling Hércules a caricature. This distorted and

155 O'Connor, *Myth and Mythology*, p. 27.
156 Ibid., p. 154.   157 Arellano, 'Comicidad escénica', p. 72.
158 Calderón de la Barca, *Fieras*, p. 37.

unflattering profile exists even before he is subjected to a humiliating *burla* by the scheming and mischievous Yole. She is convinced by her friends not to kill Hércules,[159] and in the end cruel jokes prevail over death, providing a finish that is much closer to that of an *entremés* than that of a typical *comedia palaciega*.

While Arellano calls Hércules' appearance comical, and the audience probably would have laughed at a man clad in animal pelts, his hair sprouting beautifully braided, ribbon-filled pigtails, the reaction of the soldiers in the face of their transformed captain is quite different. Some traditions describe the surrounding people laughing at the feminised brute,[160] but in *Fieras*, the soldiers shout '¡Muera!' and they would surely kill him in the name of Queen Yole if not for the intervention of Caliope and the literal *deus ex machina* of Venus and Cupido, who arrive in a splendidly decorated carriage. The violent attack of the soldiers may seem to offset the pathetic position of Hércules by introducing the grave situation of war, but this effect of cancellation would be dependent upon resistance from the hero. Instead, he is powerless, and his position is made even more laughable as his ridiculous appearance leads to complete impotence. The man who so proudly slew the Nemean lion in the first scene of the play, and goes on to slay further monsters and seemingly unstoppable adversaries, stands powerless before a troop of ordinary soldiers.

How can we be certain that Hércules is meant to be a laughingstock when nobody in the play explicitly laughs at him? The reactions of various women[161] to the hero's appearance, whether he is feminised or 'inhumanly'

---

[159] Like Diana in *Celos*, Yole chooses transformation (or costume change) over killing her victim. Pérez de Moya (*Philosofía secreta*, p. 476) explains how this could be a fate worse than death: '. . . y con desimulación trajo a Hércules a amarla en tanto grado que no sólo le hizo desnudar de sus ásperos vestidos y que se vistiese otros muelles y mujeriles, más ponerse sortijas y anillos en los dedos, y untarse con ungüentos preciados, y peinarse, y aun tocarse cofias, y otras cosas de mujeres; y como aun con todas estas cosas no le pareciese haber satisfecho su ira, después de haberle traído a tanta blandura, le hizo que asentado como mujer en el suelo hilase con sus dueñas y contase las patrañas de sus trabajos. Parecióle a esta mujer ser mayor honra haber afeminado a un hombre tan robusto y valiente que haberle muerto con cuchillo o ponzoña.'

[160] In Ovid's *Fasti*, Hercules's feminine attire is combined with Faunus's misguided rape attempt in a scene that ends in festive and innocuous laughter directed towards both humiliated god and hero. See Ovid, *Fasti*, ed. Betty Rose Nagle (Bloomington: Indiana University Press, 1995), Book II, ll. 303–58. See also Sir Philip Sidney, *Defense of Poesie*, in *Complete Works*, vol. 3 (Cambridge: Cambridge University Press, 1962), p. 162, where he writes: 'So in Hercules, painted with his great beard, and furious countenuance, in a womans attyre, spinning, at Omphales commaundement: for the representing of so straugne a power in Love, procures delight, and the scornefulnesse of the action, stirreth laughter.' Omphale here is synonymous with Yole.

[161] Wilson, in his edition (Calderón de la Barca, *Fieras*, p. 45), writes about the audience: 'The Queen Mother probably saw in Yole a compliment to her beauty and perhaps, too, to her skill in political intrigues. Did Hércules remind her and some of the spectators of the second Don John of Austria, her political enemy? If so, there can be no doubt about which camp the royal Chaplain who wrote this play belonged to.'

masculine, offer proof that some people found him quite laughable. When Yole and Hércules first meet in person, her immediate response is to exclaim '¿Quién vio más fiero semblante, / ni más horroroso aspecto?' What follows is a comically ironic exchange among the surrounding observers:

Dama primera	¿Éste es el esposo, Flora, de nuestra ama?
Dama segunda	Sí.
Dama tercera	Por cierto, que él viene galán a vistas.
Licas	No mormuren los pellejos, que venimos de Moscovia.[162]

Licas's attempt to shrug off the *damas'* taunts with another joke only further emphasises the outlandish appearance of him and his master. Though 'de ridículo' is not used in the stage directions, in the context of the play and in the eyes of those women lucky enough *not* to be promised to Hércules, his appearance is good for a laugh. Secondly, when Hércules is asleep and prone to the 'dressing up' to which Yole and her conspirators subject him, the Hesperides crow about how they plan to aggravate his anticipated shame and embarrassment. Verusa will hold up a mirror to him 'allá para que se temple / y aquí para que se ofenda',[163] and Hesperia will taunt him and make him eat his words as she revives the subject of Achilles, the hero Hércules mercilessly berated in his tirades against love. But Egle's words are of particular interest, especially while keeping in mind how criticism is voiced in the *teatro breve*: 'Yo en satíricos baldones / motejaré su soberbia.'[164] Egle does this by singing to the newly awakened Hércules, cutting him off in mid-sentence:

Por Deidamia bella
vistió mujeriles galas,
peinando el cabello a trenzas.[165]

This technique of mockery is not inherent to mythology. It is the same taunting song sung by such women as the sassy serving wench in Quevedo's *La venta*. It is indeed a satire, one that criticises Hércules' *soberbia*. However, it is not in the form of solemn censure, but rather a playful jeer, the type of satire found in the *teatro breve* and the sarcastic verses of Quevedo, not in the dry moralising texts of Spain's clergy.[166] This time, Hércules is being laughed

---

162 Calderón de la Barca, *Fieras*, p. 108.   163 Ibid., p. 207.
164 Ibid., p. 207.   165 Ibid., p. 208.
166 Anthony Close has written extensively about the *mote* tradition in Spain (pp. 189–201), as he explores the effect of increasing religious and societal restraints placed on this technique of eliciting laughter during the decades entering the seventeenth century. What was acceptable as a form of ridicule (flagrant sexual innuendo, for example)

at to his face, and one can only imagine that the audience was encouraged to join in. All these occurrences examined so far could be considered distracting 'trees' in the vast and implicit allegorical 'forest' that Calderón has planted and tended in his mythological dramas. Certainly the 'negative aspect of demythologizing' is not the only one, and O'Connor would say that it is a small aspect at that. Yet in the case of *Fieras afemina Amor*, this aspect takes centrestage, and is itself a complex mechanism that depends on various 'negative' and humorous literary traditions for it to work. These traditions begin with the legendary figure of Hercules himself, exaggerated, larger than life and somehow ambivalent, making him easily adapted for both symbolism and caricature, both allegory and performance of the silliest and most laughable sort.

It was mentioned that the *fiesta* of *Fieras* included a *loa*, intermediate *entremés* and *sainete*, and a *fin de fiesta*. They offer the rare opportunity to compare the *teatro breve* with the *comedia* that accompanied it. Most often the *teatro breve* has nothing to do with the *comedia* in any regard, but the *loa* and the *entremés* (unlike the *sainete* and the *fin de fiesta*) in this case do seem to bear some relation to the bigger piece. The smaller pieces' authorship cannot be definitely ascribed to Calderón, but whoever wrote them seems to have had previous knowledge of the *comedia* in question and wrote with the comprehensive nature of the spectacle in mind.[167] The *loa* is important for many reasons: as a means of getting the audience's attention, as a breach into a fictional and allegorical world, as a means to praise the royal spectators in whose honour the *fiesta* was being held, and finally as a 'preview' of the action to come.[168] In its role as *prólogo*, the *loa* of *Fieras afemina Amor* produces visual clues to prepare the imagination of the audience for interpreting the action of he play. The stage directions note:

> Todo este frontispicio cerraba una cortina, en cuyo primer término, robustamente airoso, se vía Hércules, la clava en la mano, la piel al hombro y a

is later subject to religious censorship, at least as it pertains to a literature set in the courtly sphere. Regardless of these restraints, the *mote* lives on in the *teatro breve*, and can even achieve 'a sort of apotheosis', as Close points out on p. 209 of his book. In *Fieras*, Egle's *motes* are mild in relative terms, perhaps even courtly, and are directed at Hércules' vice of 'soberbia' more than they are directly *ad hominem*, yet they are *motes* nonetheless and cannot hide their affinity with the *teatro breve* and its preservation of a tradition based on humorous insults.

[167] Lobato (Calderón de la Barca, *Teatro cómico breve*, p. 553), whose criteria I mainly follow for authorship, hesitates to attribute the *entremés* (and the other pieces, I suppose) to Calderón because his name does not appear in the title. All the same, she lists five features of the *entremés* that 'defienden la atribución a Calderón'. To these features I add references to an eagle, a phoenix and the months of the year made in both the *loa* and the *entremés*. The calendar theme is also echoed in the *fin de fiesta*. I believe that the same author is responsible for all the pieces of *teatro breve*, with the possible exception of the *sainete*, which is only vaguely connected through the theme of 'lo hermoso y lo discreto' in love.

[168] Flecniakoska, p. 31.

las plantas monstruosas fieras, como despojos de sus ya vencidas luchas; pero no tan vencidas que no volase sobre él, en el segundo término, un Cupido, flechando el dardo, que en el asunto de la fiestas había de ser des-doro de sus triunfos.[169]

We also find the mottoes 'Omnia vincit Amor' and 'Fieras afemina Amor' posted above. It is also significant that after all the pomp and circumstance of the opening and middle of this introductory piece are done, the *loa* ends with a masque accompanied by 'batalla música' that shouts:

> ¡arma, arma, Guerra, guerra!
> pero guerra amorosa,
> que en paces se convierta,
> ¡arma, arma, guerra, guerra![170]

Thus the audience is prepared to watch a symbolic battle that Hércules, regardless of his strength and apparent invincibility, is bound to lose. The audience members would also doubtlessly recall these visual and aural explanations while watching the play, especially when the title of *Fieras afemina Amor* is repeated. The *teatro breve* that supplements the main action need not be funny, but neither should one think that humour must be excluded simply to ensure absolute clarity.

The *Entremés del triunfo de Juan Rana* is equally capable of 'highlighting' the themes of *Fieras* though it is full of parodic foolishness. However, after proving that Hércules was meant to be an absurd and laughable figure in the play, it may appear counterproductive to demonstrate that the *entremés* was a comic foil for Hércules. What comic relief can there be for somebody who is already bound for humiliation? However, by now it should be apparent that comic relief is not a simple process and that Calderón knew this very well. First of all, *El triunfo de Juan Rana* is a parody that fires at many targets, not only at Hércules. When the latter is a target, the technique is not aimed directly at his character, for there are no references to his brutishness, his wild abandon or his pride. These characteristics need no exaggeration, since they are funny by themselves. Instead, the *entremés* parodies Hércules' defeat at the hands of Love. Among all the joking and mugging that occur in *El triunfo de Juan Rana*, one finds a parody of the triumph (in the figurative and literal senses of the word) of Love. Juan Rana as a statue is drawn in a triumphal carriage, and at one moment he comments: 'Puesto yo de Cupidillo / parezco divinamente.'[171] One must remember that this was Juan Rana's last appear-ance. He was in his seventies, quite probably decrepit, and it was probably no accident that he was cast as a statue in this *entremés*. His sexually ambiguous

---

[169] Calderón de la Barca, *Fieras*, p. 58.
[170] Ibid., p. 74.   [171] Ibid., p. 120.

mannerisms[172] and flowery adornments[173] must have contributed somewhat to a cherubic appearance, though the overall effect was undoubtedly grotesque and degrading to Cupid's image. Any degradation of Cupid, Hércules' opponent, can only make the hero's defeat more humiliating. Seeing Hércules vanquished by the 'real' Cupid was funny enough, but imagining the raging masculine hero falling prone before the parodically and perversely 'statuesque' comedian-Cupid was also sure to cause many a chuckle. Though Juan Rana and Hércules never meet face-to-face, the imaginary connections (prompted first by the *loa*) between the themes of the main play and the accompanying *teatro breve* make this conflict (this *joke*) possible. Comic relief in this case is better described as comic accentuation, like rubbing salt in the wounds of disgrace. This articulate use of double-degradation is made possible by Hércules' ambivalent nature: he is a hero at first and a helpless victim in the end. His character's variable nature can correspond to the equally variable register of humour that Calderón could adjust in his plays as he saw fit. Our last example, *Los tres mayores prodigios*, puts our hero to the ultimate test of combining the laughable with the tragic.

Los tres mayores prodigios[174] has been likened to a *drama de honor*. Hércules' quest – with the assistance of Teseo and Jasón – for his kidnapped wife can be seen as Greek myth overlaid with the typically Calderonian theme of a husband's murderous jealousy coupled with a fear of his wife's infidelity.[175] Neso the centaur has stolen away Deyanira, and Hércules is not content with killing only the *raptor*, for he fears his wife did not resist losing her virtue despite her truthful arguments to contrary. Yet while a striking array of parallels can be drawn between this play and one like *El pintor de su deshonra*,[176] there are extremely critical points where these types of comparisons fall flat. Hércules' 'tunic of shame'[177] is indeed representative of the jealous rage that consumes the hero. But if this is so, he dies consumed by his own rage, because it is he himself (donning a shirt) that brings on his own death, something unprecedented in the case of the tragic protagonists of the *dramas de honor*. Even if Hércules had not died, Deyanira (who threw herself

---

172 Frédéric Serralta, 'Juan Rana homosexual', *Criticón*, 50 (1990), 90.

173 Calderón de la Barca, *Fieras*, p. 120.

174 In his edition, Valbuena Briones, in another act of *teatro breve* amputation, has eliminated the introductory *loa* from the *comedia*. I therefore refer the reader to Pedro Calderón de la Barca, *Segunda parte de las comedias*, (Madrid: 1637), a facsimile edition by D. W. Cruickshank and J. E. Varey (London: Tamesis, 1973), fols 248v–282r.

175 A. I. Watson, 'Hercules and the Tunic of Shame: Calderón's *Los tres mayores prodigios*', *Homenaje a William L. Fichter: Estudios sobre el teatro antiguo hispánico y otros ensayos* (Madrid: Castalia, 1971), p. 774.

176 Gwynne Edwards, 'Calderón's *Los tres mayores prodigios* and *El pintor de su deshonra*: The Modernization of Ancient Myth', *Bulletin of Hispanic Studies*, 61 (1984), 326–34.

177 The centaur Neso's poisoned shirt, which she thinks is a love charm, is given as a gift by Deyanira to Hércules. See Calderón de la Barca, *Prodigios*, fol. 280r.

after her husband onto a burning pyre) would have no fear for her life, unlike the murdered heroines of the *dramas de honor*. Though certainly not a happy ending, Deyanira's last days in exile would have been happier than Mencía's (of *El médico de su honra*) last hours, bleeding to death in her bed. While *Prodigios* ends tragically, its finish bears little resemblance to that of the *dramas de honor*. One must also keep in mind that these 'tragic' events 'concluyen con un fin de fiesta trágico-grotesco remedando el arte de la mojiganga'.[178] Aside from the ending, the play is rife with comic moments, prompting Constance Rose to write her article titled 'Was Calderón Serious?: Another Look at *Los tres mayores prodigios*'.[179] Rose reminds us that the play premiered on Saint John's Eve, a festive time very much akin to Carnival in its celebration of frivolity and the freedom to mock others.[180] A. I. Watson wrote in 1971 how this unconventional (performed on three separate stages that unite at the end) *fiesta* had escaped notice among studies of Calderón's mythological dramas: '. . . the principal oversight would appear to be, paradoxically, that *Los tres mayores prodigios* enjoys a certain notoriety as something of a freak'.[181] If *Los tres mayores prodigios* is a *drama de honor*, it is nonetheless freakish, festive, fun-filled and followed by a brief *mojiganga* 'built into' the main text.

Rose's article is very astute, but given the direction of this particular investigation, I would like to offer an alternate explanation to her tentative conclusion about why Calderón might portray Hércules in such a ridiculous fashion. I agree with her signalling of the comic aspects of the play, but we know these aspects are not exclusive to this work. Hércules' threat to commit suicide is indeed unheroic, and while tearing himself apart (almost literally) onstage may be justified by his reputation for wildness, I agree with Rose when she writes, 'Yet, doesn't his reaction really belong to the realm of farcical exaggeration?'[182] This 'farcical exaggeration' corresponds closely to E. M. Wilson's terms 'fantastically absurd conduct' and 'inhuman heroics', which he used in his introduction to *Fieras afemina Amor*. As shown, these characteristics are inherent in the polysemous Hercules figure with which Calderón must have been familiar. For Rose, the origin of Hércules' ridiculous treatment may lie in a Hercules series painted by Zurbarán that may have received unfavourable

178 Regalado, vol. 2, p. 692.

179 Constance H. Rose, 'Was Calderón Serious?: Another Look at *Los tres mayores prodigios*', in *Hispanic Essays in Honor of Frank P. Casa*, ed. Robert A. Lauer and Henry W. Sullivan (New York: Peter Lang, 1997), pp. 246–52.

180 Susana Hernández-Araico, in 'Política imperial en "Los tres mayores prodigios"', in *Homenaje a Hans Flasche*, ed. Karl-Hermann Körner and Günther Zimmermann (Stuttgart: F. Steiner, 1991), p. 92, sees the play as a veiled political satire against the policy of the Conde-Duque Olivares, and 'Tal éxito con sus receptores principales lo consigue a pesar de o quizá debido al mismo sentido crítico-burlesco que concuerda el ánimo carnavalesco de la noche de San Juan.'

181 Watson, p. 774.   182 Rose, p. 248.

critical attention. Though the paintings themselves were not meant to be ridiculous, Rose draws a tenuous link between the Extremaduran painter Zurbarán, who may have rendered Hercules inadequately, and 'Extremaduran peasants, the laughable Lepes who manhandle Hércules'.[183] The critic is referring to the hilarious scene in which Hércules clumsily attempts to interrogate some wily *socarrones rústicos* regarding the whereabouts of Deyanira and Neso. While the Extremaduran Zurbarán–Rústico connection is certainly a possibility, it is not a necessary explanation if one thinks back to the sixteenth-century *entretenimiento* of Hércules-versus-the-Bárbaros, and principally his comic conflict with the gypsy allegorical figures. Rose comes close to calling *Prodigios* a farce,[184] but she neglects to mention one of the important ingredients of farce: stock characters.

I consider Hércules' confrontation with the *rústicos* a very comical moment that depends on very much the same devices as the *entretenimiento* of the *Tragedia de San Hermenegildo*. The *rústicos* may not be gypsies and Calderón's raging jealous Hércules may be a far cry from the Jesuit liberator of Science, but I am not attempting to demonstrate that Calderón copied Fray Hernando de Avila's work, merely that both saw the enormous comic potential in pitting these two character types against each other onstage. This sort of comic confrontation is a well-worn technique of the *teatro breve*. In both the *entretenimiento* and the funny episode on the beach in *Los prodigios*, Hércules is 'manhandled', figuratively wrestled into submission. In the *entretenimiento*, he strides valiantly onto the scene, only to be confronted by the two negative allegories of Love masquerading as the positive ones. Their trickery and cunning use of words thwart Hércules' time-honoured strategy of bashing in his opponents' heads with a club or squeezing them to death. In *Los tres mayores prodigios*, in the third act, Hércules makes his first appearance,[185] landing on the island of Oeta and frightening the local villagers by his mere arrival. He manages to coax them forward, indicating that he does not intend to kill them off, only to ask them some questions. Narcisa, one of the *villanos*, responds:

> Pregunte lo que quisiere,
> que a todo responderemos,
> lo que sabemos, es poco;
> pero aun lo que no sabemos.[186]

This seemingly humble response is also a warning about the investigative wild goose chase that will soon follow. The phrase 'Pregunte lo que quisiere, / que

---

[183] Rose, p. 252.   [184] Ibid., p. 247.

[185] Because the first and second acts are respectively dedicated to Jasón and Teseo, we have not seen Hércules since the introductory *loa*.

[186] Calderón de la Barca, *Prodigios*, fol. 272v.

a todo responderemos' can also be seen as a veiled invitation to play a game of which, unfortunately for him, Hércules is not aware. The playful nature of the dialogue is immediately apparent when Anfriso states that Narcisa (she of 'lo que sabemos, es poco') can help Hércules in his quest for the kidnapper Neso, admitting that he heard from her some news '. . . y aun no es poco le prometo'.[187] Thus Hércules must ask Narcisa again. Now, if only she were not made nervous by the hero's appearance, she might be able to speak. When she gets her bearings, she tells of seeing Neso carrying Deyanira through the forested foothills. But before she could see where they went, she fainted, thus interrupting the narrative and leaving Hércules on the edge of this seat. Luckily, another peasant, Danteo, saw more, and the story is handed off to him. To no surprise, he only knows a portion of the story and thus hands it off to Laura, and so on. All this time, Hércules, who came to bash heads or shoot Neso full of arrows, and deal (in a way that is not yet clear) with his possibly unfaithful wife, is fretting more than ever. Each piece of news causes his jealous rage to increase, causing the *villanos* to stall even more because they fear they shall anger him further, thus delaying the process, thus causing greater anger, etc. As Constance Rose astutely observes, the hero's laughable impotence,[188] combined with his fuming anger (he says Mount Vesuvius is no match for the fire bursting from within him[189]) and sad dependence on the manipulative yokels, must have indeed been a funny scene. The *villanos* of *Prodigios* actually resemble more closely the 'Bárbaros' of the *entretenimiento* (instead of the tricky gypsies), who, with their mix of idiocy and ingenuity, and their deformed speech, are little more than *villanos* in animal skins. Just as the clever barbarian in the Jesuit piece manages to bop Amor de Sciencia and Amor de Honor on the head without immediate recrimination from the watchful Hércules, the *villanos* of *Prodigios*, who appear idiotic, get to play their cruel joke until the thoroughly enraged hero chases them offstage, just as he did to the 'Bárbaros' in the *entretenimiento*. Anfriso of *Prodigios* even calls the frightening muscle-bound visitor 'Señor Miércoles',[190] imitating the same (supposedly unwitting) mocking malapropism employed by the 'Bárbaros' in the piece written fifty years beforehand. However, unlike the allegorical savages who must all be killed off to make a point of Virtue's victory over Ignorance, the *villanos* of *Prodigios* get the last laugh, and it is Hércules who is killed off in the end.

The ending of *Los tres mayores prodigios* is very unusual, not only because the jealous husband and accused wife throw themselves onto a fire, but because of the reactions of the witnesses in the face of such a horrific sight. Also unusual is the silence from critics about what relevance the final comic

---

[187] Calderón de la Barca, *Prodigios*, fol. 273v.
[188] Hernández Araico, p. 91; Rose, p. 250.
[189] Calderón de la Barca, *Prodigios*, fol. 274r.
[190] Ibid., fol. 273r.

conversation of the play may have.[191] In order to imagine the scene, one must first imagine Deyanira and Hércules immolating themselves on the enormous bonfire that was meant for offering a sacrifice to Jupiter. The sight, sound and smell of their live burning flesh must have been more horrific than any murder witnessed by characters at the end of any *drama de honor*. Yet one must also notice the conversation that follows between the gawking *villanos*, including the chief *graciosos* – Sabañón, Pantuflo and Clarín – from each act, and the main *graciosa*, Narcisa:

Pantuflo	Lindo par de chicharrones para mi hambre se asan.
Sabañón	Lindas gallinas se queman.
Clarín	Qué aguardas Narcisa, para echarte al fuego.
Narcisa	Que tú te eches antes.
Los tres	Bien aguardas.[192]

Jasón then calls the finale *trágico*, and the play closes with the other serious characters announcing the end of the performance and begging forgiveness for faults in the production. But this 'tragedy', as I have insisted before, is quite different from others because of its ending. In *El médico de su honra*, the *gracioso* Coquín – who enjoys his own 'trágico-grotesco' role – is finally made to conform to a role as a messenger of tragic news. The circumstances at the end of the play overwhelm his jollity and the tone is one of uniform sobriety unquestioned by the only character that has the ability to inject levity. Regalado does well to call the end of *Los tres mayores prodigios* a 'fin de fiesta trágico-grotesco'. It is something akin to the *mojiganga* that finishes the *zarzuela El golfo de las sirenas*, being textually integrated with the main play, sharing characters and setting.[193] It cannot be merely accidental that Calderón includes a *gracioso* from each act in what we may call the 'mini-*mojiganga*' at the end of *Prodigios*. Three figures, along with Narcisa, that represent the comic spirit throughout the entire play, join forces to 'gang up' on the flame-broiled hero in much the same manner that the rustics (Clarín and Narcisa included) 'manhandled' the impotent hero when he first came ashore. Calderón brings back the previous scene in a different guise but with the same

---

191 Until now, I have found no comments by Greer, Hernández Araico or Watson concerning this question. Regarding the ending, Rose and Regalado mention how it occurs, but they offer no explanation as to its bizarre mix of death and joking.

192 Calderón de la Barca, *Prodigios*, fol. 282r.

193 Aside from its much greater length, the *mojiganga* from *Golfo* is different because of its 'unmasking' function, where the island of Trinacria is transformed back into the Zarzuela during the *fin de fiesta*. In *Prodigios*, the integrity of the fictional universe is maintained.

effect. The rustics staring at the bonfire play a childish game of daring each other, much as each villager passed the job of teasing Hércules off to the next person, until Clarín was left 'holding the bag' and was forced to truly assist the livid hero. This time, characters from previous acts of the play join in the fun, and it is as if all the ribbing and humiliating power that the play has to muster were focused in concentrated fashion upon Hércules, who lies burning to a crisp. This is similar to the 'comic accentuation' performed by the *loa* (something not inherently funny, yet able to establish symbols used for parody later) and the *entremés* of the *fiesta Fieras afemina Amor*, only this time there is no need to track a chain of associations among the images and parodies found in those pieces of *teatro breve*. It is 'accentuation' because at the end of both plays Hércules is being figuratively kicked when he is down. In both plays he suffers humiliation, though it comes from different forms of *teatro breve* in each play, each form adding insult to injury in its own way. The humiliation that Hércules suffers does not negate any notion of *fiesta* witnessed so far. *Los tres mayores prodigios* does end in a somewhat carnivalesque fashion. However, at the same time, the 'mini-*mojiganga*' parodies, *avant la lettre*, Bakhtin's sanguine point of view. Hércules and Deyanira are converted into 'chicharrones asados' and 'gallinas quemadas', but these barbecued items hardly represent the affirmation of a continuous cycle of regeneration and rebirth. Cannibalistic overtones do not square well with a positive view of food. The only things that the burning deaths generate are mourning on the part of the more noble characters, and glee on the part of the general populace of the play. Laughing at death, a common occurrence in the *mojiganga*, produces both humorous and macabre results when combined with the full dramatic force of the *comedia*.

4

CALDERÓN AND THE *ENTREMÉS* WITHIN THE *COMEDIA*

THE *GRACIOSO*

The history of the *gracioso* has been much studied and often debated. There is no question that this nearly indispensable stock figure is born from a number of definite literary precedents, yet how much influence each precedent exerts has always been a point of contention.[1] The issues of origins are likely never to be settled because, despite being a stock type, the *gracioso* figure

---

[1] María Azucena Penas Ibáñez, *Análisis lingüístico-semántico del lenguaje del 'Gracioso' en algunas comedias de Lope de Vega* (Madrid: Universidad Autónoma, 1992), p. 23, writes that the slave character of Greek comedy, or the 'pastor bobo' of Renaissance theatre, or the 'lacayo "real"' sidekick character are all possible sources. She also mentions the *pícaro*, a connection that Juan Portera examines in detail in 'El gracioso pícaro en Calderón', in *La picaresca: orígenes, textos y estructuras, Actas del I Congreso Internacional sobre la Picaresca organizado por el Patronato 'Arcipreste de Hita'*, ed. Manuel Criado de Val (Madrid: Fundación Universitaria Española, 1979), pp. 841–7. See also Alfredo Hermenegildo, 'El gracioso y la mutación del rol dramático: "Un bobo hace ciento"', in *Diálogos Hispánicos de Amsterdam 8*, vol. 2, ed. Javier Huerta Calvo, Harm den Boer and Fermín Sierra Martínez (Atlanta: Rodopi, 1989). Hermenegildo follows the ideas of Bakhtin and writes on p. 509: 'El bobo de la fiesta popular, reducido en el espacio y el tiempo del carnaval – primera y definitiva recuperación oficial de la locura colectiva – a las constantes definidas por Bajtín, se manifiesta de modo cómico y jocoso a través del rol [gracioso] del teatro clásico español, como signo de oposición dialéctica al espacio dramático serio y oficial.' Lewis Riccoboni, in his *An Historical Account of the Theatres in Europe viz. The Italian, Spanish, French, English, Dutch, Flemish, and German Theatres* (London: 1741), writes on p. 105: 'The *Spanish* Farces are more upon the *Italian* Taste than those of any other Nation. He that acts the principal Part is called *Gracioso*, and very much resembles the Dress and Character of our Harlequin. It is true that the *Gracioso* is not very lucky in the Subjects of his Witticisms, for on every Occasion he swears by the Saints, of which the Poet affects to chuse the most unusual Names, in order to make his Wit more comical, if it can be called Wit.' Along with establishing the *comedia nueva*, Lope de Vega is credited with giving definite form to the *gracioso* figure, principally the famous 'bobo aldeano lopesco'. Apparently more than one critic has attributed economic causes to the rise in popularity of this figure, because Maxime Chevalier, *Tipos cómicos y folklore*, p. 126, found it necessary to answer them by stating that the character's origins were to be found in the oral tradition more than anywhere else. The 'historical reality' of the *gracioso* as a profession is met with different points of view in Díez Borque (see the conclusion to *Sociología*) and in Close (p. 258).

demonstrates amazing flexibility and variation in behaviour, and boasts a freedom of action and attitude that far exceeds any found in the other standard characters within the *comedia* genre.[2] Nevertheless, critics still ascribe various attributes to the type. The *gracioso*'s literary antecedent, the *simple* (in turn related to the *pastor bobo*[3]) is simple-minded, materialistic, a glutton and a coward. The *gracioso* is invariably considered to share these attributes. However, when one considers influences outside the Spanish Renaissance *farsas* and *pasos*, one can see that earthiness is far from a restricting character trait. The more general *bobo de entremés* (who may or may not be a *pastor*) has been compared to the *servus* and the parasite of Roman comedy.[4] The clever lackey of Italo-classical plays, different in some ways from the Roman type, was also undoubtedly an influence. Naturally, the *commedia dell'arte*, with its *zanni* and their *lazzi*, must have also had an impact on the development of this Spanish theatrical figure.

One must also take into account the various traditions of fools that are so commonly associated with the *gracioso*. We may think of the trickster of Carnival time, the fool as the representative embodiment of materialist indulgence in the 'lower stratum' as described by Bakhtin. But the fool is also a permanent figure at court, and his jokes, antics and occasional jabs at the powerful can often be compared to the cracks made by the *comedia* character-type.[5] The immunity shared by both Carnival and court fools must bear some relation to the freedom of expression granted to the *gracioso*, which includes berating the *amo* and constantly rupturing the dramatic illusion in order to speak directly to the audience.[6] This rapport with the viewing public that the *gracioso* enjoys can be likened to the extra-textual commentaries made by the *prólogos* and *introitos* of old, which brings us back to both Roman Comedy and the later *pastor-bobo* figure of religious plays.[7] The *gracioso* is also a vast storehouse of *refranes* and anecdotes, often ready with a clever turn of phrase

---

[2] See Hans Flasche, 'Perspectivas de la locura en los graciosos de Calderón: *La aurora en Copacabana*', *Nueva Revista de Filología Hispánica*, 34 (1985–6), 631. He writes: 'Es por lo tanto absolutamente necesario acentuar que la figura del gracioso no es reducible a un esquema del todo simple. El gracioso ofrece aspectos muy diversos en cada autor y hasta en cada pieza de un mismo autor.' See also Georges Güntert, 'El gracioso en Calderón: disparate e ingenio', *Cuadernos hispanoamericanos*, 324 (1977), 442. Güntert claims that the complexity of the *gracioso*'s traits make him the epitome of Baroque style, and the critic cites Kellenberger, who called these characters 'chameleon-like'.

[3] John Brotherton, *The 'Pastor-Bobo' in the Spanish Theatre Before the Time of Lope de Vega* (London: Tamesis, 1975), pp. 197–8.

[4] Asensio, *Itinerario*, p. 37.

[5] Enid Wellsford, in her indispensable book *The Fool: His Social and Literary History* (New York: Farrar & Rinehart, 1935), p. 279, writes of *Pensamiento*, a *gracioso*-type in *Auto sacramental de la cena del Rey Baltazar*: '. . . the Gracioso is not merely representative of Thought in general, he is Belshazzar's court-jester in particular and as such symbolizes the fickleness and frivolity of the pagan king . . .'

[6] Arellano, 'Comicidad escénica', p. 87.   [7] Flecniakoska, p. 33.

or appropriate story used as the basis of wry commentaries about the action of the play. Likewise, when the playwright needs a mouthpiece for satire, it is often the *gracioso* that speaks harsh words with acerbic wit. The *gracioso* can also be seen as a walking parody, with every action and word a foil for the noble behaviour of the *damas y galanes de comedia*. Regarding the function of the *comedia*'s plot, the *gracioso* is most often a lackey, a go-between, free to move about without inviting too many questions, whereas a noble's constant visits would cause suspicion. In conclusion, this comic stock figure may pay tribute to any, all, or some of the above predecessors, and each borrowed characteristic may vary in its importance and emphasis.

Amar después de la muerte[8] is a *comedia histórica* that recounts the Alpujarra uprising of 1570. A community of *moriscos* living near Granada receive an edict by Felipe II stating that mere baptism of the *moriscos* is not enough and that they must abandon all of their Moorish customs. In the play, this cultural conflict is couched in terms of offended honour, and the *moriscos*, led by Don Álvaro Tuzaní, must fight against the soldiers who have been sent to enforce the king's wishes. One critic sees Calderón's noble treatment of the *moriscos* and his less-than-flattering portrayal of some of the Christian soldiers,[9] especially the rather picaresque soldier Garcés, as evidence that *Amar después de la muerte* is 'un drama subversivo'.[10] This claim to subversiveness must be taken with a grain of salt, as there are many currents at work here, not just the possibility that Calderón wished to oppose 'la política oficial'. Historians and literary scholars have noted that after the official expulsion of the *moriscos* in 1609, Spain experienced a resurgence of 'maurophilia', a romanticised image of the Moors, not as a centuries-old mortal enemy, but as an exotic and noble part of Spain's history. Even before the expulsion, this image existed. The most famous example is that of *El Abencerraje*,[11] which tells of the friendship, forged from a mutual understanding of the trials of love, between a Moorish nobleman and a Christian knight.

[8] Calderón de la Barca, *Obras*, vol. 2, pp. 349–86. The play, also titled *El Tuzaní de la Alpujarra*, is dated 1633 (p. 248) by Valbuena Briones.

[9] The *moriscos*, because they have been baptised, are technically Christian as well, but the *moro–cristiano* distinction still exists in the play, and even the hero Don Álvaro calls his opponents 'cristianos' (Calderón de la Barca, *Obras*, vol. 2, p. 378).

[10] 'Calderón ha manifestado su oposición a la política oficial, a las tendencias y usos sociales de su época y a una concepción racista de la sociedad de su tiempo. Y ha defendido la dignidad caballeresca y genealógica de los moriscos bautizados, la necesidad de su integración sin reservas y lo absurdo de unas marginaciones que no tenían el menor sentido. Este es el verdadero tema, en mi opinión, de *El Tuzaní del Alpujarra*. De nuevo un drama subversivo.' See José Miguel Caso González, 'Calderón y los moriscos de las Alpujarras', in *Calderón*, ed. Luciano García Lorenzo, p. 402.

[11] *El Abencerraje*, ed. Claudio Guillén (New York: Dell, 1966). Guillén's introduction gives a brief sketch of the chivalrous Moor, and the popularity of the type in the seventeenth century.

Amid the noble posturing, dramatic intrigue, harrowing action and sweeping scope of *comedias históricas* stands the comic contrast of the *gracioso*, and in *Amar después de la muerte* Alcuzcuz performs this contrasting function. In many ways he is the typical *gracioso*, particularly in a dramatic functional capacity. In the first place, he brings levity to what is essentially a play based on a bloody civil war. One critic has even charted Alcuzcuz's comic interventions to see exactly how his injections of levity operate chronologically and contextually to alleviate dramatic tension, as seen on a surface-level of analysis.[12] As a lackey, Alcuzcuz is also a go-between, who functions as both a messenger and amateur *alcahuete*. Like most *graciosos*, he is a coward, but he is also granted a certain level of immunity from violence. Amid all the cannon fire and crossed swords he functions as a comical figure of invulnerability who alleviates somewhat the horrors of war.[13] Fourthly, Alcuzcuz is also a prankster, full of surprises, who adds a certain element of chaos and unpredictability that, because it is humorous, adds an alternative excitement to the sort brought on by violent conflict. His typical function as an unruly helper relates nicely to that of his noble master Don Álvaro Tuzaní. Alcuzcuz is a lackey foil to the *morisco galán*, who in turn is similar in many ways to the heroes of Calderón's *comedias de capa y espada*. As can be assumed by now, Alcuzcuz is a materialistic coward, as are nearly all *graciosos*.

Yet Alcuzcuz, by virtue of being a *morisco*, is anything but a typical *gracioso*. Calderón is undoubtedly indebted to Lope's *moriscos graciosos* and Alcuzcuz bears the stamp of his predecessors, who themselves stood apart from their Christian comic brethren.[14] As we go deeper in our analysis, we

---

[12] José Alcalá Zamora, 'Individuo e historia en la estructura teatral de "El Tuzaní de Alpujarra"', *Calderón*, pp. 343–63. Among the many charts and graphs appended to his article, there is one akin to a cardiogram that shows 'peaks', 'valleys' and 'plateaus' (all my terms) of dramatic tension. The 'valleys' are most often caused by Alcuzcuz's presence. While the charts help visualise the critic's arguments, they create the illusion (an illusion corresponding to an absolute impossibility) of real 'data' taken from a hundred polygraphs hooked up to a real-live Golden Age audience. In reality, the 'data' comes from one person, single-handedly inventing 'grados de intensidad dramática' (on the critic's scale of 0 to 3) where Alcuzcuz scores a '.5' or '.6' regardless. The poor *gracioso* is made to seem as nothing more than a nearly abstract force antithetical to dramatic tension, a sad simplification of his role in the play.

[13] Calderón has many times put his *graciosos* in the crossfire of armed combat, the most notable example being Clarín of *La vida es sueño*, who actually dies from the shots he was sheepishly and comically trying to avoid.

[14] Thomas E. Case, 'El morisco gracioso en el teatro de Lope', in *Lope de Vega y los orígenes del teatro español: actas del I Congreso Internacional sobre Lope de Vega*, ed. Manuel Criado de Val (Madrid: Edi-6, 1981), p. 790. He writes that the typical *gracioso* is a 'cristiano viejo'. I do not know how well this claim is supported, for I would suggest that much less than half of the stage-*graciosos* actually reveal their ethno-religious identity. At the same time, based on their relation to the *aldeano* type, and the anti-Semitic and anti-Muslim jokes that *graciosos* often utter, Case seems to have some support for his statement.

shall see how Alcuzcuz is not entirely typical of the atypical, as well as discover how Calderón pushes this figure's personality and purpose further than Lope could ever have imagined.[15] I believe that many of Calderón's innovations display a profound understanding of the stereotype of the *moro* (our *gracioso*, though *morisco*, is virtually indistinguishable), a stereotype that was, if not born from, heavily cultivated in the *teatro breve*.

Like many *teatro breve* characters, Alcuzcuz can get laughs just by opening his mouth.[16] He is part of the tradition of dialect-comedy, which stretches from ancient Greek mimes and players in Plautus all the way to vaudeville, and even to today's television advertising.[17] His 'deformed' speech has been the subject of linguistic analysis[18] and must have been related somewhat to the way actual Moors spoke Spanish. However, the audience of the time was surely not concerned with authenticity. More than anything, they must have paid attention to the 'ugliness' of his speech,[19] finding great satisfaction in laughing at Alcuzcuz's difficulty in expressing himself in Castilian. Along with blacks, Portuguese, French, 'tudescos' (Germans), gypsies and others, the *moro* in the *teatro breve* is often funny, if only because of his means of expression and style of dress. In the burlesque *Mojiganga de la Renegada de Valladolid*[20] – a piece not so much about

---

[15] This is no mean feat considering Lope's own imagination. See Israel Burshatin, 'Playing the Moor: Parody and Performance in Lope de Vega's *El primer Fajardo*', *PMLA*, 103 (1992), 566–81. Burshatin sees Zulemilla, a *gracioso morisco*, who not only abandons but mocks his masters, as a key agent in a parody of maurophilic ideas. On p. 578, he concludes: 'Parody in *El primer Fajardo* discloses a complex attitude to the discourse of orientalism and implies an ambiguous position with regard to Moriscos and their proper place – if any at all – in Spanish society.' I find it debatable that Lope thought in terms of 'orientalism' as we do today, following Said's ideas *avante la lettre*. One does not need a mocking *gracioso* to 'disclose a complex attitude', for *moriscos* were surely still to be found in the days of writing this play (as merchants or agricultural workers), and this should have been enough in itself to remind people that not every *morisco* was a noble prince in the *Abencerraje* mold.

[16] If he dressed in a costume like Juan Rana in *Sitios*, was prone to comic gesticulation and mugging, and played by a comic actor of Juan Rana's calibre, Alcuzcuz may have even gotten laughs before opening his mouth.

[17] Probably every genre of comedy and farce has some form of dialect comedy. In recent years, I have noticed that in television advertisements, the character of the stern Japanese businessman, sometimes speaking Japanese, and when speaking English always with a strong accent, has become a choice comic figure.

[18] Luis Antonio Sánchez Domínguez, 'El lenguaje teatral del morisco', *Boletín de la Biblioteca Menéndez Pelayo*, 63 (1987), 5–16. See also Ángel Valbuena Briones, 'Los papeles cómicos y las hablas dialectales en dos comedias de Calderón', *Thesaurus: Boletín del Instituto Caro y Cuervo*, 42 (1987), 47–59.

[19] This relates to *El Pinciano*'s neo-Aristotelian notion of *deformitas* and *turpitudo*, known in his writings as simply 'lo torpe'. Valbuena Briones comments upon this relation to *El Pinciano* in 'Hablas dialectales', p. 55.

[20] Diego Granados y Mosquera, *Mojiganga cantada de la renegada de Valladolid*, in *Verdores del Parnaso*, ed. Rafael Benítez Claros (Madrid: CSIC, 1969), pp. 133–49 (modern pagination). For a burlesque extravaganza, treating the same theme, see Frédéric Serralta, '*Une tradition littéraire: La renegada de Valladolid (Etude et édition critique de*

Moors as one might expect – a group of characters strip off their costumes to reveal new ones, some changing into Moors, some into gypsies, and others into Portuguese pilgrims, all changing their dialects to match their new costumes. In an *entremés* such as *Las naciones*,[21] the language of the *moro* – mainly characterised by its use of infinitives instead of conjugated verbs, along with the transposition of certain letters – becomes just one of many speaking styles. In an *entremés* called *El gabacho*, attributed to Tirso de Molina,[22] a rather perturbed *gracioso*[23] is accosted by a series of foreigners, including 'uno de moro':

Moro   ¿Que querer bosance?
        ¿De que se admira?
        Hortelano estar, sonior,
        desta horta e desta casa,
        y ser, aunque velde assi,
        cenerrage de Granada.
        ¿Querer una ensaladica?
        Que me hazelda tan bezarra,
        que a saber sonior Mahoma,
        comemos de bona gana.
        Echar perregil, mastorzo,
        merdabona, merdolagas,
        caparretas, caporrones,
        zucar, lechuzas, borrachas.[24]

la comedia burlesque de Monteser, Solís et Silva)' (Thèse pour le Doctorat de Troisième Cycle soutenue devant la Faculté des Lettres et Sciences Humaines de Toulouse, Juin 1968). Serralta, most likely the leading expert on *comedias burlescas*, offers an outstanding study to accompany the text of the play. Along with careful explanations, it features a well-deserved vindication of the absurd and the *disparate* in the theatre of the Golden Age.

[21] Found in *Arcadia de entremeses* (Pamplona: Juan Micón, 1691). See María E. Castro de Moux, *La casa de los linajes: oficios y gentes marginados en el entremés barroco español* (New Orleans: University Press of the South, 1997), pp. 69–73, for commentary on this piece.

[22] *Entremeses del siglo XVII*, ed. el Bachiller Mantuano (Madrid: Biblioteca 'Ateneo', 1909), pp. 44–59. Castro de Moux, p. 65, cites *Entremeses nuevos de diversos autores* (Zaragoza: Pedro Lanaja, Impresor del Reyno de Aragon, y de la Universidad, 1640), where no author is mentioned. One must refer to the introduction to Bachiller Mantuano's book in order to see why Tirso is a possible author. In *Entremeses nuevos*, the particular *entremés* is titled *El Gavacho y las lenguas, ò las lenguas*.

[23] Within the sub-genres of the *teatro breve*, the term *gracioso* is ambiguous, but usually indicates the central character, who is funny for different possible reasons. He may be the butt of jokes, like an old-fashioned *bobo* (as we saw in *El dragoncillo*) or he may be the opposite, a trickster and master of his surroundings.

[24] *El gabacho*, in *Entremeses del siglo XVII*, p. 55. This ridiculous stereotype seems to have some basis in historical fact. See Antonio Domínguez Ortiz and Bernard Vincent, *Historia de los moriscos: vida y tragedia de una minoría* (Madrid: Biblioteca *Revista de Occidente*, 1978), pp. 110–12. 'Un cronista de Plasencia los describía trabajando en el cultivo de las huertas, apartados del trato de los cristianos. Otros tenían que relacionarse

In his *comedias*, Calderón would adjust his *graciosos* to fit into the historical or cultural context of the play. A play with Moors or *moriscos* as protagonists demands a corresponding *gracioso*. Yet neither Calderón nor his predecessor Lope pulled the comic *moro* type out of thin air. The character had been a recognisable figure in the *entremés* for a long time, and there existed undoubtedly many models for Alcuzcuz. At the same time, the above examples show variations in the character that would increase in number over the years as the *moro* was appropriated again and again, accompanied by a constant quest for novelty.

Let us return to the first scene of *Amar después de la muerte*. As the play opens, the sombre Moorish conspirators of the Alpujarra join together in singing and praising the old ways. Subsequently, Alcuzcuz breaks in with a musical interruption.

Cantan	'Aunque en triste cautiverio,
	de Alá, por justo misterio,
	llore el africano imperio
	su mísera suerte esquiva . . .'
Todos [*Cantando*]	¡Su ley viva!
Uno	Viva la memoria extraña
	de aquella gloriosa hazaña
	que en la libertad de España
	a España tuvo cautiva.
Todos	¡Su ley viva!
Alcuzcuz [*Cantando*]	Viva aquel escaramuza
	que hacelde Terife Muza
	cuando dalde caperuza
	al españolilio altiva.[25]

Alcuzcuz's burlesque could be considered merely the natural everyday behaviour of clowning *graciosos* from all *comedias* by all authors, or his singing could be the result of Calderón poking fun at his own fondness for musical theatre, a fondness that was to reach its logical conclusion in the lavish *fiestas palaciegas* thirty years later. But if we add what we know about

con ellos, pues tenían las mejores tiendas de comestibles; o bien se dedicaban a la trajinería y llevaban mercancías de unos puntos a otros . . . El morisco hortelano se convirtió en un tópico. No es que faltara entre ellos el agricultor de secano; pero era en el regadío donde desplegaban todas sus facultades de paciencia, destreza y laborosidad.'

[25] Calderón de la Barca, *Obras*, vol. 2, p. 351. I have yet to precisely identify 'Terife Muza'. The name may be difficult to trace because of Alcuzcuz's constant mispronunciations. One possibility is that it is a conflation of two names belonging to figures of the Moorish conquest. One is Tarif ibn Malik al-Muafari (a conqueror who gave Tarifa its name) and the other is Musa ibn Nusair (a famous North African general and Tarif's commander).

the development of the *moro* stock figure in the *teatro breve* together with Alcuzcuz's implied stage directions, his antics take on a different meaning for us, and probably for the audience of the time. Just before the singing, Alcuzcuz utters these words: 'Me pensar jacer astillas, / sé también entrar en danza.' The cue for his statement is Cadí's mention of 'ceremonias', prompting the *gracioso* to prepare a festive contrast. While this exact festive behaviour is not often attributed to the *gracioso* character-type, it is certainly part of the *moro* as he appears in the *teatro breve*. Yet one must be careful to note that this musical and choreographed cartoonish portrayal of Alcuzcuz, very much in line with the *teatro breve* tradition, only appears once in the play. This is no accident. Nor is it an accident that his pure clowning appears at the beginning. Like the *moro entremesil* over time, this *moro gracioso* demonstrates variety throughout the play. The extreme caricature that is the audience's vision of Alcuzcuz becomes more complex, though no less funny and no less *entremesil*, as his inevitable integration into the play continues. With each of his interruptions, we see a new comic side of somebody who started out as little more than a dancing Moorish puppet.

Calderón did not invent any entirely new jokes for his *morisco gracioso*, but he gave old jokes a new twist whenever possible, nearly always revealing the nature of his handiwork in combining the *gracioso* with a blatant *teatro breve* tradition. In the first act, the *moriscos* must pool all their resources in order to survive the onslaught that is to come if they resist the royal decree. Shouts of support are followed by one lady's offer of all her jewels and valuables for the cause. Alcuzcuz chimes in with his support:

> Alcuzcuz Me, que sólo tener
> una tendecilla en Bevarrambla
> de aceite, vinagre e higos,
> nueces, almendras e pasas,
> cebollas, ajos pimentos,
> cintas, escobas de palma,
> hilo, agujas, faldrequeras
> [. . .]
> Uno   Calla,
> que estás loco.[26]

Alcuzcuz's list of wares closely resembles that of the *moro* in the *Entremés del gabacho* cited earlier, and in the context of the *teatro breve*, such a list is standard fare. But now the character finds himself inside a *comedia*, and he must deal with a sombre adversary who does not appreciate the joke. While most *graciosos* would either shut their mouths or take a different joking tack after the accusation of 'locura', the impudent Alcuzcuz instead snaps back

---

[26] Calderón de la Barca, *Obras*, vol. 2, p. 353.

that he is not crazy. His verbal adversary shoots back, 'Si no loco, es cosa clara / que estás borracho',[27] taking a cheap shot at any *gracioso*'s weakness for booze.[28] But Alcuzcuz gets the last laugh (at least in this act) as he plays his *gracioso morisco* trump card, namely that, '. . . jonior Mahoma manda / en su alacrán no beber / vino, y en mi vida nada lo he bebido . . .'[29] Though a funny retort, it does bear with it a certain element of gravity from the Islamic tradition upon which it relies. It is this tension between submission to 'caricaturisation' and a shared solemnity with his noble *morisco* masters that will mark Alcuzcuz's personality throughout the play. He is more than a mere comic foil.

The second time we encounter Alcuzcuz, he is firmly entrenched in the workings of the plot. As a spy, he has been caught by the noble officer Don Juan de Mendoza, his unlikable subordinate Garcés, and none other than Don Juan de Austria. In a scene repeated in *comedias* thousands of times, the *gracioso* must get himself out of a scrape (normally being caught in a garden at night, caught stealing food, caught disguised as somebody else, etc. etc . . .) by use of his wits alone. Again, he plays the *morisco* card:

D. Juan   ¿Quién sois?

Alcuzcuz   (Aquí importar el cautela.) [*Alto*]
            Alcuzcuz, un morisquillo,
            a quien llevaron por fuerza
            al Alpujarro; que me ser
            crestiano en me conciencia,
            saber la trina cristiana,
            el Credo, la Salve Reina,
            el Pan Nostro, y el catorce
            Mandamientos de la Iglesia.[30]

This scene harkens back to plays in existence long before either Calderón or even Lope were born, those of Sánchez de Badajoz with their obstinate Moor who finally sees the light and converts to Christianity.[31] But in the firmly established *comedia nueva*, the heightened cynicism of the *gracioso* lends itself easily to a parody of the reconciled theatrical *converso*. Even at the end of *Amar después de la muerte*, it is not clear whether Alcuzcuz converts entirely or not, an ambiguity that today may surprise many readers of Calderón. The success of Alcuzcuz's trick is important for the plot, but it is equally important

---

[27] Calderón de la Barca, *Obras*, vol. 2, p. 353.
[28] A similar exchange occurs in Calderón's *El maestro de danzar*, *Obras*, vol. 2, p. 1559.
[29] Calderón de la Barca, *Obras*, vol. 2, p. 353.
[30] Ibid., vol. 2, p. 364.
[31] Jesús García-Varela, 'Para una ideología de la exclusión: El discurso del "moro" en Sánchez de Badajoz', *Criticón*, 66–67 (1996), 176.

comically because it makes the highest of Spanish nobility look like dupes. The *morisco*'s *burla*, so typical of the *entremés* – a universe so rife with caricatures and comic logic that pretending to be somebody entirely different involves little more than changing one's accent and throwing on some silly clothing[32] – is something any idiot could see through, yet his captors are ready to give him the benefit of the doubt. Don Juan de Austria, the standard for military Christian authority, stands before Alcuzcuz scratching his head, thinking: 'Como presumo que miente, / ya bien puede ser que sea verdad.'[33] At this moment, the audience is intended to be on Alcuzcuz's side, which consequently means the audience was meant to laugh at the Christian nobles just as much, if not more, than the *morisco*'s malapropisms.

Calderón exploits further the *moro gracioso*'s difficulty with Castilian in the third act, providing a situation that is at once comical and poignant. Alcuzcuz is behind enemy lines, hiding from the opposing soldiers, when suddenly his master Don Álvaro appears. He has come seeking vengeance against those who brutally killed his wife Doña Clara in the attack on the town of Galera. When Don Álvaro meets with his lackey, he confides: 'Hoy, Alcuzcuz, solo a ti / Quiero en la empresa que sigo / Por compañero y amigo.'[34] He treats his servant as an equal while enlisting him in the grave task of a revenge killing. However, Don Álvaro is not initially clear about his intent, and the suspicious Alcuzcuz has difficulty accepting his master's proposition to join him, despite the unusual respect that has been granted to the servant. What may seem like a traditional scenario, portraying a *gracioso*'s conflict of loyalty between his master and his own welfare, must be looked at more carefully. It thus becomes apparent that it is a discussion about theatrical convention itself, pertaining especially to the *moro gracioso*, the *teatro breve* as a whole, and the role of both in the *comedia*. Alcuzcuz explains that since he is an escaped prisoner of the Christians, it would be foolish for him to go wandering about their camp. This time he is the voice of reason, as much as he is a coward. Yet Don Álvaro insists that if Alcuzcuz goes disguised, he has

---

[32] Sometimes not even these are necessary. See *Mogiganga cantada de la renegada de Valladolid*, in *Verdores*, ed. Rafael Benítez Claros, p. 145. The Moor Vebali catches the tricky Sacristán, who obviously lacks the appropriate dress:

Vebali	Quien eres?
Sacristán	Hermano de Galiana.
Vebali	Moro tu?
Sacristán	Moro, y Remoro.
Veb.	Como?
Sacristán	Exsi foras sotana.

Which I take to mean, roughly, 'I am out of costume,' or more roughly and comically, 'I left my costume at home.'

[33] Calderón de la Barca, *Obras*, vol. 2, p. 364.

[34] Ibid., vol. 2, p. 377.

nothing to fear. He is invoking for his lackey the prized immunity of all *gracioso* go-betweens, who, with a clever change of appearances, or mere caution, can go everywhere and do everything.[35] Alcuzcuz, seemingly aware of the logic of Don Álvaro's implied argument, reminds his master that he himself suffers a disadvantage not felt by many of his general type. Their exchange reveals the essence of Calderón's use of the *morisco gracioso*:

Alcuzcuz	Mé, sonior, cativo he sido De un cristianilio soldado, Que si en el campo me ver, Matar.
Don Álvaro	¿Cómo puede ser, Si vienes tan disfrazado, Conocerte? Y pues mudado El traje los dos traemos, Pasar entre ellos podemos, Sin sospecha averiguada, Por cristianos, pues en nada Ya moriscos parecemos.
Alcuzcuz	Tú, que bien el lengua hablar, Tú, que cativo no ser, Tú, que español parecer, Seguro poder pasar; Mé, que no sé pernunciar, Mé que preso haber estado, Mé, que este traje no he usado, ¿Cómo excusar el castigo?[36]

In any *entremés*, Alcuzcuz would have had nothing to worry about. A simple costume change, a different accent, would have been sufficient to fool anybody. Don Álvaro wants a *burla* for very sombre reasons, but he wants a *burla* nonetheless. Yet the comic logic of *burlas* and disguises fails to operate at this moment, strangely because another *entremés* logic, that of stringent caricature, has greater power over the course of events. What is ordinarily comic in the context of the *entremés* now becomes a source of frustration for both the frightened, disadvantaged *gracioso*, and also his master, who this time cannot rely upon his lackey's tricks. Just as Calderón found ways to combine the apparently opposed features of the *teatro breve* with those of the *comedia*, he must have also noted the incongruities that lay beyond the simple and desirable comic contrast. Through the skilful manipulation of convention, Calderón could miraculously flip between comedy and tragedy in the same

[35] The *morisco* lackey Zulemilla of Lope's *El primer Fajardo* is so free that he even renounces his loyalty and his religion. See Burshatin, 'Playing the Moor'.
[36] Calderón de la Barca, *Obras*, vol. 2, p. 378.

subject in a single moment. After the scene above, Don Álvaro (not his trick-ster lackey) finds a solution to his predicament by insisting that Alcuzcuz play dumb.[37] He does so with great comic effect, thus side-stepping the problem of his accent altogether and alleviating the crisis.

In the second act, Alcuzcuz has stolen some supplies from his Christian captors, but when he shows the goods to the *criada* Beatriz (whom he calls 'Zara'), she responds in shock:

Beatriz   ¡Ay de mí! Todo
                  Cuanto traes aquí es veneno
                  Yo no lo quiero tocar
                  Ni ver, Alcuzcuz: advierte
                  Que puede darte la muerte
                  Si no llegas a probar.[38]

Though a *lacayo* may often bicker with the *criada*, Alcuzcuz cannot argue with the logic of theatrical convention as he says to himself: a materialist *criada* giving up some food can only mean that the bounty is indeed dangerous: '. . . razón más clara / Es de que el voneno vio / Zara, que no le probó, / Con ser tan golosa Zara.'[39] Thus Alcuzcuz is convinced that the wine he carries with him is poison, a belief that comes in handy when he tries to commit suicide after losing his master's horse at the worst possible moment, leaving him to fear death as a possible punishment. I will cite most of the text, which tells the story better than any description:

Alcuzcuz   Pues si habemos de morer,
           Alcuzcuz, con el acero,
           Y hay mortes en que escoger,
           Murámonos de voneno;
           Que es morte mas dolce. Vaya,
           Pues que ya el vida aborrezco.
           (*Saca una bota de la alforja, y bebe*)
           Mejor ser morer así,
           Pues no morer por el menos
           Bañado un hombre en su sangre.
           ¿Cómo estar? Bueno me siento.
           No ser el voneno fuerte;

[37] Calderón would also use this device in *El encanto sin encanto*. In the middle of the second act, Don Enrique and his lackey Franchipán are caught disguised as peasants. Franchipán cannot afford to be recognised and at first only says 'Ba, ba', then afterwards simply vigorously gestures while his master interprets. Such a comic pairing involving masquerade, pantomime and comic commentary is a great example of the noble master playing just as humorous a role as his lackey.

[38] Calderón de la Barca, *Obras*, vol. 2, pp. 368–9.

[39] Ibid., vol. 2, p. 369.

> E si es que morer pretendo,
> Más veneno es menester.
> No ser frío, a lo que bebo,
> El voneno, ser caliente:
> Si, pues arder acá dentro.
> Más veneno es menester;
> Que muy poco a poco muero
> Ya parece que se enoja,
> Pues que ya va haciendo efecto;
> Que los ojos se me turbian
> E se me traba el cerebro,
> El lengua ponerse gorda
> E saber el boca a herro.
> Ya que muero, no dejar
> Para otro matar voneno,
> Será piedad. ¿Dónde estar
> Me boca, que no la entriento?[40]

The comic effect of this sequence is heightened because it is the first time Alcuzcuz has ever found himself drunk, a stunt impossible for any indulgent run-of-the-mill *gracioso*. The particularly *entremesil* element in Alcuzcuz's situation stems from two classic devices. The first is the *burla*, or more specifically the *burlador burlado*. In this case, Alcuzcuz fools himself, thinking he is dying, while the audience is aware of the deception all along. The second and related *entremesil* element is the fake death.[41] As before, Alcuzcuz is both the perpetrator and the victim. In Calderón's *El mayorazgo*, Don Cosme's faked death was an elaborate affair. It involved two of his friends carrying out a mock vendetta and pretending to stab him to death. On top of that, Don Cosme makes a stunning return as a ghost who negotiates his marriage to Doña Sabidilla, the daughter of the greedy Don Pánfilo. Though Alcuzcuz himself is unaware that his death is faked, both 'deaths' in the *entremés* and *comedia* alike are seen as farces by the audience from the very beginning. We are not dealing with the type of surprise found in Cervantes' 'Bodas de Camacho', where even the seemingly omniscient narrator is kept in the dark until the crucial moment of discovery. The humour lies in the ability to laugh at death, to treat it as something distant and irrelevant, something that can also be turned into a conceptual plaything, as can any idea in the *teatro breve*. There should be no surprise that this scene also bears great resemblance to the drunken Caminante's experience in

---

40 Calderón de la Barca, *Obras*, vol. 2, p. 372.
41 One must recall that true death is an impossibility in the world of the *entremés*. The *gracioso* holds more tenaciously on to this custom than any other. Nevertheless, it should be no surprise that Calderón, always pushing against the boundaries, should give us the only known exception in Clarín of *La vida es sueño*.

La mojiganga de la muerte. Because Alcuzcuz does not witness any type of procession, and there is no masquerade, he is not part of any embedded *mojiganga per se*; but his personal confusion between drunkenness, dream and death is very similar to that of Caminante's. Let us compare the passage from *La muerte*:

Muerte	Hoy morirás a mis manos, pero ¿qué es lo que allí veo? ¿Qué bota es ésta?
Caminante	La almohada sobre que yo estoy durmiendo todavía, pues estoy viendo que la vida es sueño.[42]

with that of *Amar después de la muerte*:

Alcuzcuz	¿Esto es dormer o morer? Mas todo diz que es el mesmo, Y ser verdad, pues no sé Si me muero o si me duermo.[43]

Though Caminante is not dead, he is literally staring Death in the face. Although Alcuzcuz compares sleeping to dying, instead of saying that 'life is a dream', in both cases death is made into a joke, and in both cases all the laughable confusion is caused by an over-indulgence in alcohol.

Calderón could not have ignored the significance of turning death into a joke in a *comedia* with the title *Amar después de la muerte*. It is a play about warfare and bloody vengeance, and the threat of death that hangs in the air of both Calderón's comic and tragic plays alike is realised in the murder of Doña Clara and the revenge death of the soldier Garcés. Alcuzcuz, in his role as *gracioso*, does play a foil to many things, including the carnage that surrounds him. But by the end of the play, it becomes clear that he fulfils a role far beyond that of a simple 'función relajadora'.[44] The same is true of most of Calderón's *graciosos*, whom could not be considered mere antithetical agents with a singular purpose of opposing the themes and tone of the greater part of the *comedia*. However, Alcuzcuz is still rather special because he is not only a spy or a go-between, as are many of his comic counterparts, but he is also a *morisco* like his masters. By the end of the play, although Alcuzcuz's Castilian may not have improved, he has defended his status as a true Muslim, run behind enemy lines, outwitted his would-be captors face-to-face, dodged cannon fire, attempted suicide and freed his master while remaining tied up and in great

---

[42] Calderón de la Barca, *Teatro cómico breve*, p. 359.
[43] Ibid., *Obras*, vol. 2, p. 372.   [44] Alcalá Zamora, p. 354.

danger. It is fair to say that Alcuzcuz, who is only second to the two main
galanes in lines spoken,[45] is a type of hero, though he may be socially inferior
to the rest of the *moriscos* of the Alpujarra. And though he is a hero, every act
of heroism is accompanied by jokes, and every joke trades on the fact that
Alcuzcuz is ostensibly a *moro de entremés*. His comic heroism is harmonised
with that of the more 'serious' *moriscos* in the play. By giving this stock figure
a unique human face, and a mind of his own, Calderón was able to create a
character that could carry on the tradition of the *entremés* without undercutting
or nullifying the greater themes of *Amar después de la muerte*.

THE *FIGURÓN*

While the *gracioso* of the *comedia* has received an abundance of critical
attention, the *figurón* is a stock comic character who, while impossible to
miss onstage, has had relatively little written about him. By the eighteenth
century, Spain had come to know this ridiculous gentleman well enough to
name an entire genre after him: the *comedia de figurón*.[46] Though the name
of the category came later, the genre was well established by the middle of the
seventeenth century. Just as the *gracioso*'s genealogy is a patchwork of
influences stretching back into history, so is the *figurón*'s. Critics have
speculated about 'mutations' (my expression) among other stock types that
may have led to this one. Some cite the 'galán-hermano', the honour-bound
and sexually frustrated *comedia* character that most likely had heavy comic
overtones, all owing to his failure to defeat the play's hero.[47] Others cite the
ostentatious and sometimes ignorant 'indiano' character as a possible source
for the *figurón*.[48] The name *figurón* must come from *figura*, a term used in
Calderón's *Entremés del reloj y los genios de la venta*, and which goes back
to Quevedo,[49] whose usage Asensio compared to that of Theophrastes.[50]

[45] Alcalá Zamora, p. 353.

[46] Appendix: 'Calderón y la comedia de figurón', in Pedro Calderón de la Barca,
El agua mansa/Guárdate del agua mansa, ed. Ignacio Arellano and Víctor García Ruiz
(Kassel: Reichenberger, 1989), pp. 42–51. Their edition offers both the original
manuscript version of the text and the later printed edition. The differences between each
version are slight but significant when studying the jokes in the play. However, studying
these would take us far afield of our current study. For the sake of simplicity, and because
the printed version is the one usually edited elsewhere, I shall refer to the play as *Guárdate
del agua mansa*, noted further as *GAM*. All observations, unless mentioned otherwise in
the footnotes, refer to this printed version.

[47] See Frédéric Serralta's comments in the 'debate' following, Jean-Raymond Lanot,
'Para una sociología del figurón', in *Risa y sociedad en el teatro español del Siglo de Oro*,
p. 149.

[48] See Jean Canavaggio's comments in the same 'debate', p. 150.

[49] See A. P. Merimée's comments in the same 'debate', p. 149.

[50] Asensio, *Itinerario*, pp. 77–86.

Some critics see the *figurón* as a comic foil for the *galán*, the same as the *gracioso*. There are, however, different ways to work as a comic foil, related to differences in social status and degree of participation in the plot of each stock type. As with the *gracioso*, various characteristics of a *figurón* may be accentuated or attenuated, leaving plenty of room for debate among critics about whether a character is truly a *figurón* or not. This debate leads some critics to invent terms like 'embryonic' or 'not true' *figurones*.[51]

The aspects of the *figurón's* appearance, behaviour or attitude vary according to the discretion of the playwright. One type of behaviour is the obsession with lineage and purity of blood, what Lanot calls being a 'hidalgo linajudo'.[52] *Figurones* can often be *montañeses*, born in the hills and mountains of Asturias, supposedly protected over the ages against contamination by any non-Old Christian stock. Their obsession with their purity is only equalled by their desire to publicise it, never letting a moment go by without staking their claim to an untainted heritage. The appearance of the *figurón* is inevitably exaggerated, but the playwright has the option of parleying this exaggeration into grotesque repulsiveness. A *figurón* can be a hungry slob, talking about food in the most inappropriate of situations. Before we assume that he is fulfilling the same role as the *gracioso* (who also talks about food in inappropriate situations), and before we are tempted to turn to a Bakhtinian analysis, we must keep in mind the status of the *figurón*, along with the consequences of his public gluttony. His bodily needs are seen as a defect, as an obstacle to social integration, and thus they are a means to his exclusion. The *gracioso* may be scolded by his master for thinking of only food and drink, but he can nevertheless satisfy his urges because his lower-class status allows it. The *figurón's* indulgences are met with much more severe censure because they violently break the rules of behaviour proper to his class. The *figurón* can also appear grotesque – in the negative, non-positive Bakhtinian way (that is, *not* celebrating the 'ever-growing, inexhaustible, ever-laughing principle'[53]) – by suffering from one or several physical defects.[54] More commonly, however, the *figurón's*

[51] See Edwin Place, 'Notes on the Grotesque: The *Comedia de Figurón* at Home and Abroad', *PMLA*, 54 (1939), 413, 415. Jean-Raymond Lanot, 'Para una sociología del figurón', p. 114, lists the characteristics he feels are most commonly associated with the *figurón*. I will be using my own list, taken from my own observations in reading these types of plays.

[52] Lanot, p. 135. The expression 'linajudo' is actually currently used by critics to describe this character-type, but the word has old roots. Sebastián de Covarrubias y Orozco, in *Tesoro de la lengua castellana* (Barcelona: Alta Fulla, 1998), describes the expression thus: 'Vocablo bárbaro; el que se precia y jacta de su linage, dando a entender viene de la casta de los godos o de alguno de los doze pares de Francia, o de otra vanidad semejante.'   [53] Bakhtin, *Rabelais and his World*, p. 24.

[54] For an extreme example, see the *gracioso* Cabellera's description of the hideous Don Lucas in Fernando de Rojas Zorrilla, *Entre bobos anda el juego*, ed. Maria Grazia Profeti (Madrid: Taurus, 1984), pp. 77–9.

defect is in his style of dress, which may be grotesque and offensive,[55] but not necessarily so.[56] The *figurón* is often ignorant and unschooled. Although the *gracioso* was often a rustic in Lope's time, the supposedly simple nature of Calderón's *graciosos* often betrays a sophisticated wit and a literary knowledge that no *figurón* could ever hope to possess. Therefore, the two stock types are incomparable on this front, and it is difficult to say that one can easily substitute for the other in its function within the structure of a *comedia*.

Like many *comedias de figurón*, *Guárdate del agua mansa* is also a classic *comedia de capa y espada*.[57] Don Alonso, a father and 'indiano', returns from Mexico to his two daughters Doña Clara and Doña Eugenia, and promptly decides that the less obedient Eugenia should marry. There are two suitors for both women, Don Pedro and Don Juan, but the intrigue is furthered by the participation of the cynical Don Félix, the play's protagonist, who starts as a neutral go-between but ends up in love with Doña Clara. The plot is further complicated from the very beginning because, in spite of the intentions of the suitors and of the women themselves, Don Alonso has resolved that his nephew, the *figurón* Don Toribio Cuadradillos, is to marry Doña Clara. Don Toribio's meddling and generally distasteful presence create both comedy and plot complications throughout the entire play. These comic clashes can be seen as tiny *entremeses* that threaten to destabilise the normal functioning of the *comedia*. In the end, however, the *figurón* is finally put in his place, and the daughters happily marry the suitors of their choice.

Don Toribio does not make his first entrance until far past the second half of the first act, at which point the love-plot is well under way. The first words uttered at the reception after Don Toribio makes his entrance are '¡Jesús, qué rara figura!'[58] practically announcing him as an abnormality in the natural flow of the action thus far. The word 'figura' (used to describe *entremés* characters as mentioned above) signals him as a character of special comic value. His continuous clashes with those around him can be either jarring or subtle in their comic effect. The father Don Alonso says to Don Toribio: 'Llegad a vuestra primas, / deseando mucho veros, / han salido a recibiros.'[59] The *damas'* stares, which both Don Alonso and Don Toribio may think is evidence of admiration, revealing expectations fulfilled, actually demonstrate the *damas'* complete lack of interest in the *figurón* as a suitor. This contradiction between the disappointment of the women and the self-satisfaction of the men was undoubtedly intended to produce humorous results. After greetings are exchanged and Don Toribio is asked about his health, his only thought is to complain about his sore rump, having ridden 'un macho de tan mal asiento'.[60]

55 Lanot, p. 139.

56 It is possible for the *figurón* to care so much about his appearance that it reaches a laughable extreme, such as in the title figure of Agustín Moreto's *El lindo don Diego*.

57 Calderón de la Barca, *GAM*, p. 3.   58 Ibid., p. 163, l. 969.

59 Ibid., p. 165, ll. 981–5.   60 Ibid., p. 165, ll. 990–1.

Don Alonso, polite host that he is, immediately asks his newly arrived nephew to take a seat and await refreshment; but Don Toribio, his mind on food, asks for something to eat before resting his weary rear end. Next comes his attempt at praising his cousins' beauty, 'agora que caigo en ello'. He finds both Doña Clara and Doña Eugenia so beautiful that he is inspired to recount an anecdote from his homeland high in the mountains of Asturias:

Don Toribio	Escriben los naturales
	que, puesto un borrico en medio
	de dos piensos de cebada,
	se deja morir primero
	que haga de uno eleción
	por más que los mire hambriento:
	yo así en medio de las dos
	que sois mis mejores piensos,
	por no encentar a nenguna
	me quedaré de hambre muerto.
Don Alonso	¡Ah, sencillez de mi patria,
	cuánto de hallarte me güelgo!
Doña Clara	¡Buen concepto y cortesano!
Doña Eugenia	De borrico por lo menos.[61]

Don Toribio goes on to say that, since he has the money, he would like buy two papal dispensations and marry both his cousins. After he manages to mumble some greetings himself, he makes obligatory mention of his 'ejecutoria' (of 'limpieza de sangre' fame), which he has stashed away somewhere with his food for the journey to Madrid. Every utterance by Don Toribio is devoid of culture, causing laughter. Thus, before less than one hundred lines of verse have passed, Don Toribio has inadvertently made at least five jokes. One must also keep in mind the contrasting obsequiousness of Don Alonso and the constant barrage of comic asides made by the cousins, adding further jokes. The rapid-fire succession of jokes closely resembles that of the *entremés*, though only one character, the *figurón*, is the obvious motor of jocularity. More than a mere series of social blunders, Don Toribio's statements and actions are a parody of *comedia* commonplaces. As a figurón, he is a type of 'anti-*galán*'. Instead of arriving alert and ready to extol the wonders of Madrid, he complains about his bruised backside. Instead of seating himself promptly so that he and the father can get down to matters of business and marriage, he effectively asks 'Where's the food?' His cousin does not coo '¡Qué talle tan bizarro!' or some such exclamation of passionate interest. Rather she crows with amusement and repulsion '¡Jesús, que rara figura!' Instead of singling out one *dama* and subtly expressing his preference by praising her, he figuratively grabs hastily at both, comparing them to food,

---

61 Calderón de la Barca, *GAM*, p. 167, ll. 1013–26.

keeping his image of a glutton ever-present. And the list goes on. The parody would have been painfully obvious to any *comedia*-goer because he or she would have seen dozens and dozens of father–suitor–daughter scenes with their monotonous and predictable sequence of open platitudes and 'hidden' romantic messages in both poetry and asides.

For anybody careless enough to confuse Calderón's personal sensibilities with those of the protagonists in his 'honour plays', *Guárdate del agua mansa* is required reading or viewing material. The playwright himself was never obsessed with honour, but he did profoundly understand the social relevance of the concept, and also how it worked with excellent results as a versatile plot device. An artist's understanding of an idea can often be gauged by the quality of the parody that he uses to distort it.[62] While *Guárdate del agua mansa* is a *comedia de capa y espada*, and the notion of honour is occasionally used to give a brief fright or heighten suspense, honour is overwhelmingly portrayed in a ridiculous context, thanks to Don Toribio. The most blatant ridicule concerns family honour, which has its basis in lineage, embodied in the *figurón*'s 'ejecutoria'. So worried is Don Toribio that somebody might question his honour or purity – which for him are one and the same – that he carries the 'ejecutoria' with him wherever he goes, instead of having it stowed away at home or on file in the city records. For him, it is like a magical charm that wards off accusations that every Christian gentleman of Spain ought to have feared.[63] The racist paranoia in questions of honour in the *comedia*, constantly ferreted out and decried by Américo Castro,[64] actually seems criticised here by Calderón *avant la lettre*. After Don Toribio has seen the other suitors hanging about his cousins' place, he is attacked by a fit of *celos*. He demands that Eugenia and Clara stay indoors, thus parodying the 'favourite' Calderonian theme: conjugal honour. Unfortunately, there exists a 'Calderonian' conflict of interest: the cousins, good Catholic women, must go to mass. This conflict ends in laughter, for both the characters and the audience alike.

> Don Alonso   ¿Han de quedarse sin misa?
>
> Don Toribio   ¿Qué dificultad es esa?
>   Mi ejecutoria les basta
>   para ser cristianas viejas,
>   y con leer con devoción

---

[62] As an example, one may consider that Cervantes demonstrates a profound understanding, and even admiration, of the books of chivalry, which he parodies. Without such an understanding, he may not have been able to make *Don Quixote* into more than a simple parody.

[63] In fact, so much faith does Don Toribio put into his 'ejecutoria', that in the original manuscript version of the play he says no 'hidalgo solariego' should be without one, for protection against 'rayos y truenos'. See Calderón de la Barca, *GAM*, p. 168, ll. 755–8. This joke was curiously left out of the second, printed version.

[64] Américo Castro, 'El drama de la honra en la literatura dramática', in *De la edad conflictiva* (Madrid: Taurus, 1961).

	dos o tres testigos de ella
	con la fiesta habrán cumplido
	y no han menester más fiesta.
Don Alonso	¡Jesús y qué disparate!
	Venid, venid, no lo entiendan
	esos hidalgos.
Don Toribio	Par Dios,
	que si por mi voto fuera
	no habían de salir de casa
	quisieran o no quisieran.

Vanse

Don Féliz	No sé cómo fue posible . . .
Don Juan	¿Qué?
Don Félix	Que la risa detenga
	viendo al primo.
Don Pedro	¡Qué figura
	tan rara!
Don Juan	Extraña presencia
	de novio.[65]

With this exchange, Don Toribio is firmly put in his place as a complete freak, and everyone else takes the opposite side as normal individuals, laughing at his foolishness. But left on the *figurón*'s side is the question of honour (not to mention religion), an idea that itself is now blown out of freakishly grotesque proportion,[66] the sort of exaggeration that is the basis of the *entremés* sub-genre.

As shown in examples taken from Calderón's *entremeses*, the parodies of generic conventions can often overlap with social satire. The *comedia* is a genre so steeped in social context and so dependent upon an adherence to – and for dramatic effect, occasional breakage of – unwritten social rules, that it is often difficult to distinguish between a joyful criticism of stale artistic convention, and a joyful criticism of the equally stale social convention from which the artistic was born. It is therefore difficult to determine whether Calderón was poking fun at the true 'honour code'[67] or whether he was poking

[65] Calderón de la Barca, *GAM*, p. 209, ll. 1587–1601.

[66] See Barbara Mujica, 'Honor from the Comic Perspective: Calderón's *Comedias de Capa y Espada*', *Bulletin of the Comediantes*, 38 (1986), 12–13. Mujica relates this type of ridicule to the *teatro breve*: 'The *pasos* and *entremeses* abound in digs at the honor code. These ribald works often depict the cuckold as a happy accomplice to his wife's transgressions and the honor-obsessed husband as stupid and annoying . . . It seems that Calderón's more refined audiences were also capable of laughing at honor.'

[67]See Melveena McKendrick, 'Honour/Vengeance in the Spanish "Comedia": A Case of Mimetic Transference', *Modern Language Review*, 79 (1984), 313–35. She reminds us that the historical validity of the 'honour code' has been called into question, and that some have insisted on studying only its artistic use.

fun at himself as an exploiter of the idea. This question also relates to the use of stereotypes in any art form at any time and in any place. It is possible that in the *teatro breve*, stock figures eventually lose their satirical force over the years, as they become so commonplace that their implied criticism falls on deaf ears. Was Calderón sending a message to all the true-to-life 'hidalgos linajudos' in the audience to calm their racist passions? Did he quarrel with a particularly offensive Asturian he met in the street one day, and he wanted to strike back with a thinly veiled public reprimand? These very specific explanations seem unnecessary if we remember that the *figurón* was an established type at the time and used by many other playwrights, few of which had any motive other than to entertain the public. Yet this literary debt does not make Don Toribio any less of a socially relevant satirical character.

The comic centrepiece of *Guárdate del agua mansa*, as a scene, relies upon Don Toribio's well-established concern for honour coupled with his almost unbelievable stupidity. The literal centrepiece of the play's own figurative comic centrepiece is a *guardainfante*, or farthingale. The object is also the centrepiece of two *bailes entremesados*, each called *El guardainfante*, by master *entremesista* Luis Quiñones de Benavente. Hannah Bergman writes:

> La sátira contra las exageraciones de las mujeres (y los hombres) esclavizadas por la moda, tema casi constante en las obras de Benavente, llega a su apogeo en el baile bipartido *El guardainfante*. Este nombre se daba a una especie de armazón de hierro, ballena o esparto que las mujeres metían entre sus faldas para ahuecarlas. En la Primera Parte de la obrita traen presas ante el alcalde Juan Rana 'una falduda', el vuelo de cuyo vestido impedía la circulación en la plaza.[68]

These theatrical pieces, which probably premiered in the autumn of 1634,[69] were the initial rumblings of a storm of criticism that was to rain upon this fashion that, true to its name implying a hidden pregnancy, was associated by moralists with women of loose morals, if not with downright prostitutes.[70] The first version of *Guárdate del agua mansa* (simply titled *El agua mansa*) was probably penned circa 1644,[71] and by that time the satirical barrage – in poems, *pragmáticas*, epistles, and *teatro breve*, even in a novel[72] – had

[68] Bergman, *Quiñones de Benavente y sus entermeses*, p. 174. Velásquez's *Las meninas* contains a famous example of this fashion modelled by the Infanta and her ladies in waiting. On pp. 174–84, Bergman looks at satires about clothes, fashion and the figure of the *lindo*. We find one character representing this type of satire in the mad tailor of Calderón's *Entremés del reloj y los genios de la venta*, as seen in chapter 2.

[69] Bergman, *Quiñones de Benavente y sus entermeses*, p. 308.

[70] Ibid., p. 180.   [71] Calderón de la Barca, *GAM*, p. 60.

[72] Luis Vélez de Guevara, *El diablo cojuelo* ed. Blanca Periñán and Ramón Valdés (Barcelona: Crítica, 1999), p. 19. The *guaradinfante* is listed among many articles of clothing in a description of the citizens of Madrid jumping into bed. Also listed are

subsided.[73] Nevertheless, while the *guardainfante* may have no longer been an entirely fashionable subject of satire, memory of the diatribes must have still been fresh in the theatregoers' minds. Calderón uses the tiredness of the joke to his advantage by doing what he did in his *entremeses*, namely employing a comic shorthand. The mere appearance of the *guardainfante* onstage, without any explicit accompanying criticism, is enough to get a laugh. Publicly displayed undergarments make versatile material for jokes, independent of what one says about them, because they are taboo subjects whose mere mention can bring laughter. The criticism heaped upon the garment over the previous ten years could only have made it a more delightfully awkward sub--ject of discussion. In a way, the less said onstage, the better, in order to avoid killing the joke with a superfluous explanation. All that is required is for Don Toribio, a ridiculous male figure, to step onto the scene with a *guardainfante*, a ridiculous female fashion, not to be touched by men. How does Don Toribio end up holding the *guardainfante*? I reproduce the following dialogue, as it is the best explanation. Don Toribio has made a horrifying discovery while poking around Doña Eugenia's room: he has found a rope ladder.

Don Alonso	¿Escala escondida?
Don Toribio	Sí.
	de hartos pasos, con fuertes
	cuerdas y hierros atada.
Don Alonso	¡Vive Dios, si verdad fuese
	que había . . .
Don Toribio	¿Cómo verdad?
	Si solo porque la vieseis
	os traigo aquí cuando solo
	está el cuarto; un punto breve
	esperaos. Veréis cuán presto
	aquí la miréis patente. *Vase*
Don Alonso	¡Ay de mí! No en vano, cielos,
	previne ausentar prudente
	de la corte a Eugenia; pero
	si ya Don Toribio tiene
	tan vivas sospechas ¿cómo
	es posible que la lleve,
	pues ya . . .

---

basquiñas and *berdugados*, both women's clothing which, like the *guardainfante*, were subject to strict regulation (on paper anyhow) according (Guevara, *Diablo*, p. 158) to Philip IV's royal decree of 1639. *El diablo cojuelo* was first published in 1641, and the decree (or 'pregmática') must have been on Vélez de Guevara's mind at the time of writing.

[73] Bergman, *Quiñones de Benavente y sus entermeses*, p. 307.

Vuelve con un guardainfante

Don Toribio   Mirad si es verdad:
                       con más de dos mil pendientes
                       de gradas, aros, y cuerdas.

Don Alonso   ¡Necio, loco, impertiente!
                 ¿Esa es escala?[74]

Calderón has skilfully combined the ridiculous appearance of the undergarment with the combined paranoia of both a protective father and his oblivious, honour-bound, country-bumpkin nephew. The playwright has effectively 'plugged-in' the satire of the *guardainfante*, but done so in a surprising fashion that can catch everyone, even the most jaded audience, off guard. It could be expected that when those watching caught a glimpse of the item in question, all their memories of the previous years' controversies and jokes came rushing back. What saves the gag from appearing stale is that one man, the centre of attention, is not 'in on the joke'. Poor Don Toribio has been up in the mountains of Asturias, without any consciousness of ladies' fashion or the furore that it recently created, and few things can galvanise a crowd in laughter like a poor slob who just doesn't get the joke when everybody else does. It is precisely this complete lack of knowledge, not knowing that he himself is a 'walking *entremés*', which makes Don Toribio perhaps the funniest among all of Calderón's creations.

Not all borrowings from the *entremés* tradition are obvious. Browsing the notes of the 'Reichenberger' edition of *Guárdate del agua mansa*, one finds editorial references to nearly a dozen *entremeses*, each of them used to explain a particular joke, such as the derogatory use of the name 'Toribio'. With such *influencia entremesil* coursing through the play, it seems unlikely that the *figurón* can shoulder so much comic responsibility all by himself. In fact, his farcical exaggeration seems to free up some of the other characters and, surprisingly enough, give them the opportunity to play the part of the *gracioso*, a character that is conspicuously absent. In fact, after surveying every line uttered by Hernando, the *criado*, I have determined that this lackey character says nothing funny throughout the entire play. 'Silencing' the *criado* is obviously a conscious move on Calderón's part. Except for a piece of petty advice, 'obligarse a callar / solo puede ser estar / enamorado',[75] Hernando's lines are limited to stunningly dull pronouncements such as '¡Bravas damas han venido . . .!'[76]

Enter Doña Eugenia and Don Félix, two of the most wisecracking nobles ever seen onstage. Though one may find a more ingenious *dama de comedia* in Calderón, such as Ángela of *La dama duende*, one would be hard pressed to find one as sassy. She is a 'bad daughter',[77] disobedient and unwilling to marry. She is not a prude, but she is a sarcastic joker who spares nobody her barbs,

---

[74] Calderón de la Barca, *GAM*, pp. 329, 331, ll. 2897–2917.

[75] Ibid., p. 307, ll. 2616–17.   [76] Ibid., p. 109, l. 221.

[77] Ibid., p. 151, l. 819. Eugenia says so herself, though she jokes that it is more of goal to which she aspires.

particularly when the targets would seek to confine her and end her fun, be they suitors or family members. Her own sister is so shocked that she exclaims at one moment: '¿Ni aun a tu padre reserva / la sátira de tus labios? / ¡Jesús mil veces!'[78] By effectively calling Don Toribio an ass, Doña Eugenia firmly establishes her role as the play's chief satirist and audience liaison. She is not all harsh words, however, and she betrays a playful side when she leads Don Toribio into an embarrassing *burla* by simply saying to his face that he has no 'filis'.[79]

Don Félix is as cynical about love and marriage as Doña Eugenia, but instead of brandishing a rapier wit, he occasionally copies the part of a *gracioso* in other ways. In the first act, Don Juan accuses him of having a 'humor' (in the traditional Galenic sense) about women, and he agrees, saying: 'Sí, porque aunque ellas son bellas / me quiero a mí más que a ellas.'[80] His unabashed self-interest closely resembles that of the cynical *gracioso* who is always looking after himself, always showing perplexed amusement when some *galán* speaks of how he would give anything to be with a particular *dama*. Instead of sympathy for Don Juan, Don Félix dishes up nothing by mockery. While Don Juan and Don Pedro are staring slack-jawed at the beautiful newcomers, the impatient Don Félix scoffs:

> Don Félix   Vamos a comer, que aunque
>   tan enamorado esté
>   tengo más hambre que amor.[81]

That a *galán* would be so open about his hunger, and that he would give it priority over courting a beautiful woman, is a complete rupture of *comedia* decorum. While such behaviour is expected of the *gracioso*, when Félix does the same, we can only assume that Calderón is 'yanking our chains' (pointing out the folly of our expectations) while 'tickling our funny bones'.

Is there a connection between Don Toribio's extreme farcical interference in the play and the 'loosening' of the noble protagonists' behaviour? Lanot has warned us not to 'extrapolar las tendencias lúdicas del entremés a la comedia',[82] but Doña Eugenia's razor-sharp quips and Don Félix's complete disregard, if

---

[78] Calderón de la Barca, *GAM*, ll. 817–19.

[79] There is not sufficient space here to discuss this drawn-out joke.

[80] Calderón de la Barca, *GAM*, p. 121, ll. 374–5.

[81] Ibid., p. 147, ll. 740–2.

[82] See Lanot, pp. 133–4: 'De esta demasiado rápida evocación de los entremeses de figuras no se quiere deducir cualquier tipo de filiación cronológica, porque sería error pensar que se puede pasar del entremés a la comedia cuando cada género tiene sus exigencias, su norma y su función específicas. En particular no se pueden extrapolar las tendencias lúdicas del entremés a la comedia (si bien de figurón, comedia). Sin embargo, la existencia de un fondo cultural y social común, de un arsenal risible contemporáneo, no se puede ignorar a la hora de la interpretación del figurón. Menos aún si tenemos en cuenta las fechas de composición de las que ya definimos como comedia de (o con) figurón, escritas algunas de ellas a partir de 1619.'

not disdain, for the 'exigencias, norma y función' of his *papel de galán* for most of the play cannot be described in any other terms than 'lúdico'. *Guárdate del agua mansa* is completely rife with playfulness. In one fight-scene, Don Alonso and Don Juan clash their swords, only to have Don Félix join in, leading all three to fight each other at the same time. After that, Don Pedro, another suitor, appears with a pistol. A second later, Don Toribio looks over the scene and exclaims '¡Tanta gente honrada hay acá dentro!', signalling the ridiculousness of the situation.[83] As mentioned before, this play's authority on the question of honour is Don Toribio, who cannot tell a hoop skirt from a rope ladder. The threat of violence that hangs in the air of so many *comedias*, even the predominantly comic ones, has been all but washed away from *Guárdate del agua mansa*. If the 'serious' characters did not offer some form of counterpoint to the utterly silly Don Toribio, the play would be a *comedia burlesca* and not merely a *comedia de figurón*. Nevertheless, the spirit of the *entremés*, spearheaded by the *figurón*, infiltrates further into the other characters, indeed further than some unwritten rules of *comedia* decorum would seem to allow.

ENTREMESIL SITUATIONS IN THE COMEDIA

Dar tiempo al tiempo is a rather straightforward *comedia de capa y espada*, which according to Ángel Valbuena Briones pertains to Calderón's 'ciclo madrileño'.[84] He writes:

> El ciclo tiene sus características especiales: sátira de costumbres, contraste entre las leyes del noble y la reflexión de los criados, la idea del honor vista desde un ángulo cómico, tema urbano lleno de peripecias, multiplicación de intrigas que se basan en el equívoco de la apariencia, y finalmente, cierta enseñanza o moraleja . . .[85]

After stripping away the characteristics associated with the broader *capa y espada* genre, we are left with these: 'sátira de costumbres', 'reflexión de los criados', 'tema urbano', namely the core of any urban *entremés* such as Calderón's *El toreador*.[86] If we believe Luis Vélez de Guevara, the compiler

---

[83] This citation, which does not appear in the printed *GAM*, is taken from the autograph *Agua mansa*, included in the same modern edition. See p. 370, ll. 2805–6. I have not been able to determine the reason for its removal, but in general there is much fragmentation in this section of the printed version, and perhaps the line was lost amidst hasty editing that was never corrected before printing. I include the citation from the autograph version because it fits extremely well, and it seems to have been left out for no other reason than carelessness.

[84] Calderón de la Barca, *Obras*, vol. 2, p. 1331.

[85] Ibid., vol. 2, p. 1331.

[86] Other Calderonian *entremeses* in this vein include: *La premática* (both parts), *El mayorazgo*, *Don Pegote*, *La casa holgana* and *La rabia* (both parts). All can be found in Calderón de la Barca, *Teatro cómico breve*.

of Quiñones de Benavente's *Jocoseria*,[87] we may even include 'cierta enseñanza o moraleja' as a shared feature between the 'ciclo madrileño' and the 'entremés urbano'. Furthermore, Valbuena Briones writes that, in *Dar tiempo*, Calderón's less-than-flattering portrait of Madrid life 'lo hereda de Quevedo, pintor exagerado de las duras realidades de la época'.[88] As we saw in the chapter 2, the *entremés* was Quevedo's choice method of putting these 'duras realidades exageradas' on the stage.

The opening sequence of events is perhaps the most striking feature in all of *Dar tiempo al tiempo*. If the opening of a play is meant to set the tone, then this *comedia* would at first seem to offer a whisp of romantic intrigue buried under an avalanche of farcical episodes. Don Juan de Toledo and his *criado* Chacón enter the heart of Madrid as they discuss the *amo*'s plans to continue courting Doña Leonor. Chacón, a natural cynic, doubts Doña Leonor's romantic loyalty in Don Juan's absence, and he counts the 'boberías' (he also excuses the expression: 'perdona; / que no hallo nombre que darla / más decoroso'[89]) that his gushing, love-struck master declaims. At the fourth 'bobería', by Chacón's count, Don Juan can stand this wit no longer and in a comic rage yells: 'Necio estás, / no me obligues a que haga / un disparate.'[90] Unable to resist entering the *entremesil* world of 'disparates', he shoves his servant into a freezing mud puddle, hardly a noble action, soiling the poor Chacón from head to toe. It is a gag similar to the pie-in-the-face that vaudeville made famous. Drippy, gooey, shamed: Chacón is defeated and Don Juan is the victor who finally gets the 'smart aleck' to shut up.

On his master's advice, for he must keep up appearances, Chacón makes his way under the eaves of a house in order to shake off his cold mud like a wet dog. But before he can make it to safety:

A un lado echan agua de arriba, y sale una Criada a una ventana.[91]

The *criada* shouts (too late), 'Agua va', to which the shocked and exasperated Chacón responds, 'Mientes, picaña: / que esto no es agua!'[92] When chamber pots are being dumped on people's heads, we begin to see what Valbuena Briones meant by 'influencia quevedesca'. Seeming to have forgotten that he set these events in motion, Don Juan shouts at Chacón to keep quiet and tells him to leave because he cannot be seen with a *criado* in such a soiled state. Rebellious as he is, Chacón refuses and insists that they go to the house of his dear 'Juanilla', a *criada* that he claims is waiting for him more faithfully than Don Juan's own Doña Leonor. The master concedes, but when they arrive, they are not greeted by Juana but by another *criada*. Not recognising

---

87 Recall the subtitle 'Reprehension moral y festiva de los desordenes publicos'.
88 Calderón de la Barca, *Obras*, vol. 2, p. 1333.
89 Ibid., vol. 2, p. 1334.   90 Ibid., vol. 2, p. 1334.
91 Ibid., vol. 2, p. 1334.   92 Ibid., vol. 2, p. 1334.

Chacón, she promptly dumps a baby in swaddling clothes into his arms. Before disappearing, she says it is Juana's and pleads: 'Toma y gózale mil años, / que ha sido el parto terrible.'[93] When Don Juan tells Chacón that they have been gone from the city for thirteen months, the hapless *criado* realises that the 'trecemesino' in his arms cannot possibly be his. Upon this realisation, Chacón demands vengeance. At this stage, a burlesque mini-melodrama, an *entremés* divided into various episodes, begins. The first 'act' of this embedded and subdivided *entremés* ends when Chacón goes momentarily offstage, leaving the 'trecemesino' in the care of yet a third *criada*.

While this could have been the last in a series of wild events, as soon as Chacón rejoins his master, they are both subjected to further silliness as they are accosted by four soldiers. The soldiers are obviously criminal and comic 'personajes hampescos'. Instead of regaling the protagonists with stories of battles and faraway lands, they brusquely ask the protagonists for their capes. When Don Juan and his servant refuse, the anonymous 'Soldado 4°' shouts '¡Cuerpo de tal, lo que garlan!'[94] betraying his criminal status with 'germanía' speech. Stealing capes at night was such a common activity that a special verb, 'capear', was coined, along with the word for the perpetrator, 'capeador'.[95] As with many illegal professions, 'capeadores' (along with pimps, prostitutes, pickpockets, charlatans, etc.) became the subject of *entremeses*. Quiñones de Benavente wrote a two-part series entitled *La capeadora*, giving the role a further twist by making its thieving protagonist female. Don Juan and Chacón fend off the *entremesil* invasion with the help of Don Pedro and Don Diego, who arrive upon the scene at the sound of clashing swords.

The lead *galán* and his servant eventually escape the fray, and subsequently the overall 'tone' makes a transition back to that of a standard *capa y espada* play. Shadowy figures slip in and out of houses, apparent strangers call out in the darkness of the night, lights are lit and extinguished, identities are confused, suspicions mount and all the tension erupts in yet another sword fight. Gone are the slapstick scenes of before. The pace is still rapid, but this period in the play consists of 'una atmósfera lúdica generalizada' without the 'tonalidad entremesil'.[96] However, before the first act is over, the *entremés* makes one more incursion into the *comedia*, in the form of 'Alguaciles y [un] Escribano' that are searching for this evening's troublemakers. Overall,

---

93 Calderón de la Barca, *Obras*, vol. 2, p. 1335.

94 Ibid., vol. 2, p. 1335.

95 José Deleito y Piñuela, *La mala vida en la España de Felipe IV* (Madrid: Alianza Editorial, 1987), pp. 90–1.

96 I borrow this term from Ignacio Arellano, who writes in *GAM*, p. 62: '. . . sin llegar a la tonalidad entremesil, la misma dinamicidad del enredo provoca innumerables entradas y salidas, galanes que se esconden rápidamente a la llegada del padre o hermano de la dama, huidas precipitadas, etc., que producen una atmósfera lúdica generalizada'.

la justicia itself is an ambivalent entity, and not necessarily *entremesil per se*, but context makes a difference in this case, along with the subsequently comic behaviour of the city's peace-keepers. It seems strange, even comical, that it has taken them so long to show up. In fact, their appearance is almost gratuitous. It also bears mentioning that, at this point in the play, things have calmed down quite a bit. This dramatic irony is not lost on Chacón who groans: 'Esto sólo nos faltaba.'[97] When Don Juan (who has more than just a hint of *miles gloriosus* in him) draws his sword, Chacón gives in to the inevitability of the situation and wryly comments:

> Chacón   Ya van tres veces con ésta.
> Danzantes somos de espadas;
> que con cualquier mayordomo
> vuelve de nuevo la danza.[98]

For Chacón, formulaic repetition and exaggeration have brought down the art of swashbuckling to *teatro breve* status, a *baile entremesado*. The *gracioso*'s nonchalance is only matched by the *alguaciles*' cowardice, in a comical reversal of roles. 'Alguacil 1°' flees, shouting, 'Resistencia, resistencia,' and 'Alguacil 2°' makes an exit with the plea: 'Favor aquí a la justicia.'[99] Juan finally decides to make an escape, not because he fears that the clownish guard will do him harm, but because he fears that they will be able to identify him by the time reinforcements arrive. Thus Don Juan and Chacón's comic misadventures come to an end, allowing the rest of the play a 'tone' similar to that of any other *comedia de capa y espada*.

But this tone must accommodate Chacón's quest for vengeance, which started with his discovery of Juana's 'trecemesino', who was by chance dropped into his arms. Like any *entremés*, this one (divided into parts) requires a *burla* or two in order to propel the action. The first *burla* is Juana's unfaithfulness that provokes Chacón, and the clever *gracioso* decides to take revenge by planning a *burla* of his own. Ginés, the father of the baby, inadvertently explains to his friend Chacón how the baby was lost. Chacón replies that he knows an astrologer who, through divination, can find the abandoned child for the price of Juana's ring. After speaking with Ginés, the jealous Chacón shouts insults at his unfaithful girlfriend, playing the part of the offended cuckold, a stock character of the *entremés*. In a third scene, Chacón mutters threats under his breath as his master is present. In the fourth scene of this subdivided *entremés*, Chacón explains to Ginés that the astrologer has finally found the 'prenda perdida', but through a stroke of bad luck his friend was arrested for merely exercising his profession. The unlucky astrologer can only be let out of jail for a hundred *reales*, which the easily duped Ginés is

---

97 Calderón de la Barca, *Obras*, vol. 2, p. 1340.
98 Ibid., vol. 2, p. 1340.   99 Ibid., vol. 2, p. 1340.

more than willing to pay. At this point, Chacón explains to the audience the parodic nature of his actions:

> Chacón   ¿Señores,
> ¿no es venganza más sangrienta
> sacar la sangre del alma,
> que la del cuerpo, que es esta?[100]

In the fifth and final *entremesil* scene, the ruse is revealed, and Ginés and Juana discover that they have both been had. In a very traditional *entremés* ending, Ginés hits Chacón, and both father and mother yell insults at the *gracioso embustero*. The only twist is that Chacón remains onstage, instead of being chased off, for he finds himself quickly entering another scene that involves the more noble characters, making a seamless transition from *teatro breve* to *comedia*.

Why insist that all the scenes described above – the opening sequence, the battle with the *alguaciles*, and the affair of the abandoned 'trecemesino' – are part of the *entremés* tradition and should not be primarily associated with the *comedia de capa y espada*? It is well known that the love-intrigues among servants are a standard fixture of such *comedias*, and are often meant to parody or offer comic counterpoint to the relationships between the main noble characters. It could be argued that the love triangle between Ginés, Juana and Chacón is nothing more than another facet in the 'juego de espejos' of the play's intentionally tangled plot structure. The ill-paved streets, sewage disposal and marauding thieves could be considered little more than 'local flavor', whose comic tinge is merely in line with the overall light-hearted spirit of the *capa y espada* genre. The elements analysed above are *entremesiles* because of their tone, a tone deliberately chosen by Calderón, based upon a series of individual choices. The easiest way to demonstrate the consequences of these choices would be to imagine their alternatives. Luckily for us, Calderón decided to 'refundir' *Dar tiempo al tiempo* into *El maestro de danzar*, a play with a considerably different 'tonalidad'.

Ángel Valbuena Briones writes that *El maestro de danzar* is essentially *Dar tiempo al tiempo*, with the added contrivance of the *maestro* (a somewhat sloppy addition, which does not take effect until the second act) and the wholesale removal of the 'influencia quevedesca', which I freely interpret as 'influencia entremesil'.[101] At the beginning of *Maestro*, instead of a shouting match that escalates into a shoving match, which leaves Chacón soaked in mud, we find a quick exchange of three verses between master (this time Don Juan is called Don Enrique) and servant (still called Chacón). This moment is

---

[100] Calderón de la Barca, *Obras*, vol. 2, p. 1340.
[101] Ibid., vol. 2, p. 1537.

followed by a speech of almost 150 lines, explaining the play's background
and Don Enrique's love affair with Doña Leonor. Oddly enough, the speech
comes from the *gracioso* and not the *galán*. The tone of the *entremés* is
deadened because when one character dominates the stage for minutes on
end, there is no possibility left for the rapid-fire exchange of quips. Though
the initial plot exposition is peppered with witticisms and small comic
re-enactments, it leaves Chacón playing the role of the stereotypical Calderón
gracioso, full of ingenuity and lacking crudity. Needless to say, there is no
chamber pot dumped on the servant's head in *Maestro*. At the end of the
speech, Don Enrique responds:

> Don Enrique Aunque debiera no haber
> oído discurso tan necio,
> te perdono la molestia
> por el gusto de acuerdo.[102]

Let us cite again the reprimand against Chacón in *Dar tiempo*.

> Don Juan [in *Maestro*, D. Enrique] Necio estás
> no me obligues a que haga
> un disparate contigo.
> [dale un empujón, y cae][103]

The choice made by Calderón in either case, and the consequential difference
in tone, should be quite obvious to the reader. From this point in the story,
Maestro immediately jumps to the scene where Doña Beatriz (the same name
as in *Dar tiempo*) escapes her vengeful brother. In *Dar tiempo*, this was
preceded by the episode of the picaresque 'soldados capeadores'. In *Maestro*,
this funny scene of the cowardly robbers (*miles gloriosus* multiplied by four)
fleeing their would-be victims has been totally eliminated. Both plays rejoin
the same thread of action when the *alguaciles* appear on the scene and try to
uncover Doña Beatriz 'tapada'. In *Dar tiempo*, the results of the conflict are
humorous to the extreme, and nobody gets hurt: a major tenet of the *teatro
breve*. In *Maestro*, the consequences are much more dire. The tone is set in
each play by Chacón. From *Dar tiempo al tiempo*, after the fight has begun,
we remember:

> Chacón Ya van tres veces con ésta.
> Danzantes somos de espadas;
> que con cualquier mayordomo
> vuelve de nuevo la danza.[104]

[102] Calderón de la Barca, *Obras*, vol. 2, p. 1541.
[103] Ibid., vol. 2, p. 1334.   [104] Ibid., vol. 2, p. 1334.

And then from *El maestro de danzar*:

Chacón   [*Aparte*]   Malo va esto [. . .]
          [. . .] Hoy se verá por lo menos
          la novedad de un lacayo
          que no huye y tira recio.[105]

In other words: 'Here is a *gracioso* that stands his ground and is willing to kill.' 'Alguacil 1°' cries, '¡Ay infeliz me han muerto!' to which Chacón shouts: 'Ya va uno, y voy por otro.'[106] The fact that this Chacón is bloodthirsty makes him a sort of 'anti-*gracioso*', and needless to say, the *alguacil* left dead and bleeding in the street erases any vestige of 'tonalidad entremesil'. In fact, while the street in *Dar tiempo* is a place for great comedy,[107] the actual urban environs in *Maestro* are a place of mortal danger. *El maestro de danzar* is a *comedia de capa y espada* where all the laughable action is concentrated in the safety of a 'sala', where comic potential lies in disappearing through doors or hiding behind screens, but lies rarely outdoors.

Gone is the affair of the 'trecemesino'. This leaves out the burlesque quest for vengeance, the phony astrologer, and the ring or money cleverly extracted by Chacón, *al estilo entremesil*. Juana's role as *criada* is almost non-existent, and she has no relationship with Chacón. Juana's previously prominent role is replaced by Inés. She had little to say in *Dar tempo*, but is now given more lines as she sings sweet verses to cover up the noble lovers' secret conversations. Though she chats with Chacón, and he asks for her hand in marriage at the end, it would be erroneous to consider their exchanges as constituting a parodic parallel love-plot, much less an embedded and subdivided *entremés*. Calderón has effectively 'unplugged' everything *quevedesco* and *entremesil* in *Dar tiempo al tiempo*, leaving behind the main plot structure, and some 'extra space' into which he could add the scenes of Doña Leonor's dancing lessons. While these replacement scenes are funny, they are very much 'drawing-room' in their location, participants, and consequently, tone.

I argued that, in *Guárdate del agua mansa*, Don Toribio's presence allowed for a certain 'loosening' of the other characters' behaviour. Because of the *figuron*'s grotesquely absurd speech, silly clothes and lack of social skills, the general tone was brought down; and it was thus more acceptable for the *galanes* and *damas* to let fly *socarronías* or declare that food had more importance than love. Because of *Dar tiempo al tiempo*'s extremely farcical

---

[105] Calderón de la Barca, *Obras*, vol. 2, p. 1544.

[106] Ibid., vol. 2, p. 1544.

[107] Since there is no typical marketplace scene – Bakhtin's *locus* for the carnavalesque, with its laughter and bawdiness – in the *comedia* genre, the Madrid streets could be said to take its place, when possible. *Dar tiempo al tiempo* even started with 'the tossing of excrement and drenching in urine'. For this expression, see Bakthin, *Rabelais*, p. 149.

beginning, one may guess that the entire work is 'contaminated' by the spirit of the *teatro breve*, and I believe this indeed is the case. One such moment of contamination is Doña Beatriz's response to her brother Don Diego, when he threatens to stab her in order to 'silence' her dishonour. She ably turns fear into laughter by offering this mocking and self-referential remark: '¿Tú la daga para mí? / Que eres mi hermano repara, / don Diego, no mi marido.'[108] In another example of a noble's unexpectedly playful behaviour, Don Juan befuddles his friend Don Pedro by acting like an idiot, much as *graciosos* in other plays will feign stupidity in order to avoid giving away a secret. Yet these two moments hardly qualify as entire scenes, and in themselves are not enough to support the hypothesis that Calderón thought in terms of 'plugging in' entire *entremesil* episodes featuring nobles. However, there is one such episode that erupts with full force when Don Juan and Doña Leonor get into an argument at the end of the first act. I provide the entire sequence, where Chacón the observer looks on:

Juan	¿Habrá tenido,
	no digo yo el que haya sido
	noble, pero el más vil pecho,
	descaro de confesar
	a un hombre que ya engañó,
	que es verdad que se mudó?
Leonor	Pues ¿por qué lo he de negar,
	si es verdad . . .
Chacón [*Aparte*]	¡Qué bofetada!
Leonor	. . . que me mudé...
Chacón [*Aparte*]	¡Qué cachete!
Leonor	. . . por mejorar . . .
Chacón [*Aparte*]	¡Qué puñete!
Leonor	. . . comodidad?
Chacón [*Aparte*]	¿Qué patada?[109]

This entire scene is gratuitous. It is nothing but farcical violence, bopping someone on the head for a laugh. There are no clever turns of phrase, there is no hiding behind curtains or disappearing through doors. It is pure physical comedy, yet the 'figura plebeya' is out of the picture; somebody has taken his place in the role of 'ridiculizado' and it is none other than the 'primer galán'. Calderón found no difficulty in taking the 'paso de entremés' and with it 'extrapolar a la comedia'. The only thing required for successful dramatic extrapolation was to give the process few good 'whacks to the head'.

---

108 Calderón de la Barca, *Obras*, vol. 2, p. 1339.
109 Ibid., vol. 2, p. 1343.

DEATH, RELIGION AND LAUGHTER

La devoción de la cruz[110] is a *comedia religiosa* that can be further categorised as belonging to the sub-genre of 'comedias de santos y bandoleros'.[111] The ruthless criminal Eusebio, visited throughout his life by signs of the cross in various forms, begs forgiveness from God while at death's door and, through being saved, demonstrates authoritatively the power of divine mercy. The drama of the play centres on Eusebio's violent interactions with his family members, none of whom he recognises at first. He kills his brother Lisardo, almost kills his father Curcio, and while barely managing to avoid an incestuous relationship with his sister Julia, he does manage to drive her to commit heinous murders. Julia herself is redeemed at the end and makes a miraculous ascent into the sky, embracing a cross as her flabbergasted pursuers look on. *Comedias religiosas* combine elements of the standard *comedia de capa y espada* with miraculous scenes, often involving impressive stage machinery.[112] *La devoción de la cruz* relies upon *capa y espada* formulae, as it features a jealous father, more than one night-time lover's tryst, and even a duel to the death. What this *comedia* does not feature is a complicated, or even dynamic, plot. Neither does the play feature an urban setting, or the classic room with many doors allowing for the frenetic entrances and exits that provide excitement for the *capa y espada* genre. This is a religious play, and the religious theme is central. The killings and the trysts, and even the jealous father, are not primarily meant to give the audience a 'fun ride', but to instruct them in God's infinite grace, and to warn against the capital sin of despair. Nevertheless, *Devoción* is still full of funny moments, not the least of which have some religious significance.

The play begins in an unusual way because no main characters appear in the first scene. Instead, the play opens in the countryside with a fun-filled episode featuring the *villanos graciosos* Gil and his wife Menga.[113] As in *La mojiganga de la muerte*, there is trouble with a cart, and shouts of '¡Merá por dó va la burra!' and '¡Jo, dimuño, jo, malina!'[114] offstage immediately cue the audience to the rustic setting and creates the play's first

110 Calderón de la Barca, *Obras*, vol. 1, pp. 387–419. This play is a 'refundición' of *La cruz en la sepultura*. This matter will be brought up later in more detail.

111 Alexander A. Parker, 'Santos y bandoleros en el teatro español del Siglo de Oro', *Arbor*, 13 (1949), 395–416.

112 Tirso de Molina was a famous contributor to the genre, though he did want to distance himself from any responsibility concerning its excesses. See Tirso de Molina, *Deleitar aprovechando*, in *Obras completas de Tirso de Molina: prosa y verso*, ed. Pilar Palomo and Isabel Prieto, vol. 2 (Madrid: Turner, 1994), p. 8.

113 Valbuena Briones notes (Calderón de la Barca, *Obras*, vol. 2, p. 388) that these characters, with typical names to be found in many works of *teatro breve* and popular song, would return to the stage in two more of Calderón's plays.

114 Calderón de la Barca, *Obras*, vol. 2, p. 391.

tiny dramatic problem to be solved. The *graciosos* enter the stage and immediately start to bicker like any traditional *entremés* couple. Gil, too lazy to pull the mule out of the mud, decides to launch into a short tale about a certain 'coche que se atascó en la corte', managing to wax satirical while avoiding the work at hand. His exasperated wife decides to head off into town to ask for help, complaining about her husband who has 'tan pocas mañas'.[115] When Gil asks Menga if she will ever come back, she ignores her husband and cries '¡Ay burra del alma mía!'[116] While Menga is gone, Gil looks lovingly into the eyes of his mule and praises her (the mule) for being faithful as he swears that, 'ningún burro la vio / asomada a la ventana'.[117] The characters and their interactions are unmistakably *entremesil*, coarse, destitute, arguing and conniving, all the while joking with every sentence: every move is made for a laugh. It is extremely significant that this comic scene is the first thing to happen in the play. The *rústico*'s antics cannot be expected to 'relieve' anything, for nothing has yet happened. Like the *pescadores* Alfeo and Celfa who were the first people onstage in the *loa* for *El golfo de las sirenas*, the *villanos* in *Devoción de la cruz* perform a multiple function of establishing the setting, announcing themselves as the play's comic presence, and insinuating that a constant stream of comedy shall run throughout the play, just as it did in *Golfo*. The major difference between these series of interventions is that, unlike the *zarzuela*, the *comedia religiosa* does not end on a comic note.

While the opening of *Devoción* is completely disconnected from the action and other characters of the main play, Menga and Gil quickly find themselves witnesses to Eusebio's exploits and are subsequently drawn into his world of violence, simply by virtue of being in the wrong place at the wrong time. In the middle of the first act, Eusebio mortally wounds his brother (though neither knows the other is related), and carries him offstage so that he may have a decent burial. The stage is instantly cleared, and Menga and Gil (accompanied by their friends Bato, Blas and Teresa) ask exactly what happened. Uttering a macabre yet humorous riddle, Gil responds:

Gil   ¡Ay Bras; ay amigos míos!
       No lo sé más que una bestia.
       Matólo y cargó con él;
       sin duda a salar le lleva.[118]

In this case, it seems quite obvious that this joke is meant to 'relieve' some of the horror the audience may have felt after witnessing a senseless killing. A similar pairing of the tragic and the comic occurs at the end of

---

[115] Calderón de la Barca, *Obras*, vol. 2, p. 392.
[116] Ibid., vol. 2, p. 392.   [117] Ibid., vol. 2, p. 392.
[118] Ibid., vol. 2, p. 395.

the act when: 'Salen los Villanos con Lisardo en una silla, ensangrentado el rostro.'[119] The anguished father asks about the death of his son:

Curcio   [. . .]¿qué tirano rigor (¡ay hijo mío!)
          trágico monumento en las arenas
          construyó porque hiciese en quejas vanas?[. . .]
          Decid, decid, pastores, que habéis sido
          testigos fieles de mi triste llanto;
          ¿De cuál Etna crüel habéis traído
          dolor al alma, y a la vida espanto?
          ¿Quién fue el autor crüel?[120]

Menga and Gil argue over who was the witness, in the same way that the *rústicos* in *Los tres mayores prodigios* brought further frustration to Hércules through their cowardly evasions. Such a situation also bears a resemblance to the scene in which a gathering of *caballeros cristianos* in *Amar después de la muerte* was made ridiculous by Alcuzcuz's twisted repetition of their solemn words. Gil spits back *disparates* at a most inappropriate moment:

Gil   Yo, señores, no sé de fin violento,
       de cadáver, estrago, ni de braga,
       de ruin tiempo, infeliz ni, ni hado sangriento,
       ni para responder sé lo que yo haga.
       Jueves Santo conozco el monumento,
       mi Autor crüel, es el que no me paga:
       pero si me preguntas quien ha muerto
       a Lisardo, señor, eso es lo cierto[. . .][121]

This irreverence in the face of death is only less puzzling compared to Gil's jokes about religion that he makes in the second act. Menga and Gil are captured by Eusebio, who wants no news spread of his whereabouts. Gil does not realise that his captor is also the marauding killer, and he gives Eusebio this advice:

Gil   [. . .] huir
       de ese bellaco, si os coge,
       señor, aunque no le enjoje,
       ni vuestro hacer, ni decir,
       luego os matará, y creed,
       que con poner tras la ofensa
       una Cruz encima, piensa
       que os hace mucha merced.

---

[119] Calderón de la Barca, *Obras*, vol. 2, p. 398.
[120] Ibid., vol. 2, p. 399.   [121] Ibid., vol. 2, p. 399.

Considering Gil's flair for satire, it would not be far-fetched to say he is unwittingly labelling Eusebio as a religious hypocrite. Any sincere Christian would have sufficient mercy to resist going about and robbing and killing people. The cross placed over the victim, in this case, is seen as a mockery of mercy from a satirical point of view. As a proponent of satire, and an effective ambassador of the *teatro breve*, Gil is a cynic. Because the world of the *entremés* and its populace are completely devoid of any values transcending basic bodily necessity, or the need for a good laugh, Gil believes that Eusebio's gestures are empty and meaningless. But reinforcing meaningfulness is precisely the point of the play, and the point that Gil misses. The cross is not the sign of a mortal's mercy for his fellow men, and certainly not some sort of token of apology for one's victim; it is the sign of the infinite redemptive power of God. As long as some sign exists, no matter how small, or apparently hypocritical, that Eusebio has not lost faith, there is hope that he will be saved. Gil's seemingly offhand comment is actually used by Calderón to bolster a casuistic argument. Satire is at the service of theology.

When Menga and Gil are literally tied up by the *bandoleros*, and subsequently rescued by their friends Bato and Blas, the stage converts itself into a tiny scene very reminiscent of an *entremés*. Gil gets to 'play the martyr', saying 'de San Sebastián me han puesto', while Menga hints that she may enjoy being tied up, provided that nobody kills her.[122] Not content with one joke about his plight, Gil goes on to associate his and Menga's capture with that of hapless prisoners tied up at the infamous 'Peralvillo'.[123] Thus the image of the martyred Saint Sebastian fuses with that of a common criminal: both are shot full of arrows. Gil, despite his rustic upbringing, bears the mark of a true *conceptista*, and religious imagery is not off limits for his playful attacks bordering on sacrilege.

The final ridiculous religious image propagated by Gil appears in the opening of the third act.

(Monte)

Sale Gil, con muchas cruces, y una muy grande al pecho

Gil   Por leña a ese monte voy,
que Menga me lo ha mandado,
y para ir seguro, he hallado
una brava invención hoy.
Que de la cruz dicen que es
devoto Eusebio, y así
he salido armado aquí

[122] Calderón de la Barca, *Obras*, vol. 2, p. 403.
[123] Ibid., vol. 2, p. 403. Covarrubias, in *Tesoro*, describes 'Perlalvillo' as 'un pago junto a Ciudad Real, donde la Santa Hermandad haze justicia de los delincuentes que pertenecen a su jurisdición, con la pena de saetas'. Another joke with this word can be found in Rojas Zorrilla's *Entre bobos anda el juego*, l. 544.

de la cabeza a los pies.
Dicho y hecho: ¡éste es pardiez![124]

Gil's 'devotion' is pure *entremés*-style religiosity, not a question of the *devoción* mentioned in the play's title, but instead something leaning towards superstition. The *teatro breve* is a theatrical world full of charms, ghosts, spirits and magical incantations, such as those found in *El dragoncillo*, *La muerte* or *El mayorazgo*. While the *comedia* genre has its share of otherworldly encounters,[125] they are most often paradoxically 'true', or otherwise dismissed outright by the protagonists.[126] *Entremeses* depend upon a foolish and misguided religiosity in order to get a laugh out of the audience, and this exploited sentiment is what inevitably leads incorrectly devout characters into *burlas*, such as those found in the *entremeses* mentioned above. Lope de Rueda's *La carátula* relies upon this, and the *paso* even has a monologue reminiscent of Gil's in *Devoción*.[127] Miguel de Cervantes' *El retablo de las maravillas* also requires superstition of its *víctimas de la burla*, along with a healthy dose of pride and racist paranoia. Such a combination was exploited by Calderón for a joke about Don Toribio in *Guárdate del agua mansa*, who believed his *ejecutoria* would protect him against thunder and lightning while on the road. Thus Gil, ignorant of the cross-as-symbol, feels it bears inherently magical powers, like a charm or amulet. For him, the more crosses that he carries, the better. When Gil hides in a thicket, his religious joking takes another turn:

> Gil Tanta púa es la más chica:
> ¡pléguete Cristo!, más pica
> que perder una trocada,
> más que sentir un desprecio
> de una dama Fierabrás,
> que a todas admite, y más
> que tener celos de un necio.[128]

Calderón, master of Christian symbolism that he was, could not have made his character bear a cross, shout '¡pléguete Cristo!' and brush back painful thorns[129] without being aware of the image that he was creating. One question remains: aside from Gil's foolishness, what is being laughed at? Martyrdom, bearing the cross and the crown of thorns are all targets for laughter, yet the

---

[124] Calderón de la Barca, *Obras*, vol. 2, p. 410.

[125] The most famous, but far from the only, being the *convidado de piedra*.

[126] Calderón features *burlas* with spirits in *La dama duende*, *El galán fantasma* and *El encanto sin encanto*, but never do the noble protagonists fall (except for maybe a brief moment) into superstition and believe that he or she is dealing with a ghost.

[127] See Rueda, *Pasos*, pp. 121–30.

[128] Calderón de la Barca, *Obras*, vol. 2, p. 410.

[129] Hiding in the bushes (or anywhere else, for that matter) is a time-honoured activity among *graciosos*, but never before have I seen one complain of thorns.

play's main theme is one of religious devotion.[130] Thus one could speculate that all the jocular religious references are meant to degrade the main theme. This might seem shocking, especially coming from Calderón, but it should not surprise us. *La mojiganga de la muerte* was similar to a degraded and drunken *auto sacramental*, a serious genre known as 'un pequeño sermón en verso'. *La mojiganga del pésame de la viuda* made a complete mockery of one of the most solemn of religious observances. The *teatro breve*, which thrives on degradation, covers all aspects of life, including the religious. Life itself is full of religious degradation, often perpetrated by superstitious or sacrilegious fools. The easiest explanation for Gil's joking can come from following the lead of contemporary *teatro breve* apologists, who pointed out the genre's didactic usefulness in providing negative examples. They would have said that *Devoción*'s degradation instructs the audience on how *not* to behave, that is, *not* to perform any degraded religious acts themselves. The feeling of superiority, that 'sudden glory', that may cause us to laugh at Gil, is also meant to constitute a feeling of moral superiority and a desire for true devotion.

'UNPLUGGING' THE *ENTREMÉS* ONCE AGAIN

Our last example from *Devoción* is the scene immediately following Eusebio's discovery of Gil in the thorny thicket. This scene is especially intriguing because in *Devoción de la cruz* it does not exist. Now is the time to mention that our play in question is actually a *refundición* of an earlier work, also by Calderón, titled *La cruz en la sepultura*. The two plays are nearly identical, the single difference being the absence of this particular scene from *Devoción*. Melveena McKendrick has written a thorough article about the scene titled 'Los juicios de Eusebio'.[131] Her analysis takes Eusebio's perspective, and thus concerns the main themes and structures of the *comedia*. Also because of this perspective, the reasons for removing the scene are considered in these same generic terms. Despite the overall thoroughness of her analysis, McKendrick mentions only once Gil's participation in the scene, though the character has much to say. I believe that an additional explanation for the

---

[130] Recall that the theme of honour, also very present in the play, is subject to parody as well when Gil praises the faithfulness of his *burra*, or when the peasants talk about the time a bride gave birth six months after the wedding. See Calderón de la Barca, *Obras*, vol. 2, p. 404.

[131] Melveena McKendrick, 'Los juicios de Eusebio: el joven Calderón en busca de su propio estilo', in *El mundo del teatro español en su Siglo de Oro, ensayos dedicados a John E. Varey*, ed. J. M. Ruano de la Haza (Ottawa: Dovehouse, 1989), pp. 313–26. On p. 314, she writes that her thorough examination of the *ediciones sueltas* of *La cruz en la sepultura* '. . . no deja lugar a dudas de que *La cruz en la sepultura* y *La devoción de la cruz* son la misma comedia', and that all pieces of evidence '. . . se combinan para indicar que *La cruz en la sepultura* fue escrita por Calderón'.

removal of the scenes can be found if we look at the 'juicios' while employing what we know about the *entremés*.

Immediately after Eusebio has discovered Gil in the beginning of the third act, his fellow bandits bring out, along with Julia, three prisoners: a painter, a poet and an astrologer. Each states his profession and how it is performed, and each captive is subsequently criticised by Eusebio and satirised by Gil. According to McKendrick, every criticism that Eusebio offers of the prisoners' claims – the painter can copy nature, the astrologer can predict the future, the poet writes above the level of his audience – is meant to reveal 'La falsedad e insuficiencia de las percepciones del hombre [que] se entretejen tupidamente, por tanto, en la tela de la comedia'.[132] McKendrick states that Eusebio criticises the painter and the astrologer because 'han usurpado el papel de Dios',[133] and the poet because '. . . no puede considerar objetivamente la disparidad entre su opinión hinchada que tiene de sus propios talentos y su incapacidad para complacer a todo el mundo'.[134] However, these criticisms, which are meant to be infused with a religious tinge, are not explicit. Eusebio says about the painter, 'dadle paleta y colores: / coma de lo que pintare',[135] and to the astrologer, '. . . que desde el suelo / no se ha de medir el cielo / que es infinita distancia',[136] and to the poet '. . . se ve / que siempre en vosotros lidia / envidia y passion', sending him off with 'Con irte vivo, y dejarte, / tu envidia he de castigarte'.[137] This last phrase is more cryptic than the rest, and McKendrick writes, 'Hay en su modo de tratar al poeta cierto dejo de tolerancia irónica que es aclarado tal vez por una observación posterior de Gil:

Gil   Copla hay también para ti:
       'De la comedia es dudoso
       el fin; que indeterminada
       lo que al ignorante agrada
       cansa al fin al ingenioso.
       Busca, Lisardo, otros modos
       si fama quieres ganar,
       que es difícil de cortar
       vestido que venga a todos.'[138]

It is possible to see Gil as a helper who 'clarifies' Eusebio's criticisms. However, if we give weight to the quantity and quality of the lines spoken, Eusebio's comments are few in comparison to Gil's, which the *gracioso rústico* piles on with wild abandon. Gil's epigram about an astrologer who did

---

132 Calderón de la Barca, *Obras*, vol. 2, p. 319.
133 Ibid., vol. 2, p. 320.   134 Ibid., vol. 2, p. 321.
135 Ibid., vol. 2, p. 411.   136 Ibid., vol. 2, p. 411.
137 Ibid., vol. 2, p. 412.
138 McKendrick, p. 321; Calderón de la Barca, *Obras*, vol. 2, p. 412.

not foresee his own death brims with enough *desengaño* to make his remarks almost pedantic. The anecdote that Gil tells about the painter, whose picture of a cat bore the sign 'Aqueste es gato',[139] could be considered a warning of the insufficiencies of copying nature, only with a more satirical bite than the comments of his master. Indeed, if anyone is to be the voice of criticism and the bearer of *desengaño* in this scene, it would have to be Gil, not Eusebio. The *gracioso* has more lines overall, and on average, each line is much clearer in its message. Perhaps the more contemplative members of the audience would have been able to extract the lessons in Eusebio's words, while everybody (*discreto* and *necio* alike) would have noticed – and many would have laughed along with – Gil's joyful railing. Satire does not ask for subtlety, and it will triumph over vague moralising in any battle for the audience's attention.

McKendrick offers two reasons for why this scene in the first version was removed from the newly titled *La devoción de la cruz*. The first reason suggested is the 'structural intrusiveness'[140] of the scene, one that contains characters who appear only once, and which possibly 'disipa la tensión producida por la anagnórisis',[141] when Eusebio discovers Julia among the prisoners. The second reason given for excising the scene is that 'los juicios de Eusebio' may seem a bit unbelievable, given the hero's psychological development throughout the play. He would have not yet had the judgment necessary; '. . . al principio del Acto III no es un moralista racional'.[142] Taking into consideration Calderón's use of *teatro breve* elements within the *comedia*, I would offer an alternate interpretation, focusing once again on the *gracioso*. I do not believe that Gil and the satire of the prisoners dissipates the tension, because any delay caused by this interlude would only *create* tension. Were Julia to walk onstage and be the first one questioned by Eusebio, there would hardly be any tension at all. Secondly, to say that Calderón removed the scene because Eusebio was not yet a 'moralista racional' is first to assume that this was ever the case. Because deciphering Eusebio's moralising requires a good amount of thought, it is readily apparent that 'la escena anticipa el pleno desarrollo moral'. If a scene requires effort on the part of the audience to detect the 'incongruency', that might not be reason enough to remove the scene.

I do agree with McKendrick that the scene was considered 'structurally intrusive', but not because of anything that Eusebio says or does. I believe the scene mainly focuses on Gil and his relentless wit. He is almost unnaturally excessive in his satire. If any 'desarrollo' were to be thought of as unconvincing, it would have to be Gil's. He is an ostensibly illiterate country bumpkin

139 Calderón de la Barca, *Obras*, vol. 2, p. 411.
140 McKendrick, p. 322.　　　　　　　　141 Ibid., p. 322.
142 Ibid., p. 322.

who has somehow managed to pick up Quevedesque epigrams on his way to
the market. McKendrick wrote in the beginning of her article:

> Los juicios de esta índole, tanto serios como cómicos, son bastante comunes
> en la literatura de la época, lo mismo que los encuentros improvistos en un
> camino con viajeros de varias profesiones o condiciones. Pero no hay nada
> parecido a esta escena concreta, con su combinación de los dos motivos, en
> ninguna otra comedia de bandoleros que yo conozca y no he podidio encon-
> trar tal combinación en el folklore popular . . . Los indicios, por consigu-
> iente, son que la escena se escribió con destino a esta precisa comedia y que,
> en el momento de idearla, su autor la consideraba enteramente a propósito.
> Y, en efecto, la escena, aunque técnicamente intrusa a causa de su indepen-
> dencia de la acción y de los personajes del resto de la obra, revela una
> pertinencia temática que es del todo convincente.[143]

Calderón was performing an experiment when he wrote this scene, but the
ingredients were not only from the 'comedia de bandoleros' or 'el folklore
popular'. There exists another genre that consistently features 'juicos de
profesiones' or 'encuentros improvistos de viajeros de varias profesiones o
condiciones'. This genre also structurally consists of a scene with 'indepen-
dencia de la acción y de los personajes del resto de la obra'. It is a satirical
genre, full of wit and laughter and, some would claim, moral value. When plot
or dramatic tension is absent, this genre relies upon a parade of figures, likening itself to another sub-genre in its family. Naturally, we are speaking of the
entremés, and I believe this is what Calderón had in mind when he included
the scene in question in the first version of his play. He later saw that this
play-within-the-play was too intrusive. While Gil is allowed a few witticisms
throughout the play, and even a funny scene or two, this overwhelmingly satirical interlude, truly guided by Gil, and not by Eusebio, fails to fit nicely into
the rest of the action. This is (as McKendrick writes) because of many characters appearing only once, and (as I write) because of the heavy concentration of wit and even erudition in Gil's sharp criticisms. In a way, the
experiment was too successful, and the *entremés* 'up-staged' the *comedia*. In
works like *El golfo de las sirenas*, or *Guárdate del agua mansa*, the integration of a full-scale *mojiganga* piece or an *entremés* character was acceptable,
provided that one also accepted the proposition that a festive spirit would
dominate in the work from beginning to end. When *La cruz en la sepultura*
became *La devoción de la cruz*, Calderón could only leave the more subdued
interludes that corresponded to the comic misadventures of the rustic *villanos*.
This softening or polishing of the *entremés* within the *comedia* was something
that Calderón chose for most cases of comic intervention in a main play.
Occasionally, driven by the impulse to experiment and get a good laugh at

---

[143] McKendrick, p. 316.

any cost, he broke the rules to make room for some intentionally 'intrusive' situations.

BURLAS GREAT AND SMALL

Trickery or deception is not an essential element in the structure of an *entremés per se*, but it is inevitably featured if any type of plot is needed. Otherwise the *entremés* mainly consists of swapping jokes and wordplay; or it features a procession of funny characters under a flimsy pretext, and is likened to the *mojiganga*, as far as the action is structured. One of the most common *burlas* involves tricking somebody by exploiting their superstitious nature, as occurs in previously mentioned examples by Lope de Rueda, Cervantes and Calderón. During the seventeenth century, science and superstition were often mixed, and playwrights like Calderón were well aware of this tendency, giving them material for many a joke in their *entremeses*. Such a case was Chacón's use of astrology to 'recover' the abandoned 'trecemesino' in *Dar tiempo al tiempo*. In Calderón's *El astrólogo fingido*, the astrological *burla* is exploited for maximum effect.[144]

Calderón has taken a plot device found in dozens (if not hundreds) of *entremeses* and stretched it out over the last two acts of a full-length *comedia*. There is no mention of astrology until the beginning of the second act, but unlike the 'tacked-on' plot device in *El maestro de danzar*, the introduction of the phony astrologer[145] becomes expertly worked into the rest of the plot, and indeed becomes its very foundation as the play progresses. The first act establishes the intrigue by setting up various love triangles among Don Juan, Don Diego, Doña María, Don Carlos and Doña Violante. Until the beginning of the second act, this play follows the standard plotting of a *comedia de enredo*, or *comedia de capa y espada*, with night-time trysts at windows or people hiding at their friend's house because they want everyone to think that they are out of town. In the beginning of *Astrólogo*, it is purely the love-plot that sustains the action. Secret meetings and hiding places are both staples of the genre, and

---

144 See Oppenheimer, p. 245. The article is an analytical *tour de force*. About the play, he writes that the word 'burla', and synonymous or related terms, appear over *seventy* times, yet strangely he never mentions the *burla*'s comic value. In fact, perhaps because of his rigour, Oppenheimer does much to drain the levity out of *El astrólogo fingido* by making the play sound more like a discussion of casuistry and existential frustrations of the era than the good romp that it is.

145 For those who would see the play as nothing more than an indictment of astrology, it should be made clear that any satire in the play is aimed only at phony astrologers and there is no recrimination of the science itself. See Antonio Hurtado Torres, 'La astrología en el teatro de Calderón de la Barca', *Calderón*, pp. 925–37. Hurtado Torres cites Erika Lorenz who subsequently quotes Doña Violante, who warns, almost at the end of the play (*Obras*, vol. 2, p. 164): '¡Mal haya, amén, quien os cree, / astrólogos mentirosos!' Hurtado Torres concludes, on p. 937, that for the figure of 'el astrólogo fingido', 'no hay razón para pensar en una sátira de la astrología'.

both are types of *burlas*. The first hint that *Astrólogo*'s principal *burla* is different from the typical *enredo* comes from the fact that the deception starts with the *gracioso*, not a nobleman or woman. To be more precise, the trouble starts with a nobleman, but its solution, in the form of a *burla*, starts with a *gracioso*.[146] In a fit of passion, Don Diego blurts out to Doña María that he knows that she is secretly seeing Don Juan, who is not in Flanders at all. Doña María knows that her confidence has been betrayed by Beatriz, for her *criada* was the only person she told. Yet Beatriz vehemently denies having revealed the secret to anyone. It is later revealed that both the *criada* and Don Diego, as well as the *criado gracioso* Morón are implicated, for they represent the chain of gossip whose existence Beatriz denies. A few moments after his impertinent declaration, Don Diego comes to his senses and says to Morón: 'Sácame, por Dios, Morón, / de tan grande confusión / con alguna industria.' Morón balks at first, '¿A mí / me falta hoy una mentira, / no sobrándome otra cosa / todo el año?' but he finally acquiesces: 'No es muy seguro capricho, / mas por Dios, que por ahora . . .' Before the *gracioso* launches into the story of his master as astrologer, Don Diego says to him in an aside: 'Yo te ayudaré a mentir.'[147]

This is a very significant moment because effectively Don Diego is agreeing to participate in a *burla de entremés*, though he does not know it at the moment. For him, 'mentir' could be simply lying, but when Morón lets loose his tale of an astrologer who conversed with the devil, had a wizard's 'familiar', and used a magic mirror, it becomes apparent that going along with his servant's plan has put Don Diego in a situation far different from the typical intrigue of hiding behind curtains and passing love-notes in the street. What follows is curious and a further demonstration of the mixing of genres. Instead of completely denying Morón's claims, he implies that they were merely exaggerated and not *entirely* true. Don Diego tells 'his side of the story', in a monologue of seventy-five lines, about how he became a true astrologer, making sure to dismiss such nonsense as demonic pets. His speech is a parody of Morón's claims, but instead of the typical degrading type, he has refashioned the story to sound more respectable and worthy of a noble itinerant student. At this point, Don Diego is firmly in control of the *burla*, which, for the time being, has shed its 'tonalidad entremesil'.

The typical *burla de entremés* requires an extreme suspension of disbelief; the audience must believe in incredible levels of inanity. Because the sub-genre is a 'comedia breve',[148] there is never time for an elaborate 'set-up' for the deception. It is taken for granted that the victims are so incredibly stupid

---

[146] Perhaps the best-known example of the *gracioso* who saves the day is Tristán in Lope de Vega's *El perro del hortelano*. Tristán goes so far as to reinvent the family background and social status of his master. As we shall see, in *El astrólogo fingido*, there is instead a *shared* responsibility for the *burla* between master and servant.

[147] This dialogue occurs in *Astrólogo*, Calderón de la Barca, *Obras*, p. 141.

[148] Pedro Calderón de la Barca, *Entremeses y mojigangas de Calderón para sus autos sacramentales*, p. 33.

that they will believe practically anything, no matter how absurd. It is precisely this absurdity that is a staple of the *entremés* and that makes it laughable. The incredible stupidity could also be considered a function of exaggeration. Also, a stupidity so enormous is 'ugly' in the neo-Aristotelian sense, and therefore laughable. Such was demonstrated by Don Toribio in *Guárdate del agua mansa*, and used for great comic effect. However, the main victims, the dupes in *El astrólogo fingido*, do not belong to the *teatro breve*; they are 'straight' noble *comedia* characters. Calderón had an ingenious idea in mind when finding a way to uphold the *burla*, all without making his *damas* and *galanes* look like nitwits, yet still making them laughable. He chose to exploit the characters' special weakness, which resembles a type of stupidity, namely a belief in gossip.

Because the setting and number of characters in an *entremés* are usually abbreviated, all action takes place in a limited space as well as a limited time.[149] The *comedia* makes much greater use of 'latent space', whether to describe a bull fight, a battle or a ten-year journey to the Indies. This space is also used to create an implied social atmosphere, with many unnamed, unseen, additional characters, all of whom are necessary to support the ideas of 'fama' or 'qué dirán', which are essential to most plots of Golden Age romantic comedies. In the case of *El astrólogo fingido*, respect for and belief in 'fama' meet sheer stupidity as the *burla de entremés* penetrates the extended offstage social world of the *comedia*. This occurs when Don Diego worries that Doña María will soon discover that his claim to be an astrologer is ridiculous, and likewise shortly see through his entire charade. Don Diego's friend Don Antonio answers that he and Morón shall go throughout the city, spreading positive rumours about Don Diego's capacity as an astrologer. So much confidence does Don Antonio have in the power of gossip that he says only two talkers are needed to convince the entire world. Together, he and the *criado* will canvas every level of society. As Morón says,

Morón   Y yo daré
              papilla a medio Madrid.
              Pregonaré, si pregonas
              tú en salas, yo en los zaguanes,
              yo a lacayos, tú a galanes,
              tú a damas, y yo a fregonas.[150]

While it first appears to follow a standard pattern of spreading *comedia* misinformation, such as Don Juan's claim to be in Flanders, the gossip-plan quickly spirals out of control, all because the *entremesil* 'tone' persists. While

---

[149] All things are relative. The action of a *comedia* may last only a day, or a night, or two. An *entremés*, however, is ordinarily in 'real time', and the action does not usually last much longer than twenty minutes.

[150] Calderón de la Barca, *Obras*, vol. 2, p. 145.

Don Diego feared that Doña María would come to her senses, he soon learns that he has no reason to fear the general public doing the same. Soon all of Madrid is talking about the amazing feats of the astrologer who, by the beginning of the third act, can supposedly predict the future, spy on others leagues away, make portraits talk, transport bodies through the air and make people fall in and out of love. This surprising turn in his reputation is an exact opposite of Don Diego's intention to dignify Morón's original astrological 'disparates'. The nobleman wrings his hands and complains that he does not want to be known as 'mago encantador, / sino astrólogo no más', but it is all too late.[151] The comic logic and superstition of the *entremés* have won out over the carefully reasoned explanations of the *comedia*.

Not only does the spirit (or 'tonalidad') of the *entremés* permeate the play throughout, but it creates scenes that are dead ringers for the sub-genre itself. Towards the end of the play, Morón, one of the 'co-producers' of the original *burla*, decides to take the initiative and have some fun with the doddering *escudero* Otáñez. The *escudero* wants to return to his mountain home with his savings, and retire to a quiet life, a sort of reversal of the *figurón*'s emigration to the city in *Guárdate del agua mansa*. The dim-witted squire first goes to Don Diego, and asks that he be magically transported to his mountain home, so that he can save money on lodging, food and transportation. At this moment, we witness a mirrored version of what happened in the beginning of the second act of *El astrólogo fingido*. Don Diego passes back the figurative *entremés* 'baton' after Morón interjects: 'Este encanto o este hechizo [read *burla* in the subtext] / a mí me toca, señor.'[152] What follows is a truly pure *entremés* – only it is broken up in parts as was 'Chacón's revenge' in *Dar tiempo al tiempo* – that features only Morón and Otáñez in a classic pairing of dupe and duper. The collection of scenes includes the following: ridiculous clothing, covering Otáñez with a cape and tying him to a bench (his 'cabalgadura'), plenty of wordplay (including anti-Semitic *converso*-baiting against

---

[151] Calderón de la Barca, *Obras*, vol. 2, p. 155. We should also remember what Thacker (pp. 107–44) has written concerning the relationship between social roles and manipulation, or the *burla*, in the *comedia*. Works such as the *La dama duende* (p. 144), 'force the audience to look at their society by mocking its ossified roles and championing those who are willing to subvert them'. Through her use of deceptive theatre-within-theatre, Ángela is not only able to free herself of societal constraints as they present themselves in the play, but may actually lead the audience to question them in real life. In *El astrólgo fingido*, Don Diego is an entirely free man who produces metatheatre for the sake of manipulating others, but he panics when his role-play gets out of control and threatens to distort his reputation. Because of his friends' meddling, he involuntarily violates social norms by becoming the 'mago' of superstition (unfit for a *galán*) instead of the ostensibly scientific and respected 'astrólogo'. Because the topic goes beyond the scope of this investigation, I will leave it to others to explore the link between Don Diego's conundrum and the societal restraints regarding class standing, the professions, witchcraft, etc.

[152] Ibid., vol. 2, p. 159.

the *montañés*) and the inevitable laughable disgrace of *desengaño a lo entremesil* at the end, at which point Morón calls the poor squire a 'figurilla de bufete'[153] in front of everybody else. Don Leonardo greets the befuddled Otáñez, who is surprised to see his lord in the mountains with him, by saying: '¡Muy a propósito ofreces / una burla a tantas veras!'[154]

Don Leonardo is speaking of the 'burla' in the strictly comical sense of the word, not the existential or casuistic sense that intrigued Max Oppenheimer Jr. It is as though the father Don Leonardo, the most worried and frazzled of all *comedia* stock figures, were saying 'Finally, some comic relief!' But does this mean that the final 'pure' *entremés*, embedded in the *comedia*, was also meant as comic relief for the audience? Was the audience really meant to share the same anxieties as the father? I would say 'No'. I have been insisting that humour runs consistently throughout *El astrólogo fingido*, and the bulk of this humour is based on the *burla*, just as in any *entremés* with at least a minimal plot. According to a common and justified perception, *entremeses* are meant to poke fun at the *comedia*'s themes and situations. But it would be difficult to say that the 'burla de Morón' makes fun of the 'burla de Don Diego'. They are both cut from the same cloth, namely foolish superstition. If there exists a parody directed from either side to the other, then it only regards the elusive 'tonalidad'. Don Diego does not call his victims names, nor tie them to a bench. At the same time, Morón does not use his 'powers' to win the love of a woman, or defeat his romantic rival. Yet, despite a difference in 'tone', one should be careful in labelling Don Diego's antics as merely 'lúdicos generalizados'. Though critics have used the term 'lúdico',[155] I find it an excuse to avoid a more explicit term, 'risible'. It is risky to claim that a scene is meant to be funny and downright laughable, and instead the non-committal 'lúdico' or 'playful' is used. As I mentioned before, it appears as though many *comedia* critics would rather ignore the 'funny bits' than try to explain their existence. But instead of seeing *El astrólogo fingido* as a condemnation

---

153 Calderón de la Barca, *Obras*, vol. 2, p. 163.

154 Ibid., vol. 2, p. 163.

155 Aside from Arellano, 'Comicidad escénica', p. 62, we find the term 'lúdico' used to describe a tone found in Jesuit and Renaissance university theatre. See Menéndez Peláez, *Los jesuitas y el teatro en el Siglo de Oro*, p. 31. We also find it used to describe the entertainment of court spectacles. See Francisco López Estrada, 'Del "dramma pastorale" a la "comedia española" de gran espectáculo: la versión española de "Il Pastor Fido" de Guarini, por tres ingenios [Solís, Coello, Calderón]', *Actas del IX congreso de la Asociación Internacional de Hispanistas 18–23 agosto, 1986* (Frankfurt: Vervuert, 1989), p. 541. It can refer to the use of the *disparate* as well. See Blanca Periñán, *Poeta ludens: disparate, perqué y chiste en los siglos XVI y XVII* (Pisa: Giardini, 1979), p. 78. Nor do critics omit the term when studying humour in the *Autos sacramentales*. See Victor García-Ruiz, 'Elementos cómicos en los autos de Calderón', p. 138. Neither could one ignore it when describing satire in Quevedo and Góngora. See Alberto Navarro González, *Calderón de la Barca de lo trágico a lo grotesco* (Kassel: Reichenberger, 1984), p. 81.

of astrology, or a sombre lesson in 'una realidad oscilante',[156] I would like to see this particular *comedia* as a *funny* play.[157]

How can we be so sure? I shall end our analysis of the play with three of Don Antonio's comments throughout the work. Like a *gracioso* himself, this nobleman is playful, *socarrón*, mischievous and enjoys a good laugh. When he tells Don Diego how he met a man who claimed to know the 'astrologer' personally and told of his many astounding feats, Don Antonio says: 'No sé, por Dios, cómo resisto la risa.'[158] In another scene Don Diego had explained to Doña Violante that he could not magically transport Don Juan from Flanders because it was overseas. However, Doña Violante later responds that Don Juan is in Zaragoza after all, and that transporting him should offer no difficulty, thus putting Don Diego in a bind. When they recall the situation, Don Diego says to his friend: '¿Y habeís visto otro suceso / más gracioso?' Don Antonio chuckles, answering: 'Yo os confieso / que ya perdido me vi / de risa, cuando os cogió / en lo del mar.'[159] Lastly, when Doña Violante starts to question Don Diego's ability, and he finds himself in deeper water than ever, Don Antonio mentions the *dama*'s latest visit: 'Por Dios, / que si viene a consultaros, / que viene a buena ocasión. / Id astrólogo, que os llaman,' to which the now exasperated 'astrologer' responds: 'Dejad de burlas.'[160] For Don Antonio, unlike the father Don Leonardo, every 'lance', every plot complication offers a reason to laugh. It is my belief that we are to follow the jocular nobleman's lead. We are not meant to feel any *anxiety* from watching *El astrólogo fingido*. There is not a single sword fight, not a single hint of danger. Honour is only briefly mentioned at the beginning, and by the end of the first act it has become a joke unto itself.[161] Because *El astrólogo fingido* is effectively a stretched-out *entremés* in which the *comedia* love-plot is still essential, we may not laugh as much per-minute, but this fact does not stop the piece as a whole from being laughable. Oppenheimer sees the ending of the play as pessimistic because only Don Diego and Doña María get married, leaving others supposedly 'frustrated'.[162] On the other hand, Don Antonio,

---

[156] Oppenheimer, p. 246.

[157] Not *only* as a funny play, naturally. Few today would see *Don Quijote* as *only* a funny book. However, according to the reception of that novel at the time, if continuations and dramatic renditions are any evidence, most people did think of it as only funny. Likewise, it seems reasonable that the vast majority of Calderón's audience saw *Astrólogo* as a funny romp. It seems equally likely that while watching it, they did not have on their minds the technique of casuistry nor were they making calculated personal moral judgments against astrology.

[158] Calderón de la Barca, *Obras*, vol. 2, p. 138.

[159] Ibid., vol. 2, p. 150.   [160] Ibid., vol. 2, p. 155.

[161] When Morón learns from Beatriz that her lady employer is sneaking a man into her room at night, he declares (p. 138), '¿Aqueste es el santo honor / que tan caro nos vendía? / ¡Cuántas con honor de día, / y de noche con amor / habrá!'

[162] According to Oppenheimer (p. 247), the end of the play, '. . . proves the correctness of Quevedo's dictum: "El burlar llame frustrar"'.

ever ironic, makes fun of Don Carlos's frustration, by uttering his last lines, '¡Muy frío habéis quedado!'[163] This irony must have been shared by the audience. They must relish the sensation of the trickster's triumph, of the dupes' fallen faces. In order to enjoy the play (is this not what the audience wants most of all?), the audience aligns itself with the comic anti-hero and emotionally distances itself from the victims. It must enjoy its vicarious 'vacaciones morales',[164] where it is fun (and funny) to lie and deceive. In short, the audience must watch *El astrólogo fingido* almost as though it were an *entremés*, and we as critics should read it in the same vein.

A JOKE AND ITS DECORUM

As a sort of epilogue to this section on the *entremés* and the *comedia*, I would like to examine one particular joke taken from Calderón's *Luis Pérez el gallego*.[165] Before citing the joke itself, it may be useful to look at both its social and literary history. Doing so may answer some questions concerning decorum, the limits of satire and dramatic genres, and the adherence to a particular 'tonalidad' that these dramatic genres supposedly demand. The joke in question is an anti-Semitic one, or to be more precise, anti-*converso*.

As people who were often persecuted and marginalised, Jews in Spain were the subject of negative stereotypes and consequently became the butt of many jokes. Even when socially integrated, Jews would remain the target of fear and resentment, and their seemingly inevitable outsider-status continued to supply material for jokers intent on belittling those seen as a threat. The reasons for this antagonism, varying from religious intolerance to envy of superior wealth and influence, are more properly the subject of a historical or sociological study[166] and shall not be dealt with here. Anti-Semitic humour in Spain was a type of cruelly joyful attack, a type of satire based on imagined vices, and it came from a tradition that ran deep. In terms of popular literature, such humour could be found circulating in the folk tradition, in rhymes and proverbs that were originally orally transmitted but found their way into books.[167] Stereotypes found in the *refranes* are closely related to the Jew as a stock character in various forms of early literature, including theatre.

---

163 Calderón de la Barca, *Obras*, vol. 2, p. 164.

164 Asensio, *Itinerario*, p. 234.   165 Calderón de la Barca, *Obras*, vol. 1.

166 See, for example, B. Netanyahu, *Toward the Inquisition: Essays on Jewish and Converso History in Late Medieval Spain* (Ithaca: Cornell University Press, 1997).

167 See Gonzalo Correas, *Vocabulario de refranes y frases proverbiales* (Madrid: Visor, 1992), p. 253, for examples such as 'Judío ni puerco, no le metas en güerto', and 'El Judío, porque ganó la primera [mano], azota a su hijo'. Francisco Rodríguez Marín, *Más de 21.000 refranes castellanos no contenidos en la copiosa colección del Maestro Gonzalo Correas* (Madrid: Revista de Archivos, Bibliotecas y Museos, 1926), p. 228, collects such proverbs as 'Judío a caballo es querer acaballo [read 'acabarlo'] de perder', and 'Judío y trabajar, no se pueden concordar', or 'Judío de larga nariz, paga la farda a Villasís'.

In religious dramatic works, the Jew could take on allegorical significance as he represented the ignorance of those who did not recognise the arrival of the Messiah. The idea of the Jews' misguided 'waiting' was to become fodder for jokes, both religious and secular, well into the seventeenth century.[168] From the earliest examples of Spanish literature, we see Jews as the butt of jokes. In the famous epic poem of *El Cid*, a case where the oral tradition meets the written, Jewish financiers are fooled by the hero in what has been called one of the three humorous scenes in the poem.[169]

After 1492, the year of the official expulsion of the Jews from Spain, the persecution became absolute and even more complex. Aside from hating people because they were Jewish (many families tried at first to continue their religious practices), anti-Semites could target anybody who acted remotely Jewish, accusing that person of heresy, whether this was true or not. New laws for entering professions, *estatutos de limpieza de sangre*, led to the need for erasing any trace of Jewish identity, a feat most often attempted through *pruebas* and *ejecutorias*.[170] The absurd quest for 'limpieza' did not calm people's minds but, quite the opposite, only contributed to a climate of fear and suspicion, combining traditional religious anti-Semitism with a similarly irrational fear of racial contamination. Such fear provided even more fodder for jokes, and anti-*converso* humour developed, poking fun at the *cristianos nuevos*' attempts to clear their names, while the jokers continued to lampoon the 'errors' of their victims' Jewish ancestors. In fact, paranoia about 'limpieza de sangre' was so rampant, or at least was so appetising a theme, that playwrights would anachronistically superimpose these sixteenth- and seventeenth-century values on characters and settings from long before the expulsion of the Jews.[171]

Because anti-Semitism, often in a humorous form, thrived in oral folklore tradition, and because such humour was crude, based on simple puns, in a sense 'popular', it should come as no surprise that the *teatro breve* is rife with jokes about *conversos* and Jews. Most often, the victim's status is originally ambiguous, but the attacker's insinuations seem to indicate that the victim has something to hide. The thinly veiled attacks put the victim on the defensive, making him often seem 'guilty' of being a *cristiano nuevo*. In the *teatro breve*, the

---

168 Edward Glaser, 'Referencias antisemitas en la literatura peninsular de la Edad de Oro', *Nueva revista de filología española*, 8 (1954), 54–9.

169 Josep M. Sola-Solé, 'De nuevo sobre las arcas del Cid', in his book, *Sobre árabes, judíos y marranos y su impacto en la lengua y literatura españolas* (Barcelona: Puvill, 1983), p. 132.

170 Albert A. Sicroff, *Los estatutos de limpieza de sangre: controversias entre los siglos XV y XVII*, trans. Mauro Armiño (Madrid: Taurus, 1985).

171 Salomon Noël, *Lo villano en el teatro del Siglo de Oro*, trans. Beatriz Chenot (Madrid: Castalia, 1985). Salomon writes of Lope's *Fuenteovejuna* (p. 690), where, 'La alusión de los villanos de Fuenteovejuna a las cruces del Comendador, atribuidas ilegítimamente a personas cuya limpieza de sangre no es patente, era reflejo de una preocupación propia de los años 1610–1615, mucho más que del año 1476, fecha en la que se sitúa históricamente la insurrección.'

figures of the *caballero ridículo* and the *cristiano nuevo* often intersect. During Calderón's time, many *cristianos nuevos* sought to clear their names by purchasing noble titles and thus establishing their *hidalguía*, though the whole system of *estatutos de limpieza de sangre* itself was fraught with problems.[172] At the same time, the purchase of titles, together with diminished land holdings, was leading to a devaluation of the title 'don'. Ironic titles such as Don Vinoso[173] or Don Pegote[174] may have made light of this fact. Thus, along with being a general disgrace, like the *escudero* of *Lazarillo de Tormes*, many a poor 'hidalgo' was also suspected of having a less-than-pure lineage. Because it seems to have been rare to openly condemn someone as a *converso* in public (thus furnishing much material for allusive satirical works, like those of Quevedo), and the *teatro breve* reflected this custom to some degree, the art of innuendo became more elaborate. This elaboration meant that the jokes' level of wit also increased as attacks became more and more varied and allusive. The case of the *Alcaldes encontrados*[175] series is a prime example. These six *entremeses* demonstrate the tremendous popularity of anti-*converso* humour, for the latter five surely followed the unmitigated success of the first. These pieces continually pit the sarcastic and apparently 'limpio' Domingo against the suspect Mojarrilla in a battle of wits where Mojarrilla is constantly forced to defend himself against accusations of being a crypto-Jew. Here is a sample taken from the *segunda parte*. In this case, Mojarrilla is also a defendant in a legal battle.

Escribano   Aquí se queja
                una mujer casada de Domiño,
                que cantando a su puerta la inquietaba.

---

[172] See Castro, *De la edad conflictiva*, p. 208. He writes: 'A medida que avanzaba el siglo XVI las situaciones se hacían más complejas y exacerbadas con los pruritos de limpieza de sangre, vivísimos en todas las regiones, también en Cataluña. Los "impuros" sabían que lo eran. Pese a su nueva cristiandad, a menudo sincera; no obstante las ejecutorias de hidalguía, tan solicitadas entre ellos, y su frecuente bienestar económico, la verdad es que los "no limpios" veían consumiéndose.' See also Antonio Domínguez Ortiz, *La clase social de los conversos en Castilla en la edad moderna* (Granada: Universidad de Granada, 1991), p. 98, who cites a report from 1618: 'Porque según el modo que hoy se guarda en el hacer de las dichas informaciones [for the verification of *limpieza de sangre*], son innumerables las falsedades de escrituras, perjurios, sobornos, maldades y agravios que pasan en ellas [. . .] que nos es notorio que todas las venganzas de nuestros naturales, que antiguamente se solían tomar con espada y lanza, feneciéndose brevísimamente con la composición de la pendencia, las libran ahora en la lengua como mujeres para decir mal contra el enemigo o prójimo que imagina le ha hecho alguna ofensa en cualquier información que haya de hacerse del o de alguno de su linaje . . .'

[173] From Quiñones de Benavente's *Los coches*, in *Joco seria*.

[174] The title character of one of Calderón's *entremeses*.

[175] The authorship, once thought to belong to Quiñones de Benavente alone, is now very much in question, and the pieces are now considered anonymously written. All six can be found in Cotarelo, *Colección de entremeses*, but I shall use the edition *Teatro breve de los siglos XVI y XVII*, ed. Javier Huerta Calvo (Madrid: Taurus, 1985), pp. 190–8.

Mojarrilla	¿Como? Esperad[176] un poco; ¿quién cantaba?
Domingo	Pues ¿quién cantaba? Yo.
Mojarrilla	¡Lindo Becerro!
Domingo	Haceos allá, no me adoréis por yerro.[177]
Mojarrilla	Yo os hiciera becerro si pudiera.
Domingo	No os faltará de qué, porque a manadas dará vuestra mujer las arracadas.
Mojarrilla	Sois villano, harto de ajos y cebollas.
Domingo	Y vos no, que aun echáis menos las ollas.
Mojarrilla	Echar menos las ollas ¿es delito?
Domingo	No, señor, si no fueran las de Egito.[178]

[Later, the tables turn, and Domingo is accused of stealing bacon from Mojarrilla.]

Domingo	Yo cumplí en eso con lo que debía en desear vuestros sucesos buenos, que de los enemigos . . .
Mojarrilla	. . . ¿Qué?
Domingo	Los menos.[179]
Mojarrilla	Pagaréis el tocino por entero.
Domingo	Sé que más lo queréis vos en dinero.[180]
Mojarrilla	Muchos humos tenéis.
Domingo	Pues no es por tema. Debo estar junto alguno que se quema.[181]

And the list of jokes goes on. Calderón did not ignore the popularity of this comic pairing, and he features two 'alcaldes' in his *Entremés de los instrumentos*. Rechonchón takes the place of Domingo, and Oruga takes the place of Mojarrilla, but the jokes are very much the same. The two 'alcaldes' have arrived to arrest a band of unruly musicians. Here is a small sample:

Rechonchón	Oíd, alcalde Oruga, y ¿con qué hurtan?
Oruga	Con escalas y llaves.
Rechonchón	Mas ¿de veras? Pensé que con agujas y tijeras.[182]

---

[176] An anti-Semitic 'waiting' reference.

[177] A reference to the Golden Calf.

[178] The Jews who wandered in the desert, even after being freed by Moses, still thought back hungrily to the fleshpots of Egypt.

[179] That is, the less bacon for Mojarrilla (accused of being a Jew), the better.

[180] A reference to the supposed obsession Jews had for money.

[181] A reference to being burned at the stake for heresy. This text is taken from *Teatro breve de los siglos XVI y XVII*, pp. 193–4, ll. 66–75, 81–8.

[182] Tailor was a common profession among *conversos*.

Oruga	Eso no, no he de creello, camarada.
Rechonchón	Vos no estáis obligado a creer nada.
Oruga	Yo, ¿pues por qué? No entiendo este enredo.
Rechonchón	Porque en vuestro linaje no hubo Credo.[183]

Though Calderón employs an allusion requiring some thought to decipher, he also includes 'straight insults' that are crass and blatant.

We are in the world of the *entremés*, the most freely expressive dramatic art form of the time, where hateful sentiments and the desire for a good time would come together in an explosion of cruel laughter. Was such 'tonalidad' permissible in the *comedia*? Conventional *comedia* criticism seems to imply that the *entremés* stands for all that the *comedia* is not. The *entremés* is a manifestation of popular sentiment, with humble rag-tag characters, coarse language, debased themes and much more of a connection to 'real life', though its plots may be as unbelievable as those of any *comedia*. If part of this popular sentiment is a current of anti-*converso* feeling, then one would assume that such feeling is impossible to detect in the *comedia*. The *damas* and the *galanes* may very well feel hatred towards *conversos* and their descendants, but they would never openly express it. This is generally true, but not entirely so.

One must keep in mind that, aside from the *nobles*, most *comedias* are populated by humble people who accompany their noble masters, and some of these humble (and often comic) folks are more closely associated with the *entremés* tradition, not the least of whom is the *gracioso*. Many of these characters enjoy a type of immunity from the unwritten laws of decorum that appear to keep the noble protagonists from saying anything indiscreet. Witness this brief exchange between Morón (the *gracioso*) and Otáñez (the *montañés*) from *El astrólogo fingido*. The *gracioso* gives his client-victim this advice before magically sending him through the air:

Morón	. . . que es menester
	que llevéis muy grande abrigo,
	porque en las sierras de Aspa
	hace temerario frío;
	aunque vos en esta vida
	más veces habréis temido
	aspa y fuego, que aspa y nieve.
Otáñez	Mentís, que no soy judío.[184]

---

[183] This joke should be self-explanatory by this point. Citation from Calderón de la Barca, *Teatro cómico breve*, p. 308, ll. 39–45.

[184] Calderón de la Barca, *Obras*, vol. 2, p. 159. According to *Autoridades*, the 'Aspa de San Andrés' is 'La cruz de paño o bayeta colorada, que en el capotillo amarillo del mismo material manda poner el Santo Oficio de la Inquisición a los reconciliados con la Iglesia, en penitencia, y para que sean reconocidos por tales'. The 'fuego' refers to being burnt at the stake.

The dignified labourers of such *comedias* as *Fuenteovejuna* and *Peribáñez y el comendador de Ocaña* often share the same sentiments as Morón and other *graciosos*, only they are not as humorous in their means of expression. In *Fuenteovejuna*, when the villagers speak of their 'honor', the *comendador* responds haughtily: '¿Vosotros honor tenéis? / ¡Qué freiles de Calatrava!' to which the village *regidor* answers, 'Alguno acaso se alaba / de la Cruz que le ponéis, / que no es de sangre tan limpia.'[185] The comment evokes a crisis of the early seventeenth century, when many people of suspect lineage joined military orders in order to clear their family name.[186] The audience hardly would have cared that such worries were out of place in a play set in the fifteenth century. That is because anachronistic *comedias* were standard fare, and an irrational dislike of the *converso*, which required only the flimsiest justification, was the order of the day. While dignified labourers were able to defame their opponents, never would they unleash a torrent of slurs and insults like those found in the *Entremeses de los alcaldes encontrados*.[187] In Golden Age theatre at least, it appears that the higher the character's social standing, the more restricted he or she was in openly expressing anti-*converso* sentiment.

When looking at the words of the noble *comedia* characters, little mention of 'limpieza' is found, and certainly there are no jokes about bacon or burnings at the stake. The historiographer Américo Castro suggested in the 1960s that all the talk in the *comedia* about *honor* and *honra* was really a veiled reference to one's racial purity. He argued that defending one's honour against attack was effectively the same as 'clearing one's name' in racial terms, denying ascendancy from any Moorish or Jewish ancestry.[188] This constant denial also explains why the defence of the 'honra' (often synonymous with chastity) of daughters by over-protective fathers in the *comedia* is such a common theme. It is an irrational fear of 'contamination of lineage'. Such a hypothesis explains situations as when, for example, the father is relieved that his daughter, though having a love affair behind his back, had at least good enough judgment to pick a 'noble y honrado' suitor. It could mean that the father is simply afraid that his daughter will marry a ne'er-do-well, but Castro has argued convincingly that the fear runs much deeper than this. McKendrick goes one step further, postulating that, because racial purity in the individual is impossible to change, a 'mimetic transference' is necessary to put this concept into a more dynamic context that lends itself to theatre:

> An area of vulnerability is at the same time an arena for action. The theatre therefore transposes the vulnerable area of concern from an

---

[185] Salomon, p. 690.   [186] Ibid, p. 690.

[187] One case of blatant name-calling can be found in the climactic battle sequence of Lope's *Peribáñez y el comendador de Ocaña* (Madrid: Castalia, 1985), where one of the peasants speaks of his noble opponents: '¡Que piensen estos judíos / que os mean la pajuela [have an advantage]!'   [188] See Castro.

arena where action is impossible – race – to one where action is feasible – sex.[189]

Social insecurity is articulated as sexual insecurity, the real-life *caballero* hostage to his heredity becomes the stage gallant hostage to his wife's or his daughter's or his sister's virtue . . . Obviously an obsession with racial origins and social lineage is not nearly as fertile a source of dramatic intrigue as an obsession with sexual honor . . .[190]

Thus, through a series of twists and turns, anti-*converso* sentiment becomes 'a source of dramatic intrigue'. In a fashion, it becomes a disguised literary trope.

Literary and rhetorical convention also contributed heavily to the absence of raucous anti-Semitic and anti-*converso* statements in the mouths of noble characters. It scarcely requires mentioning that the heroes and heroines of the *comedia* are less crass in general, and thus every level of insult and innuendo is toned down. They are courtiers, stock figures in their own right, and thus follow certain rules of decorum, particularly those concerning humour. Though *comedia* playwrights are famous for shirking Renaissance and neo-Aristotelian restrictions,[191] many rules regarding decorum were still maintained. Theatre can be a combination of both lyric poetry and oratory, and undoubtedly Cicero's *De Oratore* exerted great influence on the creation of characters who were supposed to follow some standard of classical rhetoric:

All matter for ridicule is therefore found to lie in such defects as are to be observed in the characters of men not in universal esteem, nor in calamitous circumstances, and who do not appear deserving to be dragged to punishment for their crimes; such topics nicely managed create laughter . . . In this respect it is not only directed that the orator should say nothing impertinently, but also that, even if he can say any thing very ridiculously, he should avoid both errors, lest his jokes become either buffoonery or mimicry . . .[192]

In the tense atmosphere of the *comedia*, the utter undesirability of being a *converso* would make it a 'calamitous circumstance' and true offenders,

---

[189] McKendrick, 'Honour/Vengeance in the Spanish "Comedia"', p. 323.

[190] Ibid., p. 331.

[191] Lope's *Arte nuevo de hacer comedias* is considered the manifesto for this rejection. A case in point for the *comedia* genre is the loose treatment of the 'unities' of time and space. *Luis Pérez el gallego* itself takes place on the Portuguese border in the first act, and in Andalucía in the second and third.

[192] Cicero, *De Oratore*, trans. J. S. Watson (Carbondale: Southern Illinois University Press, 1970), p. 151.

secretly practising Jews, would certainly 'appear deserving to be dragged to punishment for their crimes'. In either case, while punishment may be apt in some circumstances, practising ridicule always appears 'off limits' for all except 'mimics and buffoons'. Assuming the playwrights indeed (consciously or unconsciously) followed Cicero's *schema*, then the *graciosos* of the *comedia* would fit nicely into the category of 'mimics and buffoons'.

Baldassare Castiglione was evidently indebted to Cicero in writing *Il Cortegiano*, and he follows closely the orator's precepts concerning who may be the chosen victims of ridicule. I quote from Boscán's translation:

> La medida también y el término de hacer reír mordiendo, cumple que sea diligentemente considerado, y se mire la calidad de la persona que mordéis. Porque claro está que lastimar a un triste, cargado de dos mil desventuras, o burlar de un gran bellaco y malvado público, sería ninguna gracia ni movería risa en nadie. Que destos así tan malos, pues que merecen mayor castigo que ser burlados, y de aquellos tan miserables no sufren nuestros corazones que se haga burla dellos, salvo si no son tan locos que en mitad de sus miserias estén muy vanos y se muestren soberbios.[193]

And, when one must 'tachar':

> Débese tambien en esto tener ojo a no burlar pesado contrahaciendo perjudicialmente algunas tachas, en especial unas fealdades que hay de rostro o de cuerpo, porque, así como las disformidades de la persona dan muchas veces grande y graciosa materia de risa a quien discretamente sabe burlar dellas, así tambien el que lo hace descardamente y con aspereza, no solamente es habido por truhán, mas por enemigo.[194]

Yet one may 'tachar' anybody, provided one has the right touch:

> Por eso cumple, aunque sea dificultoso, tener en esto, como he dicho el arte de nuestro micer Roberto, el cual remeda a todos los que quiere, tocándoles en sus tachas; mas hácelo tan sotilmente, que aunque ellos estén presentes y lo vean, no se corren dello, antes gustan ni más ni menos como si la fiesta se hiciese en otros . . .[195]

If Castiglione could have seen Calderón's *comedias* and *entremeses*, he would have deemed the 'retalhía de pullas' heaped against the hapless Oruga in *Los instrumentos* unacceptable, while the witty asides about Don Toribio's appearance by all the nobles of *Guárdate del agua mansa* would have been

---

[193] Baldassare Castiglione, *Los cuatro libros del Cortesano, compuestos en italiano por el Conde Baltasar Castellón, y agora nuevamente traducidos en lengua castellana por Boscán* (Madrid: Librería de los Bibliófilos, 1873), p. 214.

[194] Castiglione, p. 219.   [195] Ibid., p. 220.

completely in line with correct courtly behaviour.[196] Thus we come full circle and find ourselves staring at the classic division between *entremés* and *comedia*. Both *entremés* and *comedia* feature anti-*converso* sentiment, though the first is aggressive and 'over-the-top' in its exaggeration, while the second is subdued and infrequent, employing in its most humorous moments only a touch of mild irony. As with other cases, one finds exceptions, thanks to the behaviour of the *graciosos*,[197] who seem to carry with them the comically hostile tradition of the *entremés*. Yet even if one draws the line at minor humble characters, stating that the noble protagonists bear no resemblance to *entremés* characters, and never find themselves in farcical situations (beyond the 'tono lúdico generalizado'), one may still find exceptions. The joke from *Luis Pérez el gallego* is one such exception. In order to understand the circumstances, I shall quote the plot summary taken from a 1925 edition.

> Habiendo defendido á un amigo que ha muerto á otro en un duelo letal, y habiéndolo defendido con las armas en la mano, Luis debe de huir momentáneamente para que no le metan en la cárcel. Su primera huida al monte se debe pues á una acción noble y caballeresca. Cuando regresa sabe que un vecino ha declarado en contra suya, en la causa que se le sigue, elevándole una calúmnia atroz, pues lo presenta como cómplice de un asesinato. El alma pura de Luis Pérez se indigna, arde en su pecho el furor, va á casa del juez instructor con rara audacia, en plena luz del día y á sus ojos arranca del proceso la hoja en que la falsa declaración figura.[198]

What the editor, along with many others, has neglected to mention, is that the traitor (the 'bad guy') of this *comedia* is a *converso* named

---

[196] Readers interested in the social contexts and changing licitness of insults, *motes* and *apodos* as part of a shifting 'sociolect' and their relation to an evolving comic mindset are strongly encouraged to read chapters six and seven of Close. I agree with Close's statement that (p. 189), '. . . the Aristophanic spirit survived within the new framework of restraint'. That is, *motes* and other techniques in themselves thought indecorous, especially in the mouths of nobles, found new life in works where the narrator (or in our case playwright) 'adopts a buffoonish mask' or uses 'satire . . . governed by moralistic purposes' (Close, p. 211). I would argue that while playwrights were surely aware of the restraints of decorum, they were willing to push its limits for the sake of novelty and entertainment. One such means of straining against decorum was to blur the line between the noble and the buffoonish, between the acceptably satirical and the crudely spiteful. One easy means to accomplish this was simply injecting the behaviour or comments expected of a *teatro breve* comic type into an ostensibly noble character.

[197] As McKendrick writes in 'Honour/Vengeance', p. 319: 'There are plenty of *gracioso*'s jokes about Judaizers and racial purity, jokes about pork and *casticismo*, puns on *raza* and *tribu*, and there are plenty of plays where the implications of racial purity are there for those in tune with the ethos of the day . . .'

[198] *Teatro de Calderón de la Barca*, ed. García Ramón (París: Garnier, 1925), vol. 3, p. 239. Valbuena Briones (p. 280), instead of using García Ramón's term 'furor', cites Luis Pérez's 'malicia ingenua'.

Juan Bautista.[199] Let us look at what Luis Pérez has to say when he runs across the false testimony in the Judge's records,

Luis Pérez   ¡Vive Dios que miente![. . .][reads more]
             [. . .] Este es un judío.
             Dad licencia que me lleve
             esta hoja; que yo mismo
                        Quita una hoja
             la volveré cuando fuere
             menester, porque he de hacer
             a este perro que confiese
             la verdad; aunque no es mucho,
             en verdad, que no supiese
             confesar este judío,
             porque ha poco que lo aprende.[200]

One finds no subtlety here, neither in the workings of the joke, nor in the virulence of the anti-Semitism behind it. This is not the relatively gentle needling by the *regidor* of *Fuenteovejuna*, this is the pure 'pulla' found in great quantities in the *Alcaldes encontrados* series. In fact, calling Juan Bautista a 'dog' may be considered strong even by *entremés* standards.[201] Perhaps this protagonist is able to get away with a virtually *entremesil* joke because Luis Pérez is not exactly a typical *galán de comedia*. While many a *galán* has been a fugitive of the law, he much more fits into the *valiente* type,[202] rather than that of a *caballero*. In strict terms, he is not even a noble

---

[199] The only exception that I can find comes from Valbuena Briones in his edition, where he writes, on p. 280: 'Tópico de alusión literaria ocurre en el episodio en el que Luis Pérez arranca la hoja del proceso que contiene la declaración del judío Juan Bautista. El osado personaje se define como un: "curioso impertinente," llamando la atención sobre la novela ejemplar cervantina.' Strangely, this is all that is said about Juan Bautista. The extraordinary appearance of a 'judío' in a 'comedia de capa y espada' (p. 279) receives less attention than a rather trite allusion to Cervantes' novella.

[200]Calderón de la Barca, *Obras*, vol. 1, p. 303.

[201] Questions then arise about drawing distinctions between laughable 'pullas' and humourless invective. I believe that Luis Pérez's comment contains some element of humour, and has some ability to make an audience laugh, because of the play of words on 'confesar' that goes beyond the straight insult of 'perro'. I believe that the wordplay is gratuitous for merely wanting to cause injury, and therefore must have some comic value.

[202] Take, for example, the title character analysed by Glen F. Dille, 'The Tragedy of Don Pedro: Old and New Christian Conflict in *El valiente Campuzano*', *Bulletin of the Comediantes*, 35 (1983), 97–109. Dille writes, p. 98: 'The action of the play follows the adventures of Pedro de Alvarado y Campuzano, a penniless, Old Christian *hidalgo* whose sole occupation consists of brawling through the streets of Granada with his servant-*gracioso*, Pimiento, and his girlfriend, Catuja de la Ronda.' Like Luis Pérez, Campuzano worries about the courting of his sister as a source of racial contamination. In the play, when he learns from his *lacayo* that his sister was being visited by the New Christian Don Pedro, Campuzano recriminates his servant for not having taken violent action, and says

because he has no 'Don' before his name. He is a rebel, and as such, it is more acceptable for him to rebel against *comedia* convention. This much is evident at the end of the play, when he shoots a defenceless Juan Bautista at point blank with a pistol, instead of duelling him with swords.

Why did Calderón choose to make this protagonist an anti-Semite? Why did the 'bad guy' have to be a crypto-Jew? I believe the answer lies in the historical setting of the play. In his edition, Valbuena Briones mentions that the action takes place circa 1588,[203] during the preparations for the Great Armada.[204] As it happens, in 1580 Spain allowed for the free travel of *conversos* who beforehand were forced to remain in Portugal. Domínguez Ortiz writes:

> La más visible repercusión de la entrada de los conversos portugueses la encontramos en el recrudecimiento de las actividades de la Inquisición española, que, a fines del XVI, sofocados los brotes de luteranismo, ya cada vez más raros los casos de judaizantes, apenas encontraba materia en que ejercer su jurisdicción; pero ya en un auto de 1595 aparecen 98 judaizantes en Sevilla, y durante todo el siglo XVII no deja de encontrárseles en ningún auto; casi todos eran de procedencia portuguesa, de manera que portugués y judío llegaron a ser para el vulgo palabras casi equivalentes.[205]

The first recorded performance of *Luis Pérez el gallego* occurred in 1629,[206] almost fifty years after Felipe II's decree, but the event must have been fresh in the collective memory of Calderón's audience, for they saw reminders of its repercussions all around them. It appears as though Luis Pérez personifies a widespread resentment that was contemporary with his era, the 1580s, yet which lasted into Calderón's time. In the widest literary sense, the *gallego* protagonist was not alone in his vicious attack, in spite of its crudity relative

---

(*Biblioteca de Autores Españoles*, 49, p. 570): 'Mira Pimiento, a mi hermana, / A don Pedro y al morisco / De su padre, al berberisco / De su abuelo, cosa es llana / Que si los cojo este día, / Sin que lleguen a ser dos, / He de dar, si vive Dios, / Con ellos en Berbería / Y a ti te arroje también.' The word 'valiente' most often has positive moral connotations and is thus used in other *comedias* such as *El valiente justiciero*, and *El negro valiente de Flandes*, by Agustín Moreto and Andrés de Claramonte respectively. Yet *Autoridades* reminds us that 'valiente' can also be a synonym for 'Valentón: El arrogante, o que se jacta de guapo, u valiente'.

203 Calderón de la Barca, *Obras*, vol. 1, p. 280.

204 Valbuena Briones signals these lines from *Luis Pérez* in Calderón de la Barca, *Obras*, vol. 1, p. 291: 'espuma y sal a las islas / del Norte . . . / . . . besen sus doradas torres / las católicas banderas'.

205 Domínguez Ortiz, *La clase social de los conversos*, p. 82. I gratefully thank Professor Ronald Surtz of Princeton University for pointing out the historical significance in having a *converso* in a play set by the Portuguese border.

206 Calderón de la Barca, *Obras*, vol. 1, p. 280. Valbuena Briones cites N. D. Shergold and J. E. Varey, 'Some Early Calderón Dates', *Bulletin of Hispanic Studies*, 38 (1961), 280–1.

to his higher-than-normal social standing. However, Luis Pérez does appear alone, or at least in rare company, in that he tells his acrimonious joke from inside a *comedia*. More than mere chance must be responsible for allowing this exceptional event to occur. Somehow, the setting, coupled with Luis Pérez's rebellious nature,[207] allowed Calderón to break the rules as he did in other *comedias*. The eruption of Luis Pérez's deadly wrath at the end of the second act depends on an obvious rupture with decorum, but beyond that, the joke requires little invention. All Calderón needed to do was borrow the time-honoured technique of anti-*converso* and anti-Semitic *pullas* from the *entremés* tradition and stick them in the mouth of his hero. In the end, however, such jokes are no laughing matter. Luis Pérez's quip is a warning about vengeance, something taken very seriously in the *comedia* genre. The worst that the victim of the *entremés* may endure is humiliation. Indeed humiliation is often the goal, for it is the most common basis for laughter. The victim of ridicule in *Luis Pérez el gallego* suffers a pistol shot that drops him to the ground, giving him a few precious seconds to confess his treachery before he dies. Does this choice of ending mean that the audience may first laugh at the wit of Luis Pérez's threat, only to reconsider its humour when the threat becomes deadly, and finally fulfilled? Did they cheer when the *converso* Juan Bautista was shot? Did they laugh? Is it possible to laugh at such painful violence? Many say that violence is also a basis for humour. What is the relation between violence and laughter? To answer this question in the context of the *teatro breve*, we must leave the realm of both the *mojiganga* and the *entremés* – where nobody dies – and enter the world of the *jácara*. There, death is usually inescapable, while laughter is meant to be ever-present.

---

[207] In the play, rebellion against authority is seen under a positive light and, by the third act, Luis Pérez approaches the status of a folk hero. In fact, one could say that he also falls into another category of typical heroes, the fugitive, a type that has recently made a return to television in a remake of the old series. Like the television hero, Luis Pérez has been accused of a crime he did not commit, and must rely upon the kindness of local townsfolk while staying one step ahead of the law. He nobly declares (p. 302): '. . . pediremos / sustento a los villanos / de estas aldeas; pero no tiranos / hemos de ser con ellos . . .'.

5

CALDERÓN AND THE *JÁCARA*

Humour in the *comedia* and the *teatro breve* alike allowed the theatre audiences of the time to escape the worries of the workaday world, and all its seriousness, by experiencing the soothing pleasure of a good laugh. The ridiculous processions of the *mojigangas* rarely contained any inkling of a plot or deep exploration of character motivations. The essence of the *mojiganga* was much less complicated than anything with a foundation in real-life mimesis. The logic behind its presentation was also simple: A figure dressed in a silly costume was funny, but *many* figures dressed in silly costumes were even *funnier*. The funnier the better; hence a procession. The *entremés* usually relied upon some sort of plot and character motivation, yet all efforts in dramatic craftsmanship were inevitably dedicated to getting a laugh. In general, *entremés*-characters' actions were meant to deceive others and make them look ridiculous. Actions that were not inherently funny (taking a pulse, eating dinner, looking at the stars) still eventually served that end. Plot points creating suspense (such as the panic accompanying the husband's return in *El dragoncillo*) always called for a comical resolution, whose comic 'pay-off' (the release from suspense) was only heightened by the delay. Nevertheless, though the *teatro breve* may be frivolous on the surface, one is quick to discover a wealth of more serious material lying underneath. Parody and satire are always present, and, given their power to criticise art and society, cannot be considered entirely frivolous. In fact, when one begins to examine the 'essence' of many of the *teatro breve*'s jokes, it becomes evident that this 'essence' is actually quite a serious matter.

While many *entremés* tricksters pull pranks only to entertain themselves (and the audience, of course), an equal number of *burlas* are driven by deeper motivations, namely hunger and poverty. The low-life world of the *entremés* is indeed a parodical answer to the high-class court society of the *comedia*, but the *entremés* cannot survive on parody alone. However distorted its vision of society may be, and however much everything is bent towards getting a laugh, the *entremés* still represents a world where people are sick, poor and starving in the streets. Even in a 'classic' *entremés* by Lope de Rueda,

'La tierra de Jauja',[1] the rustic simple's dream of a land with rivers of honey and trees of bacon is more than a consequence of a laughable naïveté. The 'simple's overactive imagination is based on real hunger. He and his wife are poor, and because she is in jail, he has brought her a modest 'cazuela' of rice, eggs and cheese. As for the two smooth-talking thieves in the *entremés*, they make no mention of money; they only want the food. While the *burla* is funny, it is based on a less-than-funny reality. The same could be said of Calderón's *El mayorazgo*, where squandering money, crushing debt and falling sick are all the subjects of jokes; or *La mojiganga del pésame de la viuda*, which exploits the curious oscillation between celebration and mourning. Often what seems like frivolity could be better described as 'putting a happy (or funny) face on a sad situation'. This notion of superimposition complicates matters because now one must determine what is sad alongside (or perhaps behind) that which is funny. This complication occurred in the last example taken from Calderón's *comedia*, *Luis Pérez el gallego*. Luis Pérez's 'crack' about Juan Bautisa learning to confess was completely in the vein of *entremés* humour, but from the perspective of the *conversos* of the time, the comment was perhaps less likely to be considered funny. This necessary distancing from the joke's victim may have been similar to the distancing between starving rustics onstage and an audience with enough money to go to a show in order to laugh at a caricatured personification of want.[2]

The technique of joining laughter (associated with delight, pleasure and freedom) with elements of pain, suffering, sadness and repression, has often been called 'black humour'[3] or 'dark humour'. Unfortunately, a concise and solid definition of black or dark humour is difficult to maintain. In the case of prose fiction, the specific linking between laughter and grievous bodily harm may not always be 'dark'. Two examples from Rabelais's *Gargantua* are enough to show this. Rarely can one witness so much death and destruction in an overwhelmingly humorous work as when Frere Jean slaughters 13,622 men in the great battle to save the Abbey of Dindenault. Mikhail Bakhtin explains that this event is anything but dark in tone, that in fact it is yet another example of the endless cycle of life, death and rebirth.[4] Gregory de Rocher, in *Rabelais's Laughers and Joubert's* Traité du Ris, finds another moment of mass death in *Gargantua* and contrasts it with the battle scene.

[1] Rueda, *Pasos*, pp. 175–7.

[2] Bergson, p. 63, writes of: 'the *absence of feeling* which usually accompanies laughter . . . I do not mean that we could not laugh at a person who inspires us with pity, for instance, or even with affection, but in such a case we must, for the moment, put our affection out of court and impose silence upon our pity . . . To produce the whole of its effect, then, the comic demands something like a momentary anesthesia of the heart.'

[3] This term was popularly coined in the introduction to André Breton, *Anthologie de l'humour noir* (Paris: Éditions du Sagittaire, 1950).

[4] Bakhtin, *Rabelais*, p. 211.

He refers to the 'Gargantuan urinary cataract'[5] in which 260,418 Parisians perish, awash in the tremendous flood:

> Here the modern reader is able to cope with their death because it does not seem as real. The destruction is not total because there are survivors and even laughers. In the case of the utter destruction of Dindenault, however, the modern reader cannot laugh, because this death is seen as real . . . These two episodes are poles apart for today's reader. According to Joubert, however, and Rabelais, both episodes are clearly laughable . . . ambivalence is the very fountainhead of Renaissance laughter.[6]

What may seem like dark humour (heavily reliant on ambivalence or 'suspension' between disgust and joy) today may not have been seen as such at the time of Rabelais's writing. The matter becomes even more complicated if the work is a later one, and cannot necessarily be explained in terms of 'Renaissance laughter'. Take, as another example, chapter 52 of the first part of *Don Quixote*, where the Knight of the Sad Countenance and a goat-herd engage in an out-and-out brawl, with fists flying and blood spraying. Few of the audience within the book seem to be in a grim mood.

> Reventaban de risa el canónigo y el cura, saltaban los cuadrilleros de gozo, zuzaban los unos y los otros, como hacen a los perros cuando en pendencia están trabados; sólo Sancho Panza se desesperaba, porque no se podía desasir de un criado del canónigo, que le estorbaba que a su amo no ayudase.[7]

Only Sancho, often associated with 'comic relief', fails to see the humour in the situation. Among the contradicting points of view from the fictional witnesses, how should the reader react? The situation is different from that in the inn at the beginning of the novel, where the elements of fighting and massive vomiting were mixed in with shouts, stumbling in the dark and lustful fantasies, all combined in a hilarious mess similar to an *entremés*. In chapter 52, there exist only two elements: bloody pummelling and laughter. Whether we are expected to indulge in the ambivalence of 'Renaissance laughter' is difficult to say. Regardless of how we react, it remains likely that some feeling of ambivalence, or at least varied reactions, are called for. It could not have been accidental that Cervantes included a grim dissenter among the chorus of laughers.

Thus, the simple joining of violence and humour, at least as found in seventeenth-century Spanish literature, is not an easy subject to study, though

---

[5] Gregory de Rocher, *Rabelais's* Laughers *and Joubert's* Traité du Ris (University) [sic]: University of Alabama Press, 1979), p. 66.

[6] de Rocher, p. 67.

[7] Miguel de Cervantes Saavedra, *El ingenioso hidalgo Don Quijote de la Mancha*, ed. Luis Andrés Murillo (Madrid: Castalia, 1978), part (vol.) I, p. 578.

its literary manifestations are quite common. We may even err in associating situations like the above-mentioned brawl with 'black' or 'dark' humour as it is understood today. All the same, several points remain clear. The violence involved is unambiguous and explicit, not figurative. Somebody must suffer damage to their person. By the same token, the humour involved is ambiguous in its source, in the reaction it causes and in its possible meaning. This is because the object of the violence may not find the event funny, but somebody else may. Or perhaps the object finds it funny, but the witnesses do not, or some do and some do not. Also, even though one finds humour in the violence, there may be no explicit laughter. It may be a case of appreciating shocking incongruities (like a satirist happily criticising a surprising act of backstabbing) or a particularly violent poetic justice (somebody 'hoisted with their own petard') that are sufficient to provoke a knowing smile but not enough to release a guffaw. In another example, a victim of painful punishment may seek solace in treating the situation in a humorous manner, an act that may not yield laughter, but may soothe the suffering somewhat.[8] Without bringing up any theories,[9] it should be mentioned in passing that both violence and humour are closely related. Something underlies their juxtaposition in literature. Both deal with various forms of rupture, defiance, contradiction, discomfort, and both beg for some sort of visceral reaction.

Perhaps no art form during Spain's Golden Age better exemplified this strange combination of humour and violence than the *jácara*.

From *Romances En Germanía* to the *Jácara*

What is a *jácara*? It seems certain that the genre existed before the name came along.[10] The deeper origins of the name are obscure, but it undoubtedly is derived from the word *jaque*, a criminal (generally a thief or a pimp) who is most often the protagonist in the piece's narration.[11] Before the expression *jácara* was in current use, Juan Hidalgo published a collection titled

---

[8] This is a particular form of black humour called 'gallows humour'. Literal gallows humour (jokes told from the gallows) is described in Stefano Brugnolo, *La tradizione dell'umorismo nero* (Rome: Bulzoni, 1994), p. 69.

[9] A comparison between some types of black humour and sado-masochism could be made through their shared association of pleasure with bodily violence. Indeed, Brugnolo cites the Marquis de Sade as an example. But because investigating profoundly the psychology of laughter is not the goal of this study, I shall leave the topic to others.

[10] Cotarelo, *Colección de entremeses*, vol. 17, p. clxxiv.

[11] In the *Diccionario crítico etimológico castellano e hispánico* (Madrid: Gredos, 1980–91), under the heading of 'jaque', one finds an explanation in terms of a connection between chess terminology and the criminal underworld: 'De ahí . . . viene el germanesco *jaque* como nombre del rufián o matón que adopta continuamente esta actitud de reto y amenaza.'

Romances de germanía de varios autores in Barcelona in 1609.[12] These *romances*, or ballads, had been in existence since the time of the *Romancero general*, and indeed such *romances* – though not found in Hidalgo – can be found within that earlier collection, where they are described as *canciones* or *cantares* 'en germanía'.[13] *Germanía*, also called 'lengua germana' or 'gerigonza',[14] was supposedly the secret language of the criminal underworld, a special vocabulary used so that outsiders (paricularly *la justicia*) would be oblivious to conversations concerning illegal activities of all sorts. Because literature seems to be our only source for this vocabulary, it is difficult to gauge its authenticity, but because criminals (and members of all other sub-cultures, for that matter) do have their own jargon, even to this day, there is little doubt that such a vocabulary did exist. Whether that which is found in the *romances de germanía* faithfully reflects how criminals spoke depends on whether one believes what Juan Hidalgo himself wrote:

> Justamente (o amigo Lector), fuera digno de toda reprehensión, por dar al vulgo haciendo alarde de esos Germanicos romances, hechos más para pasar tiempo, que para ofender con ellos el oído del virtuoso. Verdad es, que la estrañeza de la lengua, y el mal nombre de los que la usan, eran bastantes causa para condenarla, si no me valiera de mi buen celo: que es advertir de ella por el daño que de no saberse, resulta. Y si le fuera permitidio a la brevedad deste prólogo, alargarme en razones, yo las diera tan eficaces, que al más justo, al más sabio, y al mas poderoso le obligara, a favorecer mi parte, y a deprender de ella, pues no se pierde nada de saberla, y se arriesga mucho de ignorarla especialmente a los Jueces, ya ministros de la justicia: a cuyo cargo está limpiar las Repúblicas desta perniciosa gente.[15]

To lend credence to his stated mission of educating the purveyors of justice, Hidalgo included at the end of his collection a *vocabulario*, explaining all the words of *germanía* featured in the ballads. Yet for all the stated altruism, it is impossible to ignore that reading these ballads, or hearing them sung, was *entertaining* ('para pasar tiempo'). The Horatian maxim of 'omne tulit punctum qui miscuit utile dulci', could easily be applied to *Romances en germanía*, though Hidalgo chooses to emphasise the 'utile' part.

How were these *romances* (later called *jácaras*) violent? They were violent in their narrative, always by virtue of subject matter if rarely through graphic description. Thieves may steal quietly and unseen, but thieves may also rob at knifepoint, and if the victim is unwilling, violence may ensue. Thieves can also get caught. Being caught stealing in seventeenth-century Spain meant

---

[12] See the introductory notes to John M. Hill, *Poesías germanescas del s. XVI, Romances de germanía de varios autores; Jácaras y Bailes de Quevedo* (Bloomington: Indiana University Publications, Humanities Series, 1945).

[13] Hill, pp. 29–30.   [14] Ibid., p. vii.

[15] Ibid., p. 54. I have modernised the spelling.

beatings, whippings and often hangings, all certainly violent activities. Thieves also fight among themselves and slash each other in the face. Those *jaques* who are not thieves may be *rufianes* or pimps, who lead equally violent lives. They may defend their prostitutes from abusive clients, or the pimps may physically abuse the prostitutes themselves. These *marcas*[16] are not necessarily passive victims and may strike back on their own, against customers or employers, with the swipe of a sharp blade. Both men and women embroiled in the seamy world of prostitution are at great risk for catching syphilis, and many become victims of the violent onslaught of the disease, losing their teeth at an early age, their bodies covered with sores. Male criminals who were caught and prosecuted, yet lucky enough to avoid the hangman's noose, are often condemned to galley slavery, forced to endure the elements and the *cómitre*'s lash, and often doomed to die under a sentence too long for them to survive.

Where does the humour come from? It comes mainly from two sources, often interrelated. The first is the ingenious wordplay that is the hallmark of these ballads. *Germanía* has its own double meanings 'built in' for the express purpose of avoiding intelligibility. These *vocablos* or 'code words' are often playful in nature. Here are some examples from Hidalgo's own 'vocabulario', taken only from words under the heading 'A': 'Aduana, mancebía', 'Anillos, grillos de Prisión', 'Apaleador de sardinas, galeote', 'Asas, orejas'.[17] These examples often belong to the art of euphemism, where something negative is made to sound more agreeable through word substitution. A *mancebía* (i.e., 'lupanar', *prostibulum*) is somewhat like a customs office, at least for a pimp or a madam, who collect 'tariffs' or 'duties', i.e., a percentage on the 'merchandise' that passes through. Prison irons are technically rings because they are ring-shaped, but they are not quite the type of ring one would enjoy wearing or feel proud to show in public. Perhaps the most common wordplay is that of the *jubón* or doublet, which does not refer to an actual piece of clothing, but rather to the densely packed scars of a hundred lashes, given as a standard punishment for robbery. Poets (probably none of them actual criminals) delighted in finding new ways to exploit the double meaning:

> Fue desnudo, que es vergüenza,
> y en el camino le han dado
> un jubón, que por las sisas
> diz que le viene muy ancho.[18]

---

[16] *Marca* is just one common term. Deleito y Piñuela lists many others: 'En *germanía*: *cisne, consejil, iza, urgamandera, coima, gaya, germana, marca, marquida, marquisa, maraña, pelota, pencuria, tributo, moza de partido, sirena de respigón, niña del agarro,* etc.' See Deleito y Piñuela, p. 43.

[17] Hill, pp. 106–7.

[18] Hill LV, using his own number system for the poems in his compilation.

Another piece tells a different story of El Zurdillo de la Costa, a famous *jaque* who was also the protagonist in the above *romance*.

> Al Zurdillo de la Costa
> hoy otra vez le azotaron,
> con que tiene los jubones
> a pares, como zapatos.[19]

Even more irony can be found in yet another example taken from many that are similar.

> Si me ponen el jubón,
> por mi provecho lo hacen,
> porque estaba acatarrado,
> del mal que me hizo el aire.[20]

The 'aire' that El Zurdillo suffers refers to a 'soplón', in English a 'rat', 'snitch' or 'stool pigeon', who informed on him and led to his capture and painful punishment. The second type of humour is also manifest in the examples above: it is the incongruously mild and ironic reaction in the face of great pain. This incongruity is even stronger when the victim, as in the last example, is the one making the joke. This is called 'gallows humour' in English, and it is the other main ingredient constituting the humorous nature of the form.

Generally, the *romances* found in Hidalgo's collection (the first of its sort) fall into one of three categories according to the events narrated therein. The first category relates exploits, which can range from violent street brawls to ingenious feats of 'breaking and entering'. The second category narrates the relationship between a *rufián* and his *marca*, which may take either dialogued or epistolary form, or may be described by a third-person narrator. The third category tells the story of a *jaque*'s (and occasionally a *marca*'s) capture, prosecution and punishment. This may be described in its entirety, or only parts of the legal process may be shown. This third type is usually set in an interrogation chamber, at a whipping post, on the gallows or a galley, or en route to any of these. Each of these three types of narratives may be combined in various manners. Undoubtedly the audiences and readers of the time delighted in the stories told in these *romances* as much as they delighted in the fanciful vocabulary and wordplay that bore the alluring stamp of the criminal underworld.

> Such was the appeal of the *romance de germanía* and so acceptable did the reading public of the first half of the seventeenth century find it that

---

[19] Hill LIX.   [20] Hill LVII.

> Quevedo, the greatest contemporary satirist and insuperable master of the
> Spanish language, used it freely as a vehicle of literary expression . . . [with
> the following note in page] Though Quevedo's compositions in this genre
> are called *jácaras* and *bailes*, technically they are little, if at all, different
> from the *romances*.[21]

Indeed, with Quevedo came a new stage in the history of the *jácara*, not only
increasing greatly its popularity, but also multiplying its formal aspects. His
'Carta de Escarramán a la Méndez'[22] is a letter from prison that contains both
a description of the *jaque*'s violent deeds, as well as pleas that are both tender
and cynical, as Escarramán asks for money to bribe the 'verdugo' (so the
lashes will not be so harsh), and asks La Méndez to say hello to all the *jaques*
and *marcas* back home. The *jácara* was a smashing success, and went
through at least seven editions, most of them *sueltas*. The popularity was also
enduring, as Blecua writes:

> Lo curioso es que este éxito durará más de medio siglo, puesto que en cierta
> información que mandó hacer el Santo Oficio, posterior a 1663, sobre
> los 'cantos a lo divino' y sus excesos, se dice que 'asimismo se cantan
> jácaras, y el Escarramán, y cuantas seguidillas lascivas se cantan en la
> comedia . . .'[23]

From this last citation it becomes clear that two things have occurred by 1663.
First, the *jácara* has become a genre so popular that the singular character
who made it famous, Escarramán, is awarded his own sub-genre of song or
ballad. Secondly, and more importantly, the *jácara* has established itself in
the arena of the *corrales* where publicity, popularity and less-then-savoury
subject matter combine to threaten public decency in the eyes of some
moralists. The conversion of the *jácara* into a theatrical phenomenon actually
began quite soon after Juan Hidalgo published his *Romances en germanía*.
The transition from a *romance* in a book to a *jácara* on a stage occurred
through several means. The audience had always enjoyed hearing these pieces
simply sung by one woman, as mentioned in the analysis of *Céfalo y Pocris*.
However, the search for novelty led playwrights to elaborate on the simple
'solo performance' of a *jácara*. Hill may write that Quevedo's *bailes* are
technically equivalent to the *romances*, but at the end of the *baile* 'Los
valientes y tomayonas',[24] the over 200 lines of song are suddenly greeted by
a brief chorus of 'otras', an obvious sign that this is a performance piece with

---

[21] Hill, p. ix.

[22] Written sometime between 1610 and 1612. See Francisco de Quevedo y Villegas,
Obra poética, ed. José M. Blecua, vol. 3 (Madrid: Castalia, 1969), p. 261.

[23] Quevedo, *Obra poética*, vol. 3, p. 262.

[24] Written after 1615, though the exact date is not certain. Quevedo, *Obra poética*, vol.
3, p. 351.

multiple parts. 'Las Valentonas y destreza'[25] presents an even more obvious example. After 100 lines of standard *jácara* narrative, told from one point of view, the characters mentioned in the song join in briefly and share a dialogue with the narrator. Because these were titled *bailes*, most of the participants, if not the singer, would have been dancing about the stage, adding extra entertainment. Even Escarramán's first recorded appearance onstage was accompanied by his own dancing.[26]

By the time Luis Quiñones de Benavente was achieving fame as an *entremesista*, the *jácara*, in its ever-varying forms, had become a staple of the *corrales*. His so-called '*Jácara que se cantó en la compañía de Bartolomé Romero*',[27] does not initially appear at all to be a *jácara*, but rather a boisterous scene of actors planted in the audience, clamouring for a *jácara*. The *gracioso* Tomás refuses to bow to the audience's and other actors' whims, as he declares to the insistent Juliana, 'cántala tu si la quieres, / o calla con Barrabás'.[28] Juliana begins to sing in 'tono de jácara', but her lyrics are nothing but taunts meant for Tomás. He still refuses to sing, and the piece ends without an actual *jácara*, though everybody bids farewell by saying, 'Aquí jácara, y después / baile, y más si queréis más'.[29] That this ridiculously self-referential and intentionally sabotaged piece is called a *jácara* demonstrates how loose the term had become. Still, though no mention of the criminal underworld is made, the figurative 'brawling' between the actors and with the audience offers compensation for omitting the narrative of outlaws. While the theatrical manifestation of the sub-genre was being twisted into new shapes, the traditionally violent style of *jácara* that dated back to the last century still persisted. 'Jácara de doña Isabel, la ladrona que azotaron, y cortaron las orejas', is such a song, as one can guess from the title. What is notable is that this *jácara* and the piece mentioned beforehand both appear in Quiñones de Benavente's *Joco seria*, offering a testament to the popularity of both songs in the original format, along with a metatheatrical *entremés* that is more about the popularity of the *jácara* and its associations with rowdiness.

Between the *jácaras* in the old style and *jácaras* that simply were not, the *teatro breve* was filled with a variety of forms that fed off of the genre's immense popularity. Quevedo's simple *bailes* had become an elaborate affair. In *El baile del Zurdillo*,[30] two women crisscross the stage, dancing and singing, as the famous *jaque* and an *escribano* step forth and engage in a battle of wits in which El Zurdillo answers the *escribano*'s accusations with one

---

[25] Quevedo, *Obra poética*, vol. 3, p. 361.

[26] Cervantes' *Rufián viudo*, an *entremés* written near 1615, which features a dancing and singing Escarramán, attests to this fact. See Miguel de Cervantes Saavedra, *Entremeses*, ed. Nicholas Spadaccini (Madrid: Cátedra, 2000).

[27] Quiñones de Benavente, *Joco seria*, fols 109r–11r.

[28] Ibid., fol. 109v.   [29] Ibid., fol. 111r.

[30] Gaspar Merino Quijano, 'Los bailes dramáticos del siglo XVII' (PhD Dissertation, Madrid: Universidad Complutense, 1981), pp. 55–8.

malicious wordplay after another. Later in the *baile*, the two women combine to sing a 'jácara nueva', more precisely a 'carta de la Rubilla'. This name refers to the *marca* of El Zurdillo, who has been sentenced to *la galera*, the nickname for Madrid's women's prison.[31] A strange twist to this *jácara–baile* hybrid occurs when El Zurdillo wins his freedom at the hands of the *escribano*, who shouts, 'Pues, ¡ea; a su libertad, / ¡vaya de baile y de fiesta!'[32] something completely unthinkable in the old *romances de germanía*. Evidently, the *teatro breve* had a way of toning down the horror of the *jácara* genre and accentuating its wit, which the audience enjoyed more as an abstraction, instead of as a foil against the unimaginable pain of being flogged or put in chains. Needless to say, even those characters condemned to death onstage were never actually seen dead. Other *bailes*, such as *Los galeotes*[33] and *Los forzados de amor*,[34] turn the living hell of the galleys into a festive place of song, dance and contests of wit. These pieces resemble a strange cross between Gilbert and Sullivan's *H.M.S. Pinafore* and Newman and Benton's *Bonnie and Clyde*.

Apart from the *bailes*, there existed another sub-genre best called the *jácara entremesada*.[35] It combined the brawling and badmouthing of the first part of its namesake with the rapid action, physical comedy and war of words of the latter part. Agustín de Moreto wrote several such pieces,[36] each varying in the amount of *jácara* source material (characters, settings, songs, *germanía*) included. In Moreto's *entremeses*, the character-types of the *jaque* and the *valiente* are often confused, repeating the overlap previously found between especially jargon-free *romances en germanía*[37] and *romances de guapos o valentones* found in the *Romancero*. In *El cortacaras*, we learn that the title figure 'Lorenzo es valiente del hampa', making him the very representative of these mixed ballad-inspired genres that found their way onto the Spanish stage. Considering the overlap between *entremeses* and *mojigangas*, it should come as no surprise that theatrical *jácaras* were also subject to all sorts of mixture and hybridisation. Aside from the confusion between *jaque* and *valiente*, the ever-rising popularity of the *bandolero* figure added yet another element of characterisation that could easily be confused with the other two. Though a *jaque* could generally be considered an urban type, his constant

---

31 María Luisa Meijide Pardo, 'Mendacidad, vagancia, y prostitución en la España del siglo XVIII: la casa galera y los departamentos de corrección de mujeres' (PhD Dissertation, Madrid: Universidad Complutense de Madrid, 1992), p. 4.

32 Merino Quijano, *Bailes dramáticos*, p. 58.

33 Ibid., pp. 35–7.   34 Ibid., pp. 204–7.

35 Cotarelo, *Colección de entremeses*, vol. 17, p. cclxxxiii.

36 *Baile entremesado del Mellado, El cortacaras, Las galeras de la honra*, which can be found in Robert J., Carner, 'The *Loas, Entremeses* and *Bailes* of D. Agustín Moreto' (PhD Dissertation, Cambridge, Mass.: Harvard University, 1940).

37 Hill X is completely intelligible, without 'code words', but still tells of a *jaque*'s exploits.

flights from one city to the other, and robberies along the way, gave him a certain affinity to his pistol-wielding, hillside-roaming brethren. The world of the *hampa* is also considered an integral feature of picaresque fiction, and the division is not always clear between *pícaros de cocina* or ambitious cutpurses, and those who rob at knifepoint.[38] Yet another figure that may bear resemblance to the *jaque* is the 'soldado apicarado',[39] such as the type represented by the cape-stealing soldiers in Calderón's own *Dar tiempo al tiempo*. Despite all the confusion caused by many playwrights' freewheeling use of the constituent elements found in the original *jácaras*, the term still retains significant meaning and evokes a particular literary world. When people shouted '¡Jácara!' from the audience, they knew what they wanted. They wanted thieves, pimps, prostitutes and brawlers to come alive in their imaginations through a singer's narration, or, better yet, alive onstage. They also wanted stories of slashed faces and whipped backs, of hospitalised syphilitics, broken galley slaves and hanged men. But the audience also wanted their killers to dance, they wanted their galley slaves to sing. They wanted to see the seamiest side of the criminal underworld, but they wanted it to be full of wit, even *funny*; because above all they wanted to be entertained. How could the playwrights of the time have denied the audience this pleasure?

CALDERÓN'S *LA JÁCARA DEL MELLADO*

Though effectively singular in the Calderonian *corpus*,[40] *El Mellado* is a perfect specimen and demonstrates the playwright's complete understanding of the sub-genre. This *jácara* in theatrical form features two of the three major types of situations, namely the interaction between a *marca* and her *rufián*, and the story of the punishment of the latter:

> *Sale el Mellado con grillos, y la Chaves llorando, y un músico*
>
> Músico   'Para ahorcar está el Mellado
>   por cobrar de otros la renta,
>   y la Chaves le lloraba,
>   que su mal la desconsuela.'[41]

The initial sight of El Mellado and La Chaves makes most of the information described in the 'estribillo' superfluous. The 'grillos' not only label him as a

---

[38] See Albert J. Bagby Jr, 'The Conventional Golden Age *Pícaro* and Quevedo's Criminal *Pícaro*', *Kentucky Romance Quarterly*, 14 (1967), 311–19.

[39] Edward Nagy, 'La picardía militar y su utilización por Calderón de la Barca', in *Calderón*, pp. 963–73.

[40] It is the only theatrical *jácara* authored by Calderón, according to Lobato's criteria for attribution.

[41] Calderón de la Barca, *Teatro cómico breve*, p. 333.

criminal; they also evoke the standard procedures of his prosecution with which the audience must have been familiar. He must have been hunted down, thrown into a dark prison, interrogated and probably tortured for a confession. He will later be led on a 'walk of shame'[42] to whatever may be his final destination. In *El Mellado*, when the first two words of 'Para ahorcar . . .' join the significance of the 'grillos', the genre becomes recognisable and 'activated' in the imagination of the audience, supplementing any missing information through convention. With these elements combined, El Mellado's recent history and near future are made abundantly clear, almost from capture to death-sentence. From the details revealed by Músico and the Alcalde of this *jácara*, we learn that El Mellado has yet to arrive at the gallows. Therefore the piece is not meant to simulate any type of bold public declaration on the part of the criminal before death. It seems more likely that this exact scene takes place during the transfer of the criminal from one place to another, where the public, including the criminal's admirers, were able to approach and offer words of consolation.

La Chaves' sobs instantly evoke another 'back story' belonging to the scene, that of the strange relationship between a *jaque* and his *marca*. Because she is crying, it is obvious that she feels close to him, and has likely stayed in contact, perhaps writing him letters while he was in prison. This calls to mind the sub-genre of the *jácara* made wildly popular by Quevedo in his 'Carta de Escarramán a la Méndez'. If *El Mellado* follows in this vein, it means that La Chaves is a prostitute and that her love for the *jaque* is not the sort ordinarily expressed in most love poems. When Músico sings for the second time, 'Y la Chaves le lloraba . . .' El Mellado cynically responds: 'Con razón, / que yo le daba aún más de lo que podía, / y cuando no lo tenía, / para dárselo, lo hurtaba.'[43] It now appears as though El Mellado is the smitten one, and La Chaves is in it just for the money, betraying a cynicism typical of the genre. In Quevedo's *jácara*, when Escarramán asks La Méndez for money to bribe the hangman, she writes back saying that she cannot give him any money, only advice, because she is destitute, syphilitic and must remain hospitalised while receiving treatment (the infamous 'sudores') for her disease. While neither are victims of personal cynicism, both Escarramán and La Méndez are victims of that strange *jácara*-love, a love that combines the dangers of commerical sex with the awkwardness of intimate employee–employer relations. All these associations would have been instantly evident to those in the audience familiar with the genre, merely upon seeing the 'grillos' and hearing the sobs of La Chaves.

[42] See Pedro Herrera Puga, *Sociedad y delincuencia en el Siglo de Oro, aspectos de la vida sevillana en los siglos XVI y XVII* (Granada: Universidad de Granada, 1972), pp. 255–68. From Herrera Puga's examples, one sees how theatrical a procession and actual execution could be.
[43] Calderón de la Barca, *Teatro cómico breve*, p. 333.

This work is also generically exemplary because both El Mellado and his *marca* La Chaves are well-recognised characters from *jácaras* past. True fanatics of the *jácara* would undoubtedly have been excited by the mention of the characters' names. 'El Mellado' refers to none other than 'El Mellado de Antequera', a famous *jaque* and name that appears relatively frequently in the *jácaras* that made it into print.[44] Aside from Calderón's *El Mellado*, Lobato lists three other staged works by other authors about the same character,[45] demonstrating this *jaque*'s popularity in theatrical versions as well. Each poet or playwright felt no obligation to rigorously serialise the lives of *jaques*, though sometimes this was done,[46] and we should not believe that Calderón's *El Mellado* falls into any chronological scheme of the character's life. Nevertheless, the names often evoked memories of *jácaras* past, and if a poet or playwright were feeling particularly inventive, he or she might make allusions to events in previous works. La Chaves does not appear as often in other pieces,[47] whether merely sung or theatrical, but her repeated appearances probably would have gained some recognition from audience members and thus grabbed their attention. It is difficult to say whether or not these *jaques* and *marcas* were real figures that enjoyed notoriety without the aid of literary embellishment.[48] Yet the pure truth of their lives could not have held much interest for the audience, any more than did historical accuracy in the lives of kings or princes from *comedias históricas*. Just like famous nobility, alive or long dead, the anti-heroes of the *jácaras* achieved a life of their own in song and theatre.

A third reason for seeing *El Mellado* as a good example of the genre is its musical accompaniment, reminding us that the *jácara* was always a sung art form. Because of their *rasgueado* style, *jácaras* are relatively jaunty, not delicate or soothing,[49] and the melody is meant to match the rowdiness of the subject matter. Though he is constantly interrupted, *El Mellado*'s Músico is finally able to finish singing twenty verses of a *jácara* in the appropriate

[44] He appears five times in Hill's modern compilation.

[45] Calderón de la Barca, *Teatro cómico breve*, p. 332.

[46] Quevedo's paired letters between La Méndez and Escarramán are necessarily chronologically linked.

[47] She appears twice in Hill, as well in Moreto's *Baile del Mellado* (found in Carner), and not at all in Cardona's *El Mellado*, in Cotarelo, *Colección de entremeses*, vol. 17, p. cclxxxiii.

[48] Take, for example, the 'Curiosa xacara nueva, que haze relacion de vn pasmoso caso, sucedido en el Reyno de Aragón, cerca de la Villa de Grades, condado de Ribagorça, en la venta de Horguena, donde el Ventero Francisco Pablo, y nueve ladrones hazian en los caminos robos diversos . . .' (Málaga: por Pedro Castera, 1672). The work can be found in the Biblioteca Nacional, under the call number VE / 114 / 1. This *jácara* has many vivid details regarding its location, and it seems hard to believe that it is a complete fabrication.

[49] Stein, pp. 232–3. There are also a number of recordings available these days that feature seventeenth- and eighteenth-century *jácaras* played on guitar. Although these refined versions are not exactly violent in their strumming, I still recommend listening to them in order to get a feeling of what audiences of the time might have heard.

manner. The fact that a man, not a woman, sings does make this accompaniment different from the norm, but it bears some resemblance to the common
sight of the theatrical company's best female singer stepping forth to sing. At
the same time, the presence of 'músicos' at the beginning of *teatro breve*
pieces also pertains to another phenomenon, that of a love song or lament that
foretells a burlesque scene of anguished passion, as occurred in Calderón's
El toreador. In a sense, Músico in *La jácara del Mellado* fulfils both this
aforementioned *entremesil* function along with treating the audience to a real
old-fashioned *romance en germanía*.

Contemplating mixtures brings us to our fourth point. *El Mellado* is a perfect
mixture. It is both a sung monologue and a spoken dialogue, each perfectly
integrated with the other. Every time the Músico sings, either El Mellado or
La Chaves has something to say about it:

Mellado	Repita usted ese tono,
	aunque el alma me penetra.
Chaves	Repita usted esa letra,
	que quiero hablar en su abono.
Músico	'Para ahorcar está el Mellado . . .'
Mellado	¿Soy yo verdugo, menguado?
	¡Qué lindo modo de hablar!
	¿Estoy para ahorcar
	o para ser ahorcado?[50]

The dialogue between *jaque* and *marca* is not a new concept, but rather an
extension of the original epistolary exchanges that Quevedo had made so
popular. Also, that a song about the hero's demise is sung to the hero himself is
not new. In fact, it is this technique that gives the climactic scene of Lope's
El caballero de Olmedo its eerie quality. However, that the actual subject of the
jácara is able to *debate* with the narrator of his own life is rather innovative in
any genre. As a result, La Chaves and El Mellado's constant interruptions make
up a three-part joke. At first they take the verses with good humour,
embellishing them with witty glosses, but soon they lose patience. Thus, they
become a symbol of defiance in the face of the inevitable death of El Mellado,
representing the kind of impudence that provides humour for any *jácara*.
Though their barbs may not halt the execution, at least they keep somebody
from singing about it. They bully Músico into submission (he finally says, 'Yo
callaré. . .'[51]) the same way Juan Rana threatens to have his 'músicos' thrown
out the window in *El toreador*. When the low-life couple has figuratively
wrested the narration away from the hands of Músico, and the ensuing lines
are purely spoken, it becomes evident that Calderón is actually calling attention

[50] Calderón de la Barca, *Teatro cómico breve*, p. 333.
[51] Ibid., p. 334.

to his mixing of genres, cracking a sort of 'meta-joke' about the eagerness with which playwrights included *jacarandino* elements in their works.

A fifth reason *El Mellado* is successful is that the spirit of the *jácara* is maintained despite its theatricalisation and self-mockery. After all, nothing changes the fact that El Mellado is going to be hanged the next day. Though we may question La Chaves' motives and sincerity, she still bawls to the best of her ability, contributing to the melodrama[52] of her *jaque*'s plight. It may even be reasonable to assume that this *jácara* contains a modulation between melodrama and farce. At the end, before Músico sings his final verses, a scene of apparent tenderness occurs between the two:

Chaves	¡Qué pesar!
	¿Que colgado te he de ver?
Mellado	Paciencia. ¿Qué le he de hacer?
	No me tengo de ahorcar.
Chaves	Vivirás en mi memoria.
Mellado	Tuyo seré eternamente.[53]

Naturally, whether this scene was made funny or not was nearly entirely left up to the theatrical company. The rest was left up to the audience's reaction. The woman who played La Chaves could have swooned with the back of her hand to her forehead, gasping, sobbing and bellowing her lines. He who played El Mellado could have shrugged his shoulders, stuck his thumbs under his belt (difficult in chains), and given the look of a man who just missed the bus and knows there is nothing left to do but wait another half-hour. This is the risk of 'deformation' that is run by putting such a *jácara* on stage. Nevertheless, the words in the text convey the spirit felt in previous romanticised images of pimps and prostitutes. Aside from the three characters mentioned so far, we also hear from an Alcalde, who has only one line, uttered offstage: 'Recójanle al calabozo.'[54] Though brief, the voice of the Alcalde and his mention of 'calabozo' instantly call to mind scenes of imprisonment, interrogation and torture that were often mentioned briefly in the original sung *jácaras*. The Alcalde is a theatrical device that works to vocally separate El Mellado and La Chaves against their will (El Mellado himself could have easily said something like: 'tiempo es que me vaya') and heighten the *pathos* of the final lines of the piece. The inclusion of this fourth figure also exemplifies Calderón's attention to detail and is a token of his appreciation for the standardised elements of the *jácara* universe.

Is there any commonly occurring element that has been left out of this *jácara*? It does lack a conflict between two *jaques*, though such a scene is by

---

[52] See Rodríguez, 'Del teatro tosco al melodrama'.
[53] Calderón de la Barca, *Teatro cómico breve*, p. 336.
[54] Ibid., p. 335.

no means required. Indeed, it would be difficult to have El Mellado fight, get captured and be at the eve of his execution, all in the same piece. Justice may have been swift, but not *that* swift, even in the *teatro breve*. Though we hear the voice of the Alcalde, both *alguaciles* and *escribanos*, the true antagonists of the *jácara*, are conspicuous in their absence. Also, because of El Mellado's final destination (the gallows), there exists little opportunity to present a galley scene, a common setting in works of this sort. Leaving out these elements was no doubt a conscious choice by Calderón, who is shown to have a thorough knowledge of the genre through his playful and masterful treatment of the *jácara*'s *topoi* in *El Mellado*. For a piece of *teatro breve* that is only 120 lines long, about a third the length of most *entremeses*,[55] *El Mellado* manages to pack in a wealth of material, humorous and violent, all recognisable and appreciated by audiences crowding the *corrales* during a time when the *jácara*'s popularity approached its peak.[56]

[55] It is not necessarily a characteristic of the theatrical *jácara* to be shorter than an *entremés*, though such is the case here.

[56] Stein, p. 233, cites María Cruz García de Enterría, and writes: 'After 1650 the vogue of the *jácara-romances* reached its height.' Though we do not know the exact date for *El Mellado*, it is reasonable to assume that it was written between 1635 and 1650, the time of production for Calderón's other works of *teatro breve*.

6

CALDERÓN AND THE *JÁCARA* WITHIN THE *COMEDIA*

THE *JÁCARA*'S ROLE IN A SEQUENCE OF JOKES

In chapter 3, we encountered two sung *jácaras* embedded within larger works, namely *Celos, aun del aire matan* and its rough parody, *Céfalo y Pocris*. In *Celos*, an opera, Clarín sings a *jácara*, expressing his tough and streetwise demeanour in a musical way. The action takes place in a mythical place at a mythical time, and the jaunty *tono* of his song style (with its contemporary urban connotations) may seem out of place, but Clarín's occasional taste for blood, generally disruptive behaviour and good humour give him dramatic licence to sing this type of song that fits his personality. In *Céfalo y Pocris*, the entire notion of *jácara* as a theatrical form is made into a joke, from beginning to end. First, Céfalo comments that somebody must want one of the actresses to come out and sing a *jácara* because they all shout 'échala fuera' from inside the castle. Suddenly, Aura steps forth and makes Céfalo's joke into a reality by singing a *jácara*. Unfortunately, she has an identity crisis onstage, and cannot remember whether she is the mythical Aura or the mundane 'María, hija de Luis López', asked by the audience to sing for them. Finally the Capitán comes along, reprimanding everyone for 'making a neighbourhood disturbance', and he takes all of them prisoner, as though he were *la justicia* in an actual *jácara*. Both of these examples demonstrate the creative freedom enjoyed by a playwright when including the popular sub-genre in the *comedia*. The inclusion of the *jácara* could be played for a joke, or it could be used to bolster the violent image of a particular character, or it could be used for both. Either way, when the *jácara* appears in a *comedia*, inevitably violence, criminality and humour, in various measures, are part of the setting.

Calderón de la Barca's *El alcaide de sí mismo* is set nowhere near an urban environment, yet it should not surprise us completely that the play contains a 'jacarilla',[1] after witnessing the seemingly incongruous appearances of

[1] Such a felicitous term for this particular song comes from Diego Catalán, 'Una jacarilla barroca hoy tradicional en Extremadura y en Oriente', *Revista de estudios extremeños*, 8 (1952), 377–87. For the conclusive connection between this 'jacarilla' and the song in *El alcaide de sí mismo*, see Jesús Antonio Cid, 'Calderón y el romancillo de "El bonetero de la Trapería"', *Hispanic Review*, 45 (1977), 421–34. In the play, there is no

jácaras in the two *comedias* previously mentioned. Also, as in *Céfalo y Pocris* and *Celos*, the lyrics of this song do not contain the traditional types of wordplay and subject matter of the original *romances en germanía*. The song makes fun of Morales, who, after climbing on his horse, falls deep into a mud puddle, and must be drawn out with the help of ropes. Sung together by the rustic couple of Benito and Antonia, the main comic figures of *El alcaide de sí mismo*, this 'jacarilla' makes no reference to urban life. The two sing of a rustic subject, to the tune of a song most certainly first written by a city dweller, at least in its 'original' (first printed in 1654) version, one which bore much closer resemblance to a standard *jácara* in setting, characterisation and wordplay.[2] As shown by Diego Catalán, the song's popularity spread so far that in the twentieth century it was thought to have been invented by an 'ingenio extremeño', somewhere near the rural area of Arroyo del Puerco, while other versions were being sung by Sephardic Jews in Sarajevo.[3] Over three hundred years ago, Calderón chose a particularly appropriate rendition, or he altered the subject matter of this widespread 'jacarilla' so that it conformed to the setting in which it was sung, much as he did with the lyrics found in *Celos, aun al aire matan* and *Céfalo y Pocris*.

Yet Calderón's 'jacarilla', despite its dominating rusticity, still pays homage to the violence inherent in the genre, reinforcing a *tonalidad* perhaps not sufficiently evoked by the melody alone. While falling off a horse, though funny, can barely be called a violent occurrence, the last verses of the song in *El alcaide de sí mismo* do seem a bit disturbing and funny, if not entirely intelligible to us nowadays:

> Sogas y maromas
> tiran a sacarlo:
> sácanle una asadura
> que había merendado.[4]

It is not entirely clear what is happening here, but there exists some connection between the ropes and Morales throwing up his lunch on the street. It is quite possible that after wrapping a slipknot around his waist, the mighty pull of his rescuers tightened the rope, constricted the stomach, and squeezed out its contents, 'asadura' (roasted entrails) and all. Morales figuratively (or in a particularly violent interpretative fantasy, literally) vomits

---

explicit reference made to 'jácara' as a genre for the song, but the song names itself a 'sonsoneta' in its refrain. See Calderón de la Barca, *Obras*, vol. 2, p. 812. Later, p. 829, Benito calls it a 'letrilla'. Following the definition of 'sonsoneta/e' in *Autoridades*, one concludes that it is the equivalent of a 'tonilllo' or 'tonadilla', which are often synonymous with the melody type played in *jácaras*. One may recall El Mellado (Calderón de la Barca, *Teatro cómico breve*, p. 334), who says to the musician: 'Repita usted ese tono . . .'

  2 Catalán, pp. 379–80.   3 Ibid., p. 378.
  4 Calderón de la Barca, *Obras*, vol. 2, p. 812.

his guts out. Thus, we find some textual 'reinforcement' of the jaunty melody linked musically to the greater corpus of the popular *jácara* genre.

Claiming that Benito and Antonia's mostly rambunctious song evokes an atmosphere of humour and violence might seem farfetched, were it not for the conversation between them that follows. Though the structure of *Alcaide* is incapable of the sort of free association and movement between genres found in *Céfalo y Pocris*, Calderón still manages to construct a three-part string of jokes, each more violent than the next, all for which the 'jacarilla' is the beginning. When Antonia finishes singing, Benito 'praises' her, saying that no frying pan, no organ, no wagon(wheel) could screech better and louder than she. This comment sparks an *entremesil* bickering war as Antonia responds that no ox, no hound dog, not even a puppy, grunted finer than he.[5] The malicious insults must be ironic, for Antonia speaks next of how anxious she is to marry Benito, though the later statement might be the ironic one. Benito, playing the misogynistic *entremesil* husband role to the hilt, begins to rant about how he will never give in, that the time for a wedding has come and gone, and that he should beat Antonia to death with a large stick instead. He goes on to decry the crushing monotony of marriage and laments how he could not stand seeing her face every day. What follows is an exchange that can only be described as humorous and violent:

Antonia	¡Vos darme palos a mí!
	¡Malos años para vos!
	No en mis días, a la he.
Benito	Yo desenojarte quiero.
	Si no es el día primero,
	en mi vida te daré.
Antonia	¿Por qué el primero?
Benito	Azotó
	la justicia cierto día
	un hombre: y él, que
	temía la penca, al verdugo dio
	tal cantidad de dinero,
	porque ablandase la mano
	la solfa de canto llano.
	Tomólos, pues, y el primero
	azote fué tan cruel,
	que la sangre reventó:
	y cuando de probar hiel,
	le dijo: "Con tales modos
	vuestra deuda satisfago:
	ved el amistad que os hago
	que así habían de ser todos."

---

5 Calderón de la Barca, *Obras*, vol. 2, p. 812.

Ansí tu conocerás,
pegándote el primer día,
la amistad y cortesía
que te hago en los demás.[6]

Thus, we have arrived at wife-beating jokes (something few of us consider funny
today), ending a chain of associations that started with a seemingly frivolous
'jacarilla'. In *Alcaide*, one finds a much darker tone than the one associated with
the compound *jácara* joke of Calderón's *comedia burlesca*, *Céfalo y Pocris*.
Although *Alcaide*'s most violent joke lacks any reference to hanged men and
prisons, the single mention of the whipped prisoner seems to carry great weight.
Related to this chain of associations is the jump from one genre to the next. The
'jacarilla' belongs to the *jácara*, the squabbling and threats of 'palos' belong to
the *entremés*, and the story of whipping to the *cuentecillo*, a form commonly
embedded in the *comedia*. When Benito, refusing to renege on his threats (ironic
or not) to beat his wife to death, compares himself to the remorseless (though
joking) hangman, what was once fantasy for the sake of a joke now enters the
more real plane of the play's setting. The 'jacarilla' first appeared ambivalent,
hardly a harbinger of discord, but now it is clear that if Benito and Antonia had
not sung together, he would have had no pretext to tell her to shut up, and he
would not have insulted her. Consequently she would not have become incensed,
and his playful taunts would not have escalated into threats of physical violence.
The entire sequence in this scene between the two rustics is actually a skilfully
orchestrated manipulation of the humour and violence inherent in each
embedded genre. The 'jacarilla' acts as a sort of 'atmospheric introduction' to a
hybrid rustic *jácara entremesada*, full of love, laughter and violence.

The influence of the *jácaras* in Calderonian *comedias* examined so far has
been mostly incidental, limited to isolated episodes or confined to the shaping
of a single character. In *Celos, aun al aire matan*, Clarín sang a *jácara* to give
greater relief to his role as a troublemaker and dangerous fellow. He was not
an ordinary *gracioso*, but something approaching a *jaque*, in his posturing and
attitude if not in strictly violent behaviour. Aura's *jácara* in *Céfalao y Pocris*
had multiple functions, as befits the abundantly playful and scatterbrained
comedia burlesca. The stereotype of the *jácara* performance itself is
hilariously scrutinised as Aura breaks character and momentarily imitates the
actress who typically comes out after the show to appease the audience when
'jácaras piden'. When Aura changes from noblewoman into prisoner, evoking
her criminal 'enjaulada' status through a rowdy song, the Capitán and his
assistants are subsequently transformed into *alguaciles* and *corchetes* by
association, ready to quash public disturbances and eager to participate in an
imaginary world of the *hampa* that has been temporarily created. But like all

---

6 Calderón de la Barca, *Obras*, vol. 2, p. 812. See Maxime Chevalier, *El cuentecillo
tradicional en la España del Siglo de Oro* (Madrid: Gredos, 1975), p. 109. Chevalier notes
that his anecdote is also found in a *comedia* by Lope de Vega.

embedded literary references and shifts in genre, the *jácara* episode in *Céfalo y Pocris* quickly fades away without a trace, as other types of jokes appear onstage in a relentless barrage of theatrical comic madness. *El alcaide de sí mismo* contains a 'jacarilla' that might have seemed far removed from the world described in Juan Hidalgo's collection or Quevedo's wildly popular *sueltas*, were it not for the violent references that follow it in the conversation between Antonia and Benito. As reflected in the initial song, their relationship in that moment achieves a partially morbid tone, though they tease each other and are certainly in love. In none of these *comedias* is lawlessness a major theme, nor are any of the heroes criminals or even proponents of violence. It seems as though the spirit of the *jácara*, though not neutralised, does not strongly affect the behaviour of the major characters as the *tonalidad entremesil* did in *Guárdate del agua mansa*, *Dar tiempo al tiempo* and *El astrólogo fingido*. Not only is true violence absent, but its witty treatment (with irony and wordplay), even as an abstraction, is limited to the mostly humorous characters. In *Celos* and *Alcaide*, the serious plays, it is left to the *graciosos* to make references (humorous ones, naturally) about hangings, jailings and beatings and whippings, while the more 'noble' characters fail to follow suit. Calderón did go beyond the use of the *jácara* described above, in characterisation, situations and themes. However, in approaching the last Calderonian *comedia* for this entire study, it would be worthwhile to first look at two other playwrights and their technique. Each wrote a *comedia* that exploited the full dramatic potential of the *jácara*.

JAQUES AND *VALIENTES*

El valiente Campuzano by Fernando de Zárate[7] is a *comedia de valentón*,[8] as one can guess from its title. In these types of *comedias*, the central figure is the *valiente*, one who enjoys a special freedom from society's laws because

---

[7] The author is also known as Antonio Enríquez Gómez. I shall be using the edition from *Biblioteca de Autores Españoles*, vol. 47, pp. 569–86. Glen F. Dille, *Antonio Enríquez Gómez* (Boston: Twayne, 1988), dates the play as printed and performed in 1660 in the 'Chronology' at the beginning of the book.

[8] While not an often-used term (Dille uses it on p. 160), *comedia de valentón* describes a genre that is easily delimited by its distinct main character, much as a *santo* defines the *comedia de santo*. Emilio Cotarelo, in his edition of Lope de Vega, *El valiente Juan de Heredia*, in *Obras de Lope de Vega,* vol. 2 (Madrid: Revista de los Archivos, Bibliotecas y Museos, 1916), p. xv, writes of such plays, which he calls 'comedias de guapos': 'Tales como *El Valiente sevillano*, de Enciso; *El Valiente Diego de Camas*, de Enríquez Gómez; *El Valiente toledano*, de Luis Vélez; *Afanador el de Utrera*, de Belmonte; *Añasco el de Talavera*, de Cubillo; *El más valiente andaluz, Antón Bravo*, de Monroy; *Pero Vázquez de Escamilla*, de Quevedo; *El Valiente Barrionuevo*, de Cantón Salazar; *El Valiente Campuzano*, de Zárate, hasta llegar a la famosa del *Guapo Francisco Estevan*, al *Valiente Pedro Ponce*, al *Valor nunca vencido, hazañas de Juan de Arévalo* y otras aún más disparatadas del siglo XVIII.' See the note on p. 182 for the use of the word *valiente*.

of his extraordinary valour and willingness to fight.[9] Though many *comedias de capa y espada* are full of furious swordplay, these violent situations stem out of love intrigues and miscommunication, both staples of that genre. The staple of the *comedia de valentón* genre, however, is the fighting itself, and the complications with the law (difficult to call 'intrigues') that arise from the fighting. The *valiente* enjoys quarrelling, mostly for its own sake, and needs only a pretext (defending accosted women on the street, for example) to draw his sword. In this sense, he closely resembles the *jaque*, especially under the title of 'valiente del hampa'.[10] Yet the *valiente* does differ from the *jaque* in one important way. He is never a thief or a pimp. He fights to defend and avenge, to achieve glory and renown, and if ever to make money, only by legal means. Still, the 'overlap' between the two character-types remains, because not all *jaques* and *rufianes* fight in expectation of remuneration. They may want to kill just for the thrill, just like a *valiente*. Secondly, because of this constant killing (something quite illegal, despite being forgiven in the end), the *valiente* is always in trouble with the law, even if he does not steal money or prostitute women. He does not like *la justicia* any more than a *jaque*, for both types of protagonist see the law as an impediment to doing what makes them happy. Glen Dille describes Zárate's *El valiente Campuzano* thus:

> The action of the play follows the adventures of Pedro de Alvarado y Campuzano, a penniless, Old Christian hidalgo whose sole occupation consists of brawling through the streets of Granada with his servant-gracioso, Pimiento, and his girlfriend, Catuja de la Ronda. Catuja is a varonil maja, as quick and sure with her dagger as is Campuzano with his sword.[11]

Let us first look more closely at Campuzano. He may be no *jaque* in name, but he does have wit, and he does seem to enjoy killing people, provided he has at least a small pretext. In the beginning of the play, Campuzano finds himself in a situation similar to the initial conflict of *Luis Pérez el gallego* when his cousin, Doña Leonor, reveals that she wants to marry Don Pedro, the descendant of *moriscos*. Like Luis Pérez, Campuzano wants to kill off any threat to his family 'honour' (that is, racial purity), and like his Galician counterpart, he also makes fun of his rival's ethno-religious background. The revelation of Doña Leonor and Don Pedro's relationship comes by way of the *gracioso* Pimiento:

Campuzano	Abreviemos; ¿Cómo lo sabes?
Pimiento	Yo hallé Al tal Don Pedro, que estaba En tu casa y que la hablaba.

---

[9] Belmonte's *El afanador de Utrera* (Madrid: 1669) features one of the most violent protagonists imaginable. For *El afanador*, fighting is practically his state of rest.

[10] In Moreto's *El cortacaras* (see Carner) the violent protagonist, not quite a *jaque*, though very close, is so called. '. . . que Lorenzo es valiente del ampa'.

[11] Dille, p. 98.

Campuzano	Y tú, ¿qué hiciste?
Pimiento	Callé.
Campuzano	Pues infame, ¿así profanas
	El valor? ¿Por que no fuiste
	Y treinta heridas le diste?[12]

Campuzano goes on to sarcastically threaten to toss Don Pedro, as well as his 'morisco' father and his 'berberisco' grandfather, back over to 'Berbería'. While Luis Pérez made his anti-*converso* joke in front of the judge, and not his rival Juan Bautista himself, Campuzano assaults Don Pedro directly with a tirade mocking the noble's father and grandfather. The *valiente* even manages to slip in a bit of 'habla dialectal morisco' by imitating Don Pedro's grandfather's supposed manner of speech.[13]

While *El valiente Campuzano*'s minor love intrigues give the protagonist a pretext to both kill and joke, there are plenty of other pretexts as well. When *la justicia* comes to arrest La Catuja, she naturally resists and is joined by Campuzano. When the *alguacil* barks to the *escribano*, 'Escriba esta resistencia', Campuzano responds 'Escriba, seo secretario, / Pero con aquesta pluma', promptly drawing his sword and dealing the *escribano* a fatal blow. Both *valiente* and *guapa* escape defiantly, proudly shouting their names as Pimiento trails close behind muttering: 'Sé que si os cogen, seréis / dos muy lindos ahorcados.'[14] Now facing the threat of being hanged, the demise of most *jaques*, Campuzano and La Catuja have undoubtedly become 'valientes del hampa'. They are later caught, only to escape once more, slicing their way through yet another onslaught of *ministros de la justicia*.

When the outlaw party arrives at the inn of the keeper Maladros, he offers them not only food and lodging, but also safety from the authorities. Little do they know that Maladros has 'sold them out'[15] to the local judge who is approaching the inn, accompanied by men heavily armed with muskets and carbines. As the men approach the inn, the protagonists realise that they are

---

[12] Fernando de Zárate, *El valiente Campuzano*, in *Dramáticos posteriores a Lope de Vega*, ed. Ramón de Mesonero y Romanos, 2 vols, in the series *Biblioteca de autores españoles* [*BAE*], vols 47–48 (Madrid: M. Rivadeneyra, 1858–9), p. 570.

[13] In the *comedia* genre, it is usually the *gracioso* who recounts amusing anecdotes, but Campuzano's abundant wit allows him to play the joker on numerous occasions.

[14] Both of the above citations are from Zárate, p. 571.

[15] La Catuja later exclaims (Zárate, p. 576): 'Vendidos / Estamos a muy bien precio.' The names mentioned in this adventure are not chosen carelessly. Maladros is the hero of the extraordinarily lengthy 'Romance de la vida, y muerte de Maladros' (Hill XXXII) which recounts '. . . toda su Germana vida / desde el principio hasta el cabo . . .' The poem begins with 'Cante mi Germana Lyra / en canto godo, altano . . .' announcing a curious mix of *germanesco* and *culto* styles. Among the pursuers in the play is a certain Periquillo who shares his name with Periquillo el de Baeza (Hill XC) and Periquillo el de Madrid (Hill XCI), two *jaques* immortalised in song. Zárate's purpose in associating certain members of *la justicia* with criminals is not entirely clear, although it certainly gives even greater emphasis to the atmosphere of violence and lawlessness.

the victims of a judicial *burla*, of which the 'soplón'[16] Maladros is the main author. Not to be outdone, with quick movements and harsh threats, Campuzano and his friends are able to 'pre-empt' the ambush and steal arms from their would-be attackers. They also capture Maladros, turning him into a *burlador burlado*. Upon the arrival of the judge, Campuzano explains in a lengthy diatribe how he is not only an honourable man,[17] but also the victim of treachery. The 'conversation' ends with the following plea:

Campuzano	He reñido como noble
	Y sin gavilla de escolta
	Algunas cuarenta veces,
	Y esto sin llevar pistolas,
	Sino mi capa y mi espada.
	Di de palos a Lobona,
	Por maldiciente y traidor;
	Corté las orejas sordas
	Al Mellado de Antequera
	Por falsario de la costa,
	Maté a Chirinos, porque
	Dentro de mi casa propia
	Él y Angulo mi quisieron
	Prender sin culpa; hasta
	Ahora en mi vida robé a
	Nadie ni dije mal de persona;
	Por dinero a nadie he muerto.
	Y sobre todas mis glorias,
	Empresas y valentías,
	Una quiero contar sola.
	Dígame el señor-Juez:
	Si usté con llaneza propia
	Entrara en cas de un amigo
	Y le fiara su honra,
	Y este amigo le entregara
	En las manos rigurosas
	De su enemigo, ¿qué hiciera?
Juez	La venganza era forzosa
Campuzano	Pues levántese, y repare
	Sin pasion ni ceremonia,
	Criminal en este infame

(*Aparece el ventero, como dado garrote en un palo*)

Ventero, que ya no sopla,

---

[16] Even today, one of the greatest villains for criminals in fiction is the 'soplón', 'rat' or 'snitch' (to use modern jargon), he who informs on his fellow lawbreaker.

[17] Among *jaques*, the word 'honrado' means brave and itching for a fight. Because Campuzano lives to fight, it seems likely that 'honrado' refers just as much to his worries of appearing cowardly as it refers to his reputation as an honest man.

> Si está como debe; ¡mire
> Qué tragedia tan gustosa!
> ¿No está galán?

Juez   Sí por cierto.

Campuzano   En un tálamo la novia
> No está mejor que él está;
> Tengale Dios en su gloria . . .[18]

This scene of the garroted victim makes burlesque reference to the 'tragedias' of vengeance such as Calderón's *Las tres justicias en una*, where the angered protagonist takes 'justice' into his own hands and appoints himself judge, jailer and executioner. But the notion of 'justice' in the case of *El valiente Campuzano* is of a much different sort, speaking in generic terms. It is the notion of justice in a world of 'soplones', 'malsines', over-zealous or corrupt *alguaciles, corchetes, escribanos* and even judges. Though there is no proof that the Juez is corrupt, Campuzano will not trust him at all, and he will not give in to *la justicia*'s demands. As seen in the end of the diatribe above, Campuzano is much more a part of the *hampa* than civil society. All his problems are best solved by cutting people up with his sword, beating them to death with a pole or strangling them with a garrotte. His cynicism towards the justice system is accompanied by bitter laughter; his killings are coupled with glee. The only defence that Campuzano gives against being hanged,[19] the only effort he makes at disassociating himself from *jaques* like El Mellado, is to say: 'At least I'm no thief.'

If Campuzano, now easily identified as a 'valiente del hampa', comes dangerously close to being a *jaque*, La Catuja comes even closer.[20] Although she is indeed a woman, and though she is in fact able to wield a sword,[21] it would be generically confusing to simply call her a 'mujer varonil'.[22] She is neither an Amazonian warrior nor a wronged lover breaking societal rules in

---

[18] Zárate, p. 577.

[19] The judge says to himself that Campuzano should be hanged, but because he fears retribution, he wisely leaves all the criminal protagonists alone.

[20] The character of Campuzano is supposed to originate from a 'historia verdadera' as mentioned at the end of the play, and cannot be found in any *jácaras* theatrical or otherwise. La Catuja, on the other hand, appears in the *baile* titled *Los forzados de amor* (Merino Quijano, pp. 204–7), a piece with strong *jácara* influences, leading one to believe that she is more of a literary than historical figure.

[21] She is usually found wielding a dagger, however. Such a weapon, often of choice among *jaques*, distinguishes her from the typical *mujer varonil* who models herself on the *galán de comedia*. By definition, heroes and heroines of the *comedias de capa y espada* do not fight with knives, something too vulgar for their status.

[22] Generally, these women dress as men. See Carmen Bravo-Villasante, *La mujer vestida de hombre en el teatro español (Siglos XVI–XVII)* (Madrid: Revista de Occidente, 1955), pp. 223–4. In Bravo-Villasante's appendix, she lists thirteen different 'motivos' for dressing up (and one assumes, acting) like men, including 'Amazonas', yet none of these 'motivos' corresponds to the brawling life led by La Catuja.

order to fight for her honour. La Catuja exclaims that it is laughable to think
of how God made her a woman, considering her violent nature. Humour and
violence seem to be the basis for her very existence. For fans of the original
jácaras, La Catuja ought to be the favourite, instead of Campuzano, and here
is why. In telling stories of bravery, she is at least of equal stature to her
valiente friend, if one measures by the number and length of her tales, as well
as the violence contained therein. What is more, when enjoying the lengthy
description of her adventures, we notice key *jacarandino* elements in her tales
that are missing from Campuzano's. The male *valiente* does scatter a few
violent jokes throughout his one story, yet few could be called worthy of the
jácara. La Catuja's speech, on the other hand, contains sections that could
have been lifted straight from Hidalgo's *Romances en germanía*:

> La Catuja   [El Juez] me dijo que confesase
>   Tus cuatro muertes no más;
>   Yo dije que en el Rosario
>   Hiciste dos en Milan,
>   En Granada una de hueso,
>   Y otra, en Cádiz, de cristal;
>   Enojóse, y manda luego
>   Al músico criminal
>   Que me apretase las cuerdas,
>   Porque pudiese cantar [. . .][23]

On her travels, she meets a 'milanés', who asks her for money when she asks
him for a piece of bread:

>   [. . .] por aquesta cruz,
>   Que sobre esta daga está,
>   Que al estómago le vino
>   El milanés tan igual,
>   Que, si no es por él, no alcanzo,
>   Y eso sin poner un real
>   De mi casa, un jarro de agua,
>   Esto es hablar de la mar.[24]

In the beginning of the first act, she tells Campuzano of a fight she had on the
street on the way to meet him:

> Catuja   Llegué a la calle Real,
>   Sin un real, porque yo
>   Hago del poco caudal.
>   Y al darle limosna a un pobre,
>   Un maravedí no más,

---

[23] Zárate, p. 581.   [24] Ibid., p. 579.

Que acaso en la faltriquera
Le guardó la voluntad,
Vi a Juanilla y a Jusefa,
Estanques de solimán
Obligadas del pecado,
Que es renta de Barrabás.
Se llegaron Escamilla,
Soria Angulo, Sebastián,
Disgustados con el vino,
Aunque no le quieren mal;
Y viéndome sola, dijo
Escamilla: '¿Por acá
Seora Catuja?' y yo dije:
'¿Vióme usarcé por allá?'
Respondióme: 'Ya la veo;
Que con agua de fregar
Lava platos Campuzano,
En agravio de cristal.' [. . .]

[. . .] De espacio
Lleguéme a Escamilla, y zas [. . .]

   [. . .] Digo que apenas
Les desnaricé la faz,
Cuando el señor alguacil,
Que estaba pesando pan
(Que en Granada, esto es seguro,
La justicia, esto es verdad,
Por lo que tiene de Dios,
En todas partes está),
Quiso prenderme; yo dije
Que estaba prendida ya:
No me entendió, la mantilla
Tercié con lindo ademán,
Y como por línea recta,
Si no es tú, no pudo entrar
En mi pecho otro ninguno,
Le di con la universal
A un corchete, y se la hice
Luego al punto confesar [. . .]25

Both *romances* cited above, with their constant violent references, with each comment wrapped in witticisms or wordplay, would have made perfect stand-alone *jácaras*. The only missing ingredient is music. Luckily, Fernando de Zárate, so obviously indebted to the ballad genre in writing *El valiente Campuzano*, did not pass up the opportunity to include at least one sung

25 Zárate, p. 570.

jácara in his play. Amid the din of battle in the beginning of the third act, a new sound is heard:

> (*Por el otro lado del monte baja la Catuja, cantando esta jácara*)
>
> La Catuja   Hoy con mi hombre he reñido
>   Sobre qué me quiso dar,
>   Y si él diera muchos menos,
>   Yo se lo estimara más;
>   Al campo quiere sacarme
>   Para que estemos en paz,
>   Y como si fuera a Roma,
>   Me envía con cardenal.[26]

Thus, the audience, were it clamouring for *jácaras*, would get exactly what it wanted. Though this is the only sung *jácara*, and the only one recognised as such in the *acotaciones*, the song is part of the overwhelming manifestation of the genre in the entire play's setting, characterisation, action, entire lyric passages, jokes and *tonalidad*. Whereas the *jácaras* in *Celos*, *Céfalo y Pocris* and *Alcaide* exerted a limited sphere of influence, Zárate has allowed the influence of the *jácara* to seep into every aspect of the *comedia*. The world of *El valiente Campuzano*, before it is consumed by the warfare that will redeem the protagonist from his many murders, is a place where justice is treated as the butt of a cruel joke. *Alguaciles*, *corchetes* and *escribanos* are treated as annoying flies that must be squashed. Judges are not to be trusted, and executions are to be carried out personally by the offended party, without the intervention of corrupt or pusillanimous legal authorities. The obvious difference between *El valiente Campuzano* and a hypothetical *jácara–comedia* hybrid is that the protagonist, as mentioned, does not steal, and just as importantly, avoids punishment. In fact, the *jácara* convention of a suffering and often unredeemed protagonist would have been completely neglected at the end, were it not for La Catuja, a true representative of the genre. Unlike Campuzano, she is both put on the rack and later forced to steal. At the end of the play, the Marqués de Leganés pardons Campuzano, because of his valour in battle, and grants him the title of captain, lifting the man up in the social hierarchy and giving him an honest profession. La Catuja, though she led a squadron of *mochileros* into battle, fiercely fighting off her French adversaries, is awarded no prize, and must return to Granada and resume a life of brawling. She is forever trapped in the *hampa* that Fernando de Zárate has created for the setting of this *comedia*. Resigned to a life of stealing and stabbing, La Catuja will manage to enjoy it all the same, thanks to her ever-flowing wit that manages to make light of even the most violent situations.

---

[26] Zárate, p. 580.

Zárate's *comedia* demonstrates clearly how the elements of the *jácara* as song can be the inspiration for an entire work, but it does not go so far as to include what could be called a *jácara entremesada*. This extra-generic transformation from *romance* to *entremés* would require something more. The jokes in *El valiente Campuzano* were aimed at acts of violence, but never at the genre itself. The irony of the *jácara*[27] is generally used to counter the pain and suffering felt by the criminal, to decry the cruelty or arbitrariness of his or her captors, or to simply add literal 'insult to injury' to the victim of a slashing or robbery. The *jácara* integrated with an *entremés* enjoys an extra level of irony that is very much related to the metatheatrical awareness of the *teatro breve*. In that genre as a whole, the entire notion of the *jácara*, and even its theatricalisation, can become the object of joyous disrespect.

THE *JÁCARA ENTREMESADA* WITHIN THE *COMEDIA*

Luis Vélez de Guevara's *El águila del agua*, written about thirty years before *El valiente Campuzano*,[28] shares many characteristics with the Zárate's later play, but significantly stands apart because it contains an embedded *jácara entremesada*. The title *El águila del agua* refers to Don Juan de Austria, a military leader who fought in the famous naval battle of Lepanto. Like *El valiente Campuzano*, Guevara's *comedia* ends with a pitched battle, something exciting to watch onstage and which yields 'heroicos premios'[29] for the *valiente* protagonist. While the figure of Zárate's Campuzano is supposedly born of a unique 'historia verdadera', the *valiente* in *Águila* is none other than Pero Vázquez de Escamilla, virtually the embodiment of all *valientes*.[30]

[27] The irony of the *jácara* is very well cultivated though it tends to be of the same type. Exceptions include extreme self-reference, such as the *jaque* who refers to the performance of a theatrical *jácara* in Hill LXXVIII. Parodies of the *genre* such as *jácaras a lo divino* use the 'tough guy' image of the *jaque* to portray somebody whose 'criminal' nature is ironically used for virtue, not crime.

[28] Luis Vélez de Guevara, *El águila del agua in Lepanto: Fact, Fiction and Fantasy, with a critical edition of Luis Vélez de Guevara's* El águila del agua, *a play in three acts*, ed. Michael G. Paulson and Tamara Alvarez-Detrell (New York: University Press of America, 1986), p. 48.

[29] Vélez de Guevara, *Águila*, p. 173. I side with Edward Nagy, who writes that, in spite of its title, the valiente Escamilla, not Don Juan, is the true hero of the play. See Edward Nagy, 'El galeote de Lepanto de Luis Vélez de Guevara: la diversión en vez del escarmiento picaresco', *Bulletin of the Comediantes*, 29 (1977), 28–34. The editors of the version cited here do not agree with the ideas of Nagy or myself, and they say as much in their introduction. They may feel this way because it is difficult to imagine that a less sombre character could be the centre of attention. However, as we have seen before, when the influence of the *teatro breve* is strong, such a not-so-sombre hero is entirely appropriate.

[30] See the note in Lope de Vega, *La gatomaquia*, ed. Celina Sabor de Cortazar (Madrid: Castalia, 1982), p. 135.

Like Campuzano, Escamilla is accompanied by a brawling and joking woman who, like La Catuja, is even more of a *jaque* than her male counterpart.

In an omission unusual for most *comedias*, Guevara has provided no *gracioso*, no counterpart to *El valiente Campuzano*'s Pimiento, leaving the burden of eliciting laughter to rest upon the shoulders of others. A strange consequence of this strategy is that one of the characters that ought to be the most sombre is actually the funniest. One such person is the captain Don Lope de Figueroa, a historical figure who appears in many *comedias*, including Calderón's own *Amar después de la muerte* and *El alcalde de Zalamea*. Two important facts about Don Lope, surely known by the audience, were that his leg had gout and that he was an inveterate swearer of oaths. Instead of 'toning down' these well-known attributes, Guevara chooses to blow them up into comic proportions. After Don Lope faces Escamilla in armed combat, he declares: 'Valiente es el picarazo / como mil Héctores . . . / . . . ¡Voto a Dios! / que temo más que a mi pierna / a este caballero.'[31] During the climactic battle scene, when he brags of 'Ese brazo sobra / contra mundos de Turquías . . .' and when the equally hot-tempered yet serious Don Juan advises him, 'Las turcas galeras todas / palotean,' Don Lope responds: 'Palotee / esta pierna en una orca.'[32] When the enemy galleys are finally driven off and cheers of victory erupt, Don Lope mutters: 'Eso sí, cuerpo de Cristo, / que es lo que ha de ser, y agora, / más que con mi pierna juegue / Lucifer a la pelota.'[33] Many in the audience would have undoubtedly chuckled at these comically cantankerous comments, and even more would have done so were the actor brave enough to ignore the censor's admonitions to leave out all the swearing.[34] Don Lope swears so much that the king Felipe II himself must tell the nobleman to watch his mouth. Don Lope attempts to excuse himself:

> Don Lope   Es tacha
> en mí, señor, muy antigua,
> de una costumbre endiablada,
> pero yo la mudaré,
> ¡juro a Dios!
>
> Rey   ¿Eso es mudalla?
> Don Lope   Señor, no sé.[35]

Who could imagine that Don Lope de Figueroa could function comically in any genre other than a *comedia burlesca*? He comes as close to any character in this play to being a *gracioso*, though his love of fighting is in no way diminished. Not only is he laughable for his foibles, but he intentionally

---

[31] Vélez de Guevara, *Águila*, p. 103.
[32] Ibid., p. 169.   [33] Ibid., p. 172.
[34] The editors wisely included these details found in the margins of the original manuscript.   [35] Vélez de Guevara, *Águila*, p. 91.

makes jokes as well. Whether it is a joke about Jews or *castrati*,[36] Don Lope has a masterful grasp of standard joking techniques, a skill that is rare among noble *comedia* characters. As witnessed, the rupture of decorum is so drastic that even the king himself finds it necessary to intervene, although it is to no avail. This jocular *valiente* characterisation of such a noble figure is typical of the generic 'loosening' of the restrictions in a play that otherwise would have been a typical *comedia histórica*. Such 'loosening' is also emblematic of an atmosphere in which humour and violence are constantly related.

How did Escamilla and Almendruca become 'valientes del hampa?' Like Campuzano and La Catuja, brawling is their way of life, but eventually the law has come too near and they must flee to Madrid, 'laying low' for a while. Once there, instead of picking fights on the street, they get mixed up with some noble adversaries. This occurs when Escamilla joins a 'pelota' match during which a fight breaks out between the two teams.[37] Escamilla and Almendruca's constant involvement in the 'pendencias' between the noblemen brings unwanted attention from *la justicia*, forcing them to flee the scene once more. Their constant flight eventually leads them to stumble into Don Juan de Austria, unconscious and dreaming prophetically in his chair. After waking and shaking off his vision, he says:

Don Juan	Escamilla, escusar lances
	con la justicia y temella
	es cosa muy saludable,
	que es su majestad muy justo.
Escamilla	Mientras ponerme en la cárcel
	no quieran esos señores
	de las ropas venerables,
	soy una paloma, soy
	a Filis muy semejante,
	soy un cordero, unas natas,
	dos libras de uvas mollares;
	mas para que el verduguito
	conmigo brinque a ganarme,
	la defensa es natural,
	que no tengo dos gaznates.[38]

Escamilla's cheerful irony in reference to hangings, and his vocal disrespect for the law, make him very much akin to a *jaque*. It is an association emphasised

---

36 Vélez de Guevara, *Águila*, pp. 156, 158, respectively.
37 Not only is the 'pelota' scene a piece of Madrid *costumbrismo*, it could also be considered quite humorous, with its contestants bickering like modern-day school children about whether or not a ball went out of bounds.
38 Vélez de Guevara, *Águila*, p. 109.

further when Don Juan, in an act of relative clemency, sentences Escamilla to the galleys later destined for the dangers of Lepanto. Despite the fact that Don Juan recognises equal 'valor' (that is, brawling ability) in Almendruca, he lets her off the hook, and instead gives her a small bag of money to spend on nicer clothing.[39]

When she learns of the galley's destination, Almendruca makes another appearance in order to appeal Don Juan's decision, but we see no sign of Escamilla until later in the act. When he finally appears, his *jacarandino* status is made abundantly clear:

> *Éntrense todos* [the king and his subjects]. *Y salgan en una cadena larga asidos todos los que pudieran salir de galeotes, y lo último Pero Vásquez* [i.e., Escamilla] *y mujeres tras ellos y un alguacil con un bastón detrás y Almendruca muy llorosa.*[40]

It is a scene nearly identical to Calderón's *La jácara del Mellado*, only multiplied onstage with more prisoners and more weeping women. The main difference between the two scenes is that Escamilla will escape being hanged. Like El Mellado unto La Chaves, Escamilla tries to console Almendruca (she wanted to die with 'honour' like him), making light of his situation:

Escamilla   No hay honor como vivir;
                mejor podré con las olas
                averiguarme después,
                que no dando con los pies
                en la orca cabriolas;
                mejor quiero ir a remar
                que dar con humilde exceso
                en los del verdugo un beso
                y a todo el lugar.[41]

They continue their exchange, as though she were an overly emotional *marca* and he were her braggart *rufián*, halfway between stoicism and farce, until the *alguaciles* attempt to break up the conversation and move the prisoners along. Escamilla threatens one of the *alguaciles*, 'que estos eslabones / haré centellas carbones / de cólera sobre ti',[42] and he continues to think up new threats until he is eventually marched off the stage. Thus ends the relatively serious prelude to the entirely humorous *jácara entremesada* that is to follow.

[39] She complains (Vélez de Guevara, *Águila*, p. 108): '¿Y quédase en el tintero / Almendruca, inexorable / parca de todo viviente / si me hace el son Pedro Vázquez?' A similar favour is done by Campuzano to La Catuja, who wants a nice dress.
[40] Vélez de Guevara, *Águila*, p. 128.
[41] Ibid., p. 128.   [42] Ibid., p. 129.

We see neither sign of Escamilla nor Almendruca until the opening of the third act, which follows directly on the heels of the second, as indicated by the stage directions:

En acabándose la segunda jornada salga Almendruca cantando por una parte.

Almendruca   Galericas de España, tened los remos
               para que descanse mi amado preso.

               (Salgan del mismo modo que Almenduca)

Otra I   Galericas vienen, galericas van
               y en la mar parecen olas de la mar.

Otra II   Galericas de España, bajad las velas,
               porque el bien de mi vida se queda en tierra.

Almendruca   Mientras que sobre la playa
               descansando están los remos
               y el gusto en popa tenemos,
               vaya de jácara.

Las Dos   ¡Vaya!

Alemendruca   Escribano era Maladros
               del charco de los atunes,
               que en la salobre le tienen
               delitos del agua dulce.[43]

All three women keep singing, trading verses with each other and recounting the fate of *jaques*, *marcas* and even *renegados*, all in true *jácara* style, constantly joking about the hellish life of galley slavery. They continue until Escamilla steps forth, 'de galeote con arropea y camisola y bonete',[44] and scoffs: 'No está mal la capilla / de las ninfas de galera.'[45] After this unmistakable introduction to an embedded piece of *teatro breve*, the 'tonalidad jacarandina-entremesil' is briefly interrupted as Escamilla and Almendruca converse for the sake of narrative exposition, explaining the 'rollo de Lepanto'[46] and naming their Turkish adversaries. But the thread of the *jácara entremesada* is quickly retaken as Escamilla announces the arrival of several more *galeotes*.[47] The first is Argandona, who had eight of his teeth ripped out as punishment for testifying falsely. In a bizarre act of futile defiance, only understandable if one is familiar with the extreme irony of *jácaras*, Argandona

---

[43] Vélez de Guevara, *Águila*, p. 140.   [44] Ibid., p. 141.
[45] Ibid., p. 142. Both 'galera' and 'ninfa' have double meanings. The 'galera' was Madrid's infamous women's prison and 'ninfa' could mean prostitute. See José Luis Alonso Hernández, *El léxico del marginalismo del siglo de oro* (Salamanca: Universidad de Salamanca, 1976).   [46] Ibid., p. 143.
[47] The following scene bears some resemblance to another one with 'galeotes' found in chapter 22 of the first part of *Don Quijote*.

busies himself by making his own toothpicks, for which he has no use. When Escamilla asks him what he had for lunch, Argandona responds, 'Unas gachas [a type of soft griddle cake] / que sirviendo reverendas / de turrón [toffee] para la calva de mis dientes'.[48] Next is El Zurdillo de la Costa, a *jaque* so famous that he needs no introduction. Nevertheless he gets one from Escamilla all the same:

> Escamilla Este que viene se llama
> el Zurdillo de la costa,
> el que en las jácaras anda
> desde Sevilla a Madrid,
> ladrón cuatero hasta el alma,
> palmeando cuatro veces
> y ternas de dados labra.[49]

For lack of ivory, El Zurdillo must carve his dice out of sheep and cow's horn. The silliness of the scene increases greatly when the next *galeote* arrives. He is a poet, imprisoned for writing satires, and for the first time Almendruca passes judgment on a prisoner, scolding him with: 'Malhaya / quien en tan infame cosa / tiempo y consonantes gasta.'[50] The poet gives a flowery greeting, and Argandona responds with a mocking 'Sea bienvenido el so Petrarca'. Next is a 'vejete', imprisoned for marrying four times.[51] He carries an enormous 'libro de caballerías'. As the old man begins to read aloud, Almendruca makes the obvious comparison to Don Quixote, and the poet in turn begins to complain because the noise of the reading is distracting him from his writing.

At this point, the scene appears similar to that found in 'los juicios de Gil' in *La devoción de la Cruz*, in which a parade of satirical prisoner-*figuras* marched forward, making clear their identity as well as their vice, after which they were ridiculed by an outsider. However, as the scene in *El águila del agua* progresses, it begins to resemble more Calderón's *El entremés del reloj y los genios de la venta*, as the fixated *figuras* – the poet and the Don Quixote imitator – begin to clash as their obsessive activities interfere with one another. Yet all the while, El Zurdillo and Argandona contribute to the conversation, giving it a particular *jacarandino* slant. When the poet, after asking that all be silent, is able to bear down and squeeze out one *comedia* verse, 'Laura, / quien tal hace que tal pague', El Zurdillo (surely whipped more than a dozen times in as many *jácaras*) wryly comments: 'Más veces a las espaldas / lo he escuchado que él lo ha dicho.'[52] When all grow tired of

---

48 Vélez de Guevara, *Águila*, p. 144.

49 Ibid., p. 145.   50 Ibid., p. 145.

51 This may have been an inside joke on Guevara's part, if one considers that he himself married four times. See Vélez de Guevara, *Águila*, p. 46.

52 Ibid., p. 147.

the poet's pathetic attempts at artistry and they lose interest in the 'vejete's readings, Escamilla suggests that it is time for some good old-fashioned back-biting. El Zurdillo suggests that they start verbally attacking the *cómitre*, the man in charge of the ship's discipline. El Zurdillo and Argandona make jokes with references to Judas and hangings, as can be expected of their characters. Obeying his own character traits, the poet threatens to write 'un soneto que trata / de su vida y sus costumbres' when Escamilla confirms that he once smashed in the *cómitre*'s face. The 'vejete' laments that 'que tras cómitres no salga / ningún caballero andante', pointing out the inherent incompatibility of the *caballería* and *jácara* genres. The backbiting then broaches the subject of a 'mozuelo', '. . . que hace / con el patrón camarada, / muy presumido y muy crudo, / vizco de un hombro y espalda, / muy novicio en la milicia, / muy profeso en la hampa'. The *jaques* insinuate that he is more than a mere 'camarada' of the hated *cómitre*:

Zurdillo	Trae lindo dinero y gasta largamente.
Argandona	No quisiera que el patrón se desposara con él, aunque está casado en Porto Venere.
Vejete	Bravas caricias le hacen, mas yo por la persona gallarda he llegado a imaginar que es algún príncipe que anda encubierto en aventuras como otros tiempos se usaba . . .[53]

The 'vejete' refuses to believe that the 'mozuelo' could be a young 'puto', once again pointing out the clash between the romanticised innocence of the *Libros de caballerías* and the seedy, and for some, unimaginable, reality of the *hampa* found in the *jácaras*.[54] The generic fusion of this *jácara entremesada* begins to break up as the outside setting of Lepanto takes precedence. Doña Hipólita, dressed as a man in classic *mujer varonil de comedia* fashion, strikes up a conversation with Escamilla, thus directing the audience's attention back to the main plot of the play. Argandola then shouts some final threats to the poet, and Zurdillo does likewise to the drowsy 'vejete'.

[53] Vélez de Guevara, *Águila*, p. 149.
[54] For a literary reference to this type of male-to-male prostitution, see Quevedo's 'Respuesta de la Méndez a Escarramán' in Quevedo, *Obra poética*, vol. 3. For a historical example (which is quite theatrical in its own right) see the case of the *alcahuete* Mayuca found in Herrera Puga, p. 266.

Meanwhile, a 'Sargento', as if conscious of his role in switching genres, asks those present:

Sargento	¿No se sabe que es la causa, otras pláticas dejando que son de poca importancia, que para esta liga obliga a Venecia al rey y al papa?
Escamilla	La original es aquésta, si escucháis atentos.
Todos	¡Vaya![55]

Escamilla then launches into a *romance*, not about *jaques*, but about the war, like a traditional lyric messenger in any *comedia histórica*, thereby marking the definitive end of the embedded *jácara entremesada*. The editors of the edition used here have commented that at 3,700 lines, *El águila del agua* must have been cut for performance,[56] but the stage directions suggest something else. One must remember that the directions initiating the third act indicate: 'En acabándose la segunda jornada salga Almendruca cantando por una parte.'[57] Likewise, the directions starting the second act indicate: 'Salgan a cantar a cuatro, sin haber cantado entre las dos jornadas otra cosa, lo siguiente,'[58] followed by a song of war that accompanies Don Juan's violent dream foreshadowing the naval battle. These direct transitions from act to act can only mean that any supplementary *teatro breve* between these acts was intentionally omitted at the request of the playwright. If one adds up the verses of the singing sequence in the second act with those from the *jácara entremesada* – up until the Sargento's request to stop talking of matters of 'poca importancia', that is, stop the embedded *teatro breve* – one arrives at a total of 536 verses. Removing these leaves 3,164 verses for the *comedia*, which *comedia* scholars will recognise as only slightly above the standard amount. Thus one can conclude that Luis Vélez de Guevara himself supplied the *teatro breve* between acts by embedding it in the *comedia*. Don Juan's musical dream sequence is not a funny episode, but it would have served the purpose of a non-jocular *baile* or other such type of piece. There is no doubt that the episode aboard the galley is meant to be funny and contains its share of violence in the characters' narration, if not so much in their actions.[59] It seems certain that Luis Vélez de Guevara wanted to find ways of integrating both the *jácara* ballad and its *teatro breve* counterpart into a *comedia*. Evidence of such

---

55 Vélez de Guevara, *Águila*, p. 152.   56 Ibid., p. 51.
57 Ibid., p. 140.   58 Ibid., p. 104.
59 The amount of bickering among characters, particularly the satirical *galeotes*, could allow for much scuffling and comically violent 'stage business' though none is expressly mentioned in the 'acotaciones'.

integration can be obvious, as in specific mention of the word 'jácara', or it may be more subtle, as in the increased humour and violence found in certain noble characters' behaviour. After proving how such integration was made possible by Guevara and Zárate, each with different results, it is now time to analyse Calderón's own dramaturgical operation of this sort in *El alcalde de Zalamea*.

EL ALCALDE DE ZALAMEA AND THE JÁCARA

El alcalde de Zalamea is one of Calderón's most-studied works, and when studying it, the majority of *comedia* scholars tend to place emphasis on tragedy, justice, vengeance and honour as the fundamental themes of the play.[60] While it would be intriguing to study how these sombre themes are able to relate to the overwhelmingly humorous *teatro breve*, we shall have to be content with studying the presence of the *teatro breve* and its effects on the more immediate features of setting, characterisation and *tonalidad*. While the play's themes are undoubtedly linked to these features, the scope and length of this study unfortunately does not allow for much thematic analysis, and instead we shall simply begin by looking at the *teatro breve* itself as it appears.

El alcalde de Zalamea[61] contains no less than three *jácaras* to be studied, but in addition one must not ignore the straight *entremés*, untainted by references to the *hampa*, at the beginning of the play. The character of Don Mendo, forming one half of the comic scene, has been alternately described as a *figurón* or a direct literary descendant of the ragged *escudero* of *Lazarillo de Tormes*.[62] Nuño, his servant and the other half of the pair, is an ironic joker who obliquely complains about their lack of food and who delights in deflating his master's pathetic attempts at self-promotion. After the first scene of the first act, they enter the stage after the soldiers exit. Don Mendo goes through a 'checklist' of items indicating his 'hidalguía': a horse to be fed, hounds to be tied up, gloves and an ornamental toothpick (a sign of having recently attended a banquet) to be worn and a lady to court. Each item is roundly mocked by Nuño, who finds such pretence of nobility quite laughable, as the audience must have done as well. Even when, for purposes of exposition, mention is made of the visiting soldiers, Nuño finds an occasion to joke. He explains that it should come as no surprise that none of them lodge in the house of a 'hidalgo' because no soldier wants to die from lack

---

[60] For a summary of important critics' opinions, see the first part of Isaac Benabu, 'La inconclusividad de un fin: Pedro Crespo y la problematización del género en una lectura teatral de *El alcalde de Zalamea*', in *Texto e imagen en Calderón: Undécimo Coloquio Anglogermano sobre Calderón, St Andrews, Escocia, 17–20 de julio de 1996* (Stuttgart: Franz Steiner, 1998), pp. 37–45.

[61] Calderón de la Barca, *El alcalde de Zalamea*, ed. José María Diez Borque (Madrid: Castilla, 1976).   [62] Calderón de la Barca, *Alcalde*, p. 71.

of food.[63] As an 'hidalgo de figura', like Don Toribio de Cuadradillos of *Guárdate del agua mansa*, Don Mendo cannot help but bring up the subject of his 'ejecutoria tan grande, / pintada de oro y azul, / exención de mi linaje', to which Nuño responds '¡Tomáramos que dejara / un poco del oro aparte!'[64] The fact that Don Mendo is a laughable *figura* makes it clear that this conversation is not the typical *amo–criado* exchange found in *comedias de capa y espada*, but rather a scene typical of the constant stream of joking dialogue found in all *entremeses*. As the banter between Don Mendo and Nuño continues, they head towards Pedro Crespo's house, with the intention of visiting his daughter Isabel. While there, Don Mendo is made to look even more foolish as his ridiculous declarations of love fail to impress Isabel. It is almost as though she thought of him as a walking *entremés*,[65] not a real man, and she refuses to have anything to do with him. Both 'hidalgote'[66] and servant scatter at the sight of the protective father Crespo and his overly protective son, Juan.

While the comic pair did not start off the first act, they do initiate the second one. In the first forty lines, they review the important events of the previous act, and Nuño manages to make yet another joke about his master's infatuation with Isabel. Don Mendo responds with a slap to the face, breaking some of Nuño's teeth, and enlivening the scene with some physical comedy. When the vicious Capitán (Don Mendo's imagined rival) appears on stage, the two *entremesil* characters become frightened and run away. They make a second brief appearance in the second act, when tensions in the main plot have increased considerably. Don Mendo carries a small shield to protect himself in yet another futile attempt to join the (increasingly violent) action around him. Yet, when the Capitán reappears, the 'hidalgote' and his servant go running scared once more. After this scene, exactly midway through the *comedia*, the two are never again seen onstage. Thus we can conclude that, despite the coherent scene in the first act, the overall presence of the *entremés* is incidental and limited in influence. Don Mendo and Nuño are always frightened off the stage before they can affect any relevant action, and they disappear altogether after one half of the play has finished. All the same, the two characters do offer 'comic relief' and Don Mendo does relate thematically and parodically to other characters in the play. The 'hidalgote' parodies the nobility of the other characters and offers a comic contrast that may make the more serious characters seem more exalted. It is highly unlikely that Don Mendo's

[63] Calderón de la Barca, *Alcalde*, p. 140.   [64] Ibid., p. 140.

[65] That other characters compare him to Don Quixote helps consolidate this image, as the Manchegan gentleman was always presented as *entremesil* when featured in plays great and small. Also, the name 'Don Mendo' is rather humble, though it does not reach the level of absurdity enjoyed by such *caballeros entremesiles* as Don Pegote and Don Vinoso.

[66] So Pedro Crespo himself calls him, in an aside. See Calderón de la Barca, *Alcalde*, p. 151.

minor presence is strong enough to 'contaminate' the truly noble characters with a constantly parodical point of view. Neither Don Mendo nor Nuño make direct fun of others, and Don Mendo is the ultimate butt of jokes regarding the theme of 'hidalguía'. When Pedro Crespo himself speaks of true honour versus 'hidalgos postizos', he alludes to – though he does not mention him by name – the obvious example of Don Mendo. There is absolutely no confusing Don Mendo with Pedro Crespo. Therefore, the scenes of 'hidalgote' and servant are akin to *entremeses* in an extremely strict sense; they offer jokes and parody, but they are rather disconnected from the main play with respect to their ultimate effect on its characters, action, setting, *tonalidad* and even theme, the last of which is only further supported (not undercut) by parody.

The limited role that Don Mendo and Nuño play in *El alcalde de Zalamea* suggests that bringing humour to the work is mainly the duty of other characters, and perhaps these characters play a greater role in the plot, contributing more to the setting and tone. The most obvious provocateurs of laughter are Rebolledo and La Chispa, and all critics appear to agree on this point. Some, like Parker, have given further responsibility to these characters beyond just that of 'comic relief':

> They are subordinate characters in the action, but they serve to present the tone and the setting of military life, with its disorderly conduct, carefree and unruly, which is the background against which a dramatic conflict will unfold. La Chispa is a cheerful woman of loose life, who is to serve as the contrast with the modest and demure Isabel. Against this background, the principal characters appear one by one, this being a structure that completes the thematic exposition by the continuous addition of new elements.[67]

Rebolledo, it must be mentioned, is a *soldado apicarado–gracioso* hybrid. Though his name makes him seem like a *gracioso*, he is not listed as such among the *dramatis personae*, and he lacks cowardice and gluttony: two principal *gracioso* traits. He is, however, a witty lackey that enjoys a good time and poking fun at others, characteristics common among *graciosos*. Both La Chispa and Rebolledo are 'cheerful' and both represent 'disorderly conduct', 'carefree and unruly', something that unsurprisingly involves violence.[68] This mixture of violence and humour – for that is what these two characters enjoy – can be typified by the *jácaras* they sing in *El alcalde de Zalamea*.

The first *jácara* is sung at the very beginning of the play, as the rag-tag soldiers march into town, all soon to join the command of Don Lope de

[67] Alexander A. Parker, *The Mind and Art of Calderón: Essays on the Comedias* (Cambridge: Cambridge University Press, 1988), p. 45.

[68] Diez Borque in 'Fuentes históricas y de la realidad circundante', Calderón de la Barca, *Alcalde*, pp. 61–6, describes the 'disorderly conduct' and destruction at the hands of soldiers among civilians as a sad reality of sixteenth-century Spain.

Figueroa. When La Chispa shouts among them that she has no complaints about the march, one soldier praises her fortitude and Rebelledo chimes in:

Rebolledo   ¡Reviva!
                  Y más, si por divertir
                  esta fatiga de ir
                  cuesta abajo y cuesta arriba,
                  con su voz el aire inquieta
                  una jácara o canción.[69]

La Chispa complies enthusiastically and Rebolledo joins in as they trade verses. However, the day's entertainment is suddenly interrupted by one of the soldiers shouting that he has spied something in the distance. Rebolledo asks:

Rebolledo   ¿Es aquélla Zalamea?
La Chispa   Dígalo su campanario.
             No sienta tanto vusé
             que cese el cántico ya:
             mil ocasiones habrá
             en que lograrle, porque
             esto me divierte tanto,
             que como de otras no ignoran
             que a cada cosica lloran,
             yo a cada cosica canto,
             y oirá ucé jácaras ciento.[70]

Unlike the *gracioso* Tomás in one of Quiñones de Benavente's *jácaras*, who shouts back at his audience, '. . . cántalla yo es por demás / cántela quien la pidió / o juro a Dios que han de aullar',[71] La Chispa is a true crowd pleaser and would sing 'jácaras ciento' without any difficulty. All the same, the words to La Chispa's first *jácara* are not typical of the genre. They start with the refrain, 'Yo soy, titiritaina, / flor de la jacarandaina', followed by two humorous verses about not wanting to go to war, and then two more verses about eating, combined with a double entendre about marital infidelity. All in all, though it is full of wit and irony, there is very little violence inherent in the first song. At this point, both Rebolledo and La Chispa appear to be mere entertainers, refreshing the audience in the same way that they raise the spirits of the tired troops. The problem with this explanation of refreshing 'comic relief' lies in the fact that this is only the beginning of the play, and the audience could hardly have been expected to be tired of the action onstage so soon. Instead, those who were paying attention to the *comedia* – those not

---

69 Calderón de la Barca, *Alcalde*, p. 125.   70 Ibid., p. 128.
71 Quiñones de Benavente, *Joco seria*, fol. 109v.

snacking, gossiping, drinking, sleeping, etc. – must have been looking and listening intently, watching the scene unfold, and searching for clues that might foreshadow what was to happen later. Exposition describing Pedro Crespo and his daughter Isabel develops in later conversations with other characters. In the plot of *El alcalde de Zalameas*, the villagers make up only half the story. The other half consists of the unruly military presence that clashes with the tranquil life of the village. That the play will be about soldiers is abundantly clear from the first moments of the opening act. What type of soldiers these are, and what havoc they are capable of wreaking, are foreshadowed when La Chispa belts out her *jácara*. In hindsight of the tragic events that unfold later on, the lyrics are not as innocuous as they first appeared.

> Vaya a la guerra, el alférez
> y embárquese el capitán.
> Mate moros quien quisiere,
> que a mí no me han hecho mal.
> Vaya y venga la tabla al horno,
> y a mí no me falte pan.
> Huéspeda, máteme una gallina;
> que el carnero me hace mal.[72]

The first four lines, though comical, still refer to dissension in the ranks, something that has a grave effect on later events in the play. The second half of the *jácara*, the one about satisfying hunger, is actually taken from a larger song, a version of which is found in Quiñones de Benavente's *Entremés cantado de la visita a la cárcel*.[73] In the *entremés* version, a 'capigarrón' sings most of the verses, and he is later joined by an *alcalde* who sets him free and joins in a bagpipe song-and-dance routine.[74] If Calderón had lifted this song directly from Benavente's *entremés*, audience members who had seen both pieces would be party to a somewhat exclusive joke and understood the allusion to *alcaldes*[75] and criminal activity. Even if the song had originally been written by somebody else, and *La visita a la cárcel* was unknown to Calderón and his audience, people still would have noticed the illicit twist, the reference to 'carnero', that Calderón added to the song. At first glance, the twist, which Rebolledo sings, is both laughable and commonplace. It pokes fun at the archetypal dupe husband, but it also evokes the image of a dishonourable woman.

---

[72] Calderón de la Barca, *Alcalde*, p. 127.
[73] Sage and Wilson, p. 137.
[74] Quiñones de Benavente, *Joco seria*, fol. 34r.
[75] In Madrid, the *alcaldes* were the head justice officials, similar to today's police chiefs, who headed each of the *cuarteles* into which the city's jurisdiction was divided. See Eudosio Varón Vallejo, 'Rondas de los alcaldes de casa y corte en los siglos XVII y XVII', *Revista de Archivos, Bibliotecas y Museos*, 45 (1924) 149.

In the presence of Rebolledo's lover La Chispa, a woman of loose morals, such a joke seems to be in good fun, in step with the irony of both comical characters. But if one thinks of the *jácara*'s ability to set the scene, to foreshadow violence as it did in other *comedias*, we may also remember Parker's words that La Chispa, 'is to serve as the contrast with the modest and demure Isabel'.[76] Though cuckoldry is never a theme in *El alcalde de Zalamea*, that of a woman's honour is, along with that of injustice due to the conflict between badly behaved soldiers and innocent villagers. Both themes, which are the mainstay of this play's tragedy, get oblique treatment in this seemingly purely festive *jácara* that opens up *El alcalde de Zalamea*. Yet it is no accident that the tune of a *jácara* is chosen, because in that genre and song-style laughter is tied to the threat of violence and often promises its fulfilment.

The second *jácara* is not explicitly announced, but its identity can easily be deduced by what the characters say beforehand. First of all, the *jácara* is the song of choice among the soldiers. Rebolledo mentions it by name without mentioning any other type as an option except a vague reference to 'canción'. This preference is corroborated by La Chispa, the troops' 'lead singer', who says that she loves to sing *jácaras* and she would sing a hundred if she had the chance. Secondly, in the beginning of the second act, when the Capitán is trying to think of a way to get close to Isabel, Rebolledo suggests a plan. As it happens, the plan involves singing *jácaras*:

> Rebolledo   En la compañía hay soldado [that is, himself]
> que canta por excelencia;
> y la Chispa, que es mi alcaida
> del boliche, es la primera
> mujer en jacarear.
> Haya, señor, jira y fiesta
> y música a su ventana;
> que con esto podrás verla [meaning Isabel],
> y aun hablarla.[77]

Thus we can conclude that when the 'jira y fiesta' arrives at Isabel's (also Pedro Crespo's) house, La Chispa will be there too, singing plenty of *jácaras*. That night, we learn from Don Lope and Pedro Crespo's conversation about a conflict between two types of music. The first type is figurative and can be found in Crespo's garden. It is the music of the 'viento suave / que en las blandas hojas suena'[78] and the 'compás desta fuente, / cítara de plata y perlas'.[79] The unusually apologetic Pedro Crespo begs Don Lope's pardon for the lack of singers, 'que como músicos son / los pájaros que gorjean, / no quieren cantar

---

[76] Parker, *The Mind and Art of Calderón*, p. 45.
[77] Calderón de la Barca, *Alcalde*, pp. 198–9.
[78] Ibid., p. 202.   [79] Ibid., pp. 202–3.

de noche, / ni yo puedo hacerles fuerza'.[80] His house and garden are the model
of domestic tranquillity and almost literal harmony. Crespo himself is
unusually calm, as Don Lope himself observes.[81] There is certainly tension
between these two, but both of their good natures prevail as Pedro Crespo's son
and daughter, along with their maid, join them for dinner at the father's behest.
As soon as all are seated and their meal in this island of tranquillity is about
to begin, a raucous din of music and merrymaking is heard approaching
the house.

Don Lope explains to Pedro Crespo that the rigid life of a soldier requires
some occasional festivity. An unexpected part of this merrymaking involves
launching more than just verses into the night air:

Rebolledo   ¡Vaya a Isabel una letra!
             Para que despierte, tira
             a su ventana una piedra.[82]

There are no stage directions indicating if the soldiers throw a pebble to make
a sound, or rather a good-sized rock to smash against the window. But given
a choice and the *autor*'s discretion, it would likely be the latter, considering
the tone of the scene and the need for a sound big enough for the audience to
hear it.

Don Lope (*aparte*)   Música, vaya; mas esto
                      de tirar es desvergüenza.[83]

In other words, merrymaking is acceptable, but disruptive and possibly violent behaviour is intolerable. In generic terms, Don Lope is only willing to
accept one aspect (merrymaking) of the theatrical *jácara*, not allowing for the
other (violence), a near impossibility because the two are so closely linked in
the sub-genre's tradition. The tension in the room between the previous tranquillity and the impending chaos begins to mount. The rowdy soldier–
musicians roughly fit to their to boisterous strumming and singing the 'letra'
of a traditional *romance* honouring 'Isabel'.[84] Pedro Crespo mutters under his
breath that he would do something unmentionable to the soldiers were it not

---

[80] Calderón de la Barca, *Alcalde*, p. 203.
[81] Ibid., p. 205.   [82] Ibid., p. 213.
[83] Ibid., p. 214.
[84] On the notes to this page in his edition, Díez Borque lists Lope de Vega and Góngora
as poets who have also used this song that begins with the verse: 'Las flores del romero'.
Given the rowdiness of the soldiers, it is most likely that the melody for this *romance* has
been changed from a sweetly gentle serenade to something much more lively and raucous.
Don Lope himself (ibid) calls the singing 'cantaletas', which Díez Borque (citing the
Diccionario de autoridades) describes as: 'El ruido que se forma cantando y metiendo bulla
desordenada con algunos instrumentos desconcertados.'

for Don Lope's presence. Juan, itching for a fight, decides to go arm himself
with a shield. When his father asks him where he is going, the son responds
that he is off to make sure that food is brought forth. Pedro Crespo, in a subtle
attempt to calm his son (who lacks his self-control), says that somebody else
can take care of the food. The tension rises higher as the soldiers sing,
'¡Despierta, Isabel, despierta!'[85] Isabel asks herself nervously what she has
done to deserve this serenade, an activity entertaining for the soldiers yet
nightmarish for her. At that moment, as if to break the tension slightly, Don
Lope overturns a table and declares: 'Ya no se puede sufrir, / porque es cosa
muy mal hecha.'[86] Pedro Crespo, thinking his guest is referring to the disturbance, throws a chair to the floor in agreement. Don Lope responds that he
was only complaining about his gout and gives, through defeated expectations
and incongruity, a comic tinge to the frustrated tossing of furniture. But this
comic tinge does not alleviate the tension much. The spirit of the *jácaras* is
having an effect on the main players of the *comedia*. In fact, both Don Lope
and Pedro Crespo's foolishly violent acts make them look a bit like rowdy
character-types themselves, somewhat similar to *valientes* who see violent
behaviour as the only way to soothe their frustrations. Meanwhile, the
jácaras, the generic harbingers of violence, show no sign of abating. The
climax of this scene occurs when dinner is cancelled and Don Lope and Pedro
Crespo respectively notice that a small shield and a family sword are missing.
Starting from the very beginning of the scene, the *jácaras* in the street foreshadowed the coming violence under the guise of merrymaking.[87] But the
songs, though influential, were still peripheral, offstage and unseen: a lurking
menace. When the scene concludes, the threat of violence is finally made
manifest in the main action of the *comedia*, through the disappearance of the
sword and the shield.

The third and final *jácara* in *El alcalde de Zalamea* appears in the scene
following the one described above, after Don Lope and the Crespo family
have left the stage. The first stage directions exemplify the unruly and festive
behaviour of the troops in the street:

Salen el Capitán, Sargento, Chispa, Rebolledo, con guitarras, y soldados.[88]

The collective armed musical menace waits expectantly for Isabel to open a
window, as Don Mendo and Nuño make an ever-so-brief entrance. Afraid of
the disturbance, they stupidly try to hide themselves by sitting on the ground,
as the nearby Rebolledo whispers a joke to La Chispa about Don Mendo's

---

85 Calderón de la Barca, *Alcalde*, p. 215.
86 Ibid., p. 215.
87 Recall the sudden arrival of 'la justicia' after Aura sings her *jácara* in *Céfalo y Pocris*.
88 Calderón de la Barca, *Alcalde*, p. 218.

laughable appearance and behaviour. As if oblivious to this minor comic interruption, the looming threat of violence is greater than ever. Pedro Crespo has gone to 'encerrar'[89] his children, to make sure that nobody can reach Isabel and that Juan does nothing rash like attack somebody. It is night, and were Zalamea a city, it would be the time for criminals, *capeadores* and the like, to come out from their hiding places in the shadows and terrorise the populace. Despite its size, the village still suffers from its own brand of urban peril: the *soldados apicarados*, one of whom will prove to be the villain of the play. The *hampa*, though obscured by a strange festive–military guise, has come to the sleepy little town of Zalamea. After a lull, when the guitars and shouts have died down for a moment, Rebolledo calls for a song in a way that is both humorous and chilling:

Rebolledo   Va una jácara tan nueva
                  que corra sangre.

La Chispa   Sí hará.

Salen don Lope y Pedro Crespo a un tiempo con broqueles

La Chispa, *canta*   Érase cierto Sampayo,
                 la flor de los andaluces
                 el jaque de mayor porte
                 y el rufo de mayor lustre.
                 Éste, pues, a la Chillona
                 topó un dia . . .

Rebolledo   No le culpen
                 la fecha; que el asonante
                 quiere que haya sido en lunes.

La Chispa   Topó, digo, a la Chillona,
                 que brindando entre dos luces,
                 ocupaba con el Garlo
                 la casa de los azumbres.
                 El Garlo, que siempre fue,
                 en todo lo que le cumple,
                 rayo de tejado abajo,
                 porque era rayo sin nube,
                 sacó la espada y a un tiempo
                 un tajo y revés sacude.

Acuchillándolos don Lope y Pedro Crespo

Crepso   Sería desta manera.

Don Lope   Que sería así no duden.

Métenlos a cuchilladas y sale don Lope[90]

[89] Pedro Crespo (Calderón de la Barca, *Alcalde*, p. 217) uses this word himself.
[90] Calderón de la Barca, *Alcalde*, pp. 223–5.

TED L. L. BERGMAN

The scene is a *tour de force* of dramatic timing and mixed genres. From the very disappearance of the sword and shield that signalled the end of the last scene, to Don Mendo's later appearance with shield in hand, the threat of a sword fight has been implied. It is only a question of when the fight will begin and who will be involved. Soon after Rebolledo's signal of 'que corra sangre', Don Lope and Pedro Crespo enter the scene, both armed and ready to beat back the mounting menace of the unruly troops. They fight against the invaders as La Chispa, 'flor de la jacarandina', launches into the most traditional *jácara* so far, its lyrics brimming with *germanía* and characters from the criminal under-world.[91] The lively music of the *jácara* itself – we can imagine Rebolledo and La Chispa rapidly 'rasgueando'[92] their guitars as a sort of 'sound track' to the ensuing fight scene – must have added additional excitement, and like nearly all *jácaras*, this whole event is also rife with irony. Both Don Lope and Pedro Crespo feared that people on a criminal rampage would invade the house and cause trouble. Therefore they armed themselves and went in search of these lurking criminals. After the real enemy is defeated, the protagonists stumble upon each other in the dark, and their first assumption is that the other man is a criminal, not a crime-fighter. The following dialogue and action ensues:

Don Lope	¡Gran valor! Uno ha quedado de ellos, que es el que está aquí.

Sale Pedro Crespo

Crespo	Cierto es que el que queda ahí sin duda es algún soldado.
Don Lope	Ni aun éste no ha de escapar sin almagre.
Crespo	Ni éste quiero que quede sin que mi acero la calle le haga dejar.
Don Lope	¿No huís con los otros?
Crespo	¡Huid vos, que sabréis hüír más bien!

Riñen

Don Lope	¡Voto a Dios, que riñe bien!
Crespo	¡Bien pelea, voto a Dios![93]

---

[91] I have not been able to find other songs with the *jaques* Sampayo and El Garlo, though El Garlo's name certainly sounds authentic, given the word 'garlar', which in *germanía* means 'hablar'. See Alonso Hernández, *Léxico*. La Chillona, on the other hand, must have been a well-known *marca*, as she appears three times (in *romances*) in Hill, and four times (in *teatro breve*) in Recoules.

[92] Stein, p. 232.

[93] Calderón de la Barca, *Alcalde*, pp. 225–6.

The audience watches from an ironic perspective and is able to see that each protagonist is doing just the opposite of what they ought to be doing. Effectively, each protector becomes (for a moment) a violent criminal himself, almost a *jaque*, in the other's mind's eye.

Thus, it requires very little imagination to conclude that Don Lope and Pedro Crespo, for a brief moment in time, are actually made unwitting participants in a *jácara entremesada* that Calderón has embedded in the *comedia*. All the trappings of the humorous and violent 'minor' genre are there. Like the Músico's song in Calderón's *La jácara del Mellado*, La Chispa's *jácara* is interrupted by commentary from a joking second party. This self-reflection and rupture of illusion, almost for their own sake, are hallmarks of the *teatro breve*, now mixed with the purely sung *jácara*. But a greater self-reflexive element, or metatheatrical comment, can be found in the lyrics themselves. Of the three types of *jácara* mentioned in the beginning of this section, La Chispa chooses the type that tells the story of a battle between *jaques*. In this case they are Sampayo and El Garlo, who fight over the possession of the *marca* La Chillona. The very words 'sacó la espada, y a un tiempo / un tajo y revés sacude', which describe the *jaques*' swordplay, perfectly match the subsequent actions of Don Lope and Pedro Crespo, completely confusing the imagined criminals onstage with the fictional ones in the narration. Just as the Músico in *El Mellado* sang 'Para ahorcar está el Mellado . . .' as El Mellado stepped forward in chains, La Chispa's words serve as a connecting point between the tired commonplaces of the *jácara* and their renovation onstage. The novelty of the *comedia*'s main characters being completely dominated by both the humour (manifest in the audience's own ironic perspective) and violence (obvious enough) of the *jácara* must have caused great joy and excitement among the spectators. The two men keep fighting after the music has stopped, until Juan Crespo appears, speaking aloud to his father and consequently shattering the *hampesca* illusion that had enveloped the entire scene. The father and his previously threatening 'adversary', Don Lope, awkwardly identify each other and apologise, creating a comic anti-climax to the excitement brought on by the embedded *jácara entremesada*. They make amends as Pedro Crespo explains that, '. . . yo he salido a reñir / por haceros compañía', affirming his solidarity with Don Lope and perhaps even promising a future harmony between the village and the visiting troops. This possibility for harmony is quickly dispelled as shouts from the soldiers are heard. But instead of the raucous *jácaras* and strumming of guitars, these are shouts of another kind, violent, but not offset by any humour whatsoever:

> ¡A dar muerte nos juntemos
> a estos villanos![94]

---

[94] Calderón de la Barca, *Alcalde*, p. 227.

This call, occurring soon after the last *jácara* of *El alcalde de Zalamea*, marks a definitive change in the play's *tonalidad*. From the cheerful 'unruly and carefree' presence of the soldiers at the opening of the play, to their increased rowdiness in their serenade of Isabel, and ending with a frenzied fight between the keepers of the peace on either side (military and domestic), each *jácara* signalled an increased threat of violence, undiminished by its humorous nature. The *jácaras*, and their proponents, El Rebolledo and Las Chispa, are more than just 'background', as Parker (the critic who grants them the biggest role) wrote. It may have been true during the first *jácara*, which sets the scene, but it is not so for the second two. It is Rebolledo himself who suggests to the Capitán that they visit the Crespo family house at night, thus influencing the action of the soldiers that causes Pedro Crespo so much alarm. The *jácaras* they sing could not have calmed anybody down, especially the soldiers, who start throwing rocks and shouting at Isabel to wake up.

To sum up, the third *jácara* does offer 'background' because it functions as a sort of 'soundtrack' to the fight scene. However, La Chispa does more than merely 'present the tone and the setting of military life', because for the time being, the military is out of the picture. Instead, she is presenting within the *comedia* the recognisable sub-genre of the *jácara entremesada*. More than just background, the singing converts the rural domestic setting into the *hampa* and the characters into, if not *jaques*, 'valientes del hampa' themselves. The *tonalidad* becomes so strong, and its generic origins become so blatant, that everything is affected, and some of these aspects, like the threat of violence, are obviously lasting. It would be intriguing to study how even the sombre themes of tragedy, justice, vengeance and honour are able to relate to the *teatro breve*. When we now possess a new perspective, we could revisit previous character studies of Pedro Crespo, armed with knowledge of the *jácara*'s ironic and often cynical point of view concerning the delivery of justice. There can be no doubt that Pedro Crespo is a wit, but neither can one doubt that he has the capacity to commit extreme acts of violence. Death by garrotte occurs in other plays where justice and treachery among nobles play a role,[95] but beyond these examples, one must also remember the garrotting carried out by Fernando de Zárate's *valiente* Campuzano, a man who also took justice into his own hands. Pedro Crespo's defence in front of Felipe II at the end of the play is not without humour, though the subject itself is of the utmost violence. Though he is not as openly sarcastic as Campuzano in his

[95] Calderón himself uses the device elsewhere in *Las tres justicias en una*. In Diego Ximénez de Enciso's *El Príncipe don Carlos* (first published in 1634), no less than Felipe II himself orders that a treacherous Italian ambassador be strangled in his chair. As in *Tres justicias*, the hapless victim is 'descubierto' in the play's most shocking scene. It is tempting to think that there is some connection between the king's garrotting in *El Príncipe don Carlos* and the approval he gives for a similar act in *El alcalde de Zalamea*, although the two events may be pure coincidence, and neither playwright may have seen or heard the other's play.

defence of such a 'just' strangulation, Crespo cannot help but gloat a little in his own subtle way. Pedro Crespo is no *jaque*,[96] but there is something about his personality that evokes the world of the *jácara*, and not only because such a world surrounds him throughout the play. When he makes his first obvious joke, long before the garrotting, one critic felt compelled to write:

> Es totalmente inhabitual que los parlamentos o actuaciones de los caracteres principales cumplan – en algún momento – funciones cómicas, misión reservada al gracioso (en este caso Rebolledo y la Chispa). Incumple aquí Calderón esta suerte de *decorum* que, a su modo, también cumplía el teatro del siglo XVII, aunque se apartara de las reglas clásicas.[97]

Perhaps there is another decorum at work here, as well as in many other plays: a decorum based on the mixing of genres, one that makes particular demands on characters, resulting in seemingly 'inhabitual' behaviour. Of all the 'caracteres principales' mentioned throughout this study, we must recall that many performed 'funciones cómicas'. Were all these characters acting 'inhabitually' as well, or were they acting in accordance with other standards, those of the *teatro breve*? Did the 'loosening up' of the *comedia* (as when Don Félix says that he's hungry, or Doña Leonor kicks Don Juan) correspond to the imposition of another set of unwritten rules? When rules are broken, perhaps the result is not chaos, but rather the imposition of other rules that take their place. Like Pedro Crespo's own carefully planned lawlessness, or the three-part incremental violence brought on by successive *jácaras*, Calderón de la Barca, in *El alcalde de Zalamea* and many other plays, has a method to his madness, his own 'inhabitual' behaviour. The non-stop humour of the *teatro breve*, controlled and limited, is used to create something 'inhabitual' yet recognisable, accepted yet surprising, and most important of all, still able to get a laugh.

---

[96] Though, curiously, his name does appear in a list of *jaques* found in one *jácara*. See Hill LXIX, which is taken from *Romances varios*, published in 1655. Of course, it may have been some other Pedro Crespo who happened to be a *jaque*. In a *baile* (with *hampesca* subject matter) called *La galera*, by Suárez Deza y Avila, we find a man simply called Crespo, alongside Añasco and Chillona, famous names for a *jaque* and *marca*, respectively.

[97] Calderón de la Barca, *Alcalde*, p. 203.

CONCLUSION

Calderón de la Barca certainly had a sense of humour, along with most of his audience. Nevertheless, many unanswered questions remain concerning exactly why an audience may have laughed at certain moments. Psychologists have theorised much about why people laugh, tell jokes and the circumstances under which they feel they can or cannot do either of these. A psychological study, without attempting to plumb the depths of an abstract and/or collective unconscious, could still be valuable in discovering further unwritten rules (derived from behavioural observations) for telling jokes onstage. Such an investigation can also demonstrate how these rules may relate to the audience's own expectations of what can and cannot be done, as well as the emotional satisfaction that comes from (directly or vicariously) following, breaking or circumventing these rules. Psychological studies can also be helpful, particularly those regarding humour and group dynamics. One such study[1] has demonstrated that a crowd is more likely to laugh at humorous performances if it has recently undergone a similar experience – such as being caught in the rain – that creates some sort of sympathy among the group. Such data may help us better imagine how different audiences might have responded to the same joke. Yet this information also humbles us by proving that something nearly impossible to ascertain in historic terms, such as the weather, could have been the determining factor in the success of an *entremés*.

I mention this example, and the following one, because while we know that humour does not exist in a vacuum, we must be careful whenever examining the phenomenon in wider contexts, particularly after becoming aware of the complexities in the 'vacuum' of the works themselves. Sociological, anthropological, philosophical, religious, etymological, gastronomical and any other approaches to humour in the *comedias* and *teatro breve* of Calderón are intriguing and certainly should be carried out, but they should also be accompanied by a consideration of the generic and literary conventions at work. Whether one wishes to demonstrate that, at a given time, humour (trying to get a laugh) is a tool for social control, subversion, self-reflection on language or merely an excuse to wear a hat made of sausages, the most convincing arguments will be those that include the context of the *teatro breve* and *comedia* as works of art,

---

[1] Antony J. Chapman and Hugh C. Foot, *Humor and Laughter: Theory, Research, and Applications* (New York: John Wiley & Sons, 1976), p. 237.

along with social contexts. I myself would require more than just one example of a theatrical device if I were to believe that it was a means to social control. One single joke, running a few times in repeat performances of a *comedia*, would hardly have this effect. Twenty such jokes might do. The same joke, drawn out over an entire act, or embedded in a character with great stage presence, might also be sufficient to 'control' members of the audience. Regardless of the circumstances, the structure as well as the literary and theatrical context of the joke cannot be ignored if we are to examine sociological implications.

After seeing the *teatro breve*'s influence at work in Calderón's *comedias*, it seems logical to look for the same influence in the *comedias* of dozens of other playwrights, especially those who wrote pieces belonging to both genres. Calderón is undoubtedly not alone in mixing them together. As it happens, Agustín de Moreto's *entremés* called *La burla de Pantoja* is nothing more than a separately published scene taken directly from the same playwright's *comedia* titled *Las travesuras de Pantoja*. In one scene of Guillén de Castro's *comedia*, *Los malcasados de Valencia*, a group of *damas* and *galanes* are on their way to see a *comedia* themselves. Before they arrive, two *graciosos* create a comic disturbance and splash paint all over, leading one of the *galanes* to remark: 'De la comedia a que vamos éste ha sido el entremés.'[2] Can we not find further examples, some more obvious than others, of this mixing of two genres thought by most to be entirely separate and distinct? I selected Calderón for this study because he is both well-known and generally considered a serious playwright. It is quite possible that 'less serious' playwrights, such as Moreto and others notoriously dubbed 'de segundo o tercer rango', are even freer with their use of the *teatro breve* in their *comedias*. Perhaps they even went further in stretching the supposed limitations of the larger genre. Perhaps their open dedication to exploiting the less prestigious (then as now) *teatro breve* allowed them to accomplish peculiar dramaturgical feats of which only playwrights 'de segundo o tercer rango' were capable.

Despite the *teatro breve*'s lack of prestige – the master Quiñones de Benavente himself would not publish his own works – it was as much a part of the theatregoer's life as was the *comedia*, whether at the king's *coliseo*, or the *corral*, or in the confines of a private home. *Entremeses*, *jácaras* and *mojigangas* were not just tiny titbits; they constituted a hefty portion of a typical *tarde de comedia*. If one believes Quiñones de Benavente's friend and editor, then a good *entremés* was enough to give a bad *comedia* crutches and give a good *comedia* wings with which to fly. The *teatro breve* was anything but minor in its popularity and undoubtedly had no small effect on the imagination of the audience. They knew and understood the silly costumes of the *mojiganga* as well as they did the allegorical figures of the *auto sacramental*. They recognised and comprehended the character-types of the

2 Guillén de Castro, *Los malcasados de Valencia* in *Obras completas*, vol. 1, ed. Joan Oleza (Madrid: Fundación José Antonio de Castro, 1997), p. 711.

entremés as well as they did those in the *comedia*. During the baroque, an age so strongly associated with admixture, movement, confusion (and even ugliness) in art, how can it be that the *teatro breve* and the *comedia* remained side by side in the imaginations of theatregoers (not to mention playwrights), without any 'contamination' between the two? Nowadays, there exists a well-founded opinion that a play's text is but one of many intersecting 'discourses,' some themselves literary and others social, political, religious, etc. Perhaps the most neglected 'discourse' so far has been that of the *teatro breve*, in its literary and other significances. However this neglect may only refer to us nowadays, because while Early Modern theatregoers likely saw at least two *teatro breve* pieces for every single *comedia*, modern scholars have probably read only one *teatro breve* piece for every five *comedias*. For a richer understanding of humour in the *comedias* of Calderón, and of theatre in general, I urge the reader to pick up a few *mojigangas*, *entremeses* or *jácaras*, study them for a moment or two, and enjoy a few good laughs. I am sure that Calderón would approve.

SELECT BIBLIOGRAPHY

PRIMARY TEXTS

Alonso Asenjo, Julio, ed., *La tragedia de San Hermenegildo y otras obras del teatro español de colegio*, 2 vols (Madrid: UNED, 1995)

Benítez Claros, Rafael, ed., *Verdores del Parnaso* (Madrid: CSIC, 1969)

Calderón de la Barca, Pedro, *El agua mansa/Guárdate del agua mansa*, ed. Ignacio Arellano and Víctor García Ruiz (Kassel: Reichenberger, 1989)

——, *Céfalo y Pocris*, ed. Alberto Navarro González (Salamanca: Almar, 1979)

——, *Comedias: a facsimile edition*, ed. D.W. Cruickshank and J.E. Varey, 19 vols (Farnborough, England: Gregg International, 1973)

——, *Entremeses, jácaras y mojigangas*, ed. Evangelina Rodríguez and Antonio Tordera (Madrid: Castalia, 1983)

——, *Entremeses y mojigangas de Calderón para sus autos sacramentales*, ed. Agustín de la Granja (Granada: Universidad de Granada, Curso de Estudios Hispánicos, 1981)

——, *Fieras afemina amor*, ed. Edward M. Wilson (Kassel: Reichenberger, 1984)

——, *Una fiesta sacramental barroca*, ed. José María Díez Borque (Madrid: Taurus, 1984)

——, *El golfo de las sirenas*, ed. Sandra L. Nielsen (Kassel: Reichenberger, 1989)

——, *Obras completas*, 3 vols, ed. Ángel Valbuena Briones (Madrid: Aguilar, 1960–7)

——, *Teatro cómico breve*, ed. María Luisa Lobato (Kassel: Reichenberger, 1989)

Cervantes Saavedra, Miguel de, *Entremeses*, ed. Nicholas Spadaccini (Madrid: Cátedra, 2000)

——, *El ingenioso hidalgo Don Quijote de la Mancha*, ed. Luis Andrés Murillo, 2 vols (Madrid: Castalia, 1978)

Cicero, *De Oratore*, translated by J.S. Watson (Carbondale: Southern Illinois University Press, 1970)

Cotarelo y Mori, Emilio ed., *Colección de entremeses, loas, bailes, jácaras y mojigangas desde fines del siglo XVI á mediados del siglo XVIII*, in the series *Nueva biblioteca de autores españoles*, vols 17, 18 (Madrid: Bailly y Baillere, 1911)

Gracián y Morales, Baltasar, *Agudeza y arte de ingenio*, ed. Emilio Blanco (Madrid: Cátedra, 1998)

Hill, John M. ed., *Poesías germanescas del s. XVI, Romances de germanía de varios autores*; *Jácaras y Bailes de Quevedo, Poesías germanescas del s. XVII* (Bloomington: Indiana University Publications, Humanities Series, 1945)

Hobbes, Thomas, *Human Nature, or, The Fundamental Elements of Policy* (Oxford: Oxford University Press, 1994)

Huerta Calvo, Javier, ed., *Una fiesta burlesca del siglo de oro*: Las bodas de Orlando (*comedia, loa, y entremeses*) (Lucca: Mauro Baroni, 1997)

——, *Teatro breve de los siglos XVI y XVII: entremeses, loas, bailes, jácaras y mojigangas* (Madrid: Taurus, 1985)

Mantuano, el Bachiller, ed., *Entremeses del siglo XVII* (Madrid: Biblioteca 'Ateneo', 1909)

Matos Fragoso, Juan de, Juan Bautista Diamante and Juan Vélez de Guevara, *El hidalgo de La Mancha*, ed. Manuel García Martín (Salamanca: Ediciones Universidad de Salamanca, 1982)

Molière, *Five Plays* (London: Methuen, 1981)

Molina, Tirso de, *Obras completas de Tirso de Molina: prosa y verso*, ed. Pilar Palomo and Isabel Prieto, 3 vols (Madrid: Turner, 1994)

Monteser, Francisco Antonio de, *El caballero de Olmedo*, ed. Celsa Carmen García Valdés (Pamplona: Universidad de Navarra, 1991)

Ovid, *Fasti*, ed. Betty Rose Nagle (Bloomington: Indiana University Press, 1995)

Pérez de Moya, Juan, *Philosofía secreta de la gentilidad*, ed. Carlos Clavería (Madrid: Cátedra, 1995)

Plautus, *The Pot of Gold*, ed. Peter D. Arnott (Arlington Heights: AHM, 1967)

Quevedo y Villegas, Francisco de, *Obra poética*, ed. José Manuel Blecua, 4 vols (Madrid: Castalia, 1969–81)

——, *Obras completas*, ed. Felicidad Buendía, 2 vols (Madrid: Aguilar, 1978)

——, *Sueños y discursos*, ed. James O. Crosby, 2 vols (Madrid: Castalia, 1993)

Quiñones de Benavente, Luis, *Colección de piezas dramáticas (entremeses, loas, y jácaras) escritas por el licenciado Luis Quiñones de Benavente*, 2 vols (Madrid: Librería de Biliófilos, 1874)

——, *Joco seria: burlas veras o reprehensión moral festiva de los desórdenes públicos, recopilados por Manuel Antonio de Vargas* (New York: G. Olms, 1985)

Quirós, Francisco Bernardo de, *Obras, Aventuras de don Fruela*, ed. Celsa Carmen García Valdés (Madrid: Instituto de Estudios Madrileños, 1984)

Rojas Zorrilla, Francisco de, *Entre bobos anda el juego*, ed. Maria Grazia Profeti (Madrid: Taurus, 1984)

Rueda, Lope de, *Pasos*, ed. José Luis Canet Vallés (Madrid: Castalia, 1992)

Sidney, Philip, Sir, *The Complete Works of Sir Philip Sidney*, ed. Albert Feuillerat, 3 vols (Cambridge: Cambridge University Press, 1962)

Vega, Lope de, *El caballero de Olmedo*, ed. Francisco Rico (Madrid: Cátedra, 1981)

——, *La gatomaquia*, ed. Celina Sabor de Cortazar (Madrid: Castalia, 1982)

——, *Peribáñez y el comendador de Ocaña*, ed. Felipe B. Pedraza Jiménez (Madrid: Castalia, 1985)

Vélez de Guevara, Luis, *El águila del agua*, in *Lepanto: Fact, Fiction and Fantasy, with a critical edition of Luis Vélez de Guevara's* El águila del agua, *a play in three acts*, ed. Michael G. Paulson and Tamara Alvarez-Detrell (New York: University Press of America, 1986)

——, *El diablo cojuelo*, ed. Blanca Periñán and Ramón Valdés (Barcelona: Crítica, 1999)

Villena, Enrique de, *Obras completas*, ed. Pedro M. Cátedra, 3 vols (Madrid: Turner, 1991)

Ximénez de Enciso, Diego, *El príncipe don Carlos* (Madrid: Bruno del Amo, 1925)

Zárate, Fernando de, *El valiente Campuzano*, in *Dramáticos posteriores a Lope de Vega*, ed. Ramón de Mesonero y Romanos, 2 vols, in the series *Biblioteca de autores españoles* [*BAE*], vols 47–8 (Madrid: M. Rivadeneyra, 1858–9)

SECONDARY SOURCES

Alcalá Zamora, José, 'Individuo e historia en la estructura teatral de "El Tuzaní de Alpujarra" ', in *Calderón: actas del Congreso internacional sobre Calderón y el teatro español del Siglo de Oro*, ed. Luciano García Lorenzo, 3 vols (Madrid: Consejo Superior de Investigaciones Científicas, 1983), pp. 343–63

Alonso Hernández, José Luis, *El léxico del marginalismo del siglo de oro* (Salamanca: Universidad de Salamanca, 1976)

Arellano, Ignacio, 'La comicidad escénica en Calderón', *Bulletin Hispanique*, 88 (1986), 47–92

Asensio, Eugenio, *Itinerario del entremés desde Lope de Rueda a Quiñones de Benavente: con cinco entremeses inéditos de D. Francisco de Quevedo* (Madrid: Gredos, 1971)

Bagby, Albert J. Jr, 'The Conventional Golden Age *Pícaro* and Quevedo's Criminal *Pícaro*', *Kentucky Romance Quarterly*, 14 (1967), 311–19

Bakhtin, Mikhail M., *The Dialogic Imagination*, ed. Caryl Emerson and Michael Holmquist (Austin: University of Texas Press, 1989)

——, *Rabelais and His World*, ed. Hélène Iswolsky (Bloomington: Indiana University Press, 1984)

Benabu, Isaac, 'La inconclusividad de un fin: Pedro Crespo y la problematización del género en una lectura teatral de *El alcalde de Zalamea*', in *Texto e imagen en Calderón: Undécimo Coloquio Anglogermano sobre Calderón* (Stuttgart: Franz Steiner, 1998), pp. 37–45

Bergman, Hannah E., *Luis Quiñones de Benavente* (New York: Twayne, 1972)

——, *Luis Quiñones de Benavente y sus entremeses: con un catálogo biográfico de los actores citados en sus obras* (Madrid: Castalia, 1965)

Bravo-Villasante, Carmen, *La mujer vestida de hombre en el teatro español* (*siglos XVI–XVII*) (Madrid: Revista de Occidente, 1955)

Breton, André, *Anthologie de l'humour noir* (Paris: Éditions du Sagittaire, 1950)

Brotherton, John, *The 'Pastor-Bobo' in the Spanish Theatre Before the Time of Lope de Vega* (London: Tamesis, 1975)

Brugnolo, Stefano, *La tradizione dell'umorismo nero* (Rome: Bulzoni, 1994)

Buezo, Catalina, *La mojiganga dramática: de la fiesta al teatro* (Kassel: Reichenberger, 1993)

Burshatin, Israel, 'Playing the Moor: Parody and Performance in Lope de Vega's *El primer Fajardo*', *Publications of the Modern Language Association of America* (*PMLA*), 103 (1992), 566–81

Canavaggio, Jean, 'En torno al "Dragoncillo": nuevo examen de una reescritura', in *Estudios sobre Calderón: actas del Coloquio Calderoniano, Salamanca*

1985, ed. Alberto Navarro González (Salamanca: Universidad de Salamanca, 1985), pp. 9–16

Carner, Robert J., 'The *Loas*, *Entremeses* and *Bailes* of D. Agustín Moreto' (PhD Dissertation, Cambridge, Mass.: Harvard University, 1940)

Caro Baroja, Julio, *El carnaval: análisis histórico-cultural* (Madrid: Taurus, 1965)

Case, Thomas E., 'El morisco gracioso en el teatro de Lope', in *Lope de Vega y los orígenes del teatro español: actas del I congreso Internacional sobre Lope de Vega*, ed. Manuel Criado de Val (Madrid: EDI–6, 1981), pp. 785–90

Caso González, José Miguel, 'Calderón y los moriscos de las Alpujarras', in *Calderón*, pp. 393–402

Castiglione, Baldassare, *Los cuatro libros del Cortesano, compuestos en italiano por el Conde Baltasar Castellón, y agora nuevamente traducidos en lengua castellana por Boscán* (Madrid: Librería de los Bibliófilos, 1873)

Castro, Américo, *De la edad conflictiva* (Madrid: Taurus, 1961)

Castro de Moux, María E., *La casa de los linajes: oficios y gentes marginados en el entremés barroco español* (New Orleans: University Press of the South, 1997)

Catalán, Diego, 'Una jacarilla barroca hoy tradicional en Extremadura y en Oriente', *Revista de estudios extremeños*, 8 (1952), 377–87

Chevalier, Maxime, *El cuentecillo tradicional en la España del Siglo de Oro* (Madrid: Gredos, 1975)

——, *Tipos cómicos y folklore (siglos XVI–XVII)* (Madrid: EDI–6, 1982)

Cid, Jesús Antonio, 'Calderón y el romancillo de "El bonetero de la Trapería"', *Hispanic Review*, 45 (1977), 421–34

Close, Anthony, *Cervantes and the Comic Mind of his Age* (Oxford: Oxford University Press, 2000)

Cotarelo y Mori, Emilio, *Don Enrique de Villena: su vida y obras* (Madrid: Sucesores de Rivadeneyra, 1896)

——, *Ensayo sobre la vida y obras de D. Pedro Calderón de la Barca, Parte primera (Biografía)* (Madrid: Tip. de la 'Rev. de Arch., Bibl. y Museos', 1924)

Covarrubias y Orozco, Sebastián de, *Tesoro de la lengua castellana* (Barcelona: Alta Fulla, 1998)

Davies, Christie, *Ethnic Humor Around the World: A Comparative Analysis* (Bloomington: Indiana University Press, 1990)

Deleito y Piñuela, José, *La mala vida en la España de Felipe IV* (Madrid: Alianza Editorial, 1987)

Díez Borque, José María, *Sociología de la comedia española del siglo XVII* (Madrid: Cátedra, 1976)

Dille, Glen F., 'The Tragedy of Don Pedro: Old and New Christian Conflict in *El valiente Campuzano*', *Bulletin of the Comediantes*, 35 (1983), 97–109

Domínguez Ortiz, Antonio, *La clase social de los conversos en Castilla en la edad moderna* (Granada: Universidad de Granada, 1991)

Domínguez Ortiz, Antonio and Bernard Vincent, *Historia de los moriscos: vida y tragedia de una minoría* (Madrid: Biblioteca *Revista de Occidente*, 1978)

Edwards, Gwynne, 'Calderón's *Los tres mayores prodigios* and *El pintor de su deshonra*: The Modernization of Ancient Myth', *Bulletin of Hispanic Studies*, 61 (1984), 326–34

Elizalde, Ignacio, 'El teatro escolar jesuítico en el siglo XVII', in *Teatro del siglo de oro: homenaje a Alberto Navarro González*, ed. Victor G. de la Concha, Jean

Canavaggio, Theodor Berchem and María-Luisa Lobato (Kassel: Reichenberger, 1990), pp. 109–39

Elliot, Robert C., *The Power of Satire: Magic, Ritual, Art* (Princeton: Princeton University Press, 1960)

Flasche, Hans, 'Perspectivas de la locura en los graciosos de Calderón: *La aurora en Copacabana*', *Nueva Revista de Filología Hispánica*, 34 (1986), 631–53

Flecniakoska, Jean-Louis, *La loa* (Madrid: Sociedad General Español de Librería, S. A., 1975)

Frye, Northrop, *Anatomy of Criticism: Four Essays* (Princeton: Princeton University Press, 1957)

Gaetano, Armand L. de, 'Gelli's *Circe* and Boaistuau's *Theatrum mundi*', *Forum Italicum*, 7 (1973), 441–54

García Soriano, Justo, 'El teatro de colegio en España', *Boletín de la Real Académia Española*, 14, 15, 16, 19 (1927–)

García-Varela, Jesús, 'Para una ideología de la exclusión: El discurso del "moro" en Sánchez de Badajoz', *Criticón*, 66 (1996), 171–8

Glaser, Edward, 'Referencias antisemitas en la literatura peninsular de la Edad de Oro', *Nueva Revista de Filología Española*, 8 (1954), 54–9

Gómez-Torres, David, 'La función de la risa en el discurso de la comedia: absorción y manipulación de los rasgos grotescos y carnavalescos' (PhD Dissertation, University of Tennessee, 1994)

González, Eloy R., 'Carnival on the Stage: *Céfalo y Pocris*, a *Comedia Burlesca*', *Bulletin of the Comediantes*, 30 (1978), 3–12

González Gutiérrez, Cayo, *El Códice de Villagarcía del P. Juan Bonifacio: teatro clásico del siglo XVI* (Madrid: Universidad Nacional de Educación a Distancia, 2000)

——, *El teatro escolar de los jesuitas: 1555–1640 y edición de la* Tragedia de San Hermenegildo (Universidad de Oviedo: Servicio de Publicaciones, 1997)

Grant, Helen F., 'El mundo al revés', in *Hispanic Studies in Honour of Joseph Manson*, ed. Dorothy M. Atkinson and Anthony H. Clarke (Oxford: Dolphin, 1972), pp. 119–38

Greer, Margaret, *The Play of Power: Mythological Court Dramas of Calderón de la Barca* (Princeton: Princeton University Press, 1991)

——, '"¿La vida es sueño? ¿o risa?" Calderón Parodies the *Auto*', *Bulletin of Hispanic Studies*, 72 (1995), 313–25

Griffin N.H., 'Some Aspects of Jesuit School Drama, 1550–1600, with Special Reference to Spain and Portugal' (PhD Dissertation, Oxford, 1975)

Güntert, Georges, 'El gracioso en Calderón: disparate e ingenio', *Cuadernos hispanoamericanos*, 324 (1977), 440–53

Hermenegildo, Alfredo, 'El gracioso y la mutación del rol dramático: "Un bobo hace Ciento"', in *Diálogos Hispánicos de Amsterdam 8*, ed. Javier Huerta Calvo, Harm den Boer and Fermín Sierra Martínez, 3 vols (Atlanta: Rodopi, 1989), vol. 2, pp. 503–26

——, 'La marginación del carnaval: *Celos, aun del aire, matan* de Pedro Calderón de la Barca', *Bulletin of the Comediantes*, 40 (1988), 103–20

Hernández-Araico, Susana, 'Política imperial en "Los tres mayores prodigios"', in *Homenaje a Hans Flasche*, ed. Karl-Hermann Körner and Günther Zimmermann (Stuttgart: F. Steiner, 1991), pp. 83–94

Herrera Puga, Pedro, *Sociedad y delincuencia en el Siglo de Oro, aspectos de la vida sevillana en los siglos XVI y XVII* (Granada: Universidad de Granada, 1972)

Highet, Gilbert, *The Anatomy of Satire* (Princeton: Princeton University Press, 1962)

Holgueras Pecharromán, Loly, 'La comedia burlesca: estado actual de la investigación', in *Diálogos Hispánicos de Amsterdam 8*, vol. 2, 467–80

Hurtado Torres, Antonio, 'La astrología en el teatro de Calderón de la Barca', in *Calderón*, pp. 925–37

Issacharoff, Michael, *Discourse as Performance* (Stanford: Stanford University Press, 1989)

Jolles, André, *Las formas simples* (*Einfache Formen*), translated by Rosemary Kempf Titze (Santiago de Chile: Editorial Universitaria, 1971)

Kalnein, Albrecht von, 'Teatro y política: Calderón como arma polémica en las sátiras de los años 1670', in *Teatro del Siglo de Oro: homenaje a Alberto Navarro* (Kassel: Reichenberger, 1990), pp. 297–320

Kamen, Henry, *The Spanish Inquisition: An Historical Revision* (London: Weidenfeld & Nicolson, 1997)

Kellenberger, Jakob, *Calderón de la Barca und das Komische: unter besonderer Berücksichtigung der ernsten Schauspiele* (Frankfurt: Peter Lang, 1975)

Kernan, Alvin, *The Cankered Muse: Satire of the English Renaissance* (New Haven: Yale University Press, 1959)

Kurtz, Barbara E., 'Guilty Pleasure: The Comic, the Sacred, and Placer(es) in the Autos Sacramentales of Calderón de la Barca', in *Play, Literature, Religion: Essays in Cultural Intertextuality*, ed. Virgil Nemoianu and Robert Royal (Albany: State University of New York Press, 1992), pp. 61–75

Lanot, Jean-Raymond, 'Para una sociología del figurón', in *Risa y sociedad en el teatro español del Siglo de Oro/Rire et société dans le théâtre espagnol du Siècle d'Or* (Paris: Centre Nat. de la Recherche Scientifique, 1980), pp. 131–48

Larson, Catherine, 'Metatheater and the *Comedia*: Past, Present, and Future', in *The Golden Age Comedia: Text, Theory, and Performance*, ed. Charles Ganelin and Howard Mancing (West Lafayette, Indiana: Purdue University Press, 1994), pp. 204–21

Laurie, Joe Jr, *Vaudeville: From the Honky-Tonks to the Palace* (New York: Henry Holt and Co., 1953)

López Pinciano, Alonso, *Philosophia antigua poetica*, ed. A. Carballo Picazo, 3 vols (Madrid: CSIC, 1953)

Maqueda Abreu, Consuelo, *El auto de fe* (Madrid: Istmo, 1992)

Marsh, David, *Lucian and the Latins: Humor and Humanism in the Early Renaissance* (Ann Arbor: University of Michigan Press, 1998)

McKendrick, Melveena, 'Honour/Vengeance in the Spanish "Comedia": A Case of Mimetic Transference', *Modern Language Review*, 79 (1984), 313–35

——, 'Los juicios de Eusebio: el joven Calderón en busca de su propio estilo', in *El mundo del teatro español en su Siglo de Oro, ensayos dedicados a John E. Varey*, ed. J.M. Ruano de la Haza (Ottawa: Dovehouse, 1989), pp. 313–26

Meijide Pardo, María Luisa, 'Mendacidad, vagancia, y prostitución en la España del siglo XVIII: la casa galera y los departamentos de corrección de mujeres' (Doctoral dissertation, Madrid: Universidad Complutense de Madrid, 1992)

Menéndez Peláez, Jesús, *Los jesuitas y el teatro en el Siglo de Oro* (Oviedo: Servicio de Publicaciones de la Universidad de Oviedo, 1995)

Meregalli, Franco, 'Cervantes in Calderón', in *Atti delle giornate cervantine* (Padova: Unipress, 1995), pp. 129–35

Merino Quijano, Gaspar, 'Los bailes dramáticos del siglo XVII' (Doctoral dissertation, Madrid: Universidad Complutense, 1981)

Mommsen, Theodor E., 'Petrarch and the Story of the Choice of Hercules', in *Medieval and Renaissance Studies*, ed. Eugene F. Rice, Jr (Ithaca: Cornell University 1959), pp. 175–96

Mujica, Barbara, 'Honor from the Comic Perspective: Calderón's *Comedias de Capa y Espada*', *Bulletin of the Comediantes*, 38 (1986), 7–24

Mussachio, Enrico and Sandro Cordeschi, eds, *Il riso nelle poetiche rinascimentali* (Bologna: Lapelli, 1985)

Nagy, Edward, 'El galeote de Lepanto de Luis Vélez de Guevara: la diversión en vez del escarmiento picaresco', *Bulletin of the Comediantes*, 29 (1977), 28–34

——, 'La picardía militar y su utilización por Calderón de la Barca', in *Calderón*, pp. 963–73

Navarro González, Alberto, *Calderón de la Barca de lo trágico a lo grotesco* (Kassel: Reichenberger, 1984)

——, 'Comicidad del lenguaje en el teatro de Calderón', *Iberoromania*, 14 (1981), 116–32

Nees, Lawrence, *A Tainted Mantle: Hercules and the Classical Tradition at Carolingian Court* (Philadelphia: University of Pennsylvania Press, 1991)

Netanyahu B., *Toward the Inquisition: Essays on Jewish and Converso History in Late Medieval Spain* (Ithaca: Cornell University Press, 1997)

Oblanca Fernández, Justo, *Literatura y sociedad en los entremeses del siglo XVII* (Universidad de Oviedo: Servicio de Publicaciones, 1992)

O'Connor, Thomas Austin, 'Formula Thinking/Formula Writing in Calderón de la Barca's *El golfo de las sirenas*', *Bulletin of the Comediantes*, 38 (1986), 25–38

——, *Myth and Mythology In the Theater of Pedro Calderón de la Barca* (San Antonio: Trinity University Press, 1988)

Oppenheimer, Max Jr, 'The *Burla* in Calderón's *El astrólogo fingido*', *Philological Quarterly*, 27 (1948), 241–63

Pailler, Claire, 'El gracioso y los "guiños" de Calderón: apuntes sobre la "autoburla" e ironía crítica', in *Risa y sociedad en el teatro español del Siglo de Oro* (Paris: Centre Nat. de la Recherche Scientifique, 1980), p. 33–48

Parker, Alexander A., *The Mind and Art of Calderón: Essays on the Comedias* (Cambridge: Cambridge University Press, 1988)

——, 'Santos y bandoleros en el teatro español del Siglo de Oro', *Arbor*, 13 (1949), 395–416

Pedrosa, Jose Manuel, 'La oración del peregrino y la comedia de *Céfalo y Procris* de Calderón', *Neophilologus*, 82 (1998), 403–10

Penas Ibáñez, María Azucena, *Análisis lingüístico-semántico del lenguaje del 'Gracioso' en algunas comedias de Lope de Vega* (Madrid: Universidad Autónoma, 1992)

Pollin A.M., 'Judaísmo y Sinagoga en Calderón: recreación de un tema alegórico medieval', *Revista de Literatura*, 54 (1992), 149–81

Portera, Juan, 'El gracioso pícaro en Calderón', in *La picaresca: orígenes, textos y estructuras, Actas del I Congreso Internacional sobre la picaresca organizado por el patronato 'Arcipreste de Hita'*, ed. Manuel Criado de Val (Madrid: Fundación Universitaria Española, 1979), pp. 841–7

Portús Pérez, Javier, *La antigua procesión del Corpus Christi en Madrid* (Madrid: Consejería de Educación y Cultura, 1993)

Recoules, Henri, 'Les intermèdes des collections imprimées: vision caricaturale de la société espagnole au XVIIᵉ siècle', 2 vols (Lille: Service de reproduction des thèses, Université de Lille III, 1973)

Redfern, Walter, *Puns* (New York: Basil Blackwell, 1984)

Reed, Cory A., *The Novelist as Playwright: Cervantes and the Entremés Nuevo* (New York: Peter Lang, 1993)

Regalado García, Antonio, *Calderón: los orígenes de la modernidad en la España del Siglo de Oro*, 2 vols (Barcelona: Ediciones Destino, 1995)

Reichenberger, Kurt, *Bibliographisches Handbuch der Calderón-Forschung* (Kassel: Theiele & Schwarz, 1979–)

Riccoboni, Lewis, *An Historical Account of the Theatres in Europe viz. The Italian, Spanish, French, English, Dutch, Flemish, and German Theatres* (London, 1741)

de Rocher, Gregory, *Rabelais's Laughers and Joubert's* Traité du Ris (University [sic]: University of Alabama Press, 1979)

Rodríguez, Evangelina. 'Del teatro tosco al melodrama: la jácara', in *Actas de las jornadas sobre teatro popular en España*, ed. Joaquin Alvarez Barrientos and Antonio Cea Gutiérrez (Madrid: CSIC, 1987), pp. 227–47

——, 'Gesto, movimiento, palabra: el actor en el entremés del Siglo de Oro', in *Los géneros menores en el teatro español del Siglo de Oro* (*Jornadas de Almagro 1987*), ed. Luciano García Lorenzo (Madrid: Ministerio de Cultura, 1988), pp. 47–93

Rodríguez, Evangelina and Antonio Tordera, *Calderón de la Barca y la dramaturgia corta del siglo XVII* (London: Tamesis, 1985)

——, *Escritura y palacio: el toreador de Calderón* (Kassel: Reichenberger, 1985)

——, 'Intención y morfología de la mojiganga en Calderón de la Barca', in *Calderón*, pp. 817–24

Rose, Constance H., 'Was Calderón Serious? Another Look at *Los tres mayores prodigios*', in *Hispanic Essays in Honor of Frank P. Casa*, ed. Robert A. Lauer and Henry W. Sullivan (New York: Peter Lang, 1997), pp. 246–52

Sage, Jack and Edward M. Wilson, *Poesías líricas en las obras dramáticas de Calderón* (London: Tamesis, 1964)

Salomon, Noël, *Lo villano en el teatro del Siglo de Oro*, translated by Beatriz Chenot (Madrid: Castalia, 1985)

Sánchez Domínguez, Luis Antonio, 'El lenguaje teatral del morisco', *Boletín de la Biblioteca Menéndez Pelayo*, 63 (1987), 5–16

Segal, Erich, *Roman Laughter: The Comedy of Plautus* (Cambridge, Mass.: Harvard University Press, 1968)

Serralta, Frédéric, 'Juan Rana homosexual', *Criticón*, 50 (1990), 81–92

——, 'Une tradition littéraire: *La renegada de Valladolid* (Etude et édition critique de la comedia burlesque de Monteser, Solís et Silva)' (Doctoral Dissertation, Toulouse, 1968)

Sicroff, Albert A., *Los estatutos de limpieza de sangre: controversias entre los siglos XV y XVII*, translated by Mauro Armiño (Madrid: Taurus, 1985)

Slawinski, Maurice, 'Comedy of Words and Comedy of Things: A Renaissance Commedia and its Plautine Models', *New Comparison*, 3 (1987), 5–18

Sola-Solé, Josep M., *Sobre árabes, judíos y marranos y su impacto en la lengua y literatura españolas* (Barcelona: Puvill, 1983)

Stein, Louise K., *Songs of Mortals, Dialogues of the Gods: Music and Theatre in Seventeenth-Century Spain* (Oxford: Clarendon, 1993)

Sullivan, Michael R., 'A Study of the Paired Sonnets in the Plays of Pedro Calderón de la Barca' (PhD Dissertation, The University of Missouri, 1998)

Sypher, Wylie, *Comedy: 'An essay on Comedy' by George Meredith. 'Laughter' by Henri Bergson* (Baltimore: Johns Hopkins University Press, 1980)

Tapia Bolívar, Daniel, *Breve historia del toreo* (México: Editorial México, 1947)

ter Horst, Robert, 'The Origin and Meaning of Comedy in Calderón', in *Studies in Honor of Everett W. Hess*, ed. William C. McCrary and Jose A. Madrigal (Lincoln, Nebraska: Society of Spanish and Spanish-American Studies, 1981)

Thacker, Jonathan, *Role-Play and the World as Stage in the 'Comedia'* (Liverpool, Liverpool University Press: 2002)

Toro-Garland, Fernando de, 'El "entremés" como origen de la "comedia nueva" según Lope', in *Lope de Vega y los orígenes del teatro español: actas del I congreso internacional sobre Lope de Vega*, pp. 103–9

Tyler, Richard W. and Sergio D. Elizondo, *The Characters, Plots, and Settings of Calderón's Comedias* (Lincoln, Nebraska: Society of Spanish and Spanish-American Studies, 1981)

Valbuena Briones, Ángel, 'Calderón y las fiestas de carnaval', *Bulletin of the Comediantes*, 39 (1987), 165–74

——, 'Los papeles cómicos y las hablas dialectales en dos comedias de Calderón', *Thesaurus: Boletín del Instituto Caro y Cuervo*, 42 (1987), 47–59

Varón Vallejo, Eudosio, 'Rondas de los alcaldes de casa y corte en los siglos XVI y XVII', *Revista de Archivos, Bibliotecas, y Museos*, 45 (1924), 148–55

Watson A.I., 'Hercules and the Tunic of Shame: Calderón's *Los tres mayors prodigios*', in *Homenaje a William L. Fichter: estudios sobre el teatro antiguo hispánico y otros ensayos* (Madrid: Castalia, 1971), pp. 773–83

Wilson, Edward M., 'Calderón y Cervantes', in *Archivum Calderonianum, Hacia Calderón: Quinto Coloquio Anglogermano, Oxford 1978* (Wiesbaden: Franz Steiner, 1982), pp. 9–20

INDEX